INNATE HAPPINESS

Realizing
Compassion-Emptiness

Khenpo Drimed Dawa

Innate Happiness: Realizing Compassion-Emptiness

© 2013 Khenpo Drimed Dawa

This book is dedicated to all beings.

May you experience lovingkindness and compassion for all.
May you experience the deep inner peace of transcendent wisdom.
May you experience the innate happiness of compassion and wisdom
for all ... always and all ways!

Table of Contents

Preface

Reasons for Writing This Book

The Western householder faces a very different experience and set of challenges than the monks and nuns living in a monastic community in Tibet, India, Nepal and so forth. While some lamas have made an effort to adopt their teachings to the West, most have largely approached teaching here in the same way as in the East as if for the same audience, and often with the same expectations.

In contrast, other lamas have learned to speak English and use Western stories and metaphors to supplement traditional ones. His Holiness the Dalai Lama has said that Western students tend to be very intelligent and learn dharma very quickly. Still, few lamas have learned Western pedagogical methods and scientifically-researched techniques that may expedite the learning and the process of realization, particularly using these methods to adapt the teachings and practices to the Western householder lifestyle. While teaching in the West, many persist in attempting to fit students into a traditional mold. Too often we hear, "If you *really* want to achieve enlightenment in this lifetime, you need to ___." Fill in the blank: complete a three-year retreat, practice in a cave for many years or even for your lifetime, etc. Really? Why then are there stories of householders (and rather unremarkable or even lesser lamas for that matter) who did achieve enlightenment outside or in spite of the establishment? What's *really* possible here? The Dzogchen Ponlop Rinpoche adds,

> It's like saying to our ourselves, "Yes, you're a buddha too. You have the same enlightened potential. You can wake up any minute, just like Shakyamuni Buddha and many others." … We're trying to see how all of these teachings exist in our everyday life: taking piano lessons, driving our kids to school, walking home from the bar, or locking ourselves up in a three-year retreat – they're all the same.

In discussions with students, lamas, and others, I have found two predominant views of dharma in the West. One view is that of maintaining the tradition in a fairly rigorous manner, even though much of it is focused on monk and nun practitioners living in monasteries. The other view is the secularization of the tradition, removing the "cultural" and "mythical" elements down to the essence of the teachings, but at the same time stripping it of the rich and vibrant character and, most importantly, their benefits for helping us achieve realization.

When the Buddha first taught the Middle Way, he emphasized the middle between asceticism and indulgence. When he next taught the Middle Way, he emphasized the middle between the extremes of permanence and nothingness. In this text I have approached the tradition with a focus on a middle way between the monastic tradition taught in the East and the attempts to secularize that tradition in the West. My position is that while the West has much to offer the tradition, particularly through our scientific and inquiring minds, we must be careful not to exorcise too much of the character that makes the actual process of training the mind effective.

For example, we have no deity tradition in the West and it can be very tempting to consider all the deity practices as nothing more than mythical stories of an ancient civilization that are no longer relevant in the modern world. But as tools for training the mind, these practices have been shown for centuries to be highly effective. Furthermore, I would argue from experience, as well as the instruction of my teachers, that there is a great value in the rich and varied wealth of material in the dharma, even that which seems beyond credibility to the modern Western mind when viewed from a very literal interpretation and presentation, as often happens.

Thus, I have taken somewhat different approach that seeks to include a balance between the two extremes, while also focusing on the heart of the path with a comprehensive series of trainings appropriate for the Western householder with limited time for "formal" training and practice. At the same time, I have selected those practices that are consistent with the scientific support for efficiency and effectiveness towards achieving the traditional goal of enlightenment in this lifetime.

In this context, it is important to understand that Buddhism as a practice is largely a matter of training the mind, although there is ample opportunity for elaborate ritual and other elements of religion that may also appeal to practitioners. Mind training is not unlike that of an athlete or a musician. It takes hours and hours of practice. Some techniques are more effective than others, but there is no shortcut. Some say that one needs at least 10,000 hours of meditation to achieve a significant level of realization. If you only practice 20 minutes a day, that will take 30,000 days or about 82 years (with no vacations). On the other hand, if you sit in a 3-year retreat with 10 hours per day of actual practice, you will achieve that goal before the end of the retreat.

Lest you be discouraged by this, reframe the "problem." We each have 24 hours per day, whether we are lamas in retreat or busy Western professionals. Twenty-four hours! You, me, Rinpoche, all of us. So how do we take advantage of this opportunity? You make *everything* practice. Instead of focusing only on what you do on the cushion, as most Western practitioners tend to do, you expand your view of practice to literally everything you do. Thich Nhat Hanh (pronounced "tik not hon"), for example, teaches this through numerous little prayers and sayings that apply to dozens of activities we all do every day.

That is one approach. My approach, however, comes directly from the teachings in the Tibetan tradition. It takes a while to master, so it is not like you can start doing it from day one, but it is a very realistic accomplishment. And doing so levels the playing field for Western practitioners, many of whom are very intelligent and deeply committed to this goal, a significant advantage. At 24 hours per day, 10,000 hours can take as little as 416 days! Just over one year. And you can do this all without giving up your job, your family, or moving to Tibet or India.

One of the reasons that I have chosen to follow the teachings of Padmasambhava in this text is that he recommends doing nearly all of the practices for a period of three days. I have extended this in light of the fact that we may only be doing the practices for shorter periods of time than for a full day. Nevertheless, it does become possible, if not advantageous, to do a very good job of completing these practices and achieving the signs of realization for each incremental practice within one to three weeks.

Now, before you get too excited – or critical – keep in mind that this requires a level of focused attention that takes time to develop. So in reality it is likely to take longer. It took the Buddha himself 6 years after having already mastered the teachings of two other gurus. And most of the great Mahasiddhas took at least 12 years, often after considerable previous training. So unless you consider yourself to have skills beyond the best of the best, a little humility and patience are warranted.

As I said, it takes some effort and practice to achieve that level of experience. So we still need *patience* and *persistence*, the hallmarks of training the mind and two of the Six Perfections. My hope is that this book can help you expedite the process. The faster you can get there, the sooner you can potentially achieve enlightenment. We have the advantage of hundreds of years of experience and recent scientific inquiry. Nevertheless, we still need patience and persistence regardless of our capabilities.

So whether you have zero experience or several decades, it is within this context that I invite you to participate in this marvelous experience we call Buddhism. You may do so as a religious or secular practitioner. That, as His Holiness the Dalai Lama frequently points out, is of little consequence. What does matter is how this experience can help you and others benefit in the quality of your life in this world and the next, whatever that might be.

Buddhism has been very good to me. So much so, that I agreed to share what little expertise I have developed in my study and practice. It began when my teacher, Tulku Khenchen Paljea Dorjee Rinpoche, asked me to teach. I began teaching and developing courses for Dharmakirti College and eCollege (now the Awam Tibetan Buddhist Institute). After a while, I was named President, and two years later I was given the title *Khenpo*, as nearly as we can tell, the first American to receive that title in the United States. Rinpoche has continued to ask that I teach more, as well as begin to write. My students, too, asked that I write to benefit them in their studies and understanding. Thus, I humbly dedicate this text to all sentient beings. May it be of some small benefit.

My Story

My interest in Buddhism began in junior high school in a small rural town in Idaho, where I grew up. I was raised in the American Baptist tradition. One day a friend of mine came to school talking about metaphysics. It piqued my interest, so I began to read what little I could find. This led to reading about other religions of which Buddhism held the greatest appeal. This continued in college, reinforced by my philosophy teacher and working in the library where I had regular access to what seemed at the time to be a very large collection of related books.

Although I changed majors and universities, I stumbled across the books of Alan Watts and others and began to read more. I was fascinated by Zen and Taoism at the time. Sitting naturally came easy and I delighted in the paradox of the koans. I had no teacher and was never aware of any in Oregon at that time – the late 60s.

The young pastor and a progressive youth leader at a church in Oregon helped stimulate my questioning and openness to other traditions. As often happens, I graduated, later got married, eventually started a family, and life "got in the way." Buddhism slowly faded into the background, though I continued a casual interest from time to time.

Eventually I moved to a new job in Arizona. During a summer a couple of years later, one of the directors at my new college invited others to come to a weekly discussion and meditation session during the lunch hour. I decided to participate, but quickly read the book and looked for more. I went back to some of the Zen books I had read years before.

Another job change resulted in me moving away from my family for an extended period with occasional weekend trips to visit, so I had a lot of time on my hands. I discovered Lama Surya Das' *Awakening the Buddha Within*. I began reading everything I could find on *Dzogchen*[1]– the Great Perfection, which wasn't a lot at that time. A friend suggested a book by Thich Nhat Hanh, and I added him to my list. I was reading at least one book a week and doing daily meditation practice at that time.

Still, there were no teachers nearby. Some research led me to learn about the Garchen Institute in Chino Valley, Arizona. As fate (karma?) would have it, I was transferred nearby by my university, and I began to attend regular meditations on Sundays, as well as the summer and winter retreats and other teachings. This exposed me to a broader array of Tibetan Buddhist practices, but I continued my primary interest in *Dzogchen*. Fortunately, we were able to get some very good *Dzogchen* teachers in addition to Garchen Rinpoche, including *Dzogchen* masters Ven. Gyalpo Rinpoche and Ven. Traga Rinpoche. The latter began a series of weekly teachings on *Dzogchen* that continued until I was once again transferred, this time to Tucson, Arizona.

Several individuals from Tucson regularly attended events at the Garchen Institute, about a four-and-a-half hour drive away. I was able to connect with some of them and learned about the Awam Tibetan Buddhist Institute (Dharmakirti College at that time) in Tucson. A class on the *Yangzab* Three Roots practice was starting with *Acharya* Cliff Leftwich and I began attending. As we got acquainted, he shared his vision of the Institute with me, and we began to discuss the dream. The following summer, I was invited to join the board of directors and helped develop a full curriculum and a business plan.

---

[1] Pronounced close to "zoke-chen" (the "g" is somewhere between a "g" and a "k").

The next year, *Acharya* invited Khenchen Paljea Dorjee Rinpoche (Khenchen Lama) to come to Tucson from Nepal and teach. A small group of us met in the dining room every day for a few hours as he gave us a wealth of detailed instructions for several months through a translator who had come to Arizona with Rinpoche. He also gave several public talks, transmissions and empowerments. Rinpoche left for Asia for several long months, but then returned and continued to teach. It was during this second visit that he named me President of Awam Tibetan Buddhist Institute on Losar, 2007. Rinpoche continued to ask me to teach. I was teaching two classes each week in Tucson as well as one or two online. Then, I also started a series of monthly "dharma talks." During my summer retreat in 2008 at a center in Colorado, Rinpoche communicated with me via Skype that he was going to give me the title of *Khenpo* during his planned fall visit, which was later postponed until spring 2009. Although I continue to learn from Khenchen Lama, he also introduced me to His Eminence Jigme Lodro Rinpoche, whom we have invited to give a number of teachings at the Institute.

I continue to teach and develop programs for the Awam Tibetan Buddhist Institute, including the development of Western teachers and advanced practitioners, in addition to basic instruction in meditation and Tibetan Buddhism. At the request of Khenchen Lama and my students, I am also now writing this text to further benefit others. I hope you enjoy it!

Part 1 –Introduction

This introduction asks several questions important in considering the practices described: Why should you practice Buddhism? What is your intention? Why practice this form of Buddhism? Can you really achieve enlightenment as a householder? It concludes with an overview of the rest of the text.

Chapter 1

Introduction

Why Should You Practice Buddhism?

Perhaps the most fundamental question is, "Why should you practice Buddhism?" And more specifically, "Why this form of Buddhism?" People come to Buddhism for many diverse reasons. They continue to practice for diverse reasons as well. Some are attracted to the "bells and smells," i.e., the costumes, the chanting, the drums and symbols, the language, the ritual. Others are attracted by the charisma of the lamas, who tend to have very amicable personalities and a good sense of humor. It can be a delight to just be in their presence. Others are attracted to the intellectual challenges posed by the scriptures and commentaries, which are exhaustive. One could never complete an examination of the ever-growing library of written texts in a long, full, and rich lifetime. Some are attracted to the benefits of meditation, well documented in the Western scientific literature, regarding well-being, health, etc. Still others are seeking solutions to personal problems such as anger, fear, anxiety, relationships, jobs, and so forth. A fairly large number are general spiritual seekers checking out Buddhism for possible answers on their personal journey. And finally, a few (or so it seems) are actually attracted to the prospect of achieving enlightenment in this lifetime.

All of these are valid reasons for an interest in Buddhism and for pursuing study and practice. Not all practitioners have the same level of commitment. Some attend mostly the highly ceremonial empowerments, even "collecting empowerments." A fair number also attend regular teachings by lamas. Fewer are attracted to teachings by Westerners, although that is changing as more Western practitioners are developed as teachers, and there are other exceptions among those who have a highly visible record of publication. A small number of students take advantage of in-depth classes to really develop understanding and realization through extensive study and practice. Fewest of all engage in full monastic participation.

The best reason to practice Buddhism, however, is that we all want to have happiness and avoid suffering. But true happiness does not come from "things" or sense pleasures. Those are simply temporary and leave us wanting more. In Buddha's time there were several schools of thought about how to achieve an ideal form of happiness they called enlightenment. As we will see, the Buddha tried two of those paths, but found them unsatisfactory in that the happiness attained during meditation was not sustained afterwards. He also tried asceticism for six years, nearly dying in the process, and was still dissatisfied with the results. He then set out to discover his own way, which became the path of Buddhism. So the reason for following the teachings of the Buddha is fundamentally to achieve the happiness of enlightenment. What the Buddha found was an *innate happiness – a deep, abiding, inner peace.* Furthermore, he concluded that we are *all* imbued with this innate happiness. We just need to wake up to it, as he did.

What is the source of such happiness? Happiness or enlightenment became articulated as the union of wisdom and compassion. This results in a deep inner peace that is undisturbed by the events that happen in our lives. "Wisdom" is the most difficult element to define or describe. It refers to a direct experiential knowing of the true *nature* of self, mind, and all things, often referred to as "emptiness." It is said that emptiness is ineffable, beyond words. Yet much has been written about it. Compassion and its partner, lovingkindness, have very specific definitions in Buddhism. Lovingkindness is the wish that all beings have happiness and its causes. Compassion is the wish that all beings *not* have suffering and its causes. Together they express the desire for all beings to achieve enlightenment. The enlightenment of Buddhahood, then, is a state of deep inner peace attained through direct experiential knowing of the true nature of things – emptiness – and simultaneously acting out of great compassion for all other beings. Pretty simple.

The path to achieve this (and there are several), while not difficult to do, does require *patience* and *persistence*. Some paths work better than others for particular individuals. But this book is not about finding the right path for you. It describes the core practices of the path known as Tibetan Buddhism[2] in a form attributed to the Second Buddha, Padmasambhava – The Lotus Born, also known as Guru Rinpoche. It is a form of this path most suitable for householders. But as noted above, it

---

[2] Tibetan Buddhism is also known as Vajrayana Buddhism, Tantrayana, Mantrayana, and other names as well.

still requires *patience* and *persistence*. This is not a magic pill. This is not a path of instant gratification. Nevertheless, the Buddha said that could be achieved for those of highest suitability. So there is reason to be optimistic at the same time. The true test is how you respond when things go bad! That is when you will know if you have achieved real enlightenment.

There are, of course, many far more detailed explanations of the stages or steps towards enlightenment, which have become significantly more complexified and nuanced over time. The Five Paths, the Ten Bhumis, the Fourteen Bhumis, and so forth are examples. Here we will focus on primarily on the practices and experiences, with just enough of the philosophy to provide a basic understand necessary to do the practices.

So attaining enlightenment in this lifetime for the benefit of all, including you, is the reason Buddhism exists. And this is the reason I am writing this text, to encourage you to actively pursue enlightenment in this lifetime for the benefit of all … here … now. Yes, there are texts that say that it will take many lifetimes. But there are also texts, including statements attributed directly to the Buddha, that say it can be done in a fairly short time, and certainly in this lifetime. I am convinced that this is indeed possible.

What Is Your Intention?

As we will see shortly, the reason the Buddha sought enlightenment in the first place was to overcome *dukkha*. While usually translated as "suffering," this term is better understood as "unhappiness," "dissatisfaction" or "imperfection," which to be sure includes what we normally think of when hearing the word suffering. But it is much broader than just that. More on that below, but suffice it to say at this point that many Westerners investigate Buddhism as "seekers" looking for answers to personal problems or spiritual concerns. Or they may see this as a personal journey on "The Spiritual Path" (notice the capital letters). While there is no "wrong" reason for practicing Buddhism in any of its forms, these can become obstacles to the path itself. Why? Because seekers and those on a path are focused on the process, not the result. Those focused on the process *can* wind up in a state of suspended animation that never arrives anywhere. It is not intended to. It is all about "the Path." So intention or motivation can make a huge difference in whether you make rapid, or indeed any, progress toward the realization of enlightenment. As the Dzogchen Ponlop Rinpoche points out, ask yourself every day, "What is my intention?" and "What do I want to achieve during my meditation *today*?"

Research on setting goals has shown that it is highly effective. Just to give one example, a long-term study was done of the Yale graduating class of 1953. At the time of the study, the 3% who set goals were worth more than the rest of the graduating class combined. Goals give us a sense of urgency, a leading edge. They give us an intensity of purpose and enthusiasm for success. But we need to decide *exactly* what we want to accomplish. Having said that, please don't be afraid to change your goals; and don't beat yourself up if you do not attain them within your expected deadline. While goals can be helpful, they can also become obstacles if you get too carried away.

One common guideline is the acronym SMART: Specific, Measurable, Attainable, Relevant, Timely. First, we need to be very clear about what it is that we intend to accomplish. Then, we need to know how we can determine whether we have actually achieved it … or how far along we are. Next, it must be challenging but realistic, what are often call "stretch" goals. It must have meaning for you. And finally, it needs to have a deadline. When do expect to achieve it?

So if you want to accelerate your progress *significantly*, set goals following these guidelines for what you expect to do both on and off of the cushion *every day*. The Buddha said, "He is able who thinks he is able." You are as able as you want to be. The word for meditation in Tibetan means "habituation." So repetition is very important to habituate or train our mind. This includes setting goals. Make a habit of refreshing your intention every day … several times each day. In *The Empire Strikes Back*, Yoda tells young Skywalker who was *trying* to master his skills, "Try not. Do or do not. There is no try." And so it is here, too.

Why Practice This Form of Buddhism?

Another "why" is regarding the particular form of Buddhism to practice. As in other religious traditions, there are several options. The Buddha said there are 84,000 paths to enlightenment. There are indeed several major branches of Buddhism, each with numerous subdivisions.

The only way to know what is best for you is to test them, which given the number of options can be an endless process. Alternately, you can look at the character of the leaders and teachers to get a feel for what they are like. You will always do better with someone you like. While I have no doubt that other Buddhist traditions have great leaders and teachers, His Holiness the Dalai Lama, and many others whom I have met, have matched my preferences. Their intellectual prowess and sense of humor, their lovingkindness and great compassion are among the qualities I most admire. Selecting a *personal* teacher or lama is another matter that we will address later on. Just be cautious about the initial enthusiasm that is often associated with the first "real" lama you meet. While I was not attracted by the ornate ritual and decorative elements of Tibetan Buddhism in the beginning, originally preferring the simplicity of Japanese Zen, I have grown to like it a great deal, particularly after learning much of the symbolic representation embodied in it.

According to the tradition itself, Tantra as practiced in Tibetan Buddhism is the most expedient of the different vehicles (*yanas*). It is said to produce results faster through the use of the tantric methods than the approaches used in the other branches. I am sure that those branches may well disagree. However, there are at least some valid scientific reasons to support this contention beyond the claims of the tradition itself as we will learn later on.

On the other hand, there are certainly arguments against Tantra based on questions regarding the "authenticity" of the teachings, i.e., the *source* of the teachings. These critics believe that only the teachings of the historical Buddha himself should be the basis for the teachings. The Tantric teachings, which are generally not traced directly to the historical Buddha, are said to have come from other Buddhas. And those teachings accept and build upon the foundational principles of the other traditions that are claimed to have come from the historical Buddha. But as we will see shortly, those claims are open to question as well. One of the features of the Tantric approach is that it became a *living* tradition, unlike those that established a *fixed* cannon.[3] Thus, Tantra is open to a continuing revelation, which is particularly beneficial when a tradition moves into a new cultural setting like the West.

---

[3] To be fair, the various branches of the Tibetan Buddhist tradition have now established their own cannon as well.

Can You Really Attain Enlightenment as a Householder?

The realistic answer is, of course, not necessarily. But *can* you? Yes! Mipham Rinpoche said that according to the sutras, "One can become enlightened in one week." It is possible, just not likely. This is not really about actually achieving enlightenment in that time. It *is* about really understanding in that time exactly *how* to do it, cognitively and experientially. This text captures the essential elements of the tradition from a Tibetan or Tantric Buddhism perspective based on essential teachings attributed to Padmasambhava, the great Indian yogi who is largely credited with establishing Buddhism in Tibet.

The work best known in the West attributed to Padmasambhava, also known as Guru Rinpoche, is *The Tibetan Book of the Dead*. The root text source for much of this book is a companion volume known in the West as *Natural Liberation*, the teachings on the Six Bardos by Guru Rinpoche. The problem with that text for a beginner is that it is organized around the six bardos. Consequently, the order of the practices does not present a systematic path toward enlightenment. Of course, it was not intended to. But the practices listed are ideal for householders. They are short and easy to do.

After teaching three, year-long courses on these teachings, it became clear to me that the order was a problem for students. So I set out to re-order them into a series more closely aligned with traditional path of learning. In that process, I found that I needed to provide some introductory material, as well as fill in a few gaps. The result has been very favorable, based on a new class spread over four semesters, with more breaks to allow students to catch up or catch their breath, as the case may be. At the same time, at the request of my students, I committed to writing this book for them … and you.

So by studying this text and following the simple instructions for each of the practices, you will gain a clear understanding of exactly what needs to be done to attain enlightenment in this life. Furthermore, you will have the practical experience from a systematic approach for actually doing the practices and understand how to do it from an experiential level as well. When combined with the proper motivation, this can become a powerful drive to realize the goal in this lifetime. That, too, is my goal for you!

Content Overview

"You wake up in the morning and it's so beautiful you can hardly stand it!" – Zen student

Buddha means one who is awake! Our innate Buddhanature is already within, we only need to "wake up" to it – to a correct understanding of it, to a direct experience of it, and to its application every moment of our lives to be fully awake. And it is beautiful! Everything is seen as part of the spontaneous radiant display of the transcendent wisdom – the sacred outlook or Pure View. Abiding in that Pure View, one also manifests immeasurable lovingkindness, compassion, joy and equanimity for the benefit of others. We are all interrelated, interconnected and interdependent. Through this we achieve the Great Compassion of a Buddha. When combined with transcendent wisdom, we achieve the union of compassion and wisdom – *innate happiness.*

How does one awaken? While we may spontaneously experience brief moments of being awake, full development of awakened consciousness requires practice – much like learning to play a musical instrument. And to be truly great at it requires committed, persistent practice over an extended time. Brain research shows that parts of the brain are physically changed from these practices – musical, spiritual or other – with long-term effects. These changes facilitate growth and development in the practice. This book is about how to do that … as a householder.

This book uses traditional sources, primarily from Padmasambhava's Six Bardo teachings[4], that fit into the householder lifestyle in a way that we can achieve enlightenment in this lifetime. While, once again, it still takes patience and persistence, it is realistically achievable according to the texts themselves. The root text was attributed to Padmasambhava (8th century) and written down by his consort, Yeshe Tsogyal, as a heart-essence teaching containing pith instructions essential for swift enlightenment. It was discovered by the great treasure revealer

---

[4] These may be found in *Natural Liberation: Padmasambhava's Teachings on the Six Bardos*, with commentary by Gyatrul Rinpoche and translated by B. Alan Wallace, and *Mind Beyond Death*, by The Dzogchen Ponlop Rinpoche.

Karma Lingpa (14th century). This is a very concise set of teachings based
on the Great Perfection or highest Tantric view. The primary focus is on
practices for the six bardos or intermediate states: this life, dreaming,
meditation, dying, Dharmata[5] and the process of next rebirth.

These teachings on the six bardos were intended for times of
hardship in dharma practice. In addition, this very concise text includes
all the practices essential to achieving enlightenment. Thus, the practice
of these teachings is especially relevant to the situation of householder
practitioners in the West, when the time for dharma practice is limited.
The text summarizes the essential points on the nature of samsara and
nirvana, and thus enables you to achieve swift liberation even during our
busy lives.

As previously noted, the order of the practices in the root text is
based the six bardos is not the same order in which they are normally
taught and practiced for greatest effectiveness. Thus, the order in this text
has been more closely aligned with the traditional sequence taught in
Tantric Buddhism. The exact content and order will vary from one
lineage to another. In a few cases I have elaborated upon the original
descriptions where a more detailed understanding has only been
inferred. I have added practices from the tradition to fill in gaps or
facilitate transitions and direct experiential understanding.

In addition to the rearranged root practices from
Padmasambhava, I have included commentaries to help Western
householders understand the context and the practice – some based on
traditional views or explanations but also many Western and scientific
views or explanations and approaches based on brain and behavioral
research – to facilitate learning and using these practices to expedite your
development along the path.

Thus, I have attempted to bring together the heart-essence of the
teachings and practices in a concise and easy to understand set of
instructions for busy Western householders who really do want to
achieve enlightenment in this life.

While some traditionalists may not approve of this approach, I
am following the advice of the Buddha to not accept his word (or that of
others) without testing, just as a goldsmith tests the purity of gold before
buying it. Furthermore, I am following the Buddha's advice when his
followers asked about how to they were to tell whether a teaching is
authentic after he died. He told them to see if the teaching is consistent

---

[5] An experience of the ultimate nature of things – emptiness.

with the dharma and not to challenge it based only on the source. At the same time, I do believe that many of the practices that some Westerners have eliminated from their approach as just "cultural" elements have actual benefits for your practice. This is a complete and systematic path to enlightenment, but it has been streamlined to meet the needs of those of us in the West, while accelerating the efficiency and effectiveness of learning and practice so as to achieve comparable realizations to many monks and nuns who follow a slower, more traditional approach to learning and practice. This is the path of the householder – the yogi and yogini.

The choice is up to you, and only you. The only way to know what approach works best for you is to actually follow the instructions and test them for yourself. This, of course, requires a degree of faith that they will in fact work. If you doubt, it is likely that they will not work. If you trust, it is likely that they will. The mind is a powerful thing. Use it to your advantage.

Organization of the Book

The remaining parts of the book are briefly described below. Each path is explained in more detail in Part 2.

Part 2 — Background gives a short historical perspective on the life and teachings of the Buddha, the influence of the Second Buddha – Padmasambhava, and a brief discussion of the second dissemination of Buddhism into Tibet. This is followed by a chapter on the Three Trainings – ethics, meditation, and wisdom – and Four Paths – the Path of Individual Liberation, the Path of Altruism, the Path of Tantra, and the Path of Great Perfection – which form the basic structure of the core of the book. There is a part in the text for each path and, within that one or more chapters on each of the Three Trainings for that path. This part concludes with a discussion regarding the qualifications for and process of following a dharma teacher.

Part 3 — The Path of Individual Liberation focuses on the ethical views, practices, and view regarding wisdom for this path. These are the most direct teachings of the historical Buddha and form the foundation for the other paths.

Part 4 — The Path of Altruism describes the ethical views, key practices, and view of wisdom in this path. This expands upon the Path of Individual Liberation to include the altruistic goal of enlightenment for all beings.

Part 5—The Path of Tantra describes the ethics, core practices, and view of wisdom for this path. This introduces the deity yogas, as well as the somewhat secret practices of sexual yoga that are more suitable for householders than monks and nuns who take vows of celibacy.

Part 6—The Path of Great Perfection is generally the most advanced path and normally considered part of the Path of Tantra. It has been distinguished here as a separate path due to its unique approach to ethics, meditation, and view of wisdom.

Part 7—Enlightenment brings together these four paths to describe their unique understandings of the goal of enlightenment. It concludes with a discussion on using the practices in this book, based on the teachings of Padmasambhava, for achieving enlightenment in this life.

Part 8 includes appendices with a few more detailed practice texts (*sadhanas*) that may be helpful in your development.

I recommend that to you begin by reading the entire text. Most Westerners don't have the patience to read just a few pages and do the practices for a week or more without peeking ahead. I don't! This is in effect like a "glance" meditation, which is used to review and remind practitioners of the whole path. Then go back and actually do each of the practices for a week or more as needed to develop mastery or a degree of certainty in each practice. You have to master the practices to attain enlightenment. Study alone does not work. Periodically scanning the whole path as you do the practices is also helpful. You need to know where you have been, as well as where you are going.

While this text is grounded in many fundamental principles from the Buddhist tradition, these practices are not limited to Buddhism. As His Holiness the Dalai Lama frequently points out, many of these practices are also applicable to other religious traditions or even outside of religions. Readers so inclined are encouraged to find those that may be applicable to their particular religious or secular spiritual needs.

In addition, I have minimized the use of Tibetan and Sanskrit language as much as practical to convey a Western approach to these practices, and to facilitate extending them into other religious or spiritual traditions. However, I have noted the source terms to ensure academic clarity. In a few cases where there is not an easy and reasonably accurate translation possible, I have continued to use the Tibetan or Sanskrit words.

It is important to recognize that teachings are often best communicated directly from master to student. Texts have long been a part of the tradition and facilitate both consistency and diversity in the tradition. Still, it is recommended that those who can, find a qualified master from whom to receive these teachings directly, along with ongoing direction in your spiritual development.

There are others, no doubt, more qualified with greater understanding and realizations than me. I deeply appreciate what they offer to help my own learning and practice. Nevertheless, I offer this simple text for those who find it to be of some benefit for their particular needs. And while my intentions are pure, I take personal responsibility for any errors in my thinking, descriptions or recommendations contained herein.

Homage to Samantabhadra and Samantabhadri! May any errors in understanding or transmission regarding these contents be forgiven. May this text be of some benefit in your practice. May we all wake up to our enlightened state of being in this lifetime for the benefit of others! EMAHO!

Part 2 –Background

This part of the text gives a short historical perspective on the Buddha and some of the fundamental teachings and principles of the Buddhist practices. These include the preliminaries of ethics, motionlessness, and breath control. It goes on to describe the levels of attainment achieved by the Buddha prior to his enlightenment. Then, I review the teachings that followed, including the Four Noble Truths, The Three Turnings of the Wheel, the four Paths of Individual Liberation, the Bodhisattva, Tantra, and the Great Perfection, a brief history of the Second Buddha – Padmasambhava, and a brief review of the second dissemination of Buddhism into Tibet.

Chapter 2

A Concise Historical Background

A Brief Life Story of the Historical Buddha

There are numerous stories about the historical Buddha. Most of them include considerable amounts of "legend" or "myth" about him and his accomplishments. After all, nothing was written down for hundreds of years after he died. Here I will only give a short synopsis of his life and look at that from a scholarly perspective of what do we really know? It is important to realize that there was little concern about "history" in ancient times. It was the "story" that was important. After the death of a founder, the followers would recall the deeds and sayings. Great figures were often assigned to distant antiquity to enhance their status. Stories became embellished and augmented by being entwined with the lives of other important figures. There were often meetings with luminaries of the past.

Within Buddhism, there are variations in the approach to the story of the Buddha. The Theravada tradition tells the story of a human teacher with human limitations, abilities and death. In the Mahayana tradition, the Buddha becomes a transcendent cosmic figure who appeared among humans, but surpassed even the great gods of India in wisdom and power. He did not really die and still appears to those who need help. There are, of course, countless variations and stories as Buddha was remembered for how he personified the myths and symbols of the particular group's assumptions, doctrines and practices. These then reflect the shared paradigms in Indian and, later, Tibetan cultures.

Historians believe Shakyamuni Buddha was born in 563 BCE, although exact dates vary. At that time what we now call India was somewhat larger than now and included Nepal, Pakistan and so forth, representing the subcontinent rather than a country. It consisted of small principalities with significant and growing differences between rich and poor, due to a growing merchant class.

The ancient Vedas (ca. 16th-6th centuries BCE) dominated the culture. Among the Vedic principles was the concept of Brahman – the ultimate out of which comes all things and into which all things return. The Vedics also believed in a permanent soul or "self," which was identical with Brahman. But one must pursue *moksha* – liberation – to free the self from attachment that binds it to *samsara* – the endless cycle of life and source of unhappiness – following the laws of *karma*. In addition to following the rigid caste system and other rules and rites of the Vedas, one should follow the way of *dharma* to achieve liberation. The spiritual life was primarily the focus of the Brahmin class according the Vedic tradition. But the Bramins had come to focus mostly on ritual and during this time of social turmoil, people were becoming discontent.

The Vedas increasingly competed with other philosophical and religious views, including the *shramana* movement of wandering ascetic monks that reflected many of the views adopted by the Buddha. The *shramanans* did not accept the Vedic class structure and ritual, lived an ascetic lifestyle, believed in reincarnation and karma, and sought liberation from *samsara* through meditation and asceticism. They believed that it was through intentional suffering that its opposite, nirvana, was achieved. The more ascetic your life; the more transcendent happiness you realized. One who achieved that was called an *Arhat*.

It was into this environment that Siddhartha Gautama was born in the foothills of what is now Nepal. It is said that he was the son of a king, although some recent archeological evidence suggests that this area was governed by a council form of government (a new and emerging form of governance at this time in India), in which case he may actually been the son of the head of this council. Keep in mind that this is not particularly important as it is all about the story, not the historical facts. He was born into the Shakya clan, hence became known as Shakyamuni, Sage of the Shakyas.

According to the story, his mother had a dream before Siddhartha was born, a dream of a white elephant entering her side to impregnate her. This was interpreted to mean that the child would become a great king or a great sage.[6] His father sought to protect him and guide him into the former role. But at age 29 he experienced (the details vary) seeing old age, sickness and death for the first time in his life, which had a profound impact on him. In addition, he is said to have encountered one of these wondering ascetics, which struck him with a

---

[6] This kind of dream also appears in Vedic literature from which it may have originated into the story of the Buddha.

strong desire to pursue a spiritual life. At that time his own wife (or one of his wives) had a baby, both of whom he left to seek enlightenment. He shaved his head and took up the yellow robe of a yogi.

He then sought out a teacher. The initial requirement at that time was to begin with *ethics*. Ethical behavior is the foundation upon which the practices are built. If one cannot behave in an ethical manner, then the practices will have no benefit. Later, as the Buddha, ethics was included into the expectations of monks, nuns, and lay practitioners.

The second prerequisite was the preliminary practice of *motionlessness*. The yogi needed to be able to sit completely still without distraction for extended periods of time. The Buddha also adopted this principle, which is found in the descriptions of several forms of meditation. Tibetan Buddhism is not as rigorous in this matter as some other branches of the Buddhist tradition. However, there are certain practices in which this is included. The ability to sit in stillness can be very beneficial to one's meditation.

Stillness leads into the third prerequisite, which is *breath control*. Some forms of meditation make this a major point of emphasis. It is used in several of the Buddhist meditations, though many simply relax the breath rather than controlling it. But learning to use long, slow breaths can be beneficial to meditation generally. In that regard, it is helpful to practice intentional breath control in the beginning, until it becomes habituated and no longer requires focused attention. At that point it becomes natural and can be applied both during and after meditation.

I would like to make a critical point here. While these three prerequisites are done intentionally as a practice, the purpose is to develop skills and a way of seeing things, a worldview, that affects us *all the time*. Meditation is not about becoming a great meditator. It is about becoming a buddha. One is not a buddha just during meditation, but *all the time*. I will continue to drive home the point that to follow the Buddhist path means to make *everything* practice ... always and all ways. You will benefit from this only in very limited ways if you only do it as a meditation 20 minutes a day, while sitting on the cushion. Intention is critical.

Siddhartha mastered these three prerequisites and then learned the first four concentrations (*jhanas*) or meditations on "form" from his guru:

1. Focus on an object (e.g., the breath) leading to calm happiness, but still with some thoughts.

2. Withdrawal of the senses through concentration leading to a sense of joy.

3. Single-pointed concentration on the "ground of being" transcending joy.

4. Stop thinking, becoming one with object of focus in single-pointed equanimity.

According to tradition, Siddhartha easily mastered these and was still dissatisfied. So he sought another guru who taught him four higher meditative states or "formless" meditations (*ayatanas*) :

1. Sense of vastness or openness beyond an object of focus

2. Pure consciousness (awareness of awareness) beyond space

3. Nothingness

4. "Neither perception nor non-perception"

Still dissatisfied, Siddhartha decided to follow the path of asceticism and with five other yogis went into the forest to seek enlightenment. After nearly six years of extreme asceticism, he again became dissatisfied and was on the verge of death. Upon leaving the forest, a compassionate girl gave him some nourishment[7] from which he recovered his strength and set out to attain enlightenment on his own. Neither the indulgence of his previous life in the palace nor the extreme asceticism was the way to enlightenment. He sought a "middle way."

He sat under the Bodhi Tree (a fig tree) in what is now Bodhgaya, India. Here he committed to staying until he achieved enlightenment. All night he sat. According to some stories he faced many challenges from the demon *Mara*. These were, of course, his own inner demons. Whether attacked by warriors and their arrows, which he turned into flowers, or seduced by temptresses, which he turned into old hags, he remained unfazed, much as one does during dream yoga when facing various afflictive emotions or other mental obscurations that manifest as bad dreams. Finally, as Mara was preparing another onslaught, Siddhartha showed him the ruin he was about to suffer, and he withdrew. Siddhartha remained calm and sat in stillness, meditating through the night.

---

[7] Rice milk, rice porridge, or rice pudding – stories vary.

He recalled an experience as a child. His father had taken him to a planting festival. Sitting under a rose-apple tree and watching, he noticed how the earthworms writhed in agony as they were unearthed by the plow, and he developed deep compassion for them. His mind wandered and he began to feel an *innate happiness* spontaneously arise. He had found a third alternative, a Middle Way between the extremes of indulgence and asceticism. And this transcendent happiness was innate. We already have it. We just need to relax, be quiet, and calm the mind, and it will reveal itself.

We are told that having this realization, he continued to meditate under the Bodhi tree and recalled all of his prior lives, the cycle of birth and death, and the workings of the universe. Then as the dark of night was replaced by the first light of dawn, Siddhartha is said to have achieved complete enlightenment.

In Tibetan Buddhism, this experience of the first light of dawn is often used as a metaphor for the dawning of *clear light*. In fact the dark blue-black color of first light is often used for the skin color of personifications of the ultimate, such as *Samantabhadra* or *Vajradhara*. However, clear light is neither clear nor light. It is better to think of the "clear" aspect as "pure" and the "light" aspect as "awareness" (lighting the way). In this sense, clear light is a metaphor for *pure awareness - rigpa*.

In this state of pure awareness the Buddha once again experienced *innate happiness*. This is what had been missing in all of those prior attempts. The Buddha remained for seven weeks, thinking no one would believe his story. Then, according to some sources, the gods Indra and Brahma appealed to him, and he finally agreed to share his insights.

Walking along the road he was asked, "What are you?" He responded, "I am awake!" Buddha means one who is awake. Thus, he became known as the Buddha. He is said to have then approached his five former companions with whom he practiced asceticism. Upon seeing him at a distance, they resolved not to speak to him; but as he approached, they were overwhelmed by his peaceful radiance and they asked him to teach them. Thus, they became his first disciples or *sangha*.[8]

The first teachings of the Buddha became known as the Four Noble Truths: (1) the truth of "suffering" (unhappiness), (2) the truth of the source of suffering (fundamental ignorance), (3) the truth of cessation (enlightenment), and (4) the truth of the path (training the mind). Since

---

[8] Today, a group requires at least 5 members to start a *sangha*.

much has been written on these, I will provide only a summary, including a Western view on these four truths.

The Four Noble Truths

The First Truth - Suffering, Unhappiness, Dissatisfaction and/or Imperfection

A perfect world! Wouldn't that be ... perfect?! Unfortunately, most of us experience a variety of less than perfect events in our lives. We may get sick or be injured. We may experience the loss of a loved one. We may go hungry or in need of clothing or shelter. If not us, we may see others suffering in these ways. At another level our picnic may be interrupted by rain. Our crops may suffer from lack of moisture. We may wake up with a hangover from having too much fun. We may be anxious about closing a big deal with a client or getting a raise or promotion at work. We may worry about our stock portfolio. We may have an argument with a spouse or be frustrated by actions of our children. There are countless forms of unhappiness in this material universe.

These are all examples of "suffering" or *dukkha* as noted before. I pointed out that this is broader than our normal understanding of the word suffering in the West, which tends to focus on pain and mental anguish. Recall the experience of Siddhartha seeing the sufferings of old age, sickness, and death. Often birth is added to this list, the same list found in the Vedas. The suffering of pain and mental anguish is classified as the *suffering of suffering*. But in the broader perspective of unhappiness, it may include not getting what we want or getting what we do not want. We may get too much or too little. These are classified as the *suffering of change*. But there is an even more subtle form - imperfection. "Why can't we all just get along?" "Why can't we all love each other?" This is classified as *all-pervasive suffering*.

When we don't get what we want - a raise or promotion, a new house, the man or woman of our dreams, and so forth - we experience unrequited *desire*. Such desire comes from our *attachment* to the objects of our desire. We may experience *envy* toward those who do have or get what we want. We may develop such a strong desire that it manifests as *greed* or *jealousy*. If we do get what we desire, we may also hold it up for others to envy, experiencing *pride* or *arrogance* in our achievements. When we desire something or someone, our focus is on self. What's in it for *me*? This is our *ego* talking.

When any of these qualities become excessive – and most of them are – then they become sources of imperfection in our lives and/or in the lives of others. We suffer … or we cause others to suffer. In such instances, desire is another source of imperfection on our sacred journey. Ego and ignorance are the two most significant barriers on the spiritual path to enlightenment.

If we become sufficiently frustrated, anxious, or restricted – particularly by others – we may also become *angry*. In some cases this may extend to hatred. Anger and hatred are significant barriers to spiritual development. They interfere with our ability to relate effectively with others. They can even debilitate our personal effectiveness. In either case, they prevent us from attaining or maintaining a spiritual outlook, another imperfection on our sacred journey. Ignorance, desire, anger and their related manifestations are forms of *poison* to those who seek spiritual enlightenment, in whatever form we practice. Along with *ego* they create much of the imperfection that we experience in our lives.

In the West our regular mind is understood largely as a function of our brain. Our brain affects our experience in the form of mind, and our mind affects our brain. They are interdependent. Our brain developed into three major parts. The most ancient of those is the primitive or reptilian brain, the brain-stem. Its function is pretty much focused on survival – fight or flight. It is extraordinarily anxious, fast, and always alert to danger. The second part to develop was the subcortical structure. It is also fast, holds both short and long-term memory and processes emotions. It, too, is closely engaged in fight or flight. The "modern" part of the brain and the last to develop is called the cortex. It is slower and allows us to think, communicate, bond, collaborate, and love. It can also calm the anxiety of the reptilian and subcortical brain.

Part of the thinking process includes our senses: seeing, hearing, smelling, tasting, and touching. Tibetans include thinking (and feelings) as a sixth sense. Each then is described as a form of consciousness. Recall that the brain evolved to focus on survival. As a part of that, there is a significant emphasis on the negative – dangers to our survival. The brain processes negative information faster. It leaves a stronger imprint or memory. And it takes as many as five positive interactions to overcome a single negative one. You could say we are programmed for suffering!

The Second Truth - The Source of Suffering

So certainly our brain structure is one source of our suffering. But the Buddha knew nothing of modern neuro-science. What he did know from the shramana tradition is that our senses (including thinking) lead us into misunderstanding the nature of our mind. He called this our fundamental ignorance. Furthermore, all sentient beings[9] are said to want happiness and to avoid suffering that are caused by this ignorance. In other words, our unhappiness is caused by nothing other than our own mind.

The Buddha added that our sense of self or our ego, due to this ignorance, is what leads us to desire and attachment, anger and aversion. We act as if we have some form of permanent or "inherent" existence. The brain feeds this by helping us construct boundaries that differentiate our "self" from what is outside of us, the "other." This leads us to "want" or as my Mother used to tell me as a young child (especially around Christmas), "Want, want, want; all you do is want!" So we believe consumerism is the answer. If only we had ___. This would bring us the happiness we desire. As the bumper sticker says, "He who dies with the most toys wins!" Or in the movie Wall Street, Mr. Gecko tells us, "Greed is good." Yes, the wealthy can buy themselves out of some problems. But they are also able to hide behind their wealth, enabling their problems to get even worse! This just digs us in deeper and deeper. Look at the recent global financial meltdown. It was fueled by greed. Greed at the top. Greed at the bottom. Greed everywhere in between. We just don't get it! So we suffer from our own fundamental ignorance.

This sense of imperfection is a form of perception. We perceive it that way. The rain on our picnic is moisture for thirsty crops to the farmer. The deal that we were able to close, shut out another competitor. We are focused on our self-interest over that of others, more often than

---

[9] A sentient being is any living being capable of experiencing happiness and suffering. The Buddha knew nothing of microbes. Scientists are not in agreement as to exactly what life forms do experience happiness or suffering. There is even debate about at what point the human embryo is capable of those experiences. In general, sentient beings are interpreted to include insects and higher forms of life.

not. We do not see the bigger picture, the *true nature* of what we call reality.

Most religious and spiritual traditions posit a nonmaterial reality, something beyond what we can experience through our five senses or what we call "empirical" reality. What is it? Some give it a name – God, Allah, Brahman, the Tao, Dharmakaya, and so forth. Conceptualizations may vary somewhat, some described with more personified characteristics and others as more ineffable. But none of them can be observed through ordinary senses. This ultimate reality is the focus of *wisdom* within each of these traditions. Lack of this wisdom is ignorance. Ignorance is a source of imperfection on the sacred journey.

The Third Truth - The Truth of Cessation

In achieving enlightenment, the Buddha found a truth that was not present in the other teachings he mastered from his previous gurus. Something had been missing. He felt good during the meditative experience, but that disappeared afterwards. He sought something more permanent. The answer was found in addressing our ignorance of the true nature of mind, and the true nature of things, our worldview. He compared it to a candle burning out when the fuel is used up. In this analogy, what is being burned up is our negative karma and habitual tendencies. He specifically addresses them as ignorance (delusion), attachment (desire), and aversion (hatred). These are the three fires[10] described by the Buddha in what is known as his Fire Sermon, which need to be extinguished. These are the roots or most basic causes of our suffering. And nirvana literally means "blowing out" those fires.

At the same time, he noted that change happens. Nothing seems permanent. And indeed this is true. Science tells us that systems entropy – decline in their energy over time. Seasons change. The earth continues to rotate through a cycle of day and night. Time marches on. The only thing permanent is change itself, or so it seems.

Impermanence allows this change to happen. If there was no change, we would be stuck in our fundamental ignorance. Enlightenment would be impossible. But because of impermanence, the Buddha was able to awaken and so can we. Although he may have initially expressed some doubts, he finally came to accept that if he could do it, so could

---

[10] Also known as the "three poisons"

others. Yes, it may be easier for some, but even the Buddha came to recognize that in fact *everyone* can eventually achieve enlightenment, even if it takes more than this lifetime or even eons. It is in the Tibetan Buddhist tradition that we are taught that you, too, can achieve enlightenment and do it within *this* lifetime.

With the cessation of suffering, our *innate happiness* blossoms. There is a deep inner peace with no attachment or aversion and with great lovingkindness and compassion for all. This, above all, is what made the message of the Buddha unique. This was the realization he finally had under the Bodhi tree. We find that much of human motivation, whether or not it is considered to be ethical, is driven by our pursuit of happiness. The founding fathers and mothers of the United States considered it to be a fundamental human right as expressed in the Declaration of Independence. His Holiness the Dalai Lama has also pointed out that it is the common denominator in most human endeavors and at the heart of our religious traditions, whether we are seeking happiness in this life or in some form of afterlife.

But happiness should not be confused with pleasure. When we pursue pleasure, we are seeking a temporary state of happiness. Happiness is certainly not about money. Studies show that except in cases of extreme poverty, there is no correlation between one's wealth and one's happiness beyond a temporary effect from a sufficient increase. The effect of a raise, a promotion, a fancy car, a beautiful home, even an intense orgasm, does not last. Then we are off on the chase after yet another level of achievement to fulfill our endless pursuit of pleasure.

True happiness comes from inner peace, contentment, and satisfaction with our lives. Inner peace best comes from developing our spirituality – learning, experiencing, and abiding in the sacred outlook. When one can remain continuously in this state, we experience blissful surrender and true inner peace. This is the goal described as nirvana, the pure lands, or heaven in various traditions. In some it is in the next life; in others it is here and now, heaven is within.

Yet even inner peace by itself is not the ultimate. Happiness for oneself fails to meet the ethical consideration of transcending self for the benefit of others. Thus, ultimate happiness engages an altruistic intention to benefit *all* others in also realizing inner peace. We have already established that we are all interdependent. Therefore, we can only achieve ultimate happiness through our intention to benefit everyone … even, as Jesus said, our enemies. That's a tough standard … to put it mildly. But we are all one in a sense – interrelated, interconnected, and interdependent. Only when we consider the common good of all can we achieve our own state of ultimate happiness.

How can this be possible? There are nearly seven billion human beings on this planet, a number that is rapidly increasing. People are starving and dying all over the globe. What can one lone person do? And that does not even begin to consider the gazillion ants and other sentient beings on this planet alone. Fortunately, interdependence works in both directions. Not only are we dependent upon others, but also they are dependent upon us. *Anything* that we do to benefit others, even one other, tends to have a beneficial effect that extends in subtle ways to others. In some cases this comes from the chain of cause and effect. We help one, who then helps another, who then … and so forth.

The Fourth Truth - Training the Mind

To achieve cessation of fundamental ignorance, one must follow a path for training the mind to see the world in a different way, a new worldview. We call this sacred outlook or Pure View. The Buddha initially taught that the way out of our fundamental ignorance is to follow what he called the Noble Eightfold Path. This consists of:

1. Right conduct

2. Right speech

3. Right thought

4. Right livelihood

5. Right effort

6. Right mindfulness

7. Right concentration

8. Right view

The first three refer to our body, speech, and mind. We use #6, right mindfulness, to help us do that, being mindful of all we think, say, and do. This is not about meditation, although that is included. It is about the rest of our lives. We engage in virtuous thoughts, words and deeds and avoid nonvirtuous thoughts, words and deeds, i.e., ethics. We make a conscious effort to pay attention to all of these throughout the day, and eventually even in our sleep. Right livelihood could be part of right

conduct. But here the essence is that we should choose jobs that follow
the ethics or moral precepts. One can see that from the very the
beginning, the Buddha addressed householders and not just monks and
nuns. Right effort, mindfulness, and concentration focus on meditation.
Right view is the result, the wisdom that overcomes fundamental
ignorance. In the Paths of Altruism and Tantra, these actions are
summarized as the Three Trainings: ethics, meditation, and wisdom.

The Three Turnings of the Wheel

The Buddha taught for over 50 years and is believed to have died
around 483 BCE at age 80. Not all of these teachings have come down to
us. And there are differences of opinion about the authenticity of what
has come down to us. We do know that he followed some of the ideas of
the Vedas and Shramanans, while rejecting others such as the concept of
Brahman, the caste system, subjugation of women, and a permanent soul,
the latter of which he replaced with nirvana – a state of inner peace, a
sense of liberation, insight into the true nature of things, the joy of
oneness with reality, and love for all sentient beings.

One of the systems of classifying his teachings has come to be
known as the Three Turnings of the Wheel of Dharma. In the first
turning, the Buddha taught the Four Noble Truths, the Noble Eightfold
Path, and so forth. These were given in and around Deer Park where he
located his main monastic community.

Later he went to Vulture Peak. There he gave a series of
teachings on emptiness. These became known as the Second Turning of
the Wheel. From these teachings, we have the concepts of emptiness of
self, emptiness of other, and so forth that led to the texts on transcendent
wisdom (prajnaparamita) such as the Heart Sutra and the Diamond
Sutra. Here the texts make use of extensive lists to show the emptiness of
things and concepts, including those of Buddhism itself.

Because of a tendency to regard "emptiness" as nothingness, the
Buddha is said to have late in life given teachings called the Third
Turning of the Wheel. These describe buddhanature – luminous
emptiness. "Luminous" here refers to illuminating or shedding light on
emptiness. It has a sense of knowing or clear understanding about it. This
is intended to show that it is not nothingness. But neither is it something.
Rather it is the Middle Way between the extremes of nothingness and
permanence. And buddhanature is innate within every sentient being. It
is like a seed waiting to be cultivated or, in another approach, it is like the

egg of a garuda[11] waiting for the shell to crack open so it can emerge fully grown and ready to fly into the sky. We will examine emptiness in more detail later in the book.

The Second Buddha

We are not sure how Buddhism first came to Tibet. There are differing stories. We do know that the Indian king, Asoka sent Buddhist emissaries throughout much of the known world in the 3rd century BCE. By the 7th century CE, Tibet had encountered Buddhism as an invading force into China and other regions. The first "definitive establishment of Buddhism in Tibet occurred during the reign of King Songtsen Gampo (c. 618-650)."[12] According to legend, he took two Buddhist wives to establish political alliances, one from Nepal and the other from China. Each brought Buddhist statues with them for which temples were built. In the latter case, the statue of Shakyamuni Buddha became known as Jowo Rinpoche and remains as one of the most sacred images in Tibet. The legends also tell us that King Songtsen Gampo sent a scholar to India to develop a script for the Tibetan language, which became the first written script and grammatical standards for the Tibetan language.

The eighth-century Tibetan King Trisong Detsen (c. 740-798) decided to construct the first Buddhist monastery in Tibet. He invited the Indian scholar Shantarakshita to oversee the construction. However, after encountering a series of natural disasters – some say evil spirits who, each night, would destroy what was built that day – and resistance from government ministers from the indigenous Bon religion, he was forced to leave Tibet. In leaving, he recommended to the king that he invite the powerful tantric adept Padmasambhava to come from India to overpower the spirits.

So the king invited Padmasambhava, who subdued many spirits along the way, as well as those obstructing the construction of Tibet's first monastery, *Samye*[13]. In addition, during his stay in Tibet, he is said to

---

[11] A *garuda* is a mythical bird that emerges from the shell fully grown and developed at birth, not unlike a Western analogy of an airplane, which emerges from the factory ready to fly.

[12] *Introduction to Tibetan Buddhism* (revised edition) by John Powers, p. 144.

[13] Pronounced "sawm-yay"

have traveled extensively and subdued more evil spirits, turning them
into "dharma protectors" who promised to protect the dharma against
other evil spirits and obstructions.[14] King Trisong Detsen was able to
invite Shantarakshita to return and the monastery was consecrated
around 767 CE, and the first seven Tibetans received monastic
ordination. The Indian *pandita* Vimalamitra was also invited to Tibet, and
together these three figures are largely credited with the establishment of
Buddhism in Tibet. Padmasambhava in particular became regarded as
the Second Buddha by Tibetans. Retroactively, during the second
dissemination, Padmasambhava become known as the "founder" of the
Nyingma School (lit. Old School) of Tibetan Buddhism. Buddhism then
spread, particularly among the educated classes for the next 50 years.

The Second Dissemination

In spite of his efforts to subdue and transform the evil spirits of
Tibet into dharma protectors, not everyone was happy about the
establishment of Buddhism in Tibet. In particular the Bon ministers
continued to resist. After King Relbachen (reigned 815-836) spent lavishly
on temples and monasteries, supported visiting teachers from India and
sent Tibetan scholars to India, all while neglecting matters of state, the
opposition intensified, and he was assassinated.

He was followed by King Lang Dharma, who was a devout Bon
follower. He closed the monasteries and temples in central Tibet,
destroyed texts and statues, and forced the monks and nuns to return to
lay life. Buddhism in that part of Tibet went underground. The harsh
policies created a backlash that led to his own assassination. This was
followed by a period of chaos until China gained control over parts of
Tibet. After the collapse of the Yang dynasty in 905 CE, the emergent
Mongol empire began to annex Tibet.

Buddhism remained relatively strong in Western Tibet.
However, it was around 1000 CE that Indian scholars again began to visit
Tibet and new monasteries began to be built. One of the most famous of
these was Atisha (982-1054). Although records from the time show him
as a minor player with little influence, he became known as a major
figure in what became known as the second dissemination of Buddhism
into Tibet. His disciples established the Kadampa order, which later

---

[14] This is reminiscent of Catholic missionaries turning Celtic gods and goddesses into
saints in Ireland to gain acceptance of the indigenous people.

became the Gelugpa order under Je Tsongkapa (1357-1419), the order of the Dalai Lamas. The second dissemination continued over the next 100 or so years, a time approximating that during which the great monasteries and Buddhist universities in India were attacked and destroyed by the Muslim invasions of India. Thus, perhaps many of these great figures and others were fleeing the Muslim invasions just as many Tibetans fled back into India during and after the invasion of Tibet by the Chinese in the 20th century.

Out of this dissemination came the other two major orders of Tibetan Buddhism as well – the Kagyus and the Sakyas. The Sakyas rose to political dominance through collaboration with the Mongols. After their empire fell apart, the Gelugpas, which had little interest in politics under Tsongkapa, ascended to power, particularly under the Great Fifth Dalai Lama (1617-1682). They retained dominance until Tibet was overthrown by the Chinese in 1950-51. His Holiness the Fourteenth Dalai Lama fled from Tibet in 1959.

The diaspora of Tibetan Buddhism, however, has led to its spread throughout the world in a way what would never have been imagined just a few decades ago. In the process, Tibetan Buddhism faces new challenges as East meets West. Some of the seemingly archaic and medieval concepts are difficult for a secular West, which was transformed through our own period of Enlightenment. The scientific worldview of the West also challenges the mythology and magic associated with Tibetan Buddhist practices. Yet, we are enthralled. The intellectual approach embraced by Tibetan Buddhism attracts many in the West. The message of lovingkindness and compassion resonates with many raised in Christian traditions. Yet not everyone is ready or willing to embrace everything taught within the tradition.

I certainly am in no position to even prophesy what will be accepted and what will be discarded along the way. But as described earlier, there are two main approaches emerging in the West, particularly the US. One seeks to maintain a very traditional approach as taught in Tibet. The other leans toward a highly "Americanized" approach that basically eliminates what is considered to be indigenous or "cultural" in nature. I pray for more of a middle way and hope that this text will not only contribute to the dialog, but also provide an example for the application of this truly remarkable path of training the mind that can benefit all beings, whether directly or indirectly, through our thoughts, words, and deeds[15].

---

[15] For those interested in a more detailed presentation of the history of Tibetan Buddhism, I recommend John Power's *Introduction to Tibetan Buddhism*.

Chapter 3

Trainings & Paths

The Three Trainings

The Buddha taught his principles according to the needs of each person. A. K. Warder described his approach this way, "It is certainly not his way to denounce the opinions and practices of another…. Rather, [it is] to adopt the other person's point of view and then by question and answer to improve on it until a position compatible with his own has been arrived at…. So that the partner seems himself to continue his own quest … to arrive at higher truths…." However, this individualized approach created an array of doctrines, discourses and approaches which disagrees with what he told another audience (not to mention the variety that inevitably manifests in recollecting teachings in an oral tradition). When asked near the end of his life how to distinguish between authentic and non-authentic teachings, the Buddha said that anything that leads to virtuous actions and decreases suffering and that accords with reality may be adopted and practiced, no matter who taught it.

Thus, in examining the three trainings in the context of each of the four paths described in this text, there is another teaching to keep in mind. It is critical to really understand each of these trainings and paths. That teaching is known as the Four Reliances. Although you can find variations in wording, they essentially go like this:

1. Rely on the teaching, not the teacher.
2. Rely on the meaning of the teaching, not the words that express it.
3. Rely on the definitive meaning, not the provisional meaning.
4. Rely on transcendent wisdom of deep experience, not ordinary knowledge.

It is very important that one not get caught up in words, concepts, or ideas. One must go beyond them to see that meaning from the view of ultimate truth. And beyond that, it is best to use that meaning to achieve transcendent wisdom through direct experience. It is very easy to get caught up in the details of Buddhism. Step back and absorb the broader meaning. Then let go of even that and abide in its suchness.

As described earlier, the traditional Eightfold Path can be divided into three trainings: ethics, meditation, and wisdom. All paths include these three elements.

The First Training - Ethics

Ethics has to do with "right" and "wrong." There are a variety of "theories" about ethics, different approaches to the issue of right vs. wrong. I make no attempt to discuss these theories or their differences, except within the four paths described in this book. In this case, each builds upon the previous, so there is no direct conflict. At the same time, each approach articulated here takes the previous version to a new level of understanding, complexity, and sophistication.

Nevertheless, within Buddhism, some of the finer points appear to contradict each other, as noted above. Ethics are not "rules." They are "guidelines." The difference is that guidelines allow for exceptions as appropriate. Rules always encounter dilemmas when they run into exceptions. Guidelines allow for some degree of flexibility. However, that flexibility also creates conflict, as people will always disagree about how they interpret the intent, always choosing to have it reflect their particular bias. For this reason, it is critical to maintain the perspective on ethics of the Four Reliances. Otherwise you can fall into the trap of using the ethical principles, particularly those of the subsequent paths, to "rationalize" your behavior.

The Second Training - Meditation

Having an understanding and commitment to the ethical standards of the path, you then apply the practices themselves, generically referred to as "meditation." Meditation in Tibetan is translated as habituation or familiarization. The idea is to use these techniques to transform our habitual way of seeing things to a new way. We have been doing it in the same or similar ways for a very long time involving thousands, if not millions, of repetitions of that way of seeing. We just take it for granted as being "real." But even the most basic analysis of that process blows that understanding away. A more scientific analysis makes it absurd. And following that up with the direct experience of meditation truly transforms our view of what we call "reality."

But changing such a fixed habitual way of seeing and understanding the world is not something that is done overnight. You will see some teachings that talk about it taking eons of time to overcome. Others still refer to multiple lifetimes. Yet others accept the possibility of achieving enlightenment in this lifetime. Still, it requires patience and persistence. Remember, it took the Buddha over 6 years and the great Mahasiddhas 12 or more. Patience and persistence … memorize that phrase and repeat it to yourself often.

The Third Training - Wisdom

The result is called "wisdom." This is not the wisdom as normally discussed in the West, where we consider it to be knowledge, expertise or experience. A better phrase is "transcendent wisdom." It transcends any ordinary conception of what it might be. To be sure, words can indeed help us understand and eventually access it directly. But one must follow the principles of the Four Reliances or it is easy to look at the tip of the finger pointing at the moon instead of looking directly at the moon itself.

Transcendent wisdom is truly ineffable, beyond words. Many terms have been used to try and capture this. Even "transcendent wisdom" is just a term. If we grasp onto the term, that is not it! It is achieved only via direct experience. Although we can point to it in many helpful ways, we must at some point let go of the instructions and just do it ourselves.

Even within Tibetan Buddhism, different "schools" developed that use different approaches to study vs. experience. On one end of the spectrum we have the Gelugpas and the Sakyapas that emphasize extensive study. On the other end of the spectrum we have the Kagyupas and the Nyingmapas that emphasize practice. Within those there are still subtler distinctions. To some extent this is a personal preference. The source for most of the practices in this text is said to be Padmasambhava. The emphasis on practice in the Nyingma tradition is particularly appropriate for Westerners as householders with little time for extensive study, or even long and detailed practices. Yet Padmasambhava included practices from each of the four paths: Individual Liberation, the Bodhisattva, Tantra, and Great Perfection.

The Four Paths

The stages of this path have been outlined into what is called the Nine Vehicles (*yanas*). There are three primary divisions within Buddhism: *Hinayana* (or *Theravada*)[16], *Mahayana*, and *Vajrayana*. (*Zen* is a major form of *Mahayana*.) Hinayana is the Path of Individual Liberation. Mahayana is the Path of Altruism. Vajrayana is the Path of Tantra. *Dzogchen*, the Path of Great Perfection is usually taught as part of the Path of Tantra. But it is also sometimes taught independently. I have elected to treat it in this text as a separate path due to its significantly different approach from the Path of Tantra. Nevertheless, I view these four paths as an integrated whole, not four separate paths.

According to Tibetan Buddhism each vehicle transcends and includes the previous division(s). Furthermore, the Path of Individual Liberation has two major divisions and the Path of Tantra has two. Each division of tantra includes three additional subdivisions. Thus, in total there are nine vehicles. Historically these were not developed in quite such a sequential manner, but were later organized in this way to systematize them and facilitate development in the practice.

There are also the four major schools within tantra: *Nyingma* (old school), *Kagyu*, *Sakya*, and *Geluk* (the new schools – *sarma*). The divisions of practice are similar among the four schools but do include some unique characteristics. As mentioned previously, the old school was founded by Padmasambhava, the source of our practices in this text. Thus, the following very brief summary of the nine vehicles is based on the Nyingma taxonomy.

The Path of Individual Liberation

1. *Shravakayana* (also known as "hearers," mostly monks and nuns) – Four Noble Truths and Eightfold Path; *vipassana* meditation; realization of selflessness; achievement of *nirvana* – peace and happiness for oneself.

2. *Pratyekabuddhayana* (also known as "solitary realizers," mostly yogis and yoginis) – *Karma*/causality; selflessness of persons and

---

[16] From the teachings of the Buddha, there were 18 major schools that developed in India. Of those, only the Theravada remain.

phenomena; *shamata* meditation; achievement of *Arhathood* for oneself.

The Path of Altruism

3. *Mahayana* – Emptiness and compassion (monks, nuns and lay people); *six perfections* of generosity, ethical discipline, patience, persistence, concentration, and wisdom; accumulation of merit and wisdom; achieve enlightenment to help all other beings to also become enlightened; altruistic achievement of the *Bodhisattva* ideal for benefit of others.

The Path of Tantra

Outer Tantras

4. *Kriyayoga* – purification of *karma* (in body, speech and mind); *absolute* and *relative truths,* but separate; deity visualization (*deity* as lord, oneself as servant).

5. *Upayoga* – same as above, but deity as friend or helper.

6. *Yogayana* – *absolute truth* as nonconceptual, empty, luminous; *relative truth* as *mandala* of *deities*; visualization of self as deity; actualization of divine body, speech, mind and actions.

Inner Tantras (Highest Yoga Tantra)

7. *Mahayoga:* Generation Stage – wrathful deities in union, *absolute truth* as the essence of mind; *relative truth* as manifestations of thoughts and appearances and as sacred aspects of divinities; indivisibility of the *two truths*; visualization of oneself as deity with *consort* – one develops as "impure" illusory body.

8. *Anuyoga:* Completion Stage – wrathful deities in union, but less emphasis; perfection of bliss-emptiness, clarity and nonthought; practice of channels, winds, and drops; practice with an actual consort using sexual tantra (*karmamudra*) or symbolic visualized consort (*jnanamudra*) – one develops "pure" illusory body.

The Path of Great Perfection

9. *Atiyoga:* Nondual Stage – nonconceptual pure awareness without attachment or aversion, realization of transcendent wisdom; manifestations are illusory, the dynamic radiant display of the ultimate heart essence; abide in "suchness" with or without meditation; practices of *khorde rushen, trekcho,* and *togal,* achievement of *Light Body* or *Rainbow Body.*

In this text, the teachings of Padmasambhava have been arranged to follow this outline. The first practices form the foundation, by encapsulating the first three vehicles into the "preliminary practices" - ngondro[17], following the sequence outlined in *The Words of My Perfect Teacher.* The outer and inner Highest Yoga Tantra generation stage practices are next, followed by the completion stage practices, and finally the pinnacle of all practices, the Great Perfection, which I treat for descriptive purposes as a separate path.

The Path of Individual Liberation

The Path of Individual Liberation is the foundation for the other three. It is the path closest to the historical Buddha. It is called by this name because of the focus on the enlightenment of ourselves as individuals. After the Buddha died, or even earlier according to some sources, Buddhism began to divide into different schools of thought and practice. There were eighteen main schools within the Path of Individual Liberation. Of those, only one has survived, Theravada. This is also known by the main practices associated with it: single-pointed calm abiding and special insight – shamata and vipassana respectively.

The practitioners were also of two types: monastics and yogis. The monastics were also sometimes referred to as hearers and the yogis as solitary realizers – shravakas and pratyekabuddhas respectively. But the Buddha also had may lay disciples. We know this from the stories about the Buddha going to lay supporters and giving teachings in return for their material support of the sangha. But we also know because of the Four Noble Truths, particularly the Noble Eightfold Path. Here the

---

[17] Pronounced "noon-dro."

Buddha addresses Right Livelihood. Since monks and nuns did not do this kind of work, this is clearly addressed to lay disciples. There are also different sets of vows for monastics and lay disciples.

According to all four Tibetan schools, the Path of Individual Liberation for monastics focused on the Four Noble Truths and Noble Eightfold Path, special insight meditation, the realization of no-self or selflessness, and the achievement of nirvana – peace and happiness for oneself. For yogis, the path focused on karma, the selflessness of persons and phenomena, single-pointed calm abiding meditation, and achievement of nirvana for oneself. These differences are not always this clear as there is considerable overlap among monastics and yogis. Thus, for the Path of Individual Liberation, I do not differentiate between these two as separate paths.

Because it is the basis upon which all the rest of Buddhism is established, the Path of Individual Liberation is always to be respected. No one is to look down upon either the path or the practitioners of this path. His Holiness Dilgo Khyentse Rinpoche is said to have folded his hands in the prostration mudra whenever he was in the presence of the saffron-robed monks, saying things like, "How fortunate we are to still have the banner of Shakyamuni Buddha, the Lion of the Shakya, Shakya Senge."[18] He showed great respect for the very root of Buddha dharma. And so should we!

The Path of Altruism

The Bodhisattva

The Path of Altruism is that of the Bodhisattva. A Bodhisattva is one who has taken a vow to remain in samsara for as long as it takes for all sentient beings to attain enlightenment. They are willing to endure whatever suffering or unhappiness they encounter because of their altruistic intention to benefit others. They choose to serve others above themselves.

With the concept of the Bodhisattva came the development of idealized beings, which we now refer to as "deities." Some of the well-

---

[18] *Brilliant Moon: An Autobiography of Dilgo Khyentse*, p. xxiv.

known deities from the Path of Altruism are Amitabha (the Buddha of Boundless Light), Maitreya (the Buddha of the Future), Avalokiteshvara (the male Buddha of Compassion), Green and White Tara (female Buddhas of Compassion), and Manjushri (the Buddha of Wisdom). In Tibetan Buddhism these appear as peaceful deities of the "outer" tantras. So we will return to them in the Path of Tantra.

Bodhicitta

Bodhicitta is also referred to as the Mind of Enlightenment. There are two parts – relative and ultimate. Relative bodhicitta is further subdivided into two parts – altruistic intention and action. Thus, we can speak of three parts.

Altruism is the intention to do something for others without any expectation of anything in return. (We may actually derive some good feelings from our actions, but we would do it anyway. The good feelings are not the reason we do these actions.) The Buddha first taught the Path of Individual Liberation. But he did so for the benefit of others. Thus, by his example, if not by his words, he taught what became the Path of Altruism – Mahayana. The Bodhisattva Vow is to attain enlightenment for the benefit of all sentient beings. This is our altruistic intent. We intend to become enlightened to benefit others.

The next part is action bodhicitta. Here we put our intention into practice. Later, we will learn specific practices to help with this development. In general terms, action bodhicitta focuses on lovingkindness and compassion or the Four Immeasurables of lovingkindness, compassion, sympathetic joy, and equanimity. We also follow the Six Perfections, the first of which is generosity. In particular, teaching the dharma is a form of generosity.

Finally, we have ultimate bodhicitta – transcendent wisdom. Here we master meditative equipoise both on and off of the cushion, awake or asleep. We abide in pure awareness in all of our activities, and spontaneously do those for the benefit of all. This is our goal … in this lifetime.

The Six Perfections

The core practices of the Six Perfections (Paramitas) are: generosity, ethics, patience, persistence, concentration (shamata), and wisdom (vipassana). The first five collectively represent skillful means. Of particular importance to the Path of Altruism is generosity. This is the heart of altruistic intention, the Bodhisattva Vow. When generosity is combined with the skillful means of ethics, patience, persistence, and concentration, one lays the foundation for transcendent wisdom, leading to full enlightenment in this lifetime.

Buddhanature

Buddhanature is also called the Buddha within. It is defined as luminous-emptiness. It is the clarity of transcendent wisdom, innate happiness. Some branches of Buddhism treat buddhanature as a seed that must be planted, watered and so forth in order to grow and produce the fruit of enlightenment. But in the Path of Great Perfection, one is considered to already be a full buddha, but that is hidden by our mental obscurations and afflictive emotions due to our karma. While the conceptualization is slightly different, the meditative paths are nearly identical in order to purify our karma, habituate ourselves in meditative equipoise, and fully realize transcendent wisdom.

It is because our buddhanature is innate in all sentient beings that we are able to achieve buddhahood. Our various obscurations and habitual tendencies are not permanent, so we can change by following the practices to achieve enlightenment.

The Path of Tantra

Tantra

Tantra refers to a loom or warp, a weaving together as in a system of principles, but also an expansion or stretching and liberation. No one knows for sure when or where it actually began, although there are several theories. But we do know that it was originally a separate movement apart from either Hinduism or Buddhism with which it is associated today. In general, it was a counter-culture movement. The early texts, which begin to appear in the mid seventh century, take a very contrarian view to that of the Vedic Indian culture at the time. That is, whatever was generally prohibited by the culture was accepted and practiced by tantricas. First, it was dominated by women in a patriarchal society, although men increasingly became part of the movement. They would go into the forest in small groups without regard to class, take off their clothes and engage in practices that included eating meat, drinking alcohol, taking drugs, and having sex outside of marriage, among others, that were prohibited by society.

This movement corresponded to another movement in Indian culture in which the female goddess rose to prominence, even becoming central figures in various rituals and practices. This transcended specific religions, so we see evidence for the movement in Buddhism, Hinduism, etc. at the same time. These religions often borrowed from each other, sometimes even retaining the names and descriptions, but other times modifying them to fit their particular view.

The result of the rise of tantra and the goddess movements led to the absorption of tantra into both Buddhism and Hinduism, with rather different approaches. In Buddhism, the movement was largely "monasticized", i.e., adapted to fit the dominant monastic tradition and Buddhist principles. Since monks (and nuns) took vows of celibacy, they were generally prohibited from participating in a literal way. So the texts were adapted to a process that involved visualization rather than actual intercourse. Other ritual elements such as eating the "five meats" and drinking the "five nectars" were also modified into symbolic representations of those. On the other hand, not all Buddhists were monastics, so celibacy did not necessarily apply. So a more literal version of these practices survived among the yogis and yoginis and was transmitted into Tibet as we will see.

The principle impact of tantra on Buddhism, however, was the use of "deities" in the meditation practices, although this began earlier during the period dominated by the Path of Altruism. However, it is important to recognize a distinction between the deities of Buddhism and those of other religions, especially Hinduism with which a number of them are shared. In Buddhism, all deities are considered to be a manifestation of one's mind. They do not "truly" exist in the same way that other religions view deities or gods. Although some teachers object to this characterization, I have found that students in the West find the characterization of deities as "tools" for meditation practice to be helpful in understanding both the role of deities in practice and their very nature in terms of training the mind.

The Three Buddha Bodies

As a buddha, one manifests in multiple forms. The primary division is into the three bodies (kayas) of a buddha. Dharmakaya (truth body) represents the ultimate nature of mind. It is not a "body" per se, but none other than pure awareness (actual clear light, ultimate bodhicitta). The sambhogakaya (enjoyment body) is a spirit or energy form. It is said to be transparent like a rainbow and invisible to all but highly realized beings. It may be thought of as something like a daydream or a reflection in a window through which you can see the things on the other side as well. This is the form of the deities visualized in the deity yoga practices of the Path of Tantra. The third form or body is the nirmanakaya (the physical form body of a buddha19). This is the form taken by Shakyamuni Buddha.

The Path of Great Perfection

While deity practices are said to enable one to achieve enlightenment in this lifetime, most branches of the tradition also include advanced practices of Mahamudra (Great Seal) or Dzogchen (Great Perfection). These practices focus on transcendent wisdom itself. The visualizations previously employed in the practices are no longer considered necessary (although some of the actual practices still use visualizations). Mahamudra and dzogchen are directed at finalizing one's attainment of enlightenment in this lifetime. The essence of the state of enlightenment is the mind of a buddha – emptiness. But this is described in various forms.

The Path of Great Perfection is considered to be the highest of all Buddhist teachings and is divided into two parts known as trekcho (break through) and togal (leap over), along with a series of preliminary practices. The preliminary practices associated with the Path of Great Perfection are directed at the separation of "samsara" from "nirvana." Basically, the idea is for the practitioner to develop a direct experiential understanding of the difference between these two concepts … and then transcend even those.

---

19 There is also another "form body" described in the texts. This is called *rupakaya*, which is a combination of the sambhogakaya and nirmanakaya.

Trekcho views the nature of mind as pure awareness (rigpa), i.e., the awareness that arises before becoming aware of anything. It is the root of awareness or consciousness itself. Thus, it is that which allows awareness of things (described as the manifestations of our mind) to happen. Trekcho is nearly identical to the practice of mahamudra. The goal of trekcho is the direct realization of dharmakaya.

Togal includes several practices, but is most noted for the "Four Visions of Togal" that describe a progressive series of visions of increasing complexity and detail, primarily during a practice called "sky gazing" that involves looking at a clear, cloudless sky in which the visions appear without any external source from which to generate them. The goal of togal is attainment of a "rainbow body," the manifestation of a sambhogakaya body of a buddha.

Chapter 4

The Teacher & Devotion

Qualifications

Before getting into the actual practices, there are two related topics that warrant some consideration. The first is the teacher, and the second is our devotion to the teacher. In the Path of Tantra, the relationship with the teacher is particularly important. For all practical purposes, they are the Buddha for us. They become our role model, as well as our teacher. They provide guidance and help us with the inevitable difficulties and questions that arise. To be effective, we need a very special relationship with our teacher. It is said that if you see the teacher as a Buddha, you will receive the benefits of the instructions from the Buddha. If you see the teacher as just a teacher, you will receive the benefits of a teacher. And if you relate to your teacher as an ordinary human, you will receive the blessing of an ordinary human being.

Finding the right teacher can be a challenge on several counts. One is access. Where do we find a teacher locally, especially if we live in a small community? And even if there is one, how do you know it is the "right" teacher for you? If you don't have regular personal access to His Holiness the Dalai Lama, there are still other options. Increasingly, teachers and teachings are available through technology. There has been an explosion in the number of books in English, many excellent, over the past 15-20 years. The Internet has become a vast reservoir of accessible resources. One may receive teachings or take classes from qualified teachers online. Nevertheless, you may need to travel from time to time to make a personal connection that will then help develop a relationship to sustain your practice between contacts. Many lamas follow the tradition of requiring that empowerments for Highest Yoga Tantra (and perhaps other practices) be done only in person due to the relationship involved in such a transmission and blessing.

A teacher may also challenge us in ways that are not usual in the West. This can cause us to question our relationship and even the teacher themselves. While there are no guarantees regarding future behaviors by a teacher, there is good advice in some of the texts that warrants our consideration. I have seen too many students who, upon going to their first teachings with a Tibetan lama, let go of all sensibilities and ask them to be their root teacher. This is not only unreasonable, it can be disastrous to your practice and even result in you leaving Buddhism due to a bad experience. DO NOT go "ga-ga" over the first Tibetan lama that you meet! Many Tibetan lamas are very personable and friendly. It is easy to love them. It is more difficult to determine whether they are qualified or, even more so, whether they are a good match for you.

As Sogyal Rinpoche writes in his book, "True teachers are kind, compassionate, tireless in their desire to share whatever wisdom they have acquired from their masters, never abuse or manipulate their students under any circumstances, never under any circumstances abandon them, serve not their own ends but the greatness of the teachings, and always remain humble."20 So what other qualifications should you look for in a teacher? There many lists in the tradition. According to The Words of My Perfect Teacher, Patrul Rinpoche (1808-1887) says that the teacher should at least be (1) pure and maintain the vows, (2) learned, (3) suffused with compassion, (4) well versed in ritual practices, (5) actualized in the meaning of the teachings, (6) generous, (7) pleasant, (8) teach each individual according to his/her needs, and (9) act in conformity with what he teaches. He then goes on to say that we should avoid those with (a) no qualities arising from study, reflection and meditation, (b) pride by the profits and honors they receive, (c) very little knowledge, (d) strong negative emotions, (e) weak mindfulness and vigilance, making them lax in their vows (samayas), (f) qualities that are not superior to your own, and (g) lack of love and compassion. Several sources indicate that love and compassion are the single most important quality of a teacher. Patrul Rinpoche cites the following text describing the ideal teacher:

> He is the great ship carrying us beyond the seas of samsaric existence,
> The true navigator, unerringly charting the sublime path,
> The rain of nectar quenching the inferno of emotions and actions,
> The sun and moon dispelling the darkness of ignorance.
> He is the earth, immensely patient,
> The wish-granting tree, source of help and happiness,
> The perfect vase containing the treasure of the Dharma.
> He provides all things, more than a wish-granting gem.

---

20 The Tibetan Book of Living and Dying, p. 130.

He is a father and mother, loving all equally.
His compassion is as vast and swift as a great river.
His joy is unchanging like the king of mountains.
His impartiality cannot be disturbed, like rain from a cloud.

He adds that "such a teacher is equal to all the Buddhas in his compassion and his blessings. Those who make a positive connection with him will attain Buddhahood in a single lifetime." Yet, it is the student's responsibility to examine the teacher. This should not be taken lightly, nor too expeditiously. Some sources say that you should examine the teacher for a period of 12 years before making a firm commitment. While this may not be necessary, it is important not to rush in. The teacher should be one that "wears well," that is, that continues to draw you in over an extended period of time. This should be someone who you are willing to be devoted to, someone whose instructions you are willing to follow even when they are not what you really want.[21]

Devotion

Devotion in Buddhism is not blind faith. As previously noted, the Buddha encouraged us to question what we are taught. Nevertheless, it does require a willingness to try it out, as long as you have a good teacher as described above. You will never know unless you follow the instructions of the teacher. In the West, we tend to make up our minds without doing it first, based on our biases, previous experiences, and our expectations. But when devotion flows naturally after a period of developing the relationship, a bond of trust is formed and you will know you have found a good teacher. Shabkar wrote:

No matter in what direction I go, I think of the master;

No matter in what solitary place I stay, I think of the master;

No matter what signs I see, I think of the master;

Always, at all times, I think of my authentic master.

---

[21] This does not mean that you should do something that your ethical sensibility says is wrong. There have been too many lamas who are willing to exploit the naïve or gullible. You need to stand up for yourself and be willing to question anything that just seems wrong.

But what if you are unable to find the right teacher? Buddhism has answers for that as well. First, Padmasambhava (Guru Rinpoche) is considered the "universal" teacher for all tantric practitioners. If you have not been able to find your "root guru" in human form, consider Padmasambhava to be your root guru, at least until you do make that special personal connection. In addition to the "outer" teacher, we each are endowed with buddhanature[22], our "inner" teacher. Even more important, though, is the teaching, not the teacher. As previously noted, the Four Reliances state that we are to:

1. Rely on the teaching, not the teacher.

2. Rely on the meaning of the teaching, not the words that express it.

3. Rely on the definitive meaning, not the provisional meaning.

4. Rely on transcendent wisdom of deep experience, not ordinary knowledge.

These guidelines help us to focus on the teachings from the perspective of Pure View. So while a close relationship with a teacher is very important, it is not the most important.

Sex and the Teacher

One potential source of problems needs special attention. Some students find teachers to be very attractive for a variety of reasons. Some teachers find certain students to be very attractive as well. And the teachings on tantra explicitly include using passion as the path. Padmasambhava, Tsongkapa, the Great Fifth Dalai Lama, and many others have either done these practices or noted their importance for enlightenment in this life. I have included basic descriptions of these practices for householders in this text, even though it is rare for a teacher

---

[22] Briefly, buddhanature is our own innate transcendent wisdom, just hidden from our ordinary consciousness. It is revealed through the process of training our mind.

to give these teachings in the West. It is even more rare for a teacher to demonstrate or practice with a student. Yet it does happen.

Assuming that neither you nor the teacher is actually attempting to exploit the other, sexual yoga practice between you and a teacher can be of great benefit in your practice. Although I am an advocate of actual sexual yoga with a qualified consort, I am cautious about students and teachers practicing together. The reason is that it has the potential to create serious obscurations for you, the teacher, as well as the sponsoring organization. The Buddha was very reluctant to ordain women, and subsequently to permit monks and nuns to even be in close proximity, due to the potential for relationship problems. He taught that desire, specifically lust, is the main obscuration of the human realm, so he was well aware of the risks. And he had to deal with the consequences. Many of the rules of conduct for monks and nuns (the *vinaya*) were created to deal with issues involving sexual behavior. While sometimes it works well for everyone, too many people have been emotionally hurt and sanghas have been torn apart because of sexual relationships that developed. Even good ones can fall apart.

People are human, even lamas. Humans may become attracted to each other, sometimes in very powerful ways. There is no simple black and white line that can be drawn. Each organization should have made a conscious policy decision regarding sex between teachers and students. On one hand, it is easy to be prescriptive. Some organizations simply say that no sexual relationships are permitted between students and teachers who are not already in a committed relationship or marriage. This, however, does not ensure that it will not happen, as the Buddha himself learned. We are people, and people have sex. Also, strict renunciation, as a policy, may seem excessive just as a matter of principle. As a culture, we tend to like our freedoms and resist prohibitions, even ones we don't intend to violate ourselves.

On the other hand, it is also easy to say there are no rules, to openly accept sex between all parties without restriction. While this may work, it is also the most vulnerable to the foibles of human behavior. So each organization should consider whether to engage in a strict, open, or middle-way policy. Furthermore, the policy should be made explicit to the sangha so the nature of any such teachings is clear and above board. Individually, each teacher should have a clear standard for their own behavior. You, as a student, should have a clear standard as well. Then don't cross that line. Don't be afraid to say, "No." Do not compromise your integrity. That would be deluded devotion.

When practice with an actual consort is taught that would involve sexual union between you and a teacher, then practice with the teacher should be requested only by you (because of the "power relationship" between you and the teacher). Be very cautious if it is requested by the teacher. This is not a good sign. Know your boundaries. But even if you make the request and it is accepted, be aware that people talk. Jealousies arise. Other un-Buddhist-like behaviors sometimes emerge that can cause a great deal of hurt among others.

Anyone who participates in such teachings and practices should know the risks involved for themselves, the teacher, and the organization. You may have only the best of intentions. But we are deluded sentient beings, and we will make mistakes or even take advantage of opportunities that were not intended. No policy in itself, whether restrictive or open, will guarantee that there will be no problems. This is samsara. There will be problems. Do your best to avoid them, but also be prepared to deal with them when they do occur. They will. This then becomes another opportunity to practice lovingkindness and compassion.

Signs of Devotion

Devotion to the lama is critical to one's progress. This is most outwardly expressed through various practices of *Guru Yoga*, presented in the Path of Tantra. It is best done as a daily practice, often with daily preliminary practices. Other signs include:

Prostrations – One stands when the lama enters the room, then prostrates three times after he/she is seated. When entering after the lama is seated, one also prostrates three times (but respect their request for you not to prostrate and to be seated).

View – Beginners see the lama as just another person. Middling practitioners see the lama as a lama and one to be respected, and showing appreciation for the precious teachings that they share. Advanced practitioners see the lama as a buddha, sharing perfect wisdom.

Practices – Beginners will commit to following the lama's instructions sometime. Middling practioners will follow all of the lama's suggestions to the best of their ability. Advanced practitioners will do all of the instructions *and more*. This may be

10%, 20%, double, triple and so forth, always finding a way to *exceed* expectations.

Transmissions – Transmissions are usually given in Tibetan, and many Western students (and even Tibetans when the text is read very quickly) may not understand. A beginner may complain about not understanding or why this is necessary. Middling practioners will sit with respect for the lama and the tradition, and appreciate the blessing and connection with the lama. An advanced practitioner will feel *great joy* at the rain of blessings and deep devotion for the lama and the precious dharma throughout the reading.

Part 3 – The Path of Individual Liberation

As noted earlier, the Path of Individual Liberation comes the closest to what was originally taught by the historical Buddha during his lifetime. It provides a solid foundation upon which to build the subsequent teachings that evolved from them. For some, it will even provide all that is necessary to achieve enlightenment. This path is respected by all Buddhist traditions and is sometimes referred to as the Path of the Elders. It should never be disparaged as "lesser" or "inferior" to the other paths for it is essential to them.

At the same time, the way this path is taught here is from the view of Tibetan Buddhism. It should not be considered to fully represent the teachings of the modern Theravada lineage that most closely aligns with this path, the only remaining of the 18 lineages based on the original teachings of the Buddha. While the original Pali Canon upon which these teachings are based are the most ancient and close to the historical Buddha, the texts currently available are only about three to five hundred years old.[23]

---

[23] Richard F. Gombrich (1996), *How Buddhism Began: The Conditioned Genesis of the Early Teachings.*

Chapter 5

The First Training on the

Path of Individual Liberation: Ethics

In the time of Shakyamuni Buddha, training in ethics was a preliminary practice to learning meditation. He continued this tradition as well. Today, there are many vows in the Buddhist tradition. But they can be summarized into three sets of vows associated with each of the three Paths of Individual Liberation, the Bodhisattva, and Tantra. And while ethics has to do with what is right and wrong, the dilemma has always been how to determine that ... and in some cases who determines that. The Buddha's approach was that you need to determine it for yourself. And the sole criterion is whether it is beneficial to your path to enlightenment.

His Holiness the Dalai Lama has summarized the three vows as (1) do good, or at least do no harm, (2) engage in altruistic intention and action, and (3) maintain Pure View. [24] But when you face difficulty in determining the right action, there are more specific guidelines that have been developed to assist you. To some degree these more specific lists of vows have become "rules" in the tradition, especially for monks and nuns. But they should not be seen that way, especially for householders. As described in Chapter 3, we must use the Four Reliances to help guide us in applying these guidelines. For us, these three simple vows are enough. Nevertheless, it does help to examine at least some of these more specific vows to see how they have been applied within the tradition.

Karma is the foundation of Buddhist ethics. It provides a basis for good or right actions and avoiding consequences of bad or wrong actions.

Other traditions posit rules of behavior as commanded by the ultimate, usually a form of God. The Ten Commandments are one example – ten of the 613 such commandments found in the Hebrew Bible

---

[24] These are the essence of the Hinayana, Mahayana, and Vajrayana vows according to HH the Dalai Lama.

and Old Testament of the Christian Bible. Yet, fixed approaches to ethical dilemmas have presented significant challenges to modern humanity. In some instances, times have simply transcended the standards. Either there are no directly applicable standards or the standards are difficult to apply in a meaningful way. One example is the Biblical commandments regarding Temple sacrifices. There is no longer a Temple. Abortion is another example where the Bible must be interpreted to find an ethical precept as there is no direct reference to abortion in the text itself. Although homosexuality is addressed in the Bible directly, the contemporary understanding of it has changed the basis upon which the original standard was created. Thus, there is a vast difference in understanding among Christians regarding this. Buddhism and other traditions have similar cases, such as some discriminatory practices regarding women that were conceived in ancient patriarchal societies but are now widely regarded as unacceptable standards of ethical behavior in contemporary societies.

Flexible approaches to ethics allow for greater interpretation to fit changing times and varying circumstances. Nevertheless, they also suffer when extended to the level of absolute relativity, i.e., nothing is right or wrong, everything is relative. The effect of this approach is that there are few, if any, guidelines for ethical behavior.

Some argue that our legal systems have replaced the need for ethical systems of behavior. With respect to some behaviors, this may be true. Still, we find that the laws are often insufficient to meet the expectations of human beings as the social animals that we are. Laws are also not always congruent with ethical standards and it can take considerable time and influence to make significant changes, especially when they reflect a majority point of view that affects a minority group in some negative way. We need higher levels of commitment to standards of behavior that permit us to live together in communities of beings.

Western philosophers have attempted to articulate such standards. These approaches tend to differentiate between means (actions) and ends (results). Deontology, for instance, focuses on the means. One version is duty-based ethics, which focuses on our duty or actions without regard to consequences. The standard is that the actions must be universal and unconditional. The problem is that there are few, if any, that can actually meet that standard. Even the most universal of all ethical standards globally – do not kill (in this case to murder another human being) – is usually exempted under some conditions, e.g., self-defense, warfare, and so forth.

Teleology focuses on the ends, the consequences of our actions for society as a whole. The most often cited version of this approach is utilitarianism. This standard considers the greatest good for the greatest number. In simple terms, the majority rules. This is common is Western society due to its correlation with democratic principles of governance. It works fine for the majority, but affords no protections for minority interests or positions. Of course, governments normally extend some form of "rights" or protections for those in minority positions as well, but we have seen numerous examples of how such "principles" have been used to discriminate against those in minority or disenfranchised positions.

We have in the West, it seems, stepped into our own trap with no way out. Nevertheless, we can find that there are some guidelines that can be beneficial in guiding our daily actions regarding others.

The *shramanans* in the time of Buddha believed in the principle of karma. As noted before, this is a form of what goes around comes around. Karma means action. So what comes around is based on our actions – cause and effect. In theory this is a direct connection. However, this does not seem to explain why bad things happen to good people or good things happen to bad people. So karma came to be thought of as a process of planting seeds. When we do something, good or bad, a seed is planted in our subconsciousness. If we repeat this, it is strengthened and may even become a habit. From brain research, we see hard evidence for this in the plasticity of the brain, which forms and strengthens neural connections based on our behaviors (including thoughts, words, and deeds). But the Law of Karma goes beyond this. This *alaya* consciousness in which the seeds are planted is said to transcend this life and become the cause for us to be reborn (reincarnation) in the next life with those same propensities based on previous actions, unless they are "burned up" through affecting our life *or* "purified" through one of many advanced practices. It is the cycle of reincarnation due to our karma that the Buddha sought to transcend through training the mind and ethical actions.

The First Vow

As mentioned above, in Tibetan Buddhism we have three sets of vows: do good or at least do no harm, engage in altruistic intention and action, and maintain Pure View.

The most basic of these Buddhist vows is to *do good*, that is, to *benefit others*. Mark Twain once said, "Always do right. This will gratify some people and astonish the rest." Here we ask, are my actions of benefit to others? As noted earlier, one must consider the issue of self-interest vs. others. As we have seen, self-interest is often a barrier to spiritual realization. Western society is heavily engaged in self-interest, often to an extreme. Some self-interest is actually of benefit to others, of course. If we do not take care of ourselves, we will be unable to be of benefit to others. It is excessive self-interest that is the barrier.

At the same time, ethics go beyond a "balance" of self and other interests. An equal distribution of effort and action is insufficient. One must go beyond self, to extinguish ego as a point of focus. Yet, when "others" become our focus, we find that we are the beneficiaries in countless ways. It may be regarded as a form of the Golden Rule[25], found in some form in all major religious traditions. Thus, we often see sacrifice, surrender, and generosity as standards of behavior in religious traditions.

As with other standards, it cannot be applied in an absolute manner. There are circumstances that sometimes may condition our ideal response. So if you are unable to do good, the precept is to *at least do no harm*. However, not causing *some* harm to an attacker may result in serious injury or death to oneself. And even if one is willing to sacrifice oneself rather than harm the other, the consequences to the attacker of their bad karma, prison, or even capital punishment might be worse, according to this standard. The classical formulation is the choice between the lesser of two evils. Either choice involves some harm. It cannot always be helped. Nevertheless, as a general guiding principle, do no harm is a helpful standard.

There is a corollary to this standard – to *prevent others from doing harm*. This extends the principle beyond our direct relationship with others to third parties that might be involved with others. The rationale

---

[25] Do to others as you would have them do to you.

and results are essentially the same for all parties to the actions as those described above. But it prevents us from ignoring inappropriate actions of others. We have some level of responsibility for the whole of our human family ... and beyond. In fact, science is increasingly finding DNA evidence that supports some altruistic behaviors even among single-cell beings, as well as behavioral evidence among "lesser" animals than humans.

These ethical principles are often articulated in terms of "virtuous" behaviors – behaviors that go beyond what is reasonable and necessary to what is ideal, the best, or exemplary. Not all will agree on these, or on their exact meaning or application. For these reasons, ethical standards are often most effective as general principles, with some specific applications. It is important to note that in Buddhism, these are articulated as vows (*samaya*). But these vows are based on what has been shown to be beneficial in training the mind, not a rigid set of standards. They are conditioned by the circumstances.

A key determinant for making ethical choices is one's *intention*. Legal systems often use this as a criterion as well. We may not always know what the right action is in a given case. As long as our intention is to do good, do no harm, or prevent others from doing harm, our intention is virtuous. In these instances, we are doing our best and should not be afraid to defend our actions in the face of others' criticism. If we honestly do our best and then find later that the action did cause harm, genuine regret and renewed intention to these principles is the best course of action. (There are also purification rituals within the tradition to assist with this process.)

As noted above, there are also several lists of virtuous behaviors and their opposites (nonvirtuous behaviors) to help guide us in deciding what may be right or wrong. These are fairly universal in many religious traditions, though some vary. Nevertheless, in Buddhism these are not prescribed. One chooses to follow those that do not interfere with spiritual practice and development. In addition, one should use "skillful means" in determining the exact choice of behavior in any given situation based on the general guiding principles (the three vows) listed above.

The most common list is that of the 10 non-virtues and 10 virtues[26]:

Ten non-virtuous actions to avoid	Ten virtuous (helpful) actions
1. Killing	1. Protect life
2. Stealing	2. Generosity
3. Sexual abuse	3. Honor sexual vows & respect others
4. Lying	4. Truth & loving speech
5. Divisiveness	5. Reconcile or harmonize
6. Harsh words	6. Pleasant words
7. Idle talk	7. Meaningful talk
8. Covetousness (jealousy)	8. Generosity (again)
9. Harmful thoughts	9. Helpful intentions to benefit others
10. Wrong views	10. Wisdom of ultimate truth and the true nature of things

Not everyone is capable of following the same level of ethical thinking and behavior. Researchers have found that humans follow a pattern of ethical and moral development just as we do with physiological development. At early stages, one makes choices based on the rewards or the risk of punishment. Our focus is on "me." Later, we consider the reciprocity of what others are willing to do for us, but the focus is still on "me." Following this stage, we begin to decide based on our need for approval of family, peers and others. Established principles of law and order guide our choices at the next stage. Here the focus is on "we." Many adults do not develop beyond this level. At the next level one tends to behave in accordance with expectations within the broader social contract of our particular society. One begins to truly transcend self-interest. Our focus shifts to "you." Finally, one may reach a stage in which fairness and need transcend the social ethic, or even legal barriers. At this level we see a very small group of extraordinary individuals who are willing even to die for a noble cause that will benefit others, even if they are in the minority. This is a state of egoless altruism for the benefit of others. While some have argued that altruism does not fit with evolutionary development of our species for survival, in fact there is evidence that altruism does help preserve and protect the group as a

---

[26] There are, of course, many more guidelines in the *Vinaya* for monks and nuns.

whole. And many of the most recent brain developments in brain evolution are focused more on group survival than individual survival.

Ethics Signs of Accomplishment

As noted above, there are three levels of ethical behavior associated with the three vows. In the Path of Individual Liberation, we focus on the first: do good, or at least not harm. We may also extend that to the application of the ten virtuous and non-virtuous actions.

The signs that one has mastered these behaviors are twofold. First, we must assess our own actions. We are the only ones who can ascertain our intention. And we are the only ones who have a collective view of all that we have done in a given day. One technique for doing this assessment is to carry a set of white and a set of black rocks or beads. Each time one does something during the day, we evaluate whether it was "good" or "bad." Then we select a white or black bead to place in our pocket (or a bag) to represent that. We do that with each action during the day. At the end of the day, we simply look at all of the beads selected to see if we did more good or bad actions. On the surface, this may seem a little silly. Nevertheless, one of the benefits of this approach, beyond the value of the assessment at the end of the day, is that it helps *focus our attention* during the day on our actions – another form of training our mind. You will get a more accurate assessment by recording your actions than just reflecting without a record at the end of the day. But with some practice, we can just take some time to review our actions during the day, having made a mental note of the good and bad actions without the beads. Do this practice daily for at least one week … or a month to develop it as a habit.

The second way to assess our behavior is based on what others perceive about us. This means we have to ask. Some people will, of course, tell us whether our actions (specific or general) are seen as good or bad. But most of the time we will get more information if we ask, over and over. There does, of course, need to be a level of trust with others that you ask. Research shows that most of us don't really know very accurately how we are perceived by others. To get them to honestly tell us requires cultivating open and honest communication with others, and then asking them with some regularity to give you some honest feedback. Beware, though. You may not like what you learn. But under *no* circumstances should there *ever* be repercussions for that honesty.

That would destroy the trust as well as undermine you ethical behavior. Thank them and bite your lip if necessary. But never ever "defend yourself," though it is okay to ask for more details or explanation.

Beyond these signs, it can be helpful to review the vows described here and evaluate yourself regarding these behaviors. If there have been missteps along the way, make a concerted effort to change. This, too, is part of training your mind. First, it necessitates paying attention. Then it requires staying focused on what you are doing, even as you do it. This means breaking away from "automatic pilot" to be *awake* at all times.

I conclude with a short story from *The Life of Shabkar* in which he states, "All that pleases the heart and mind of the spiritual masters and the Three Jewels, all that benefits others, is virtue. This is what we need to accomplish." He then continues with this story about the benefit of even small virtuous actions:

> Even a small virtuous action brings great benefit. Once an old lady offered a single butter-lamp to the Buddha, who then made the prediction that in the future she would become a Buddha named "Bright Lamp," endowed with the ten powers. The Buddha also prophesied that a village chief who kept the vow of not killing for a single day, would ultimately become enlightened as the Buddha "Beneficial Speech." A Brahmin girl offered her needle to a monk; because of that she became the noble Shariputra. A woman offered a meal to a beggar; she was reborn in a mansion made of jewels, where she enjoyed delicious food with a hundred flavors. A pig who happened to make one circumambulation around a stupa because he was chased by a dog took rebirth as the householder Palkye, who attained the level of an arhat. So it is said.

So never doubt the benefit of small actions. In spite of many stories about it taking three countless eons or other great effort and difficulties, there are also many which conclude that even simple actions yield great results. As a concluding insight, note that these stories are about ordinary people and the stories involving great effort and difficulty are about monks. This demonstrates another of the benefits of practicing Buddhism as a householder.

Chapter 6

The Second Training on the

Path of Individual Liberation:

Meditation

The second part of The Three Teachings is meditation and the longest part of each path in this book. This includes right effort, right mindfulness and right concentration. Learning to meditate – training the mind – is not always easy to accomplish. It requires rewiring our brain. This means unwiring some of our existent habits and forming new neural connections that reinforce the pattern associated with the practices of meditation. In brief, this takes patience and persistence. It does not happen overnight. It is much like learning to play a musical instrument. Unless you are a savant, it takes hours and hours of practice and rehearsal, even by great masters.

Motivation

I raised the question of "Why?" earlier in the book. It's time for some answers – your answers. Why do you want to do this? Are you really committed? You need to ask yourself these questions. As noted before, we pursue Buddhism or meditation for a variety of reasons. What are yours? What is your goal? Once you have this clearly identified it should be the first thing you think about whenever you sit down to meditate … as well as a constant reminder throughout the day. Just as we say about the best leaders, one should exhibit single-pointed focus on that goal. What if you are just exploring or find it something that you just like doing, but not something that you really want to be single-pointedly focused on? Meditation can be beneficial in many ways to many different people with different motivations. The key is knowing what your motivation is. My focus is on those who are serious practitioners whose goal is enlightenment in this lifetime. Of course, I am more than willing to help anyone who seeks my assistance to the best of my ability. But my wish is for everyone to seek enlightenment. The Dzogchen Ponlop Rinpoche wrote, "We must keep our goal of liberation in mind, or else our efforts might become half-hearted, and if they are, they won't work."

Meditation

There are many ways to categorize meditation; but for here we will examine two generic categories: shamata and vipassana. Shamata is single-pointed calm abiding. We abide in stillness of body, speech, and mind. The primary purpose is to be able to train the mind to focus one's attention and rest in that awareness. Seems simple enough. But recall that the core of our brain is structured for survival. This means that it is constantly looking for danger. Even though most of us are fortunate enough to live in a culture in which there is relatively little imminent danger, our brain is constantly firing off messages that trigger thoughts in our brain, distracting us from being able to focus our attention. This is famously known as "monkey mind." And the first goal is to train the mind to let go of that tendency and rest while remaining attentive. This takes time – patience and persistence. To do this there are many options. The most common is to focus on your breath as it goes in and out. But you can also focus on an object, real or imagined. And even the "deity" mediations of Tibetan Buddhism are a series of increasingly complex visualizations that include the purpose of training your mind to remain in single-pointed calm abiding. And this has been found to be more effective than simpler techniques such as just focusing on the breath, even though that still works. It's just slower for most of us.

Vipassana meditation is about special insight. What insight? Insight into the true nature of mind – transcendent wisdom. This is done in different ways at different levels of achievement. In the beginning this is an analytical meditation to understand the interdependent nature of all that is. As this understanding grows, it will be supplanted by a nonconceptual direct experience of the true nature of mind, until the need for analysis fades away and you gain confidence in this transcendent wisdom. Later, we will see how the Path of Tantra uses special completion stage practices of the "deity" yogas or meditations to assist with and accelerate this process so that you are more likely to attain enlightenment in this lifetime. But the practices described here are the essence of all core meditation practices and form the foundation upon which the others are built. One must first build a solid foundation before adding walls and roof.

In addition these meditations facilitate training our mind so that everything becomes meditation. This further accelerates your spiritual development, moving you closer to enlightenment in this lifetime. What you do off of the cushion is equally or even more important than what you do on the cushion.

There are some "cultural" and "ritual" elements of these practices that some in the West feel are not necessary. However, these do add to the religious climate that facilitates your spiritual development. Even if you feel that this may actually be a deterrent due to aversions you may have about religion per se, they are actually beneficial because they too are part of the process of training your mind through repetition, through habituation. So these seemingly superfluous activities actually enhance the effectiveness of your practice in ways that some consider as unnecessary ornamentation. A good test is to try it out for a few months with the "bells and smells" and then a few times without it. Most who do this find that they lose the degree of clarity and focus that they had achieved with the added ritual. Just because an element of the practice is derived from the culture or ceremonial aspects of the tradition does not automatically mean that it is not beneficial for the actual practice itself. Be very careful about dismissing these parts of the practice. Doing so can make it more difficult to achieve your goal.

It's all about meditation. That is how most new students view Buddhism. They want to learn how to meditate, and for a variety of reasons – well-being, spiritual development, health, etc. – but rarely to attain enlightenment, let alone to attain enlightenment for the benefit of all sentient beings! All of these are of value, but meditation is only a very small part of Buddhism, although an important one to be sure. We call it "practice." Why? Because it is practice for the rest of your day, what you do when you get up off of the cushion. It is *very* important to be aware of this. The idea is to do something that will change your life, every minute of every day (and night). To do this, you need to change your worldview, the way you see and experience things. That is why you train your mind through meditation *and other practices*. But for now, we focus on meditation.

This part of the text describes specific meditation practices. It begins with an explanation of the process of training the mind, followed by considerations for the "container" (environment) and use of ritual.

This is followed by a series of basic *shamata* and *vipassana* meditations to begin the process of training our mind in earnest.

Training the Mind

Training the mind is central to spiritual practice, to the process of developing awakened consciousness. The purpose is realize your innate happiness that can then be carried forward into the rest of your day (and night). Like learning any other skill, it takes time and practice for the brain to develop a new pattern of synaptic connections among the affected neurons. Both the brain and the experience grow and develop with practice. Like learning to play a musical instrument, it requires a significant commitment over a period of time, along with patience and persistence. As the brain changes over time, the practitioner will grow and develop even further.

One of the most basic of all practices is the principle of mindfulness. This principle applies both to meditation and after or post-meditation. In short, we need to be mindful of all that we think, say, and do. As it applies to daily life, this means paying attention! Focus! Our minds often wander off to memories of the past, and we may re-play them over and over. Or we may think about the future, planning, imagining, or fantasizing. We spend a great deal of time in a "daydream" state. Instead, the principle of mindfulness is to focus on the present moment. What are we doing now? Buddhist philosophy goes so far as to say that time is nothing but a series of moments. Our job is to learn to focus on each of them throughout the day and night.

You can think of the development of mindfulness as a process with levels. One such approach is:

1. Ordinary mindfulness – the baseline, not much mindfulness

2. Present moment focus – paying attention to self and other right now

3. Mental focus – paying attention to thoughts and mind itself

4. True nature of mind – paying attention to "emptiness"

5. Pure View – paying attention to the sacred nature of all beings, sounds, thoughts and phenomena

Since there are different approaches to emptiness, I have listed it before Pure View. But the most advanced forms of emptiness actually follow the development of Pure View. Each of these are first done as a practice, then they are applied off of the cushion in our daily activities. Notice the common thread – paying attention.

To apply this principle, we need to focus on one thing at a time, no "multitasking." It helps to slow down and be more deliberate, more relaxed. Thich Nhat Hanh provides a good role model in this regard, if you have ever seen him or watched one of his videos. So if you are eating, for example, begin by focusing on seeing your meal. Then smell it and deliberately raise a bite to your mouth. Taste it as it goes into your mouth and you begin to chew. Finally, feel the texture as you chew and swallow. Then begin again. Doing this and similar actions helps continue the process of training your mind.

To go a little deeper, there are two parts to the principle of mindfulness. These are usually described as mindfulness and awareness. These are synonyms in the English language, but have different applications in the context of meditation. Mindfulness refers to paying attention to the object of focus during our meditation, much like the process of focus on the present moment described above. This requires training our cerebral cortex – our ability to focus our attention. Awareness, on the other hand, means paying attention to whether we are being mindful in any moment – metacognition, thinking about thinking.27 It involves paying attention and monitoring whether we are paying attention. The latter is sometimes referred to as "the watcher." It takes some practice to develop this skill. Awareness engages the primal parts of the brain. We become alert to what is going on. (This is also our "fight or flight" mechanism.) In this case, we train our brain to be alert to whether we are remaining focused. Training our brain is all about repetition. Do many short sessions!

When we begin the process of meditation, many will experience what has often been described as "monkey mind," a mind that just won't settle down. In contrast, when one is instructed to keep the mind continuously busy, it seems there is nothing to think about! But the goal is to settle the mind so that we can begin to experience the inner peace

---

27 It may be helpful to know that some texts in English reverse the use of "mindfulness" and "awareness" as described here. Most, however, seem to follow the pattern described here. Just pay attention when reading other sources to help avoid confusion.

and joy of awakened consciousness. The process combines study, contemplation, and meditation.

The best way to train the mind is to set aside a specific time and location for regular daily practice. The best times to practice are early morning when you first get up, and late evening just before you retire. In addition, you may engage in "mini-meditations" at any time during the day, along with your present-moment mindfulness. The most advanced meditators are able to maintain a state of meditative awareness, along with innate happiness, continuously.

The best location is one that is quiet where you will not be disturbed and where you can sit comfortably. It may be in a chair with feet on the floor or cross-legged on the floor or on a cushion and pad. Some like to enhance the atmosphere with candles, incense or sacred objects, but none of these are necessary. Use them as you see fit. More on "the container" below. Wear comfortable clothing – generally something soft and loose fitting – or nothing at all. Three yards of cotton fabric in the color of your choice makes a nice meditation shawl.

Meditation can be categorized in many different ways. One is to differentiate between meditation with and without "signs." In general, meditation with signs has a specific point of focus, an object (candle, picture, cross, etc.) or thought (a saying, a chant, or a visualization). Most forms of meditation are active. Meditation without signs involves either a diffused focus or a focus on a sense of emptiness or vast openness with no object. Meditators may achieve a state known as "pure awareness" with no sense of self, time or space.

The Container

"The container" refers to the environment for meditation. As we know from many other contexts, the environment is important; it makes a difference. Some sources minimize this effect, saying that it is not necessary. Technically that may be correct, but experientially it is not. When you set up a shrine in a corner or a room for your practice, it makes a difference in how you engage in the process, as well as the quality of the outcome. That is not to say that one needs to spend a great deal of time and money on this, although that is easy to do with statues, thanka paintings, ritual items, decorations and so forth. There is a traditional model for a shrine called the "three supports." They are: (1)

images of Buddhas, Bodhisattvas, Lamas, and so forth; (2) scriptures (e.g., a copy of the Heart Sutra or other text); and (3) stupas. Such images are readily available on the Internet. A very simple, low-cost shrine can be enough. I began with a card with a picture of Buddha on it that I had received in the mail, a small holder for a tealight candle, and a holder for incense. I placed them on the top of a small bookshelf, along with a green plant. That was it, almost no cost at all. Now, of course, I have added to my collection, and I have a much more elaborate shrine, while thankas and other items fill most of my meditation space. And there are other items throughout the house. It may not be necessary, but it does help. Just be sure to stay within your means without attachment or aversion.

The key is meaning. It is not about being "right" or "decorative." It is about what it means to you. If you let it become wallpaper, it won't really matter anymore. But if you use it to help sustain your focus, your attention, then you will find it to be very worthwhile. It is one more tool in your toolbox for helping to train your mind. Use it wisely.

Ritual

Ritual is another element that some say is not necessary. They see it as just part of the culture or the tradition and not the essence of Buddhist practice.

What is ritual? It may be a prescribed order of doing things, or any regular pattern of activities. In a religious context it may be prescribed in some cases and traditional in others. In Buddhism there are elements of both.

There are different levels of ritual in Buddhism. There are some activities, such as Tantric empowerments, in which the ritual is highly prescribed or designated by tradition. Many other activities are open to the individual to decide what works best for them. This, of course, means that one need not do any ritual at all in many cases. Some argue that we should ignore the ritual elements of Buddhism and just focus on the essential elements, a minimalist approach if you will. If that is what works for you, that's fine.

However, ritual does play a role in training the mind that is often ignored. Ritual involves habituation. Training the mind involves habituation. There is a connection there which can be helpful. Of course, mindlessly following some meaningless ritual is not helpful. But if the ritual has meaning and one pays attention to that meaning, then it helps us in training our mind and reinforces the other activities such as meditation itself.

On the other hand, some people think ritual is what it is all about. I mentioned earlier that some practioners are attracted to Buddhism because they like the elaborate rituals. Just look at how many more people show up for an empowerment than for either a talk on the basics or a teaching on some fine point of Buddhist philosophy. My intent is not to criticize anyone for being drawn to the ritual aspect of Buddhism. One can receive a great blessing from participating in rituals such as an empowerment. I enjoy that myself.

Nevertheless, the benefits of Buddhism do not lie in the ritual itself. Ritual is a means to facilitate an end – enlightenment. Enjoy the ritual … but use it to help you train your mind. You can create your own, such as adjusting the heat and light, lighting some candles and incense, chanting opening prayers, and then meditating. If you do not like ritual, it is not necessary. Just remember that in discarding it you are avoiding one of the methods available to you for helping to train your mind. And most of us need all the help we can get. Now let's look at some meditation practices for training the mind based on the teachings of Padmasambhava.

Shamata - Single-Pointed Calm Abiding

Shamata is the most basic form of meditation. For some, that will be sufficient in itself. But for those who seek to achieve enlightenment, it forms the critical foundation for all that follows with one practice building systemically on the others. This foundation leads to *vipassana*. Then they will be combined to facilitate what are called the preliminary practices. These lead us into the generation stage of the deity yogas in which you begin to see yourself as the deity in union with a consort and so forth.

Padmasambhava taught this in the following stages: stillness of body, speech & mind; object; bindu; hollow body with bindu; deity; and no object. Note that Padmasambhava did not include the common meditation practice using a focus on the breath. The practical matter is that for the tantric practices, these provide more effective preparation than a focus on the breath.[28] The practice in each case is the same; only the object of your focus changes. It becomes increasingly challenging and complex, training the mind in steps. These help us on the path of realizing the true nature of mind – enlightenment.

The master teacher Pema Chodron offers this advice:

> Don't worry about perfection, just be there each moment as best you can. When you realize you've wondered off again, simply very lightly acknowledge that. This light touch is the golden key to reuniting with our openness.

As mentioned previously, perhaps the most common problem with this practice is "monkey mind." There is a tendency to try to force the mind to block thoughts. There is a story often used in the tradition that compares this with trying to tame a wild horse. If you are harsh and aggressive with the horse, it will respond in kind. However, if you are quiet and gentle, it will also respond in kind, as in the movie *Horse Whisperer*. Another analogy is trying not to think of "pink elephants." The more you try, the more they appear in your mind. Instead, just focus on the object of focus, not what you are trying to avoid. So if thoughts come up, just refocus your attention. Always focus, focus, focus … single-pointedly.

The posture is the seven-point posture of Vairocana: back straight (inner channels and energies are straight, easier to breathe properly), legs in lotus position[29] (or best you can do), hands in the mudra of meditative equipoise (right on left, thumbs together), abdomen pressed back (or some say shoulders back), neck is slightly bent forward, tongue is touching the palate behind the teeth, and the eyes are *open*[30],

---

[28] This does not in any way disparage practice with the breath. It is the way Shakyamuni Buddha taught his followers to meditate as described in the sutras.

[29] The lotus posture involves placing your feet on the opposite thigh in a cross-legged position. It is great if you can do it, but most lamas recognize that the physical structure of most Western practitioners makes this impossible. So you can sit with your legs crossed or in a chair with your feet flat on the ground.

[30] There are several reasons for meditating with open eyes instead of closed eyes as taught by some other traditions: (1) You are less likely to get drowsy, (2) you are less likely to get distracted by dream-like images that tend to appear with eyes closed, (3) open eyes help with the transition to off-the-cushion activities (the whole purpose of meditation), and (4) open eyes help prepare you for practices that can only be done with eyes open.

fixed in space, and slightly down. The most important part is keeping your back comfortably straight. It may be helpful to do a body scan (slowly scan your body down from crown to toes to relax each part while maintaining the posture).

Shamata of Body, Speech & Mind

We begin here with the *shamata* of body, speech and mind. As previously mentioned, Padmasambhava recommended doing most of these practices for three days. Because of time constraints in the lives of most householders, I recommend doing this either twice daily for one week or once daily for three weeks until you are confident in the practice.

Week 1—Shamata of Body, Speech & Mind

Practice twice daily for one week, or once daily for three weeks.

Intention: I do this practice for the benefit of all sentient beings (*or other personal intention*).

Refuge: I take refuge in the Buddha, the Dharma and the Sangha most excellent, in order to enable all sentient beings to attain enlightenment. (3X – three times)

Shamata of Body, Speech & Mind:

Settle the *body* into its natural state – a posture of stillness. On the outer level, stop all physical activity; on the inner level, stop all dharma activity (e.g., prostrations); and at the secret level, stop working with "vital energies."[31]

Settle the *speech* into its natural state (quiet). On the outer level, there is no conversation; on the inner level, no religious discussion or teaching; and on the secret level, there are no mantras, etc.

Settle the *mind* into its natural state (emptiness or at least no thoughts). On the outer level, there is no judgment or conceptualization; on the inner level, there are no good thoughts or dharma practices; and on the secret level, there is a sense of vast openness like space or the clear sky.

---

[31] "Vital energies" refers to the advanced practice of channels, winds, and drops. I'm not sure why he recommends not doing something you have not yet learned, but I have included it following his instructions nevertheless.

Don't try too hard or too aggressively. *Relax* and let it come naturally. Notice that this does *not* involve focus on breath or other object of meditation, but just "settling" or letting go. *Let go and let be.* Sit in stillness as long as you can.

Dedication: By the merit of this practice may I attain enlightenment for the benefit of all sentient beings. (3X)

Post-meditation: *Throughout the day, look for opportunities to remain still in body, speech, and/or mind. And when unable to remain still, remain* mindful *of all that you think, say, and do.*

Shamata with Small Object

The next phase is *"shamata* with signs," which refers to some object of focus, either real or imagined. So here we change our focus to a small object. It can be a pebble or other small object, but should be something simple in form. Place it a few feet away on the floor (or on a table). If thoughts or other distractions arise, just let them go and re-focus your attention on the object. It is better to do several short, quality meditations than one longer meditation during each session.

Week 2—Shamata with Small Object

Practice twice daily for one week, or once daily for three weeks.

Intention: I do this practice for the benefit of all sentient beings (*or other personal intention*).

Refuge: I take refuge in the Buddha, the Dharma and the Sangha most excellent in order to enable all sentient beings to attain enlightenment. (3X)

Shamata with Signs: Take a few deep breaths then begin with stillness of body, speech and mind. Focus your attention on a small pebble or other small object for as long as you can. If you lose your focus, re-focus and continue.

Dedication: By the merit of this practice may I attain enlightenment for the benefit of all sentient beings. (3X)

Post-meditation: *Arise gently, "leading your life in a meditative fashion."*

Stages of Shamata Meditation[32]

To better understand your progress, the following guidelines describe the stages of shamata meditative development. As one's practice develops, there are stages of growth, just as in physical, mental, and moral development. The number and descriptions vary somewhat depending on the exact meditation practice and the source describing the stages. The following adaptation provides one such example based on a metaphor in five stages:

The first stage is like a cascading waterfall.

The second stage is like a river gushing through a gorge.

The third stage is like the flow of a large river.

The fourth stage is like a wave-free ocean.

The fifth stage is like a mountain.

Another common list of stages breaks it down into nine parts:

Stage 1: Settling – attention is placed on the object of focus; effort is made to remain focused and reduce agitation or drowsiness.

Stage 2: Continuous settling – attention still moves and requires effort to stay focused; yet gives rise to a joyful persistence.

Stage 3: Resettling – develop some continuity of focus; able to use mindfulness to regain composure and resettle.

Stage 4: Completely settling – able to rest your attention in a vague manner; direct your attention inward to settle fully on the object of focus.

Stage 5: Taming – able to tame the endless movements of the prior stages; brings a small measure of joy in meditative absorption.

Stage 6: Pacifying – eliminate dullness and agitation, remain mindful while resting attentively; apply remedies as needed.

---

[32] Adapted from *Luminous Essence: A Guide to the Guhyagarbha Tantra.*

Stage 7: Completely pacifying – a peaceful state, dullness and agitation purified; thoughts and emotions nearly pacified and clearly distinguished; distraction no longer occurs.

Stage 8: Attentive – with some diligence, thoughts no longer able to create obstacles; able to rest one-pointedly on the object of focus.

Stage 9: Resting in equanimity – able to rest on the object of focus; attention is maintained uninterruptedly without effort in a state of equanimity.

You may find that one day, or even within one session, you are at one stage and the next you are at another. It is very common to move up and down from one stage to another in the process of training your mind. Consider yourself being at the lowest consistent stage over a week or two. It is of no benefit to tell yourself that you are more advanced than you really are. Remember, it takes patience and persistence. You cannot restructure your brain overnight.

Generally in the Path of Tantra, it is not necessary to go to Stage 9 before pursuing deity yoga. The focus required in those practices will further your skill at single-pointed calm abiding. Nevertheless, the further you advance on this scale, the easier and faster you will advance in the deity yoga practices. His Holiness the Twelfth Gyalwang Drukpa wrote,

I instruct my students that the natural state of mind is the main thing: awareness itself. We should not limit that to any particular object of meditation or goal or physical posture, and it has to be brought into everyday life. Of course we try to meditate daily and so forth – sitting, chanting, praying. But I would say that not doing too much is the important thing. We tend to try to overdo everything. Such conceptual actions just create more karma. Consider nondoing, nonaction, for a while, and leaving things as they are.

Retreat

There are many writings that recommend that practitioners practice in retreat, to go into the solitude of mountains or the forest and practice alone, often for long periods, even years. The main advantage, of course, is freedom from many of the distractions that fill our day-to-day lives. Also, after many years of instruction, roughly equivalent to completing high school, monks may go on a three-year retreat[33], after which they are formally recognized as a "lama."[34]

Three-year and other long retreats are not practical for most Westerners. So take heart in the many teachings that contradict the advice on retreats by pointing out that spending a lot of time away from distractions may be good to a point, but that fails to train you to deal with those daily distractions that we face in "real life." In fact, retreat is more of a state of mind than an actual practice. In that way anything and everything can be a retreat! And so it should be. Buddhism is about how we live our daily life, not being a great meditator on the cushion.

Nevertheless, it can be beneficial from time to time to reserve a block of time to focus on your practice. This can be one day, a weekend, a week, or even a month if you have the time. It can be done by camping, renting a cabin, going to a retreat center, or just staying home (leaving TV, phone, and other distractors "off" for that time. It is customary for this to be a "silent" retreat, during which you do not speak (unless really necessary) or when chanting prayers and mantras.

A typical format is to arise early for the first session. Then after breakfast, there is a longer morning session. After lunch, there is a long afternoon session. After dinner, there is an evening session. You can take breaks for tea or short walks as well. When beginning this form of practice, it may be helpful to break each day into one-hour sessions. Later on, after reciting prayers, making offerings, and visualizing, you may alternate between the meditation and reciting mantras. In long retreats, you may include some time for study and contemplation as well. It is also helpful to seek guidance from your lama or retreat master, if available.

Serious practitioners will find ways to include retreats in their lifestyle from time to time, if not on a fairly regular basis throughout the year. It is a great way to reinforce your learning and experience, as well as to return refreshed and reinvigorated to continue your development.

---

[33] Normally three years, three months, and three days.

[34] The word "lama" is used in different ways. It means teacher, so any teacher may be called lama. Great practioners are also sometimes called lama. And those who have completed a three-year retreat are often called lama.

Post-Meditation Practices

There are some additional related practices that may be of some benefit to practitioners in the full development of their calm abiding practice off the cushion.

Mindfulness is awareness of the present moment, living fully in the present moment. Following your breath at any time during the day is a basic way of increasing your mindfulness. This leads to more *innate happiness* in your life. Find joy and peace in *every* moment! When washing the dishes, take your time and focus on washing the dishes. When cleaning the house, take your time and focus on cleaning the house. When eating, eat mindfully. Enjoy the taste and texture of every bite. In general, acting more slowly and deliberately will increase your mindfulness.

Walking meditation is another variation during which you walk slowly, mindful of each step, peace in every step. This is particularly refreshing and renewing when done outdoors in nature or on a labyrinth.

As the Dzogchen Ponlop Rinpoche writes, "Once we join practice with day-to-day life, every corner of our world offers us a way to explore wakefulness, whether we're in a shrine hall or on the street." "Go outside and meditate – sit on a park bench, breathe the fresh air, look up in the sky!" Explore! Go lightly. Enjoy!

Chapter 7

The Third Training on the

Path of Individual Liberation:

Wisdom

Stages of Development

Having previously touched on the teachings of the historical Buddha, we now move into the main schools of thought regarding Buddhism that developed following the death and final nirvana (*paranirvana*) of Shakyamuni Buddha. I have mentioned some of these previously as they tie directly back to the teachings of Shakyamuni Buddha.

The Buddha himself appears to have been very much a pragmatist. He even refused to answer the big philosophical questions by maintaining a "noble silence." But with the passing of the Buddha, differences of opinion gradually emerged. These differences showed up in several Indian philosophical schools. Of these, the most notable were the *Shravakans, Cittamatrans,* and the *Madhyamikas.* Don't be overwhelmed by the names. You will get used to them.

The key focus of these schools was on the understanding of *emptiness.* There are different descriptions of this concept, which is associated with *transcendent wisdom* and is therefore beyond any accurate definition or description in words. Nevertheless, countless volumes have been composed over the centuries to do exactly that, or in some cases to say why it cannot be done.

The wisdom view of the Path of Individual Liberation may be characterized as "appearance-emptiness." The focus is on the emptiness of all appearances, commonly divided into "self" and "other." The Buddha defined emptiness as "the lack of inherent existence." But what does this mean? How are we to understand this in terms of Buddhism?

Some background in the views of the main schools and the evolution of thought regarding *emptiness* can be very beneficial when doing the actual practices. So here is my humble attempt to give an overview of their positions based primarily on the excellent text, *Progressive Stages of Meditation on Emptiness* by Khenpo Tsultrim, which was out of print at the time of this writing.

The progression in this text is described in terms of four stages of understanding: (1) listening and studying, (2) reflecting or contemplating, (3) meditating, and (4) integrating into one's being.[35] These stages help us develop certainty. The text presents a progression of increasing subtle understanding of *emptiness* in five stages:

1. Shravaka stage

2. Cittamatra stage

3. Rangtong Svatantrika Madhyamaka stage (Svatantrika stage)

4. Rangtong Prasangika Madhyamaka stage (Prasangika stage)

5. Shentong Yogacarya Madhyamaka stage (Yogacarya stage)

The original teachings of the Buddha focused on the middle way of the path between the extremes of indulgence and asceticism. But later, the Buddha taught that *emptiness* meant empty of any intrinsically existing nature. That is, things are not *self-existent*. Phenomena do not exist independent of other causes and conditions. This is based on the principles of impermanence (things change) and "dependent arising" (interdependence). *Emptiness* and dependent arising are held to have the same meaning. Things are empty of inherent existence because they are interdependent.

The teachings of the *Madhyamaka* (Middle Way school) teach the middle way of *emptiness* free of the two extremes of nihilism (nothingness) and eternalism (permanence). The *emptiness* of the *Madhyamaka* is expressed in terms of four extremes: *emptiness* is not a thing, it is not no-thing (nothing), it is not both, and it is not neither. Yet another expression of *emptiness* is that the *emptiness* of mind is vast and

---

[35] In addition, the text describes the first of these three as following three key texts in the tradition: (1) *Jewel Ornament of Liberation* by Gampopa (or other such as *Words of My Perfect Teacher* by Patrul Rinpoche), (2) *Madhyamakavatara* on the middle way by Chandrakirti, and (3) the *Mahayanaanauttaratantrasastra*, the doctrine of *buddhanature* attributed to Maitreya.

open like space. These will be explained in the Path of Altruism and the Path of Great Perfection respectively.

The Indian schools differentiated between two kinds of truth – ultimate and relative. Ultimate truth was *transcendent wisdom*; and relative truth was everything else, i.e., all concepts, labels and so forth regarding the dharma. The ultimate truth was considered absolute, whereas relative truth was provisional, that is, its "truth" depended upon the people, circumstances or context. So relative truth may or may not apply in other contexts. Since everything that can be explained in words is in some way relative, it can also be argued that all texts and teachings are forms of relative truth and only direct experience can be ultimate truth itself.

Applied to the two truths, *emptiness* refers to ultimate truth and dependent arising refers to relative truth. Echoing Nagarjuna, founder of the Middle Way school of thought, Tsongkhapa, founder of the Gelugpa school of the Dalai Lamas in Tibet, warns that complete certainty about *emptiness* and dependent arising is very rare. Conventional thoughts can be mistaken as an ultimate level, even though they may not necessarily be "wrong" at a conventional level. At the same time, we cannot ignore that we still need to make moral choices in this conventional world. Therefore, relative truth is still important. In fact, we cannot even discuss ultimate truth without using conventional concepts and labels. In other words, our understanding of ultimate truth is dependent upon our use of relative truth to attempt to describe it, limited as that effort may be.

Confused? Let's see if we can gain some clarity about these ideas by looking at the first two of the five schools of thought.

The Shravaka Approach

The Buddha defined *emptiness* as the lack of any inherent existence, i.e., not having independent, permanent existence or not being self-existent. The Shravaka approach is that of the Path of Individual Liberation with a focus on the emptiness of self or simply not-self. This involves a detailed analysis of what we mean by "self." We act as if it was a permanent, independent entity. We are very emotionally attached to this "self." It is not exactly the same as person, ego, or personality. When one is hurt or offended, who or what exactly is feeling hurt or offended? Who or what suffers? Who or what is afraid? Who or what feels bad … or good? Why does death seem like such a threat to many of us? Is it all in our mind? What is mind? Is it the brain? Are mind and the brain the same? In what ways are mind and "self" the same? Different? Etc.

We might consider Descartes' famous line, "I think, therefore I am." But "I am" is only a thought. All we can be sure of is that we have experienced the thought. I saw a t-shirt once that put a more Buddhist spin on it, "I don't think much, therefore I might not be."

When we try to find this "self" as an entity, we cannot find it. There is nothing there that has an independent, permanent existence. Anything that we can find, if anything at all, is subject to change. It is dependent upon other causes and conditions … our parents, their parents, food, clothing, shelter, and so forth. The list goes on and on and on….

The Buddha often used the example of a dream. In a dream we sense that we have a body and mind living in a world of things. But even if we drown, are burned, are eaten, etc., when we wake up, it was only a dream. The *Shravaka* concept of "self" is very much like a dream. When we "wake up," we realize that this concept of self is actually empty of any independent, permanent existence. Appearances (of self) are not what they seem.

The Buddha stated that there is no self (*anatman*[36]). In the *Shravaka* approach, we investigate our *experience* of "self" by simply being as aware as possible in every moment. One systematic way to do this is to use the traditional division into the five *skandhas*, heaps, or aggregates: form, feeling, perception, mental constructions, and consciousnesses. These were common descriptors of the "self" in the time of the Buddha.

Form refers to our body and other things "out there." We examine the concept of "self" over and over and over again and again until we gain total certainty that there is no inherent "self." Our body is not our "self." No part of our body is our "self." Nothing out there is our "self." Then we meditate in that certainty until the former habitual patterns of thought about "self" have dissolved and the direct realization of "no-self" arises.

---

[36] *Atman* means "self," whereas *anatman* means "no self." Atman is also translated as "soul." In either case it is referring to the existence of some permanent entity. These practices are designed to challenge that concept.

Feeling refers to pleasure, displeasure and indifference (positive, negative and neutral) feelings. Examining feelings, we find that they are always changing, so they cannot be a permanent "self."

Perception refers to the first recognition of input through the senses. These include the five senses of seeing, hearing, touching, tasting, and smelling, as well as thoughts – the cognition of those sensory inputs. Although we think of ourselves as perceiving, we do not think of the perceptions themselves as "self."

Mental constructions are our thoughts and emotions. Feelings and perceptions are also mental constructions, but are listed separately. So mental constructions are those thoughts and memories that come from all other mental activities of the brain. One such construct is personality. Although psychologists tell us that there are few changes in one's personality over time, there are changes. And we may behave in very different ways from time to time or context to context. Thus, although personality seems very tangible, it is not the same as the person or "self." None of the mental constructions or concepts has an independent, permanent existence that could be called "self." We do find here that "self" is indeed just another concept or mental construction that does not otherwise exist.

Consciousness means a moment of awareness.[37] It seems to be unchanging and separate, independent, and continuing from one moment to the next as a sort of stream in time and space. Since our sense of "self" is bound by time and space, it should be possible to divide that into smaller and smaller moments of time. Since it can be divided into parts, consciousness is also not "self." The *Shravaka* approach is to be aware of the smallest moments of experience in the search for a lasting, separate, permanent self. Each moment is further subdivided into subject and object. Divided consciousness is called *vijnana*. Each moment of consciousness is seen as separate and distinct. Since it is momentary, it cannot be "self" either. At the end of the analysis, we arrive at the conclusion that "self" is simply a vague and convenient concept and nothing in and of itself.

From the idea of "self" comes the concept of "other," from which our afflictive emotions and delusions arise, and then compound

---

[37] In Buddhism, there is a consciousness designated for each of the five senses, plus the mind. Thus it is said that there are six consciousnesses, e.g., eye consciousness, ear consciousness and so forth. Here we focus on mind consciousness.

themselves. We often tell ourselves stories that make things seem much worse than they really are. As Mark Twain once said, "I've had a lot of worries in my life, most of which never happened." The only way to transcend this self-inflicted suffering is to realize *anatman*, no-self. Thus, to remove our ignorance and achieve enlightenment, we must recognize the true nature of "self" as an illusory concept so that we no longer cling to it. Or as the Dzogchen Ponlop Rinpoche says, "This ignorance is a kind of blindness that leads us to believe that the movie we're watching is real."

Vipassana - Special-Insight Meditation

It is not necessary to have achieved the highest stage of development in your single-pointed calm abiding meditation practice to continue into this next practice. The teachings of Padmasambhava alternate between different forms of these two basic forms of meditation – *shamata* and *vipassana* – throughout the entire path until they merge into one. So at this point, you may begin to introduce basic special-insight meditation into your practice.

Special-insight meditation is often taught as an active contemplative process, both intellectually and experientially. Various techniques are taught for this practice, generally guiding your attention to one or more points of focus to gradually increase your awareness and understanding. One specific approach is to guide the participant through a series of questions about "self" as described above. After careful reflection, you come to the conclusion that self or I are merely concepts. And these concepts are interdependent upon other ideas as well, our notion of a body, a personality, a mind, and so forth. What is left is *suchness*, the ineffable quality of ultimate truth. "Self" and "other" have no independent or self-existence, i.e., they are empty of *inherent existence*. The Buddha called this "emptiness" (*shunyata*).

So *vipassana* meditation focuses on wisdom or ultimate truth. These practices could have been included in the previous chapter on "meditation." But because they deal specifically with wisdom, I have chosen to place them here, as it is necessary to have some cognitive background to better understand the practices. But the goal is not just cognitive understanding; rather, it focuses on developing an *experiential understanding*. We will separately examine the emptiness of "self" and the emptiness of "other."

Vipassana of Self

The *Shravaka* approach uses contemplation of "self" to achieve the wisdom of no-self. That is to say, you will examine the "self" from several views to develop both a cognitive and experiential understanding of the emptiness of self. The criteria used to whether self is *inherently existent* are that self must be (1) independent, (2) partless and (3) permanent. This meditation uses each of the five aggregates to contemplate the self and demonstrate that it is *not* inherently existent based on those criteria. In other words, self is empty of inherent existence. The approach described looks at self as a whole and then from the view of the five skandhas. An alternative approach is to select just one of the five as the point of focus for each day.

Week 3—Vipassana of Self

Practice twice daily for one week, or once daily for three weeks.

Intention: I do this practice for the benefit of all sentient beings (*or other personal intention*).

Refuge: I take refuge in the Buddha, the Dharma and the Sangha most excellent, in order to enable all sentient beings to attain enlightenment. (3X)

Vipassana of self:

Settle the body, speech and mind into the natural state as before. Then select one or follow the sequence of mental examinations listed below as your time permits. Begin by thinking about self as a whole. What is self or I? Where is it located? What shape is it? Where did it come from? Where does it go? Then continue with the five skandhas.

Examine the nature of *form*. Is our body "self"? Is the body or any part of it *independent* of anything else, e.g., food, clothing, shelter; finger, hand, arm; heart, lungs, stomach, etc? Is our body *partless*, i.e., can it be divided into other parts? Is any part of our body "self"? Is our body or any of its parts *permanent*? Continue examining the parts and the relationships until you gain confidence and understanding that your body and any of its parts are not "self."

Examine the nature of *feelings*. Is the feeling of love "self"? Is the feeling of anger "self"? Are any other feelings you experience (one at a time) "self"? Are any of these feelings *independent* of anything else, or is there a cause, such as another person or an event that triggered the feeling? Can feelings be separated into other *parts or categories*? Are there both physical and emotional components, for example? Are any of these feelings *permanent*, or do they come and go? Continue examining the feelings and the relationships until you gain confidence and understanding that your feelings are not "self."

Examine the nature of your *perceptions*. What is the nature of the things that you see, hear, smell, taste or touch? Are your perceptions (not the objects as above) "self"? Do any of them make up the "self"? Are they *dependent* upon other objects (the objects being perceived)? Can perceptions be divided into *parts*? Are the perceptions *permanent* or do they dissolve or disappear? Continue examining the perceptions and their relationships until you gain confidence and understanding that your perceptions are not "self."

Examine the nature of your *mental constructions* or thoughts. Are your thoughts "self"? Are thoughts *independent* of anything else, e.g., your brain perhaps? Are there other sources that trigger thoughts, e.g., your perceptions? Can thoughts be subdivided into *parts*? Are your thoughts *permanent* or do they arise then dissolve or disappear? Continue examining the mental constructions and their relationships until you gain confidence and understanding that your thoughts are not "self."

Examine the nature of your *consciousnesses*. Is your awareness *influenced* by other factors? Does what is happening around you change what you are conscious of? Can your awareness be broken into smaller *parts*? The context, the object, the characteristics perhaps? How many? Is there ever any finite piece which cannot be further subdivided? Is your consciousness *permanent*? Or does it come and go? How long does it last? Is it constant or does it change? Continue examining your consciousness and the moments of awareness until you exhaust all possibilities and gain confidence and understanding that your consciousness is not "self."

Once you have exhausted the possibilities, let go of all thoughts and sit in stillness as long as you can.

Dedication: By the merit of this practice may I attain enlightenment for the benefit of all sentient beings. (3X)

Post-meditation: *Throughout the day, look for opportunities to continue to reflect on the nature of form, feelings, perceptions, mental constructs and consciousness. In addition, continue to remain* mindful *of all that you think, say, and do.*

The Cittamatra Approach

Some say that the *Cittamatra* approach belongs to the Path of Altruism in which the Buddha articulated the goal of achieving enlightenment for the benefit of all sentient beings. However, the Path of Individual Liberation also uses this approach to develop a conceptual and experiential understanding of the "vipassana of other." Therefore, I have included it here. In either case, it is in the appropriate sequence regarding the wisdom aspect of these paths.

Cittamatra means "mind only." As with the *Shravaka* approach, consciousness is seen as a stream of moments of awareness. Here, too, there are six "sense" consciousnesses, one for each of the five senses and one for thoughts and feelings. These are perceived as facing "out there." However, while the *Shravakans* take the world "out there" for granted, the *Cittamatrans* question that. The division of moments into inner perceiving mind and outer perceived object is a conceptual invention. In this view there is no "outer" other than mind itself, i.e., manifestations of mind, as there is no proof that there is any substance other than mind. Solid, material things cannot get into mind; mind simply experiences mental events and interprets them, imagines them to exist outside of mind. All experience is a manifestation of mind. There is no permanent independent object. Thus, all is empty of any inherent, permanent, independent existence. Suffering itself is nothing other than the play of mind.

In the dream example, the *Cittamatrans* ask, "How do you know that you are not dreaming right now?" The six consciousnesses that usually are perceived as facing "outwards" dissolve back into the seventh consciousness, *alaya*, like waves into an ocean. This consciousness is also where the "seeds" of good and bad karma are understood to be stored and from which they "ripen" under the right circumstances or conditions in our lives. Waking experience, like the dream, is none other than the play of mind.

By resting the mind in its own nature, we see emptiness and all confusion disappears and mind becomes bright and clear and self-aware, mind experiencing mind or awareness of awareness (meta-cognition). This mind is posited as being existent, which has a self-knowing and self-illuminating aspect. When this mind recognizes there are no separate perceiver and perceived entities, one realizes the wisdom mind (*jnana*), the eighth and ultimate consciousness. Resting in its emptiness, free from dualistic concepts, one experiences the natural spaciousness and clarity of awareness.

For *Cittamatrans*, suffering cannot exist in the presence of wisdom. The *alaya* consciousness is purified of its ignorance that posits a "self," the separation into the duality of self and other, cognitive obscurations and afflictive emotions (*kleshas*) that lead to attachment and aversion resulting in our suffering. On the most subtle level every moment of consciousness is purified of all stains of ignorance and there is not even the shadow of the idea of a difference in substance between mind and its objects. The emptiness of this duality is cleared away and the light of wisdom mind is experienced as a pure stream of self-aware moments of consciousness.

Vipassana of Other

The vipassana of other meditation follows a similar pattern to that described above but with a focus on perceptions of "other" or all phenomena, i.e., the emptiness of other. Again to be *inherently existent* the object must be independent, partless and permanent. In *Luminous Essence*, Mipham Rinpoche says, "a buddha will not view any phenomenon as truly existent because it is impossible for such a being to see even the tiniest particle as truly established." There are two parts to this examination. One examines the nature of the objects themselves in terms of these criteria to show that they are all empty of inherent existence. The second examines the nature of the perception itself relative to it being "inside" or "outside."

Week 4 — Vipassana of Other

Practice twice daily for one week, or once daily for three weeks.

Intention: I do this practice for the benefit of all sentient beings (or other personal intention).

Refuge: I take refuge in the Buddha, the Dharma and the Sangha most excellent, in order to enable all sentient beings to attain enlightenment. (3X)

Vipassana of Other:

Settle the body, speech and mind into the natural state as before.

Examine the nature of phenomena that you perceive as "objects." Are any of them independent of all other phenomena? Where did they come from? How did they get there? Examine each object in great detail. Are they partless or can they be divided into parts? Can those parts be further divided into other parts? Are they permanent? Have they always been? Will they remain unchanged forever? Continue examining these objects and their relationships until you gain confidence and understanding that these objects are dependent upon other phenomena.

Now examine the nature of your *perceptions* of other phenomena. Can you tell if each object is "outside" or "inside" your mind? What evidence can you find? How do you know? Note that everything we experience is a manifestation of your mind, even if it does exist "outside" of your mind itself physically. The experience itself is *always* in your mind. Observe numerous phenomena and pay close attention to these questions in each case. Continue examining the perceptions and their relationship to inside and outside until you gain confidence and understanding that your perceptions, what you "see" as objects "out there" are not other than your mind itself.

Once you have exhausted the possibilities, let go of all thoughts and sit in stillness as long as you can.

Dedication: By the merit of this practice may I attain enlightenment for the benefit of all sentient beings. (3X)

Post-meditation: *Throughout the day, look for opportunities to continue to reflect on the nature of phenomena as the play of your mind. In addition, continue to remain* mindful *of all that you think, say, and do.*

Our society is built upon interdependence. Most of us depend on others for our food, clothing and shelter. In our global economy, the level of this interdependence has become extensive. We are all in this together! But interdependence functions at many levels. The cereal that I had for breakfast is not only dependent upon the grocer, the clerk, the truck driver, the manufacturer, and the farmer (to name only a very few of those involved), but it is also dependent up on the rain or irrigation for moisture, soil and fertilizers for nutrients, air for both nutrients and carbon dioxide, and sunlight for photosynthesis to grow, among others. Similarly, there are interdependencies at the molecular level, the atomic level, and the subatomic level.

Consider your body. The primary ingredient in our body is water. If you drink coffee or tea, it may seem like it goes directly through!

However, there is no direct link between the mouth and the bladder. Water must first be absorbed into our blood stream. It is then deposited in cells, extracted from cells, carried to our kidneys and finally to our bladder, though some may go somewhat more directly than that.

Furthermore, where was that water yesterday? In the ocean, a cloud, a stream, a lake? Might it have been in another human being, an animal, or a plant? What are we? We are part ocean, part stream, part cloud, part dolphin, part deer, part butterfly, part otter or swan, part tree or grass, and so forth. Yesterday, I was a cloud; today I am a human being. Yesterday I was a dolphin; today I am a human being. Yesterday I was a carrot; today I am a human being. What will I be tomorrow? There is interdependence among all bodies of water and living beings dependent upon water for life. A French scientist once calculated that statistically each person on earth will breathe at least one oxygen molecule breathed by every other human being who has ever lived! We are all interdependent.

Scientists tell us that we have a completely new body every seven years. Some parts change much more often. For example, our skin is replaced each month, our bones every three months. I am old enough to have gone through several bodies. So where are those previous bodies now?

Cosmologically scientists tell us that everything is interrelated, interconnected and interdependent. Fritjof Capra, a theoretical subatomic physicist, is one of a number of scientists who have written about these parallels. In *The Tao of Physics* he describes that basic phenomena cannot be understood as isolated entities, but only as integrated parts of the whole. He cites the noted physicist David Bohm's statement that the whole universe is "inseparable quantum interconnectedness," that the "parts are merely particular and contingent forms with this whole." Bohm compares reality to a hologram in which each part contains the whole. Einstein called our experience of ourselves as separate from the rest of the universe an "optical delusion of our consciousness." An electron-pair spin experiment demonstrated that the pair retains their paired-spin at any distance. But most interestingly, if the spin of one is changed, the other will change *instantly* across space and time. Even the distinction between matter and empty space was abandoned when it was discovered that "virtual particles can come into being spontaneously out of the void, and vanish again into the void." Scientists now calculate that what we perceive as "matter" only accounts for less than five percent of the matter and energy in the universe. The rest cannot, at this time, be seen or even measured. And we know almost nothing about this "dark energy" and "dark matter." But we do know that there is interdependence of this form of energy and matter with visible energy and matter.

Fascinating as cosmological interdependence may be, human and material world interdependence is of more practical significance in our daily lives. His Holiness the Dalai Lama wrote that "with awareness of the fuller picture, your outlook becomes reasonable, and your actions become practical, and in this way favorable results can be achieved." The process described above is an intellectual one. But it is also more than that. There is a *feeling* of openness and spaciousness. As the Dzogchen Ponlop Rinpoche says, "Seeing this naturally brings us a sense of relaxation, joy, and humor. We don't need to take anything too seriously, because everything we experience on the relative level is illusory." And, "We suddenly feel utterly carefree … so much more relaxed and happy."

With that in mind we move on to the Path of Altruism. But first let's look at some of the signs of accomplishment on the Path of Individual Liberation.

Signs of Accomplishment -

Path of Individual Liberation

Having completed these examinations, you should have some degree of confidence that self and other are empty of inherent existence. As you continue this outlook, you will find that it changes the way you see things, the way you understand the world. You begin to routinely see the interdependence, the composite nature, and the impermanence of self and all phenomena. This is *appearance-emptiness*.

How do we know how well we are doing or whether we are making progress? There are numerous and diverse sources that attempt to help answer those questions. The stages of *Shamata* provide one good gauge for that practice. Here are a few of the other signs of experience and accomplishment on the Path of Individual Liberation[38]:

> *Experience* – your mind is free of clinging, naturally and without any difficulty. Your mind feels at such ease that it is full of

---

[38] From *Treasures from Juniper Ridge: The Profound Treasure Instructions of Padmasambhava to the Dakini Yeshe Tsogyal*

devotion, faith, and compassion, like the sky suffused with the warmth of sunlight.

Accomplishment – You remain unaffected by the experiences of bliss, clarity, and nonthought, while being free from the two hindrances of dullness and agitation.

Further signs of progress, the feeling that:

> One does not have a body
>
> The body is firm and unwavering
>
> The body is being weighted down from above
>
> One is at ease without any pain at all
>
> It is as if one is floating in midair and the lungs and heart are all open like space
>
> The body is a visible emptiness like a haloed rainbow body
>
> There is no noticeable movement of breath
>
> The consciousness is lucid and tranquil, radiant, clear, and brilliant
>
> All perceptions are evanescent, transparent, and open, that they have the color of dawn, and that they are wobbly
>
> One is thrilled and would rather not interrupt the meditation session
>
> While in composure, all shapes are blurred
>
> All mental activity stops so that there are no perceptions
>
> The consciousness is as bright as a clear sky
>
> It is naturally lucid without any concept or clinging

Vipassana

> Remaining unmoved from the nature that never arises
>
> Confidence in the true nature of reality
>
> A total refinement of all senses and perceptions
>
> A blissful ease permeating all parts of the physical body so that there is a feeling of breaking into laughter
>
> True delight in the mind at all times

No doubt whatsoever that things don't exist and that mind cannot be bound by anything

Feeling of having turned away from attachment to appearances

Never tiring of Dharma practice

The six senses being free and unbound, like a small child or a madman

No thought whatsoever being able to cause harm

Having turned away from attachment and laziness

The mind no longer clings to mundane thrills

Every thought is recognized to be nonthought

Thoughts dissolve into *dharmata*, like bubbles dissolving back into water

Yearning for the profound teachings

Discovering one's mind, as if you were penniless and found wealth

Understanding all the profound teachings precisely

Compassion for beings who fail to realize the nature of mind

All appearances being visible and yet insubstantial

Every concrete thing dissolving as if they were a mirage

Seeing other people and all other sentient beings to be like reflections

Feeling like a cloudless sky, pure water, a clear mirror, a stainless crystal — totally bright and free of clinging

Feeling, "What else could the conquerors and their offspring have realized?" and hardly bearing to leave it

The feeling of ease continuing after standing up

There being an atmosphere of trust since you feel, "Both my body and mind are so at ease!"

Your mind being captivated by the taste of meditation, so that there is no hankering after any sense pleasure

Feeling deeply satisfied by the nature of true certainty

Through the Path of Individual Liberation we achieve *appearance-emptiness*. We see and *know* the emptiness of self and other. We abide in that knowing at all times with mindfulness of body, speech and mind. This is the true sign of individual liberation.

Part 4 –The Path of Altruism

The Path of Altruism shows signs of developing from the very beginning of Buddhism. But it was not until around the turn of the millennium that the first key texts were written. It began to flourish around the 5th-6th centuries CE, almost a thousand years after Shakyamuni Buddha.

The Path of Altruism is based on the idea of altruistic intent to achieve enlightenment for the benefit of all sentient beings. According to the Tibetan tradition, Shakyamuni Buddha taught this approach, generally referred to as *Mahayana*, to more advanced disciples. This may, of course, be a rationalization of this view as the title itself means "greater vehicle," a somewhat self-serving distinction. Nevertheless, the important development that led to this path was the idea that the Buddha himself not only attained enlightenment, but then shared that with others. That became the basis for this path – to help others attain enlightenment. Although heavily grounded in the Path of Individual Liberation, this approach adds a broader ethical perspective, some additional practices to further that view, and an elaboration of the basic philosophical view of wisdom found in The Path of Individual Liberation.

From a Western moral developmental point of view, it has been shown that people move from a focus on "me" to "we" then (in a few cases) to "you", the latter being the most altruistic in nature. In general, the Path of Individual Liberation focuses on "me" and the Path of Altruism focuses on "we" and/or "you." In this sense The Path of Altruism shows some degree of progress in understanding, whether articulated that way by Shakyamuni Buddha or elaborated upon by later followers.

The core concept on the Path of Altruism is *bodhicitta* – The Mind of Enlightenment. Bodhicitta includes both relative and ultimate, compassion and wisdom. Relative bodhicitta is further divided into altruistic intention and altruistic action. Our intention is often incorporated into the refuge vow:

> I take refuge in the Buddha, the Dharma, and the Sangha most excellent
> *In order to enable all sentient beings to attain enlightenment.*

Here it is in the second line of the vow. This may be followed by
one of the famous prayers of altruistic action, *The Four Immeasurables*:

> May all sentient beings have happiness and the causes of
> happiness.
> May they be liberated from suffering and the causes of
> suffering.
> May they never be separated from the happiness, which is
> free from sorrow.
> May they rest in equanimity, free from attachment and
> aversion.

The four verses represent the four immeasurables:
lovingkindness, compassion, joy and equanimity. Thus, we are stating
our intention to act with lovingkindness, compassion, joy and
equanimity for all beings, as well as the wish that all beings also have
that experience. "Joy" (or sometimes "sympathetic joy") also refers to the
joy of enlightenment. His Holiness the Dalai Lama often says, "My
religion is lovingkindness" or "My religion is compassion." The influence
of Buddhism in the world is largely due to its practice of love and
equality, and enlightenment for *all* beings.

The great master Shabkar said:

> One with compassion is kind even when angry, one without
> compassion kills even as he smiles. For one with compassion,
> even enemies turn into friends, without compassion, even
> friends turn into enemies. Therefore, all of you, renunciants
> and householders, cultivate compassion and you will
> achieve Buddhahood.

Therefore, compassion is the root of enlightenment because
enlightenment cannot be achieved without compassion.

In Part 4 we will examine the ethics, meditation practices and
view of wisdom on The Path of Altruism.

Chapter 8

The First Training on the

Path of Altruism: Ethics

The Two Truths

In addition to the Four Noble Truths, the Buddha differentiated between what are called the *Two Truths*: relative truth and ultimate truth. *Relative truth* has to do with samsara. Ethics and meditation fit into that category, whereas wisdom fits into the category of *ultimate truth*. Relative truths help us along the path. Ultimate truth is both the true nature of things and the fruition or result.

The pairings of relative and ultimate *bodhicitta* are similar: relative bodhicitta includes our altruistic intention and actions – lovingkindness and compassion – among others; ultimate bodhicitta is transcendent wisdom or ultimate truth.

A third pairing often found in Buddhist texts is that of the *provisional meaning* and the *ultimate meaning*. In some cases these can both be derived from the same source text. In other cases they are described separately. Provisional meaning refers to the contextual dependence of the citation. That is, it may be true for particular persons, time or place, and not be true in others. In general, relative truth matches with provisional meaning and relative bodhicitta. Ultimate meaning generally matches with ultimate truth and ultimate bodhicitta. Once again, keep the Four Reliances in mind when applying ethical guidelines (see Chapter 3).

It is particularly important to keep this ultimate nature in mind when reading texts or doing practices. Since ultimate truth, wisdom and so forth cannot be described, any ideas, concepts, words or labels applied to the practice and result of Buddhist practice is, by definition, relative or provisional in nature. No less than Je Tsongkapa, founder of the Gelugpa order, came to the same conclusion late in his life, stating that anything we can say about Buddhism is relative. Only the ineffable *direct experience* of the ultimate (labeled variously as *rigpa, dharmakaya,* clear light and so forth) can be said to actually be ultimate. Once we attempt to describe it, we enter into the realm of the relative and provisional. Nevertheless, these teachings on the ultimate are necessary and helpful in guiding our practice until we, too, are able to directly experience, stabilize and gain confidence in this experience of the ultimate itself. Hence we sometimes use of terms like suchness, thatness or isness. Yet, these too are labels. Thus, the *only* thing that can truly be said about it is that it exists.

The Six Poisons

To further examine the ethical view of The Path of Altruism, we examine the Six Poisons. To free our *innate happiness* we need to deal with our afflictive emotions and mental obscurations that keep us from realizing transcendent wisdom. *Fundamental ignorance* is the root cause or poison. From this we develop a sense of self and ego, which then leads to differentiating self from other. Having done that, we also develop desire (attachment) and anger (aversion). Together ignorance, desire and anger are the *Three Poisons*. These then lead to other related afflictions or obscurations. Among the most central of these described by the Buddha are jealousy, greed, and pride or arrogance. Together with the Three Poisons, these constitute the *Six Poisons*. Each of these is considered a "poison" on the path to enlightenment. These are frequently mentioned in Buddhist texts so it is important to be aware of them.

They are often linked to the Buddhist view of the *six realms*[39]: hell beings, hungry ghosts, animals, humans, jealous gods, and gods respectfully. But each of these clearly exists in the human realm itself. They are said to exist in your mind. They are not physical locations somewhere in this universe, although of course the human and animal realms include our physical space on the planet Earth. For example, *anger* is associated with the hell realms. There are hot and cold hell realms. We all know people who manifest anger with rage, yelling and screaming, hitting, throwing or otherwise harming things or others. This is a "hot"

---

[39] Superseding the Six Realms are the *Three Realms*. These are the *desire realm*, the *form realm*, and the *formless realm*. The Six Realms fit within the desire realm. The form and formless realms are additional "god" realms, which extend the god realm of the Six Realms.

hell. Others turn a cold shoulder and go inside, unwilling to share or communicate in any form. This is a "cold" hell.

Hungry ghosts are seen as beings with huge stomachs and tiny mouths and throats. They always want more. But even when they get it, it is slow and painful to eat or drink. Thus it is never enough, representing *greed*.

Animals live in the *ignorance* of how their own killing of others for food is harmful to those other beings. Or they are ignorant that they will be killed for food or be enslaved as work animals. Ignorance is the root of all other poisons.

Humans are characterized as having strong *sensual desires*, particularly *sexual desire*. (Note that not *all* forms of desire are necessarily a "poison" as some mistakenly say. The desire for enlightenment is a good thing, for example. You must discern whether a particular desire is helpful or harmful to your practice.) Our attachment to lust can be a huge barrier to our focus on achieving enlightenment.

When we lose something we love or wanted to have but did not get, we may suffer from *jealousy*. In extreme forms it can even lead to anger. The jealous or demi gods are said to be those who are jealous of what the gods have. And the gods themselves suffer from their *pride* or arrogance, only to fall to a lower realm after a long period of isolation from the others and their suffering.

Although the words are synonyms in the English language, gods and deities are used to indicate different categories in Tibetan Buddhism. "Gods" are a category much like the mythical gods of Hinduism, Greece or Rome. "Deities" may be similar in appearance, but are representations of Buddhas and no longer within the six realms. In tantra, we use them to help with our practice of meditation.

The practices of the *Six Perfections* help us overcome the suffering of these realms. In the process of practicing meditation and Pure View, one transforms these poisons into wisdoms. We find these matched in the Five Buddha Families, which will be discussed later.

The Second Vow

The heart of ethics in the Path of Altruism is the Bodhisattva Vow. In Part 2, I briefly described the three vows. Previously we looked at the Vows of Individual Liberation, which His Holiness the Dalai Lama summarized as "do good, or at least do no harm." Our discussion of ethics on The Path of Altruism focuses on the second vow, the Bodhisattva Vow. One form of this vow is, "May I attain Buddhahood for the benefit of all sentient beings." This is often included with the refuge vow repeated at the start of or early in a practice session as described in the beginning of Part 4.

A more detailed and poetic expression of the vow is in the form of The Four Great Vows:

However innumerable beings are, I vow to liberate them.
However inexhaustible delusions are, I vow to extinguish them.
However immeasurable the dharmas are, I vow to master them.
However incomparable enlightenment is, I vow to attain it.

There are numerous versions of the Bodhisattva Vow. Je Tsongkapa (1357-1419) lists 64 different versions of the vow. Perhaps the most popular version is taken from Shantideva's (circa 700 CE) *Guide to the Bodhisattva's Way of Life*, which is often used for the Bodhisattva Vow ceremony:

Just as all the previous Sugatas, the Buddhas,
Generated the mind of enlightenment
And accomplished all the stages
Of the Bodhisattva training,
So will I, too, for the sake of all beings,
Generate the mind of enlightenment
And accomplish all the stages
Of the Bodhisattva training.

One favorite verse often repeated by His Holiness the Dalai Lama is the following, which also comes from *Guide to The Bodhisattva's Way of Life* by Shantideva:

As long as space endures,
As long as sentient beings remain,
May I too remain for the benefit of all sentient beings.

Shantideva's text is based upon the Six Perfections (*Paramitas*): generosity, ethics, patience, persistence, meditative concentration, and wisdom. Both generosity and ethics have to do with ethics on The Path of Altruism. Generosity, of course, means giving. We can give material things, when we have them and they are needed and will help. Or we can give our time, helping others as needed. We can also give through our devotion and practice so that we can help others on their path to enlightenment. Among the verses that illustrate the ethical commitment of a bodhisattva are these, selected from Shantideva's chapter three:

May I be a guard for those who are protectorless,
A guide for those who journey on the road;
For those who wish to go across the water,
May I be a boat, a raft, a bridge.

May I be an isle for those who yearn for landfall,
And a lamp for those who long for light;
For those who need a resting place, a bed;
For all who need a servant, may I be a slave.

May I be the wish-fulfilling jewel, the vase of plenty,
A word of power, and the supreme remedy.
May I be the trees of miracles,
And for every being, the abundant cow.

Like the great earth and the other elements,
Enduring as the sky itself endures,
For the boundless multitude of living beings,
May I be the ground and vessel of their life.

Thus, for every single thing that lives,
In number like the boundless reaches of the sky,
May I be their sustenance and nourishment
Until they pass beyond the bounds of suffering.

Similarly, the following list is taken from *Lady of the Lotus-Born*, the story of Yeshe Tsogyal, the consort of Padmasambhava. Here she recites a series of verses illustrating how upon abiding in meditative equipoise, she perceived herself giving according to the needs of various beings.

To the hungry I was heaps of food and all good things, and thus I brought them joy.

To the cold and freezing I was fire and sun-warmth, thus their joy.

To the poor and needy I was wealth and riches, thus their joy.

To the naked I was every kind of raiment, thus their joy.

To the childless I was sons and daughters, thus their joy.

To those who craved a woman, I become a lovely girl and thus their joy.

To those who sought a lover, I was a handsome youth and thus their joy.

To those who wanted magic powers, I gave prowess in the eight great siddhis, and thus I brought them joy.

To the sick I was their remedy and thus their joy.

To the anguished I was all their minds desired, and thus I was their joy.

To those hard pressed by punishments of kings, I was the loving friend to lead them to the land of peace, and I was thus their joy.

To those in fear of savage beasts, I was a haven, thus their joy.

To those who fell into the depths, I was their drawing out and thus their joy.

To those tormented in the fire, I was a quenching stream and thus their joy.

To those in prey to any of the elements, I was their medicine and thus their joy.

For those who could not see, I was their eyes and brought them joy.

And for the halt and crippled I was feet and thus their joy.

I was a tongue for those who could not speak, and thus I brought them joy.

To those in fear of death I granted immortality, and thus I was their joy.

I led the dying on the path of transference and brought them joy.

To those who wandered in the bardo state, I was their yidam, bringing them to joy.

I cooled the burning heat and warmed the cold of those lost in the realms of hell.

Howsoever they were tortured, I changed myself to shield them,
  being thus their joy.

To those who lingered in the land of hungry ghosts, I was their food
  and drink and thus their joy.

I was freedom from stupidity and servitude for those caught in the
  wordless state of beasts, and thus I brought them joy.

For those beings born in savage lands, I turned them from barbarity
  and brought them joy.

I was truce from war and strife for the jealous gods and was thus
  their joy.

The gods I guarded from their bitter fall and I was thus their joy.

I shielded all from everything that tortured them and was their every
  joy.

Wherever there is space, five elements pervade,
Wherever the five elements, the homes of living beings,
Wherever living beings, karma and defilements,
Wherever is defilement, my compassion also.
Wherever is the need of beings, there I am to help them.

These verses present an example of her strong commitment to benefit others! Another set of verses related to the bodhisattva vow that are often referenced by His Holiness the Dalai Lama, and the subject of several of his teachings, is the *Eight Verses for Training the Mind*:

1. With a determination to accomplish
    The highest welfare for all sentient beings
    Who surpass even a wish-fulfilling jewel
    I will learn to hold them supremely dear.

2. Whatever I associate with others I will learn
    To think of myself as the lowest among all
    And respectfully hold others to be supreme
    From the very depths of my heart.

3. In all actions I will learn to search into my mind
    And as soon as an afflictive emotion arises
    Endangering myself and others
    Will firmly face and avert it.

4. I will learn to cherish beings of bad nature

And those pressed by strong sins and sufferings
As if I had found a precious
Treasure very difficult to find.

5. When others out of jealousy treat me badly
With abuse, slander, and so on,
I will learn to take all loss
And offer the victory to them.

6. When one whom I have benefited with great hope
Unreasonably hurts me very badly,
I will learn to view that person
As an excellent spiritual guide.

7. In short, I will learn to offer to everyone without exception
All help and happiness directly and indirectly
And respectfully take upon myself
All harm and suffering of my mothers.

8. I will learn to keep all these practices
Undefiled by the stains of the eight worldly conceptions[40]
And by understanding all phenomena as like illusions
Be released from the bondage of attachment.

Finally, another popular text related to this topic is *The 37 Practices of a Bodhisattva* by Thogmed Zangpo (1245-1369), reproduced in the Appendix A. All of these verses are intended to motivate us to make a similar commitment for the benefit of others.

These verses reflect the essence of the ethical view of The Path of Altruism. Both our intention and our actions focus on the benefit of others. But this, too, has two levels – relative and ultimate. On the relative level it refers to many of the activities reflected in the verses above in the form of ordinary acts of generosity and kindness toward others. At the ultimate level, our intention and actions focus on helping others attain enlightenment itself. To do this we still act on the relative level; only a fully enlightened Buddha can operate on the ultimate level.

There are two primary actions we can take. One is simply our own behavior as a role model. We can find countless examples of this in the literature, including those mentioned above. We act as best we can *as if we are already a buddha*. Here it is important to know that we cannot

[40] Like and dislike, gaining and losing, praise and blame, fame and disgrace.

know the causes and conditions (karma) behind another's actions. Some Buddhists say that because of this we should not engage in actions that might "interfere" with the karma of another. Perhaps. But the logical extension of this approach is that we do nothing! Ever! What about "do good"? Clearly the verses above state otherwise. Alternately, we can do what we believe in our heart is the best action to benefit others, as the most fundamental element in "doing good" is our *intention*. Never forget that!

The other action is to teach. This, of course, necessitates that we engage in extensive study and practice to become qualified to do that in a formal way. However, you can still share what you do know with others from the very beginning. In doing so, keep in mind that as a rule Buddhists do not proselytize. We do not "wear our religion on our sleeve" so to speak (some do not even practice Buddhism as a religion), but we only respond to inquiries initiated by others. We are always delighted to share when asked, but we respect the view of others and do not attempt to impose our own.

The 18 Bodhisattva Downfalls

As in The Path of Individual Liberation, The Path of Altruism summarizes our ethical actions in the form of the Ten Non-Virtues to avoid and the Ten Virtuous Actions. Furthermore, there is a list of 18 Bodhisattva Downfalls specifically for the Path of Altruism:

1. Praising yourself and denigrating others

2. Not giving wealth and dharma when requested

3. Not forgiving others who apologize

4. Abandoning the Path of Altruism

5. Taking offerings made to the Three Jewels[41]

6. Abandoning the Dharma

7. Disrobing or causing disrobing of monks and nuns

8. Committing the five heinous crimes[42]

---

[41] The Buddha, Dharma and Sangha

9.   Holding wrong views (not believing in the dharma)

10. Destroying towns or other habitat

11. Teaching emptiness to the untrained

12. Discouraging others from their aspiration for full enlightenment

13. Causing someone to abandon their individual liberation vows

14. Denigrating the Path of Individual Liberation

15. Claiming realization of emptiness when not fully realized

16. Accepting something stolen from the Three Jewels

17. Showing favoritism (attachment)

18. Giving up aspiration bodhicitta

The underlying principle is that these have been found to facilitate our progress on the path to liberation. They are not laws that must be followed dictated by some external god. In fact, for the most part we could say that they are simple common sense guidelines.

So to summarize the first and second vows together, *do good or at least do no harm for the benefit of all beings… always and all ways!* Doing this will move us much closer to the goal of freeing our *innate happiness.* In the next chapter we will learn a few of the core practices to facilitate training our mind to *be* a bodhisattva.

---

42 Killing one's father, mother, or an Arhat, wounding a Buddha, causing a division in the Sangha

Chapter 9

The Second Training on the Path of

Altruism: Meditation

There are numerous meditation practices associated with the Path of Altruism. At the core of this path are: the Six Perfections and the Four Immeasurables. I begin with the Six Perfections as they include ethics, although they include elements of the complete path all the way through wisdom. So the Six Perfections not only provide a transition from our study of the ethics on the Path of Altruism to the meditation training, it also provides a context for other meditations and a transition to the training on wisdom.

The Six Perfections

The main practices on The Path of Altruism are called the Six Perfections (Six *Paramitas*): generosity, ethics, patience, persistence, concentration (*shamata*), and wisdom (*vipassana*). The classic text on these practices is Shantideva's (8th c.) *A Guide to the Bodhisattva's Way of Life*. According to legend, Shantideva was a bit of a slacker when it came to his practice and his fellow monks looked for a way to get rid of him (not very Buddhist, but sometimes it is best not to question some of the details in these stories). They set up a challenge for him to give a teaching or leave. Then they built a very high throne for him to sit upon. Unable to climb up he touched the throne and it shrank down to a size easy for him to get up on. Once seated, he asked the monks if he should give a teaching on something that had been taught before or something new. They requested the latter and he gave the beloved teaching of this famous text. Afterwards he left the stunned sangha and set out on his own.

Another fundamental concept from the Path of Altruism is that of the *two accumulations*. The two are *merit* and *wisdom*. In terms of the Six Perfections, merit refers to the first five, while wisdom refers to the sixth. Contrary to what the term implies, one does not "accumulate" a specific amount or number of these practices. Rather, the accumulation is done in terms of accomplishments. These are seen through one's progression in the ten *bhumis*, which will be described in the wisdom chapter. For now, it is sufficient to be aware that the concept of accumulation is inherent in these practices … for the benefit of all beings.

In many ways the Six Perfections are another way of framing other teachings given by the Buddha. So while they are "new" from one view, they are based on very traditional teachings as well. Let's examine each of the components.

Generosity

There are many potential forms of generosity. The essence of this as the first of these perfections has to do with giving away or letting go. When we get caught up in our attachments, we tend to hold onto things, strengthening our ego or self and enhancing our suffering. So generosity helps us to let go of these attachments, and thus our ego-clinging as well.

Generosity may be viewed from several perspectives. One is that to pursue a spiritual practice based on altruistic consideration of others, you must also practice generosity. There is a sense of selflessness. You can, of course, give money or other resources. In the East, Buddhism was dependent upon the generosity of the population, particularly the wealthy. In the West, although there are certainly examples of great material giving, many practioners are just getting by financially and may not be in a position to give a great deal. Consequently, many Buddhist organizations struggle to get by, often supported exclusively by volunteers. Even supporting an unpaid lama can be difficult. According to the understanding of karma, those who have much have been blessed by their previous generosity. They will continue to receive such blessings through their continuing generosity. But it is the *intention* that that is the most important part of karma, not the amount.

A second form of giving is that done by the lamas, giving dharma. They give us the teachings and blessings. These are given freely. Most do not charge for these teachings. And even though dharma centers need to request donations in order to cover the costs of their operations, nearly all explain that "no one will be turned away for lack of funds."

Finally, there is what is called "giving protection from fear." *The Words of My Perfect Teacher* explains that this means helping others in difficulty. While it could refer to material giving as described above, the intention here is other forms of protection such as safety or companionship. Within the tradition of not killing, a Buddhist will also sometimes buy live animals, fish, birds or other creatures to release them instead of allowing them to be killed for food or sacrifice as an act of generosity.

As a practice we can engage in any of these forms of giving. Below I have included a practice of mentally dedicating your body, life and wealth to benefit others.

Ethics

Ethics is avoiding negative actions and engaging in positive actions for the benefit of others. Following the Three Trainings model for this text, I have already discussed the Path of Altruism's view of ethics – do good, or at least not harm, for the benefit of all beings. This is none other than *generosity*. Thus, for this meditation we use the ethics of the Bodhisattva Vow in the form of a contemplative meditation on generosity. Keep in mind that the focus is on the act of generosity, although the benefit is also relevant.

Week 5 — Generosity & Ethics

Practice twice daily for one week, or once daily for three weeks.

Intention: I do this practice for the benefit of all sentient beings (*or other personal intention*).

Refuge: I take refuge in the Buddha, the Dharma and the Sangha most excellent, in order to enable all sentient beings to attain enlightenment. (3X)

Giving:

Settle into stillness of body, speech and mind. Reflect on your body, life and wealth to get a clear understanding of all that might be included here. Imagine each thing in some detail. Then pray that someday you will be free to give them away, with no attachment whatsoever, with the pure intention that they will be of benefit for the enlightenment of other sentient beings. Continue until you feel confident that you will someday be able to give in this way.

Conclude by resting naturally in this confidence without thoughts. *Let go and let be.* Sit in stillness as long as you can.

Dedication: By the merit of this practice may I attain enlightenment for the benefit of all sentient beings. (3X)

Post-meditation: *Throughout the day, look for opportunities for giving what you can or imagining that someday you could for the benefit of every being. And continue to remain* mindful *of all that you think, say, and do.*

Patience

There is little doubt that we could all benefit from more patience in our lives. Whether we experience a flash of anger at being wronged, the desire for the latest, greatest "toy," or some other immediate gratification, we tend to be a very *im*patient society. Instead, we should always be humble, treat *everyone* with dignity and respect, lovingkindness and compassion.

One of the forms of impatience that I see often in my students is to make progress in their practice. "Khenpo, [such and such] happened! Is that a sign?" Sadly, the answer is often, "No, just keep practicing." Patience and the next perfection – persistence – are the most common instructions that I give, especially to beginners. It took the Buddha over six years to achieve enlightenment. It took the great Mahasiddhas twelve or more years, often after many years of training, to achieve enlightenment. It takes many repetitions to rewire your brain. *Practice patience.* Here is a simple meditation on patience to help in your daily life, as well as your practice.

Week 6 – Patience

Practice twice daily for one week, or once daily for three weeks.

Intention: I do this practice for the benefit of all sentient beings (*or other personal intention*).

Refuge: I take refuge in the Buddha, the Dharma and the Sangha most excellent, in order to enable all sentient beings to attain enlightenment. (3X)

Patience: Settle into stillness of body, speech and mind. Reflect on a time when you have been impatient with yourself or others. Re-imagine that experience and your impatience at that time. Once you have a clear experience, imagine yourself in the same situation responding with great patience and control. Continue until you feel confident that you will be able to respond with patience the next time you face this situation. If you have time, continue with another experience of impatience in your life.

Conclude by resting naturally in this confidence without thoughts. *Let go and let be.* Sit in stillness as long as you can.

Dedication: By the merit of this practice may I attain enlightenment for the benefit of all sentient beings. (3X)

Post-meditation: *Throughout the day, look for opportunities to show patience. And continue to remain* mindful *of all that you think, say, and do.*

Persistence

As noted above, patience and persistence often go together, especially when it comes to progress in your practice. But this is often true in other life situations as well. To better grasp the meaning of this perfection, consider another way of understanding it – *joyful effort*. It is more than just working away at it. We tend to give up on things that we don't like. Or at least we rarely do our best at them. So part of the task here is to reframe our perspective. This meditation is designed to help reframe your view of the effort involved. But be assured, it does involve effort! It took the greatest yogis of all time many years. So, too, should we expect it to take us an extended period of time. Patrul Rinpoche describes it as "diligence that cannot be stopped." Nevertheless, it is important to enjoy that experience and to *want* to make the effort. It *is* possible to achieve enlightenment in *this* lifetime.

Persistence is also about dealing with obstacles that get in the way of our practice. His Holiness Dilgo Khyentse Rinpoche explained it this way:

Obstacles can arise from good as well as bad circumstances, but they should never deter or overpower you. Be like the earth, which supports all living creatures indiscriminately, without distinguishing good from bad. The earth is simply there. Your practice should be strengthened by the difficult situations you encounter, just as the bonfire in a strong wind is not blown out, but blazes even brighter.

Or you may recall the saying, "When the going gets tough, the tough get going." Or another of my favorites, "Go on anyway; it all depends on those who go on anyway." Whatever inspires you to go on anyway, remember that *joyful effort cannot be stopped*.

Week 7 — Persistence (Joyful Effort)

Practice twice daily for one week, or once daily for three weeks.

Intention: I do this practice for the benefit of all sentient beings (*or other personal intention*).

Refuge: I take refuge in the Buddha, the Dharma and the Sangha most excellent, in order to enable all sentient beings to attain enlightenment. (3X)

Persistence: Settle into stillness of body, speech and mind. Reflect on your commitment to your practice. Do you ensure that there is time to practice *every* day? What things do you let get in the way? How much *joy* do you experience in your practice? How strong is that as a motivator for you? Are you so *compelled* to practice that it is often difficult to stop? If not, how would that feel? Imagine making a joyful effort every day and finding time to do even more until your whole life is your practice. Continue until you feel confident in your desire to make that happen with joy and devotion.

Conclude by resting naturally in this confidence without thoughts. *Let go and let be*. Sit in stillness as long as you can.

Dedication: By the merit of this practice may I attain enlightenment for the benefit of all sentient beings. (3X)

Post-meditation: *Throughout the day, make a joyful effort to reinforce your commitment to practice. And continue to remain* mindful *of all that you think, say, and do.*

Concentration

At one level this refers to avoiding all of the distractions in life, and they are countless. At a higher level it refers to the concentration of meditation (*samadhi*, literally "balanced mind") that we develop through the practice of single-pointed calm abiding (*shamata*). Yes, this is the same shamata as the Path of Individual Liberation. There are many forms of *shamata* as we will see as we progress through the Path of Tantra and the

Path of Dzogchen. But here it is the same as before. So practice the stillness of body, speech and mind, as well as the *shamata* with small object as before to continue your development of these skills, training both parts of our brain.

Wisdom

The Perfection of wisdom will be elaborated upon in Chapter 10. This is similar to the practices of wisdom in the Path of Individual Liberation. However, over time there were new developments in the understanding of the wisdom that, while fully grounded in the early sutras of the Buddha, push the envelope in terms of elaborating our understanding of those teachings. Some have, of course, disagreed with these commentaries as not being true to the "original" teachings of the Buddha. Whether or not that is factually the case, it is entirely consistent with statements attributed to the Buddha in those early texts and demonstrates the flexibility of the dharma as a living tradition that he appears to have intended even in his lifetime.

The Four Immeasurables

I introduced the Four Immeasurables in Chapter 8: lovingkindness, compassion, joy and equanimity. They are immeasurable because there are no limits to their expression. In the sutras, the Buddha teaches that these practices will bring enlightenment. So these are among the most important of all of the practices in Buddhism. There are practices associated with each of these four, usually beginning with equanimity, then following the order of the remaining three. I have selected examples among several options for each.

Equanimity

Equanimity means that we treat every sentient being equally. We don't have favorites or those we reject or ignore. As a bodhisattva we wish every being to achieve enlightenment. One of the ways that Buddhism stresses this point is by stating that with countless reincarnations, we have undoubtedly had every other sentient being as

our mother in some previous life. If by chance you have doubts about
literal reincarnation, consider it as a metaphor, which can be just as
effective. In either case when we think that every being has been our
mother (assuming that you had a loving relationship with your mother,
otherwise you might substitute another being with whom you have had
a loving relationship), it changes the way you think about and treat other
sentient beings. This includes not only humans, but all forms of beings
such as animals, birds, fish, insects and so forth.

Alternately, consider that every sentient being is a buddha, even
though they may not realize that due to their own obscurations and
habitual tendencies. How does this make you feel when you try to swat
that mosquito? Do you really want to *kill* a buddha? Or what about the
insects splattered across your windshield during a road trip in your car?
Hopefully that was not intended, but do you feel some regret for having
done that nevertheless? Or have you been indifferent? As I said, this
practice changes the way you see the world.

So what is the actual practice for equanimity? Besides
contemplating the *idea* of equanimity, there are two practices frequently
used for this purpose: (1) equalizing self and other and (2) exchanging
self and other. Below they are incorporated into one practice session. But
they may be done separately if you prefer.

Week 8 – Equanimity

Practice twice daily for one week, or once daily for three weeks.

Intention: I do this practice for the benefit of all sentient beings (*or other personal intention*).

Refuge: I take refuge in the Buddha, the Dharma and the Sangha most
excellent, in order to enable all sentient beings to attain
enlightenment. (3X)

Equanimity:

Equalizing Self and Other –

Settle into stillness of body, speech and mind. Out of that
stillness think how you and all other sentient beings want happiness
and peace. Through beginningless lifetimes we have all been stuck in
samsara because of our fundamental ignorance and the resulting
focus on ourselves. I want peace and happiness. They want peace
and happiness. We are all equal in this regard. Think specifically of
one particular individual, someone you are close to. *Feel* what that is

like for them. Then think of another and another. Each wants peace and happiness.

When you have exhausted your list of individuals, think of groups of others you do not know, e.g., neighbors, community members, state residents, country residents, global residents.

Then think of any "enemies" you may have or persons that you dislike or disagree with for any reason at all. They too want happiness and peace. Think of those enemies you know personally, those you know of but not personally, those who are members of groups with which you disagree or dislike and so forth. Continue until you are confident in knowing that all want happiness and peace and do not want suffering.

Exchanging Self and Other –

Now repeat this pattern of thought, but actually put yourself in the place of the other person or imagine yourself as a member of that group. Walk in their shoes as they walk in yours. *Feel* what they must feel in their shoes. Still they want happiness and peace. So do you. May they too have this precious opportunity for peace and happiness. Again, continue until you are confident in knowing that all want happiness and peace and do not want suffering.

Relax naturally in this confidence now without thoughts. *Let go and let be.* Sit in stillness as long as you can.

Dedication: By the merit of this practice may I attain enlightenment for the benefit of all sentient beings. (3X)

Post-meditation: *Throughout the day, look for opportunities to reflect on your wish for enlightenment for every being, no matter who or what they are. And continue to remain* mindful *of all that you think, say, and do.*

Lovingkindness

We now turn to the first of the Four Immeasurables. Having established confidence that all beings want happiness and not suffering, we now focus on lovingkindness or *metta* meditation. In Buddhism, the lovingkindness is the wish that all beings have (ultimate) happiness and its causes. Ultimate happiness is the ideal, but of course we also wish that they have relative happiness as well, to the extent that it is not harmful to them or others in some way. This practice focuses on growing our feeling of lovingkindness for all beings, whether human, animal, bird, reptile, fish, insect or other form.

Week 9 — Lovingkindness (*Metta*)

Practice twice daily for one week, or once daily for three weeks.

Intention: I do this practice for the benefit of all sentient beings (*or other personal intention*).

Refuge: I take refuge in the Buddha, the Dharma and the Sangha most excellent, in order to enable all sentient beings to attain enlightenment. (3X)

Lovingkindness:

Settle into stillness of body, speech and mind. Think of someone you love. Bring that *feeling* into your heart. Focus on it and let it grow stronger and stronger. As it grows, it expands throughout your body, filling it entirely. Soon you can no longer contain it and it radiates out to others nearby, then those in the immediate surroundings, then those in the neighborhood, the city, the state, the country, the region of the globe, all sentient beings in and around the globe ... all animate beings. This too becomes so strong that it then radiates out through the solar system, the galaxy, the universe, and all universes across time and space. Continue meditating in this state until you feel confidence in this lovingkindness for all.

Then *rest* naturally in this confidence without thoughts. *Let go and let be.* Sit in stillness as long as you can.

Dedication: By the merit of this practice may I attain enlightenment for the benefit of all sentient beings. (3X)

Post-meditation: *Throughout the day, look for opportunities to reflect on your wish for enlightenment for every being, no matter who or what they are. And continue to remain* mindful *of all that you think, say, and do.*

Compassion

The next of the Four Immeasurables is compassion. In Buddhism compassion is the wish that all sentient beings *not have* suffering and its causes. It complements lovingkindness so that together we do not want beings to suffer, and we do want them to have happiness. No "bad," all "good." We apply these principles in all of our actions, habituating our behavior in this way until it becomes natural. We wouldn't even think of doing it any other way. It changes our worldview. According to the Dalai Lama,

> The first beneficiary of compassion is always oneself. When compassion, or warm heartedness, arises in us and our focus shifts away from our own narrow self-interest, it is as if we open an inner door. It reduces fear, boosts confidence and brings us inner strength. By reducing distrust, it opens us to others and brings us a sense of connection to others, and a sense of purpose and meaning in life.

This next practice combines lovingkindness and compassion. It is called *Tonglen* – giving and taking. It can be done whenever you see suffering.

Week 10 — Compassion (*Tonglen*)

Practice twice daily for one week, or once daily for three weeks.

Intention: I do this practice for the benefit of all sentient beings (*or other personal intention*).

Refuge: I take refuge in the Buddha, the Dharma and the Sangha most excellent, in order to enable all sentient beings to attain enlightenment. (3X)

Compassion:

Settle into stillness of body, speech and mind. Think of someone you know who is suffering, whether due to pain, mental anguish or some other form. Put yourself in their place. Feel their suffering. At the same time *know* that they do not want this suffering. They just want it to go away! Imagine their suffering as a thick, black cloud clogging their mind. Breathe it in and down to your heart where it is instantly transformed into pure, warm, white light. Breathe that out sending it back to them as lovingkindness and compassion to relieve their suffering. Repeat it over and over with each breath until you *feel* that they are no longer suffering.[43] If you have time, continue with another being and so forth.

---

[43] As with prayer, many do not believe that such actions are really beneficial. H.H. the Dalai Lama says that he does not know whether it benefits the other person, but it clearly benefits the person doing the practice. There is some research that supports a small benefit to others, but that is not yet conclusive. The key is to keep in mind that this practice is for training *your* mind.

At the end of the session *relax, let go and let be*. Sit in stillness as long as you can.

Dedication: By the merit of this practice may I attain enlightenment for the benefit of all sentient beings. (3X)

Post-meditation: *Throughout the day, look for opportunities to practice compassion for others. And continue to remain* mindful *of all that you think, say, and do.*

Joy

The last of the Four Immeasurables is joy. Some translate this as *sympathetic joy*. There are two forms of it. In the first case we are indeed sympathetic to the joy of someone else, whether they graduated from school, got a new job or promotion, won the big game or whatever success they may have had. We are not jealous or envious of their joy, only sympathetic. The second form relates to enlightenment itself. It is the wish that all beings achieve enlightenment. It is often helpful to start with the first form and then move to the second.

Week 11 — Joy

Practice twice daily for one week, or once daily for three weeks.

Intention: I do this practice for the benefit of all sentient beings (*or other personal intention*).

Refuge: I take refuge in the Buddha, the Dharma and the Sangha most excellent, in order to enable all sentient beings to attain enlightenment. (3X)

Joy: Settle into stillness of body, speech and mind. Think of someone you know who has recently experienced some form of success that also made you feel good for them. Reflect on their happiness at having done so. Feel your own sympathy for their experience. Let the feeling grow until it is strong. Then think of another and another. Then move to someone for whom you did not feel quite so good at their success. Finish with someone towards whom you may have felt a bit of jealousy or envy at their success. Continue working with those visualizations until you feel a strong sense of sympathetic joy for their success.

Then switch to the wish for each of these beings to attain enlightenment. Imagine them in a state of peace and happiness in which they are also helping others achieve that same peace and happiness. Continue with this contemplation for each of those for whom you did the first form of the practice and you gain confidence in your feeling of joy for them and all sentient beings who will benefit from their success!

Conclude by resting naturally in this confidence now without thoughts. *Let go and let be.* Sit in stillness as long as you can.

Dedication: By the merit of this practice may I attain enlightenment for the benefit of all sentient beings. (3X)

Post-meditation: *Throughout the day, look for opportunities for sympathetic joy or your wish for the joy of enlightenment for every being, no matter who or what they are. And continue to remain* mindful *of all that you think, say, and do.*

The practices of the Four Immeasurables can also be combined into a single session. It is usually best to begin with a focus on just one. But once you become familiar with the practice for each of the four, they may easily be combined into a single session taking each in turn if you have sufficient time to do so. These are *wonderful* practices. Please *enjoy* doing them!

Chapter 10

The Third Training on the Path of

Altruism: Wisdom

Wisdom on the Path of Altruism is firmly grounded in the teachings of the Buddha (*sutras*). Nevertheless, there is some evolution in the conceptual explanations and texts used to explain this wisdom. There are three forms of this literature that have been collected into the Path of Altruism. The first is Buddhanature, the second is Transcendent Wisdom, and the third is the Middle Way. We will examine each of these in a summary fashion, as the literature is quite extensive. For a householder, that level of depth is not only unnecessary, but can be an obstacle to one's understanding and practice. Nevertheless, an in-depth investigation into the ideas embedded in these teachings can facilitate greater insight for those willing and able to take the time and make the effort. But that is not our level of focus in this text.

Buddhanature - *Uttaratantra*

In the First Turning of the Wheel, the Buddha taught the Four Noble Truths and the Noble Eightfold Path. In the Second Turning of the Wheel he taught emptiness – empty of inherent existence and dependent arising or interdependence of all things. In the Third Turning of the Wheel, he taught Buddhanature – *luminous-emptiness*. The text referenced here is dated to around the 5th century CE. However, it is based on statements in earlier sources going back to the Pali Canon of the Path of Individual Liberation.

All sentient beings are endowed with this luminous emptiness. Based on this and the Transcendent Wisdom literature, presented below, two interpretations emerged. The first is that all beings have the *seed* for becoming a buddha. The second is that all beings are already a buddha but have not realized that they are. In both cases they exist in samsara due to their afflictive emotions and mental obscurations (known as the two obscurations).

So what is luminous-emptiness? In the Path of Individual Liberation we saw that the Buddha defined emptiness as the lack of inherent existence. Nothing exists except in dependence upon other causes and conditions. There is nothing that exists permanently on its own. Furthermore, we did meditations to develop direct insight into this as the true nature of things.

In the *Uttaratantra* the Buddha, in the form of Maitrea – the Buddha of the Future, expands upon this view by adding the adjective "luminous." This is often described as "clarity." In other words, is this clear? Thus, it is clarity of understanding. The difference then can be understood as a *direct understanding* as opposed to an intellectual understanding – the emptiness of emptiness. This is not to say that those on the Path of Individual Liberation only understood emptiness conceptually. But it does appear to have been a serious enough issue to warrant additional clarification (no pun intended).

While the innate nature of luminous emptiness is the most critical contribution of the *Uttaratantra*, it also elaborates on views of the Buddha, the dharma, the sangha, enlightenment, the qualities of buddhahood, and buddha activities.

Transcendent Wisdom - *Prajnaparamita*

The Transcendent Wisdom (literally the "perfection of wisdom") literature is a second major contribution to the understanding of wisdom in the Path of Altruism. This is a body of literature dating from as early as 100 BCE. The best known is the *Heart Sutra* (see below), which is only 14 or 25 lines (two versions) in Sanskrit and is often included in daily recitations in monasteries. There is also a set of eight other main texts, the best known of which is the *Diamond Sutra*.

The *Heart Sutra* contains the famous lines "form is emptiness, emptiness is form; emptiness is not other than form, form is not other than emptiness." It continues through an extensive list of characteristics of what emptiness is *not*, including many of the core principles of Buddhist teaching. Using this *via negativa* approach, it attempts to give a concise sense of emptiness without saying what it is. The basic idea is that the wisdom of emptiness transcends anything that can be said about it.

Avalokiteshvara, the bodhisattva of compassion, realizing perfect wisdom, clearly saw that the five aggregates[44] are emptiness, thus transcending all suffering.

O Shariputra, form is emptiness, emptiness is form; form is not other than emptiness, emptiness is not other than form. The same is true with feelings, perceptions, thoughts, and consciousness.

O Shariputra, all phenomena are emptiness; they are not produced nor destroyed, not defiled nor pure, not deficient nor complete. Therefore, in emptiness there is no form, no feelings, no perceptions, no mental formations, and no consciousness. There is no eye, no ear, no nose, no tongue, no body, no mind. There is no seeing, no hearing, no smelling, no tasting, no touching, no thinking. There is no realm of sight and so on up to no realm of consciousness. There is no ignorance and no extinction of ignorance. There is no old age and death, and no extinction of old age and death. Likewise, there is no suffering, no origination of suffering, no extinction of suffering, no path; there is no wisdom, no attainment.

Since there is nothing to be attained, the bodhisattvas rely on this perfection of wisdom and abide in it without fear. Liberating themselves from illusion, they awaken ultimate enlightenment. All Buddhas in the past, present, and future attained ultimate enlightenment by relying on this perfect transcendent wisdom.

Therefore, one should know that perfect transcendent wisdom is the greatest mantra, the highest mantra, the incomparable mantra, the mantra that clears all suffering, the deepest truth. The mantra for perfect transcendent wisdom is proclaimed:

Gaté, gaté, paragaté, parasamgaté, bodhi svaha!

(Go, go, go beyond, go totally beyond; ultimate enlightenment, soha!)

From this text, we can see how the Path of Altruism took a philosophical position that transcended even the core philosophical tenants of the Path of Individual Liberation taught by the Buddha – no

---

[44] The five mental and physical elements that constitute the existence of an individual: form (body), feelings, perceptions, thoughts, and consciousness.

aggregates, no ignorance, no suffering, not even nirvana! How can you even call yourself a Buddhist? Well, that answer came from the Middle Way, grounded directly in the teachings of the Buddha himself.

The Middle Way - *Madhyamaka*

One of the results of this was a third major contribution to the wisdom literature, and arguably the most significant – The Middle Way. Nagarjuna (150-250 CE) is considered to be the founder of the Madhyamaka approach. Some say he was the founder of the Path of Altruism. He is sometimes referred to as a second Buddha.

He states that *emptiness* and *dependent arising* have the same importance; that they are really two ways of talking about the same view of the nature of reality. The central tenant of this approach is that emptiness is not a thing, it is not no-thing, it is not both, it is not neither (the "tetradilemma" – four-part dilemma). Thus, emptiness is beyond *any* concept or logical explanation. He summed up his reasoning in *Mulamadhyamakakarikas*. His disciple Buddhapalita wrote a famous commentary on this.

The Madhyamaka approach is divided into two groups: *Rangtong* and *Shentong*. *Rangtong* is further divided into two groups: *Svatantrika* and *Prasangika*. Bhavaviveka criticized the method of Buddhapalita and became the founder of the *Svatantrika Madhyamaka*. Chandrakirti defended Buddhapalita and became the founder of the *Prasangika Madhyamaka*.

The purpose of the *Svatantrika* approach is to establish the *emptiness of self-nature of all phenomena*. These *Madhyamikas* do not consider the mind stream of the *Cittamatrans* (see the Path of Individual Liberation) to be ultimate emptiness at all. Nevertheless, they do agree that mind is a stream of moments of consciousness. While the *Cittamatrans* found no self-nature in objects of consciousness, the *Svatantrikas* find *no self-nature in either the objects of consciousness or the consciousnesses themselves*.[45] *Madhyamikas* all agree that appearances are

---

[45] Buddhism posits that there is a consciousness for each of the five senses, as well as for thoughts and feelings, for a total of six. For example, there is eye consciousness, ear consciousness, and so forth. There are also higher levels of consciousness that vary from one school to another and are one to three in number.

only relative truth and have no ultimate reality. All *Madhyamaka* systems clarify awareness by exhausting the reasoning mind.

The Svatantrika Approach

The *Svatantrika* approach uses reason to establish that consciousness and their objects cannot be ultimately real because each arises only in dependence on the other and neither has a self-nature of its own. The *Svatantrika* approach is to use arguments to refute the self-nature of phenomena and then to establish that their true nature is emptiness. Relative truth is how things appear to the non-critical ordinary consciousness, and the absolute truth is the ultimate nature of a thing that is established through accurate and minute analysis by means of the rational mind.

In the dream example, appearances happen but have no self-nature, yet they do appear even though their absolute reality is emptiness. Thus all phenomena are emptiness. They do not accept the *Cittamatra* view that there is some truly existing substance called mind. Mind is relative, not absolute. The ultimate nature of all phenomena is emptiness because they are merely concepts. Even concepts such as emptiness itself can be established as being empty – the emptiness of emptiness. Thus, Tsongkhapa argues that everything that exists, exists only conventionally. Even the two truths (ultimate and relative) are conventional. Emptiness itself lacks any intrinsic nature. In *Madhyamaka* emptiness is the absence of any other level or type of existence. It is only *called* ultimate truth because it is realized by a mind that analyzes how things ultimately exist. The danger is reifying emptiness as something that is truly existent, the concept of emptiness rather than emptiness itself.

Ultimately the true nature of things cannot be conceptualized as either existent, non-existent, both or neither. The method is to examine all elements of existence in turn until one reaches the conviction that all without exception are empty. One approach to the analysis is to break a phenomenon into parts. Is it existent as a single entity or one made up of parts? This is known as the "one or many" system of analysis. If it can be divided into parts, each of those is further examined as one or many, and so forth. If it cannot be established as either a single self-entity nor can it be any one of its many parts, then it can be said to have no self-nature. It is simply a concept. The same argument can be applied to mental phenomena.

The second approach used is that of "dependent arising" or interdependence. If an object has self-nature, it is said to exist independently of any other phenomena, causes or conditions. Anything that arises in dependence upon any other cause or condition has no self-nature. Each object is analyzed for one or more causes and conditions until one exhausts the mind of all possible analyses and one becomes convinced of the certainty that all phenomena have no self-nature. This is done for each of the six senses: seeing, hearing, touching, tasting, smelling, and thoughts or feelings.

This meditation is another of the *Vipassana* or special insight meditations, this time following the *Svatantrika* approach. It is very similar to the *vipassana* of other that we did previously in the Path of Individual Liberation. It begins with refuge and arousing Bodhicitta, followed by the detailed analysis to exhaustion described above, this time using *the senses* one at a time to establish the lack of inherent existence. You then rest your mind in its own emptiness free of concepts in the vast open space. Then dedicate the merit. Between sessions, observe how although things appear, they are empty of any self-nature.

Week 12 — Vipassana: Svatantrika

Practice twice daily for one week, or once daily for three weeks.

Intention: I do this practice for the benefit of all sentient beings (*or other personal intention*).

Refuge: I take refuge in the Buddha, the Dharma and the Sangha most excellent, in order to enable all sentient beings to attain enlightenment. (3X)

Svatantrika: Settle into stillness of body, speech and mind. Reflect on a particular object. Begin with "seeing." Then analyze its parts – what parts can you "see"? Continue by examining each of the parts to "see" if they also consist of other parts and so forth. Follow this by examining it by "seeing" how it is dependent upon other causes and conditions. Do this for each of the parts as well. Continue until you are confident that it (the object you are "seeing") is empty of any inherent existence and/or is dependent upon other causes and conditions.

Repeat the same process for hearing, touching, tasting, smelling, and thoughts or feelings about the object. Then select another object and repeat the whole process. Do this for one or more objects in each session.

Conclude by resting naturally in your confidence without thoughts. *Let go and let be.* Sit in stillness as long as you can.

Dedication: By the merit of this practice may I attain enlightenment for the benefit of all sentient beings. (3X)

Post-meditation: *Throughout the day, continue to examine other objects as you go about other activities of daily life. And continue to remain* mindful *of all that you think, say, and do.*

Signs of Accomplishment

The Ten Bhumis

The signs of accomplishment on the Path of Altruism focus on a classification of ten levels of the Bodhisattva called the ten bhumis. Here is a brief explanation of each level of accomplishment:

1. *Very Joyous bhumi* – the practitioner seeks to perfect generosity, lose all attachment, and overcome concepts of the five aggregates[46] as constituting a truly existent person. They also train in ethics.

2. *Stainless bhumi* – the practitioner seeks to perfect the practice of ethics and engage in virtuous actions.

3. *Luminous bhumi* – the practitioner seeks the perfection of patience and equanimity. They often practice the Four Immeasurables: lovingkindness, compassion, joy, and equanimity.

4. *Radiant bhumi* – the practitioner seeks the perfection of effort (persistence), eliminates afflictions, and emits the radiance of exalted wisdom. They practice deeper meditative absorptions and the 37 Practices of a Bodhisattva.

5. *Difficult to Cultivate bhumi* – the practitioner seeks to continue perfection of effort, perfect their concentration and fully understand the meaning of the Four Noble Truths and the Two Truths (relative and ultimate).

6. *Manifest bhumi* – the practitioner seeks to clearly perceive the workings of dependent origination and directly understand

---

[46] Form, feelings, perceptions, mental formations (thoughts), and consciousness

"signlessness" (emptiness of phenomena), see phenomena as illusory and contemplate suchness.

7. *Gone Afar bhumi* – the practitioner seeks to perfect the advanced absorptions, perfect skillful means (the first five of the Six Perfections) and act spontaneously for others.

8. *Immovable bhumi* – the practitioner seeks to always be absorbed in the dharma and not be moved by "signs." Their understanding of suchness is complete and reality appears in a completely new light (worldview).

9. *Good Intelligence bhumi* – the practitioner seeks to perfect ability to teach, understand questions and answer with a single sound, which is understood. They practice without fatigue.

10. *Cloud of Doctrine bhumi* – the practitioner seeks to overcome subtlest traces, spread the doctrine, perfect their wisdom and manifest in limitless forms in all directions.

Completion of the tenth bhumi, sometimes listed as the eleventh bhumi, is buddhahood.

Luminous-Emptiness

In the Path of Individual Liberation we learned the *appearance-emptiness* of the lack of inherent existence. All phenomena – self and other – lack inherent existence, i.e., upon examination they are found not to be independent (dependent arising), not to be partless, and not to be permanent.

In the Path of Altruism, Nagarjuna took this cognitive approach to the next level by articulating the tetra-dilemma designed to create a direct experience of emptiness itself – (1) emptiness is not a thing, (2) it is not no-thing, (3) it is not both, and (4) it is not neither. Through a detailed analytical examination of the tetra-dilemma, one reaches a direct experience that is beyond all possible logical explanations – it just is! This clarity (luminosity) is the heart of buddhanature – *luminous-emptiness*.

Compassion

But wisdom alone is not enough. A bird cannot fly with one wing. Wisdom and compassion are the two wings of Buddhism. The Dalai Lama has said, "My religion is compassion." Padmasambhava told Yeshe Tsogyal, "Once you have envisioned the suffering of sentient beings ... you will feel like crying bitterly, will feel despair and fear, and will develop an intense compassion." Intense compassion and transcendent wisdom together are the heart of the Path of Altruism. Together they result in *innate happiness*.

Great Confidence

In the process of realizing enlightenment, the bodhisattva exhibits extreme humility and selflessness as seen by others. We often misjudge ourselves and our accomplishments. This is part of what are known in psychology as the self-serving bias and fundamental attribution error. Therefore, you must be cautious in even thinking you have achieved or mastered these practices. There are signs of accomplishment, and these can be helpful to us. Nevertheless, it is always better to have someone else note our achievements than to judge for ourselves. As noted above in the eighth bhumi, one must not be moved by signs.

Part 5 –The Path of Tantra

According to the Path of Tantra, the other paths are not sufficiently complete, leaving some very subtle obscurations to total enlightenment; and the other paths take too long, potentially many eons or at least several lifetimes. Tantra is said to purify all remaining subtle obscurations and enable you to achieve enlightenment in *this* lifetime or at the time of death.

The path of Tantra introduces the yogas of "deity" practices to "fast track" the process of achieving enlightenment. There are three major divisions of these practices: the preliminary practices, the generation stage, and the completion stage. There are multiple elements within each. These practices are considerably more detailed than those of the previous paths, so I have divided the material into six chapters instead of three. Most of the practices described by Padmasambhava in his *Natural Liberation* text are in this and the Path of Great Perfection part of the book.

Many sources include the Path of Great Perfection within the Path of Tantra. However, it is sufficiently unique with no deities, no generation stage, and no completion stage that I have separated it as its own path.

The root *tan* means to extend, such as to extend knowledge (as in transcendent knowledge). *Tantra* is also explained as a weaving together, such as the weaving together of ultimate and relative, personified as male and female in sexual union.

No one knows for sure when or where tantra actually began, although there are several theories. Some sources trace the origin back to the fertility rituals of pre-history. Others trace it to the indigenous Indian tradition and their Vedic religion (2nd millennium BCE to 6th century BCE). However, the evidence is that tantra and the Vedic religion coexisted independently for some time. Tantra appears most strongly in regions *not* dominated by the Vedas, i.e., Northwest, Bengal and South India, in the 4th century CE.

The emergence of tantra coincides with another movement in India, the rise of the divine feminine. Minor female spirits were elevated to goddesses during the early centuries of the Common Era. In *Buddhist Goddesses of India*, Miranda Shaw states, "[Tantra] emerges from a period of strong female participation in Buddhism from the 1st century BCE through the 1st century CE. Nuns wielded substantial political, economic, and social power through their patronage practices and imperial influence, while their literary efforts and participation in public festivals and dramatic performances signal their cultural and civic prominence."[47]

By the 6th century, there is evidence of emphasis on the divine feminine with many deities being elevated to goddess status. The first surviving written tantric texts emerged in the early to mid-seventh century, by which time the practices had been integrated into monastic Buddhism, as well as Hinduism. A Chinese Buddhist, Hiuen Tsiang, who visited India around 630 CE, found that tantra was being extensively practiced by that time.

Tantra appears to have particularly protested against the rigid structure of the Vedic tradition. The Buddha had already objected to the caste system and other characteristics of the Vedic tradition prior to any evidence of the tantra movement. We do know that it was originally a separate movement apart from either Hinduism or Buddhism. In general, it was a counter-culture movement.

The early texts take a very contrarian view to that of the Indian Vedic culture at the time. That is, whatever was generally prohibited by the culture was accepted and practiced by tantricas. First, it was dominated by women[48] in a patriarchal society, although men increasingly became part of the movement. They would go into the forest to practice in secret. Reginald Ray in *Touching Enlightenment* writes about the call of the forest, "Within Indian culture, the forest was considered the ideal place for spiritual practice because, in the forest, there are no rules and there are no presiding authorities."[49] This was an ideal place to practice tantra.

So it appears that the practice of tantra was largely dominated by females rebelling against the male-dominated culture of India and its rigid social and religious norms. Resembling the American counter-

---

[47] p. 146

[48] These are often associated with *dakinis*. Originally, dakinis were spirits blamed for many of the malicious things that happened in society. They evolved into a variety of dharma teachers and even deities within Buddhist tradition. See *Dakini's Warm Breath* by Judith Simmer-Brown and *Buddhist Goddesses of India* by Miranda Shaw for in-depth discussion and history of the dakini tradition in Buddhism.

[49] pp. 10-11

culture movement of the 1960s, when the culture told them what to wear, they went naked. When they were told not to eat meat or drink alcohol, they ate meat and drank alcohol. When they were restricted in what they could do sexually, they had sex openly and freely. The early theme seemed to be one of intentionally violating all the rules. In the beginning, it appears that males participated only to consummate the ritual sex. They were not permitted to have an orgasm, perhaps in order to have intercourse with all of the women present, although there are other ritualistic reasons that may have been factors as well.

The result of the rise of tantra and the goddess movements led to their absorption into both Buddhism and Hinduism, with rather different approaches. In Buddhism, the movement was largely "monasticized," i.e., adapted to fit the dominant monastic tradition and Buddhist principles. Since monks (and nuns) took vows of celibacy, they were generally prohibited from participating in a literal way. It became a highly symbolic practice said to significantly speed up the process of attaining enlightenment. We see the result in the generation and completion stage practices of the Path of Tantra. So the texts were adapted to a process that involved visualization rather than actual sexual union. Other ritual elements such as eating the "five meats" and drinking the "five nectars" were also modified into symbolic representations of those. Nevertheless, some leaders such as Atisha and Tsongkapa rejected or even prohibited followers from doing these practices at all.

Nevertheless, while the tantric practices in the monastic tradition became highly ritualized, the yogis and yoginis continued to do the practices in a more literal way (as did some monks and nuns, who were often criticized for having done so). The practice with an actual consort (*karmamudra*) became known as the "lower" path or the "left hand" path. While it is rarely taught by lamas, since they are largely restricted from learning or doing these practices with an actual consort, practice with a consort may be appropriate for householders, who rarely take the vows of celibacy that are taken by monks and nuns.

However, in Buddhism the core of the practice is not about sex at all. In fact, using sexual desire as the path is designed to transform the experience of sexual bliss into *transcendent bliss*, and in the process eliminate sexual desire, which is considered to be the major obscuration of the human realm on the path to enlightenment. Most teachers consider practice with an actual consort to be unnecessary and a potentially dangerous diversion. Thus, the predominant approach is through reciting and understanding the symbolic ritual to achieve transcendent bliss.

The principle impact of tantra on Buddhism, however, was the use of "deities" in the meditation practices, although this began earlier during the period dominated by the Path of Altruism. However, it is important to recognize a distinction between the deities of Buddhism and those of other religions, especially Hinduism with which a number of them are shared. In Buddhism, all deities are considered to be a manifestation of your mind. They do not exist in the same way that other religions view deities or gods.[50] Although some teachers object to this characterization, I have found that students in the West find the characterization as "tools" for meditation practice to be helpful in understanding both the role of deities in practice and their very nature in terms of training the mind.

There are vast numbers of these figures in the pantheon of Tibetan Buddhism. In general, they may be divided into "peaceful" and "wrathful" categories. Both help us to overcome our "afflictive emotions" and "mental obscurations." One key difference is in the methods they employ, i.e., peaceful or wrathful as indicated by their categories. However, the differences are not limited to that. Peaceful deities are usually also associated with the "outer" tantras, that is, they are visualized as being outside of our bodies. Whereas, wrathful deities are usually a part of the "inner" tantras in which they become embodied in us and we become them. Visualizing yourself as a buddha may be the most effective part of these practices for realizing enlightenment.

Furthermore, peaceful deities are usually visualized as single figures, whereas wrathful deities usually have a consort and are visualized in sexual union. Symbolically, the female represents transcendent wisdom and the male represents skillful means, such as lovingkindness and compassion.

Tantric practices are often further divided into generation and completion stages. In simple terms, the generation stage is the generation of a visualization of the deity and their associated environment, whereas the completion phase is the dissolution of that visualization into emptiness, at which point one rests in meditative equipoise, followed by concluding prayers. The completion stage practices are still associated with the deity, but focus on practices such as the Six Yogas of Naropa or

---

[50] Note, too, that in Buddhism there are both deities and gods, but they are not the same, even though in English the words are synonyms. Deities are buddhas or bodisattvas, whereas gods are still part of the realm of samsara or suffering. Both, however, are not "real" in the same way as perceived within other religions.

the Six Yogas of Niguma. These include practices such as inner heat (*tummo*), illusory body, dream yoga, clear light, transference (*phowa*), sexual yoga, and the *bardos*.[51]

While these practices are said to enable one to achieve enlightenment in this lifetime, most branches of the tradition also include advanced "nondual" practices of *mahamudra* or *dzogchen*. These practices focus on transcendent wisdom itself. The visualizations previously employed in the practices are no longer considered necessary (although some of the actual practices still use visualizations). *Mahamudra* and *dzogchen* are directed at finalizing one's attainment of enlightenment in this lifetime. The essence of the state of enlightenment is the mind of a buddha – emptiness.

---

[51] Here referring to the process of dying, the moment of death, and the time between death and rebirth. In the teachings, there are also references to the bardos of this life, the dream, and meditation.

Chapter 11

The First Training on the

Path of Tantra: Ethics

The Third Vow

I summarized the first two vows as *do good, or at least no harm, for the benefit of all beings.* In the third vow in Tibetan Buddhism we practice *Pure View* or *sacred outlook* – all beings are viewed as Buddhas, all sounds as mantra, all thoughts as the wisdom of Buddha, and all phenomena as a Buddhafield. All are sacred. In the beginning one "imagines" this to be the case. With practice and understanding one begins to realize that this is actually true, as it is. There is no longer any need to "imagine" it to be true. In the ground of purity and equality, everything is none other than a natural *mandala*.[52] But more on this later in the book. Here it is sufficient to note that what we do *off* of the cushion is as important as, or even more important than, what we do *on* the cushion. Ethics form the foundation for what we do during our meditation, but also what we do afterwards during the rest of our day.

In addition, there are numerous other specific vows in the tantric tradition. In attempting to apply these, keep in mind the Four Reliances (see Chapter 3). Among the most common are the Fourteen Root Downfalls (also taken by ordained lay practitioners – Ngakpas and Ngakmas[53]) and the 25 Branch Samayas (referenced in some versions of the Fourteen Root Downfalls – see #13). Because there are different versions of these, I have listed what seem to be the most common, with a few of the most common alternatives listed in brackets. A third set of

---

[52] Mandala is literally a "circle," but represents the entire environment or realm of the particular deity.

[53] Ngakpas are male and Ngakmas are female ordained lay practitioners, primarily in the Nyingma tradition.

vows included here are the Vows of the Mother Tantras[54] as an example
of practice-based vows that are often found in tantras, and may be shared
among various other tantras.

In addition, you are expected to avoid the 18 Bodhisattva
Downfalls from the Path of Altruism and the 10 Nonvirtues from the
Path of Individual Liberation. While these are fairly self-explanatory,
there are detailed teachings and/or texts available for those wanting
further explanation, although one may need to seek explanations from a
lama. A word of caution here, we are beginning to get into some very
deep levels of Buddhism that include terminology that may not be
familiar or understood by beginners. At this point, it is not important that
you grasp each point, but that you get a general idea of the kinds of
ethics that are part of this level of vows.

The Fourteen Root Downfalls

1. Criticizing your vajra master.

2. Transgressing teachings of the Buddha.

3. Out of anger, being hostile toward your vajra brothers and sisters.

4. Forsaking love for all sentient beings.

5. Abandoning Bodhicitta for the benefit of all sentient beings. [Or illicit
    sexual activity.]

6. Disparaging our own or others' beliefs.

7. Revealing secrets of the tantra to those not ready to understand.

8. Abusing your own embodied being as impure.

9. Indulging doubts about naturally pure dharma.

10. When qualified, refraining from stopping others from doing harm.

11. Claiming to be realized when not. [Or not living/practicing the view
    or emptiness, e.g., nihilism or permanence.]

---

[54] Mother Tantras are highest yoga tantras that focus primarily on the wisdom
aspect, as opposed to the Father Tantras that focus on the skillful means. The
best known of the Mother Tantras is Chakrasamvara.

12. Deriding the practices of others [including other religions].

13. Failing to understand or keep other samayas. [Or not taking what is offered as impure.]

14. Abusing or deriding a woman, the nature of wisdom.

The 25 Branch Samayas

The 25 Branch Samayas illustrate both the use of various afflictive emotions and "impure" substances that are transformed into wisdom or "pure" substances congruent with the ethical view of Pure View. Everything is pure, as it is. This also includes a "secret" element of tantra, which led to restrictions on sharing the texts and practices, e.g., see the 7th Root Downfall above. Within that context, the five sets of five branch samayas are:

1) The *five to recognize* are to realize that all the fivefold conceptions (such as the five aggregates[55] and five elements[56]) are primordially a mandala[57] of kayas[58] and wisdoms[59] (such as the five male[60] and female[61] buddhas respectively) and so forth. This is the samaya of the view.[62]

---

[55] Form, feeling, perception, thoughts and consciousness

[56] Earth, water, fire, air and space

[57] A mandala is a circular diagram. In Tantra this is usually a top-view of the universe, emphasizing the palace of the deity.

[58] The human form of a buddha (*nirmanakaya*), the spirit or "enjoyment" body (*sambhogakaya*), and the transcendent or truth-essence (*dharmakaya*). Here the reference is to the Five Buddha Families.

[59] The Five Wisdoms are Mirror-Like, Equanimity, Discriminating, All-Accomplishing and Dharmadhatu.

[60] Vairocana, Akshobhya, Ratnasambhava, Amitabha and Amoghasiddhi

[61] White Tara, Lochana, Mamaki, Pandara and Green Tara

[62] In this set of five, we see how basic concepts can be re-defined to represent a spiritual point of view – Pure View.

2) The *five not to be rejected* are not to abandon the five poisons because they become helpers [five wisdoms] on the path, when embraced by skillful means. According to *the hidden meaning*, (1) *ignorance* is the view free from partiality and the action free from differentiating through acceptance and rejection; (2) *desire* is the great nonconceptual compassion; (3) *anger* is self-knowing wakefulness which conquers conceptual thinking; (4) *pride* is the king of the view of unity which does not "cave in"; and (5) *greed* is to not allow thoughts that cling to dualistic fixation any room within the expanse of equality. By means of the practice of realizing and growing familiar with them, they should not be rejected.[63]

3) The *five to be undertaken* are to take life, to take what is not given, to engage in sexual misconduct, to lie, and to utter harsh words, when they are for the benefit of others. According to *the hidden meaning* these five are: (1) to take life is to interrupt the *pranas*, the life-force, by such means as vase breathing, or to cut the life-force of dualistic thinking by means of self-knowing wakefulness; (2) to take what is not given is to take the *shukra* of the queen or the wisdom of great bliss that is not given by anyone; (3) to engage in sexual misconduct is to practice the unchanging melting bliss by means of uniting self-knowing with the object of *mahamudra*; (4) to lie is to deliver sentient beings from a samsara that is a nonexistent presence; and (5) to utter harsh words is to talk without concealment or secrecy through realizing all sounds to be inexpressible.[64]

4) The *five to accept* are to partake of the essences of red and white bodhichitta [blood and semen], excrement, urine, and human flesh [or marrow] for the purpose of purifying concepts of clean and

---

[63] Here one can see that there is a way to take things that are normally perceived as "bad" and turn them around so that these very features may become beneficial for your practice and understanding. This is also an example of how Buddhism reinterpreted some of the original tantric practices.

[64] Similarly, these five negatives actions – those to avoid in the basic vows of lay practitioners in the path of individual liberation – may also be applied in a positive way on our spiritual path.

unclean. According to *the hidden meaning*, this means enjoying the essences of the five aggregates by binding them to be undefiling.[65]

5) The *five to be cultivated* are to correctly cultivate in one's stream-of-being the five *samayas* to recognize by means of the application of realizing and growing familiar with them [the five buddha families]. Hence, they are the samayas of meditation.[66]

The Mother Tantra Vows[67]

1.   Not to show contempt for left-handed behavior

2.   Not to enter into sexual union with one who does not have the characteristics of a qualified consort

3.   Not to lose one's meditative perspective at the time of sexual union

4.   Not to lose semen for the path of desire

5.   Not to abandon both types of consort (*karmamudra* and *jnanamudra*)

6.   Not to abandon the wisdom consort[68] without her reaching the conclusion

7.   Not to emit bodhicitta except in unusual circumstances like *abhisheka*[69]

---

[65] These five are a mix of what are known as the "the five meats" and the "five nectars." Again we see the tantric approach of taking something normally rejected and transforming them into something viewed as beneficial to our practice. Here what is being transformed is the very ideas of "attachment" and "aversion", root sources of our "suffering."

[66] In the last set of five, we are simply told to cultivate our understanding of the five Buddha Families, a representation in sets of five of many of the key concepts of Tibetan Buddhism.

[67] From an empowerment text for Chakrasamvara Tantra

[68] While the "wisdom consort" or "wisdom woman" (see #8) infer a reference to the imagined consort (*jnanamudra*), these references appear to be more general references to women as physical consorts (*karmamudras*).

8. Not to consider as impure the samaya substance which is the fluid matter appearing from the womb of the wisdom woman[70]

   The essence of these tantric vows is Pure View: all beings are buddhas, all sounds are mantras, all thoughts are wisdom of a buddha, and all phenomena are a perfect buddhafield. Everything is sacred, as it is. This is sometimes illustrated with examples of how a particular object, such as water, is viewed by beings from alternative positions:

Human beings – water

Hungry ghosts – pus and blood

Gods – nectar

Knowledge holders with Pure View – the consort Mamaki[71]

   While this may be viewed as a conceptual understanding or view, it can also be seen as a way of actually transcending those very concepts, particularly when used in conjunction with the meditations. To practice Pure View, remind yourself regularly throughout the day until it becomes second nature, i.e., habitual. It is said that once Pure View is fully established, it will never revert back.

---

[69] Bodhicitta here refers to semen. Abhisheka means an empowerment. Specifically, this is referring to the secret empowerment for sexual yoga, which sometimes involves emission of semen into the lotus of the karmamudra, although this is rarely done today.

[70] The sexual fluids of the karmamudra and/or the union of male and female fluids from the secret empowerment.

[71] Water, one of the 5 elements, from Pure View represents one of the consorts from the 5 Buddha Families. In this case, the element water is perceived as the consort Mamaki.

Chapter 12

The Second Training on the Path of Tantra: Meditation—the Preliminary Practices

The Preliminary Practices - *Ngondro*

As noted earlier, these practices are taught as preliminary to other practices. They are the very foundation for all that follows. For some, these practices are so powerful that they alone lead to enlightenment. Yet many in the West treat them lightly in order to move on to the sexier advanced practices. This may have been true at one time in Tibet as well because early masters began to require students to complete sets of 100,000 repetitions of the "uncommon" preliminary practices, perhaps as a test of their commitment. At one point, some were even requiring sets of 400,000! But this apparently did not go over well as it is rare today.

These practices are normally done by ordained monks and nuns as the first part of a 3-year retreat and are completed in 6 to 9 months. But this is a daunting challenge for most lay practitioners in the West. At only 10 per day, it would take nearly 30 years to complete! With a stronger commitment of 100 per day, it is cut to a more realistic three years. Even that can be a time challenge depending on the exact text and the ritual elements required by the teacher. At the same time, three years can seem like an eternity to someone anxious to proceed to more advanced practices.

Not all teachers require this. Some teach doing the practices daily for one year, doing as many repetitions each day as you can without any specified number required. Others look for signs of accomplishment, which improve with the degree of sincerity of the practitioner. Some require that the practices be done daily as "preliminary" to other daily meditations indefinitely. There are abbreviated "daily preliminary practices" for this purpose. Padmasambhava teaches that we are to do each of the parts for a period of only three days (although one may infer that this means three full days). One of the reasons for selecting these teachings by Padmasambhava is the practicality of his expectations in terms of householders. Still, I recommend also doing a short *daily* preliminary practice to provide a solid foundation to your other daily practices from this point forward.

Four Thoughts that Turn the Mind - *The Common Preliminaries*

The Four Thoughts that Turn the Mind are sometimes referred to as the "common ngondro." This refers to the fact that they are taught in all of the traditions. There are four parts: (1) the suffering of samsara, (2) precious human life, (3) impermanence and death, and (4) karma and reincarnation, although the order varies. The primary purpose for contemplating these four "thoughts" is as a motivation for us to do the practices of mind training. They are, to some degree, fear-based and one can argue numerous more positive reasons for doing these practices. Nevertheless, there is some value in contemplating these thoughts. And at a very minimum, they are such fundamental concepts within the tradition of which one needs at least a basic understanding and experience to understand and appreciate the more advanced preliminary practices.

Padmasambhava recommended doing most of these practices for three days each. Following his recommendation (assuming he was addressing monks and nuns with the most time to do these practices), one would complete roughly thirty hours (at ten hours per day) and twelve sessions (formal retreat meditation is often divided into four sessions each day). Since you are most likely not doing them full time, I recommend doing each of them for one week (twice each day) or for three weeks (once each day). Assuming half an hour each session, that would be seven hours and fourteen sessions in the first case or over ten hours and twenty-one sessions in the second. So while this results in fewer hours of practice, it results in *more* sessions. Research shows that the brain learns better by number of sessions than number of hours. So either of the one or three week formats of quality short sessions should have the same *or better* effect on training the mind than the three-day format suggested by Padmasambhava. More sessions can actually be even better!

There is one other recommendation to enhance training your mind. Keeping a *daily journal* of your practice and experiences will strengthen the effect of those practices. Just a few notes is all that it takes. I keep mine in my *Rigpa Calendar*, which has enough space each day for short comments. Then each week and month, go back and review what you have done and the experiences you have had. This will help give you a sense of commitment and progress. Do not expect miracles. This is a slow process, just like learning to play the piano. It takes *patience and persistence* above all. But the rewards are nothing short of amazing! Diligence does pay off. And it can take less time than some texts would have you believe. On the other hand, if you feel that you have not done well in the suggested timeframe, I recommend that you stick with that practice a bit longer until you really *feel* you have been successful. Just one word of caution – I have also seen students who have so much doubt about their progress that they also allow themselves to get "stuck" at one level, when they should be pushing on toward higher realizations. So there is a need for balance that only you will know. Of course, having a master available for consultation is also extremely beneficial and highly preferable, if you can.

The Suffering of Samsara

I described the principle of suffering and different forms of suffering in the Background chapter of this book. It may be helpful to review those before continuing. In brief, these include (1) physical pain and mental anguish, (2) the suffering of change, and (3) all-pervasive suffering. In addition, there are six "poisons" or realms of suffering: (1) anger, (2) greed, (3) ignorance, (4) desire (especially lust), (5) jealousy, and (6) pride or arrogance. These are further detailed into a list of 52 afflictive emotions as causes of our suffering. An understanding of this principle is central to all of Buddhism. Course forms of suffering are obvious, but as I pointed out, there are much more subtle forms that cause many of the problems in our life. The more we understand that, the better we are able to deal with those experiences without being caught up in them, remaining above the fray, so to speak.

Week 13 — The Suffering of Samsara

Practice twice daily for one week, or once daily for three weeks.

Intention: I do this practice for the benefit of all sentient beings (*or other personal intention*)

Refuge: Recite – "I take refuge in the Buddha, the Dharma and the Sangha most excellent in order to enable all sentient beings to attain enlightenment." (3X) [72]

Shamata: Sit in stillness of body, speech and mind. Focus on the rise and fall of your abdomen as you breathe. [5 min.]

Body: In the Milarepa posture — fold left leg in, keep right knee up, place right elbow on right knee, hold right palm at ear (or on cheek), think: "This posture of despair will lead to stark depression." [Contemplate 5 min.]

Speech: Lament, "Samsara is suffering; nirvana is happiness" [Contemplate 5 min.]

Mind: Ponder the sufferings of cyclic existence. Imagine all of existence is a terrifying fire pit … and we are caught in it. All are on fire and burning! Develop a sense of renunciation of samsara and a desire to practice, to be liberated from this suffering! [Contemplate 5 min.]

Then your spiritual guide[73] appears before you as a body of light and says, "Samsara is like a fire pit, many are suffering. Please come. I will take you from samsara." Light comes from his head to your heart and lifts you up out of the pit. But you look back and see the suffering of your mothers, your friends, etc. and feel great compassion. Light radiates out of your heart and you bring them along one by one until you bring all of them with you. [Contemplate 5 min.]

Dedication: Recite, "By the merit of this practice may I attain enlightenment for the benefit of all sentient beings." (3X)

Post-meditation: *Continually reflect on these sufferings day and night until disillusionment arises and you feel the need for dharma!*

---

[72] Three times

[73] Your spiritual guide is the lama or other teacher. If you do not have a formal teacher, visualize an image of Padmasambhava (readily available on the Internet).

Precious Human Life

While some people believe that they exist as a part of some divine plan, the scientific evidence for our physical existence is quite amazing. The odds of human existence as a species through the process of evolution are incalculably small. The odds of the atoms in our bodies ending up on this planet of all of the zillions of stars in this particular universe are even more incalculable.

Even if we choose to ignore those odds, consider the odds from our planetary ancestors. Using a very conservative estimate of only 45,000 years for the origin of "modern" man and a new generation approximately every 20 years, that is 2,250 generations. A woman releases one mature egg each month during her fertile life. In today's life spans, that could be roughly 500 eggs, though numbers decline later in life. However, in ancient times, much shorter life expectancies might produce 300 eggs. Optimistically, the odds of the particular egg that produced your body are 1 in 675,000.

On the other side, male sperm production varies considerably. Using an estimate of 6,000,000 healthy sperm per ejaculation and assuming an average of two ejaculations per week over an average ancient lifespan, we get odds of approximately 1 in 20,000,000,000. Combining that with the odds of the egg, that is, the odds that that particular sperm and that particular egg would meet at that particular time are approximately 1 in 13,500,000,000,000,000! And those odds ignore most of the history of life on this planet, not to mention the 13 billion years or so leading up to the beginning of life on this planet.

The Buddhist tradition tells the story of a blind turtle living at the bottom of the ocean. It comes to the surface only once every 100 years. On the surface, tossed about by wind and waves, is a yoke. The odds of attaining a precious human birth are the same as the odds of that blind turtle coming to the surface and poking its head through the yoke!

But that is just part of the story. For this life to be truly precious from a Buddhist point of view, we must also have the good fortune of the opportunity to practice, the advantages of being born human in a place where dharma is taught and us having the necessary sense faculties, intention and faith. In addition, we must be born with the advantage of a particular teacher with great compassion who is teaching the dharma, and where we have the time and resources to practice, among many other factors.

The point is that this human existence is *extraordinarily rare* and *most precious*. Few of us truly appreciate just how fortunate we are. And in the history of time, this life is but a flash of lightening. Every second of every day is of immeasurable value, and yet we tend to fritter it away without regard to how extraordinarily fortunate we are to even be alive. Nor do we know how much longer we will have. It may go on for years or end at any instant.

Knowing this, one *must* think of what is the best use of what little precious time we do have. One approach is to cram as much "living" into these moments as possible. This focuses on one's self-interest. Another way is to give whatever one can for the benefit of others. This is the altruistic approach. The choice, with a range of possibilities in between, is up to each of us. It is a question of what is important to us, what we value. If we seek happiness only for ourselves, we will make the first choice. But if we seek a higher purpose, particularly one that also benefits others, then we will make that latter choice.

So why seek a higher purpose? In a perfect world, there would be no need to even consider this question. However, we live in far from a perfect world.

Week 14 — Precious Human Life

Practice twice daily for one week, or once daily for three weeks.

Intention: I do this practice for the benefit of all sentient beings (*or other personal intention*).

Refuge: Recite – "I take refuge in the Buddha, the Dharma and the Sangha most excellent in order to enable all sentient beings to attain enlightenment." (3X)

Shamata: Sit in stillness of body, speech and mind. Focus on the rise and fall of your abdomen as you breathe. [5 min.]

Speech: Say, "This precious human life is just for now. If I cannot practice dharma now, it will be very difficult later. It is not enough that I have attained a human rebirth, for countless others have yet they live a life of suffering. I feel great compassion!" [3X, contemplate 5 min.]

Mind: Ponder the odds against attaining this human life. [Blind turtle, statistical odds 5 min.]

Meditate on the suffering of the three lower realms[74] [5 min.]:

> Feel the *anger* that manifests as the hell realms.

> Feel the *greed* that manifests as the hungry ghost realm.

> Feel the *ignorance* that manifests as the animal realm.

(Optional) Extend your contemplation to the three upper realms:

> Feel the *sense desires* that manifest as the human realm.

> Feel the *jealousy* that manifests as the demi-god realm.

> Feel the *pride* or *arrogance* that manifests as the god realm.

Imagine you are all alone, the *only* human being in the entire vast universe. Was this just luck or the power of virtue? What a waste to fall back now! [Contemplate 5 min.]

Your spiritual guide appears above you as before and says, "Alas! The attainment of a human life of leisure and endowment, which is difficult to find, has been obtained. It is not permanent. If something of great significance is not accomplished now, it will be very difficult to attain later." [Contemplate 5 min.]

Dedication: "By the merit of this practice may I attain enlightenment for the benefit of all sentient beings." (3X)

Post meditation: In this way, contemplate continuously on having obtained a precious human birth.

Impermanence & Death

Everything changes. Nothing stays the same. The only thing permanent is change! We have all heard these and many more similar statements. In the West, change is generally accepted as the way things are. So why is this such a big deal? Are we just more conscious of change

---

[74] The six realms are described in scriptures as physical locations, but the highly realized lamas describe these as being in our mind, that is, psychological states that we experience here and now. In either case, it is helpful to your practice to treat them as "real" from a relative truth point of view. Later, we will see that they are "illusory" in either case, so there is no point in arguing whether they really exist or not.

than the ancients? Perhaps. But recall that training the mind is about changing our worldview. How many of us are *continuously* aware of change? Do you even think about it? Regularly?

The idea of contemplating impermanence is so that it becomes a more constant part of our way of seeing things. Recall that these Four Thoughts are about increasing our motivation to practice. When we become fully aware of the impermanence of the world, of life, we are more likely to take advantage of the precious opportunity we have to practice and really make a difference in our life and the lives of others.

We can begin by reflecting on things like changes in nature, the seasons, day and night, birth and death, the weather, and so forth. Then we can reflect on our relationships. Today we have friends who we did not even know a few years ago. Other friends have gone away and we are no longer in contact with them. In other cases, our relationships may still exist, but they have their ups and downs, conflicts and resolutions, and so forth. The food we eat, the air we breathe come and go. On a larger scale, buildings are constructed, but later torn down. Even mountains and canyons come and go, though so slowly compared to our brief time here it is rarely noticeable.

By contemplating these and countless other changes we see every day, we become more sensitive to impermanence. Then we turn it inward and reflect on our own impermanence. Some of the traditional contemplations include the "three by three" contemplations. First, we focus on the impermanence of life:

1. I will definitely die.

2. The time of death is uncertain.

3. There will be no help when death comes.

The second three are the reasons for the certainty of death:

1. There is no one from the past who is alive.

2. This body is composite and all composite things are perishable.

3. Life is becoming exhausted in every moment.

Week 15 — Impermanence & Death

Practice twice daily for one week, or once daily for three weeks.

Intention: I do this practice for the benefit of all sentient beings (*or other personal intention*).

Refuge: Recite – "I take refuge in the Buddha, the Dharma and the Sangha most excellent in order to enable all sentient beings to attain enlightenment." (3X)

Shamata: Sit in stillness of body, speech and mind. Focus on the rise and fall of your abdomen as you breathe. [5 min]

Location: The text recommends a remote region, a terrifying place such as a charnel ground or cemetery … or imagine such a place and an awareness of impermanence will arise automatically.

Body: Sit cross-legged and reflect on the location. [Contemplate]

Speech: Say, "All things are impermanent. There is no time to waste!"

Mind: Ponder the changing seasons, the changes in day & night, the changes in our lives as we grow old and die. Will I die today? Tomorrow? The time of death is uncertain, so there is no time to waste! I will use this precious opportunity to pursue enlightenment for the benefit of all beings. [Contemplate]

Imagine being in an isolated place, wandering aimlessly about in a daze, when you suddenly fall into a bottomless ravine. You desperately grab onto a clump of grass on the edge. You tremble with fear! Then a white rat appears and eats away a blade of the grass on the right side, followed by a black rat doing the same on the left. They alternate bade by blade and you realize there is no escape. You are about to die. You will be separated from your friends, family, possessions and so forth, never to see them again. You say out loud, "Oh dear! Death is approaching. I will go alone. I'm afraid!"

Then imagine your spiritual guide appearing above you on a lotus and a moon disc seat, holding a *dharmaru*[75] and bell. He is dancing about and says, "This life swiftly passes by like a stream flowing down a steep mountain. There is no time to waste!" As soon as you hear these words, you regret not having practiced the dharma and generate faith and devotion. Instantly light rays from the spiritual mentor's heart lift you up to Dewachen.[76] Then incalculable

---

[75] A small two-sided ritual drum

[76] Dewachen is a pure buddhafield, somewhat like a Buddhist heaven. This one is associated with the deity Amitabha, the Buddha of Boundless Light, and perhaps the most common buddhafield in the tradition.

rays of light emanate from your heart and bring every single sentient being to Dewachen. Cultivate great compassion for all sentient beings. [Contemplate]

In this way, meditate continuously on impermanence and death!

Dedication: Recite, "By the merit of this practice may I attain enlightenment for the benefit of all sentient beings." (3X)

Post-meditation: *Continue to think about impermanence and death.*

Karma & Reincarnation

Karma means "action." Karma is a result of our actions. Many people believe in the *Law of Karma*. This law in modern parlance says that what goes around comes around. More fundamentally, it refers to the complex chain of events – cause and effect – that impact our lives in so many ways. Our actions create effects. According to karma, the effects of our actions come back to us in some way – in this life, a future life, or in some life beyond this material reality. Beneficial actions come back to us in beneficial ways. Harmful actions come back to us in harmful ways. This is the reason for pursuing ethical or virtuous behavior and avoiding harmful or nonvirtuous behavior. Of course, we often see this in our own lives and in the lives of others.

However, there are times when we see, or experience, bad things happening to good people ... or good things benefiting bad people. How can these happen? Most religious traditions either express them as being beyond human understanding, i.e., part of the spiritual realm – often articulated as part of "God's plan." Or they relate it to the Law of Karma as being a function of our actions in this life or in a prior life. This gets particularly complicated in that this perspective also necessitates that one have a sufficient store of "good" karma to have been born as a human being in this lifetime.

How, then, do these bad things happen to humans good enough to have been born as humans? The usual answer is that it is very complex, too difficult to understand and explain. Others explain that unrealized "seeds" of bad karma can still be carried forward in our "storehouse" [77] while the realized seeds of good karma enable us to attain a human rebirth. One also finds descriptions of contradictory

---

[77] *Alaya* consciousness (or a subdivision thereof)

consequences of good and bad actions should one experience a particular combination of good and bad actions. This is further complicated by "conditions" – circumstances that are said to enable these seeds to sprout or manifest. These are beyond our control (actions). These complexities are impossible to reconcile through any ordinary rational conceptualizations. Thus, it is said that only a Buddha can truly understand the karma of any one individual.

As a practical matter, it is helpful to understand four criteria for creating negative karma. All four must occur for the full effect of karma to take place. These are:

1. Intending to do the action.[78]

2. Doing the action.

3. Attaining the intended result.

4. Rejoicing or at least not regretting the action.

From this list, it is easy to see that it is not that easy to create negative karma and, accordingly, there is little need to "fear" creating negative karma. It's not that there are no negative effects from doing less than these four. But it is not nearly as serious. However, the worst actions are considered to be the five "heinous actions": to kill your father, to kill your mother, to kill an Arhat or a buddha, to divide the sangha, and to injure a buddha. Each of these is said to result in an immediate reincarnation in the hell realm.

Another way to look at karma is as a habit. Each time you engage in a particular action, it creates a neural pathway in the brain. When you repeat that action, it becomes stronger, until eventually it becomes habitual. You lie once and feel bad about it. You lie again and it becomes easier. Eventually you become a habitual liar. In Buddhist terms, you have strengthened that seed of karma and you will experience the ramifications of those actions at some point in this life or a future incarnation.

From a Western viewpoint, it seems that though cause and effect are clearly evident, it is not necessarily *purposeful* in nature. Scientists note that there is a significant level of chaos within the apparent order of the universe. While there are clearly laws or guiding principles involved, there is also a certain randomness that transcends these laws or

---

[78] Note yet again that *intention* is the key factor in Buddhist ethics.

principles. As noted above, some argue that these are not mere chance, they are just beyond our understanding, e.g., part of God's plan. Perhaps, but this appears more accurately to be a process by mere mortals of rationalization. Similarly, one could argue that to ascribe such randomness to unknown seeds of karma appears to have been derived from similar rationalization processes. It appears that while the laws of karma have some validity, they are not prescriptive. Karma indeed describes a psychosocial phenomenon, what goes around *tends* to come around. But karma, even in Buddhism, is not absolute in nature. It is relative … and, like all other phenomena in the material realm, impermanent.

His Holiness the Dalai Lama has made similar comments recently regarding catastrophic natural disasters. He has said that while this involves natural causes and effects, it has nothing to do with the karma of those affected.

Karma is *part* of cause and effect – the nature of change. Change is how we experience the impermanent and interdependent nature of material reality.

In many instances there is a cyclical nature to change. We see it in day and night, seasons, and so forth. We note patterns in birth, growth, maturing, aging, and dying. These forms of change have led us to recognize a pattern of rebirth. In human terms, we have often extended it into our conceptualizations of future rebirths either in the human realm or into a spiritual realm such as heaven.

But the change often follows a pattern beyond a cyclical one. We note that one event was caused by another, which was caused by another, and so forth to the beginning of time, if ever there was such a beginning – cause and effect. Much of science is grounded in learning the nature of these causes and effects in the material world, whether in the "hard" sciences such as physics and chemistry or in the "soft" sciences such as psychology and sociology. We have learned and benefited in innumerable ways from this learning. Of course, we have also sometimes suffered consequences of causes and effects that we did not fully understand at the time. For my students who express some doubt about karma, I tell them that it is alright to doubt, as long as you *behave as if it is true*!

Thus, the acceptance that our behaviors have consequences is an important concept in the Buddhist worldview. Our awareness and sensitivity to this view helps motivate us toward both ethical, virtuous behavior and a sense of urgency to practice, given this precious human life.

The second concept included in this practice is *reincarnation*. This is the belief that some form of our consciousness – the *alaya* consciousness – is recycled through the process of rebirth into another sentient being over and over, until we attain enlightenment. It is this *alaya* consciousness that carries the seeds of karma until all are exhausted (or purified). Because of this, we are bound to experience an inherent unhappiness with life over and over and over, unless we make a choice and pursue a path to enlightenment. Thus, karma and reincarnation are interrelated and interdependent. As one of my students noted, "It's not *me* that reincarnates. It is my *alaya* consciousness. And that means I am responsible for the karmic seeds of someone else!"

Scientists, of course, doubt reincarnation. No one has been able to validate claims of previous lives, which somehow seem to always be of some earlier famous person. However, recall of previous lives seems to be more likely very early in life. And unfortunately, babies can't talk. Nevertheless, Ian Stevenson from the University of Virginia attempted to validate such experiences among children by carefully analyzing their memories, even checking birthmarks and birth defects, to match with evidence of the person these children claimed to have been in their previous life. While he was able to document cases that could not easily be accounted for through other means, the studies remain "anecdotal" in nature. No means has yet been identified by which the *alaya* consciousness could physically leave the deceased and enter a new incarnation. His Holiness the Dalai Lama has said that until science can disprove reincarnation, which has also not yet been done, we should continue to assume that it does actually happen.

The Buddha seems to have been a very practical man. He questioned and challenged many of the beliefs and cultural standards of his time and place. And he refused to respond to several metaphysical questions posed by his followers. And yet, there is no evidence that he ever questioned or challenged the ideas of karma and reincarnation. Perhaps he did and his response has been lost. Or perhaps he thought them beyond reproach. Or perhaps he found them to be practical answers for otherwise difficult questions. We will never know.

In the simple practice below, Padmasambhava guides us to consider our actions and the cause and effect of our actions. He does not directly address reincarnation; but it is inferred from karma.

Week 16 — Karma and Reincarnation

Practice twice daily for one week, or once daily for three weeks.

Intention: I do this practice for the benefit of all sentient beings (*or other personal intention*).

Refuge: Recite – "I take refuge in the Buddha, the Dharma and the Sangha most excellent in order to enable all sentient beings to attain enlightenment." (3X)

Shamata: Sit in stillness of body, speech and mind. Focus on the rise and fall of your abdomen as you breathe. [5 min]

Speech: Say, "All actions have consequences. I will take care with all my thoughts, words, and deeds."

Mind: Contemplate your previous actions and known consequences. Think about other potential consequences from nonvirtuous thoughts, words, or deeds. Vow to only engage in virtuous actions! [Contemplate]

In this way, meditate continuously on the cause and effect of your actions!

Dedication: Recite, "By the merit of this practice may I attain enlightenment for the benefit of all sentient beings." (3X)

Post-meditation: *Continue to think about your actions and potential implications of those actions on you and others.*

The Uncommon Preliminaries

The traditional tantric path includes preliminary practices that are designed to establish one's commitment and discipline in the practice. The uncommon preliminaries are (1) refuge, (2) bodhicitta, (3) Vajrasattva purification, (4) mandala offerings, and (5) guru yoga. Each of these preliminaries is traditionally repeated 100,000 times as a preliminary to entering the tantric training. Many Western students react to this rather negatively. "Are you serious?" Keep in mind that this serves a dual purpose. One is actual preparation for the advanced practices. The other is evidence that *you* are serious! In reality, the exact number, sequence and combinations vary by school and teacher. Some of my teachers required the full 100,000 repetitions of each of their students. Another teacher required daily practice for a period of one year. Still another teacher required it only as a daily preliminary practice to other meditation practices.

As with the common preliminary practices, Padmasambhava seems to have recommended a period of at least three days for each of these. Following this pattern, I also recommend that following the one or three week model for each, lay practitioners should continue with a short preliminary practice be continued prior to any other daily practice for the rest of this life. Of course, if you can and will, completing 100,000 of each is even better! Some teachers will not accept practitioners into the higher teachings without having completed these practices. However, in the Western tradition, this is much less often followed. Within the Path of Great Perfection, this may even be transcended through other preliminaries described later. In any case, follow the instructions of your own lama, if you have one.

Refuge

The refuge vow is the first initiation into the practice. When conducted by a master, it takes the form of a simple ceremony that includes some explanation, the vow, initiation, and giving a Tibetan name. The refuge practice includes visualization, taking refuge, and doing prostrations.

The visualization is a "refuge tree." There are numerous variations and countless images can be found on the Internet. In general, they follow this design: Guru Rinpoche in center[79], buddhas on Rinpoche's right, dharma texts behind, bodhisattvas on his left, lineage figures above, primordial buddha at top, dharma protectors below, surrounded by dakas and dakinis. In addition you visualize all sentient beings in front of you, your mother and father beside you, enemies in front; all prostrate together while reciting the refuge prayer. You memorize and imagine this image while reciting the refuge prayer and make prostrations. Until then, it may be helpful to print a refuge tree picture for reference. Since Padmasambhava represents the Nyingma lineage, I recommend something from that lineage unless you are part of some other lineage. In that case, use their lineage tree.

---

[79] The central figure may be some other key figure related to the particular lineage.

In the Buddhist tradition, one takes refuge in the Buddha, the dharma and the sangha – the teacher, the teachings, and the community. Refuge is a place one goes for support, for inspiration along the path.

There are multiple levels of understanding as well. Buddha, dharma, and sangha are the *outer* level of refuge. The *inner* level includes the guru, yidam, and dakini. The guru is the teacher. The yidam is a personal deity[80] selected for advanced meditation practices with the guidance of one's spiritual master or guru. The dakini or "sky dancer" represents the feminine principle and wisdom. We will explore the dakini more, later in the text. The *secret* level of refuge is *dharmakaya*, *sambhogakaya*, and *nirmanakaya*. Kaya means "body." These are three forms of a buddha – literally the truth body, the enjoyment body, and the form body respectively. More specifically, they refer to the transcendent wisdom, energy or spirit, and the radiant display or material manifestation. These correspond closely to the Christian Trinity's Father, Holy Spirit, and Son.[81] Another analogy is water as ice, liquid, and steam. All are forms of water, appearing with different qualities. Fundamentally, the buddha is within. We just need to "wake up" to that fact, understand its true nature, and live within that reality in our daily lives. We are already buddhas. Taking refuge at the secret level acknowledges this understanding.

While taking refuge, it is customary to make prostrations. Prostrations are a tradition of reverence for the Buddha, the guru, or other significant figure. One begins by placing the hands together with the palms slightly cupped, symbolic of the lotus bud. The hands are raised overhead touching the crown saying, "I take refuge..." Then touch the "third eye" on the forehead saying, "...in the Buddha." Touch the throat saying, "... in the dharma." Touch the heart saying, "...in the sangha." (The exact wording may vary from one text to another and some versions start at the crown, skipping the forehead.) Then make the prostration by bending down onto hands and knees, then sliding the hands forward until one is prone on the ground with hands, feet and

---

[80] Tibetan Buddhism includes a vast array of deities. While "deity" literally means a "god," in Buddhist practice, the concept of god would be misleading. These are visualizations for the purpose of practice, not actual beings as gods are normally thought to be. The use of the word deity is meant to differentiate between these two conceptualizations. The word "god" is also used, but to refer to beings of the god realm, who are not considered to be deities.

[81] In this case, dharmakaya is the ineffable ultimate, not the literal form of God sometimes depicted by other religions.

forehead touching the ground. Complete the remaining part of the prayer in the process of standing up. After repeating the prostrations, conclude by folding the hands to the heart. An abbreviated version touches the forehead to the ground from the hands and knees position. It is normally repeated three times upon entering the temple, following the entry and seating of the teaching master, and/or at the beginning of one's personal practice. Here it is repeated as part of taking refuge.

Bodhicitta

This is one of a few Sanskrit words that I chose to retain due to its special meaning for me personally. It has different meanings in different teachings, which can be a source of confusion for practitioners reading different sources. As described in the Path of Altruism, this is usually translated as "the mind of enlightenment." To review, it has two parts, the first of which is further subdivided into two aspects making a total of three parts. The first part is *relative bodhicitta*. The first aspect of relative bodhicitta is to our *altruistic intention*, the intention to achieve enlightenment for the benefit of all others, or even delaying final enlightenment until all others have become enlightened. Altruistic motivation is a very high level of motivation that few in the West ever fully attain.[82]

The second part of bodhicitta is *action bodhicitta*. In this case, bodhicitta is equivalent to lovingkindness and compassion. Lovingkindness and compassion are two aspects of the same thing. Lovingkindness refers to the desire for others to achieve happiness and the causes of happiness. Compassion is the desire for others to avoid unhappiness (suffering) and the causes of unhappiness. In other words, we want them to have the good and don't want them to have the bad. Unlike the "desire" associated with negative emotions described previously, these forms of desire are okay, as they are beneficial to others. Action bodhicitta is also tied closely to the Bodhisattva Vow previously described. This deals with the application of the principle of bodhicitta in our daily behaviors, especially those involving others.

---

[82] Lawrence Kolberg described three levels of moral development: pre-conventional, conventional, and post-conventional. They correspond to a focus on me, we, and you, with the latter being altruism. We all have all three, but if we develop morally, we will shift our emphasis from me to we to you, although research shows few actually attain the highest level, that of altruism.

The third part of bodhicitta is *ultimate bodhicitta*. This is the suchness or emptiness of transcendent wisdom described previously. Relative and ultimate bodhicitta are nondual, two aspects of the same truth, the front and back of the hand.

Lovingkindness and compassion are two of the *four immeasurables*. These are immeasurable because there is no limit to their realization and application. The third is *joy*, or more specifically, sympathetic joy. At an ordinary level, this is the joy that we express toward the happiness realized by others. Rather than feeling envy or jealousy, we are deeply happy for their happiness. As described previously, our focus is on the benefits for others over self-interest or ego. At a higher level, this is the joy related to enlightenment. We wish all sentient beings to experience this joy!

The fourth immeasurable is *equanimity*. Equanimity refers to equality, treating everyone and every phenomenon the same way. Everyone is treated with lovingkindness, compassion and joy, whether they are friends or family … or even our enemies. This is a very difficult standard for most of us to achieve! It is the same standard that Jesus called on his followers to practice, i.e., to love not only God, each other (others on the path), and our neighbors (literally, those in other countries), but also our *enemies*! Previously, we did the short prayer of the Four Immeasurables that is often recited as part of the daily preliminary practice.

In some traditions refuge and bodhicitta are combined into a single practice, as we will see here. In others, they are done separately, including the additional 100,000 repetitions. For lay practitioners I recommend that you do as many repetitions of the refuge prayers with prostrations followed by the bodhicitta prayer as you can during two daily sessions for one week, or one daily session for three weeks.

Week 17—Refuge & Bodhicitta

Practice twice daily for one week, or once daily for three weeks.

Intention: I do this practice for the benefit of all sentient beings (*or other personal intention*).

Visualization: Imagine the refuge tree.

Going for Outer, Inner, and Secret Refuge with prostrations:

> I take refuge in the Buddha, the dharma, and the sangha most excellent;

I take refuge in the guru, yidam and dakini;

I take refuge in the Dharmakaya, Sambhogakaya, and Nirmanakaya

In order to enable all sentient beings to attain enlightenment.

[*Repeat with prostrations as many times as you can.*[83]]

Generating Bodhicitta – The Four Immeasurables:

May all mother sentient beings, boundless as the sky, have happiness and the causes of happiness.

May they be liberated from suffering and the causes of suffering.

May they never be separated from the happiness, which is free from sorrow.

May they rest in equanimity, free from attachment and aversion.

[*Repeat as many times as you can.*]

Dedication: Recite, "By the merit of this practice may I attain enlightenment for the benefit of all sentient beings." (3X)

Post-meditation: *Arise gently, "leading your life in a meditative fashion" as before.*

The two parts may be done sequentially, repeating them as a set instead of one at a time.

Vajrasattva Purification

One way to get rid of that negative karma previously acquired is by burning it up – the negative experiences in our lives. But karma is impermanent. We do not have to wait for that to happen. We do that through purification practices and the most significant of those is Vajrasattva, the Buddha of Purification. We do this to purify all negative karma, afflictive emotions, cognitive obscurations, and habitual tendencies and prepare ourselves as a suitable vessel for the advanced practices. This is one of the first deity practices taught in Tantric

---

[83] Note that some lamas will not permit counting repetitions done without the prostrations.

Buddhism. Deity practices may be quite simple or very complex. We will explore the more complex forms later.

Now we are ready to take the next step. The basic pattern of a short practice is (1) opening refuge prayer, (2) visualization of the deity, (3) recitation of the mantra, (4) dissolution and meditation on emptiness, and (5) closing prayers. Some short practices include other elements such as offerings and additional mantras or prayers. You may also find contradictions between practices of the same deity. In any case, it is best to follow the description in the practice text (*sadhana*[84]), which you are using.

Today, the practice text is chanted, even memorized for that purpose. However, this may not have been the case in India and early Tibet. There is some evidence that practitioners would memorize the basic structure of the process, then reflect on the meaning of that structure and do the visualizations, while reciting only the mantras. This approach also supports the approach articulated in the Four Reliances (see Chapter 3).

Each of the significant deities in the tradition has a *mantra* that is recited during the practice. The *mani* is a simple and beautiful example: *Om mani padma hum* (mani is jewel, padma[85] is lotus), the mantra of compassion, and is associated with Avalokiteshvara, the Buddha of Compassion. There are multiple levels of symbolic meaning in this simple mantra. At one level, a mantra is symbolic of the name of the deity, though not a literal translation. In this example, some say the jewel is the innate buddhanature within each of us, and the lotus is a beautiful flower that grows out of the mud (symbolizing our obscurations) below the water. In addition, the six syllables symbolically purify the six negative emotions: anger, greed, ignorance, desire, jealously, and pride. They also symbolically represent the Six Perfections of the enlightened mind: generosity, virtue, patience, persistence, meditation, and wisdom.

Om consists of three letters, A, U, and M, that symbolize both our impure body, speech, and mind and the Buddha's pure body, speech, and mind. From another perspective, *mani* (jewel) symbolizes the altruistic intent to become enlightened, as well as lovingkindness and compassion, the male principle, while *padma* (lotus) symbolizes wisdom,

---

[84] *Sadhana* means a means of accomplishing something. It is also related to *siddhi* which means accomplishment.

[85] Tibetans say *peme*, pronounced "pay-may"

the realization of suchness or emptiness, the female principle. And finally, *hum* refers to the indivisibility or nondual nature of compassion and wisdom. Thus, through the union of compassion and wisdom one can transform our impure body, speech, and mind into the pure body, speech, and mind of a buddha.

You can find various translations of the 100-Syllable Mantra of Vajrasattva on the Internet. Here is the one I first learned. (Notice that the breaks do not match the way it is actually recited in the text.)

Om – The most excellent exclamation of praise

Benza Sato Samaya – Vajrasattva's commitment

Manu Palaya / Benza Sato – Oh, Vajrasattva, protect the commitment.

Tenopa Tishta Drido Me Bhawa – May you remain firm in me.

Suto Khayo Me Bhawa – Grant me complete satisfaction.

Supo Khayo Me Bhawa – Increase the positive within me.

Anu Rakto Me Bhawa – Be loving toward me.

Sarwa Siddhi Me Pra Yatsa – Grant me all the siddhis (powers).

Sarwa Karma Sutsa Me – Show me all the activities.

Sit-Tam Shriya Kuru – Make my mind good, virtuous and auspicious.

Hung – The heart essence seed syllable of Vajrasattva

Ha Ha Ha Ha – The four immeasurables, the four empowerments, the four joys, the four kayas

Ho – The exclamation of joy at this accomplishment

Bhagavan Sarwa Tathagata – Oh, all the blessed tathagatas (buddhas)

Benza Mame Muntsa – May I be fully liberated in the Vajra (transcendent wisdom).

Benzi Bhawa – Grant me the realization of the Vajra nature.

Maha Samaya Sato Ah – Oh great Vajrasattva!

For lay practitioners, lamas sometimes permit doing a shortened version of the 100-Syllable Mantra– Om Benza Sato Ah (Om Vajrasattva

Ah).[86] In general the short mantra is recited for 600,000 repetitions instead of the 100,000 for the full 100-Syllable Mantra. As before, I recommend that lay practitioners do as many repetitions as you can during two daily sessions for one week, or one daily session for three weeks.

A *mala* or rosary, a string of usually 108 prayer beads, is used with additional counters to keep track of the number of repetitions. It is held in the left hand over the fingers. The thumb is used to pull one bead over the top of the index finger with each repetition, starting at the large "guru bead." Upon reaching the other side of the guru bead, use another counter (I use a mechanical counter like those used at sporting events to count attendance to count the number of malas). You then change directions from the guru bead and continue counting with the mala. (One never goes "over" the guru bead as a symbolic gesture of respect for the guru.)

In conjunction with Vajrasattva practice, one also includes "the four powers." They are:

1. The Power of Remorse or Regret – We regret and feel remorse for our past misdeeds.

2. The Power of Antidote – We practice as the antidote to misdeeds.

3. The Power of Resolve – We resolve never to commit misdeeds again.

4. The Power of Reliance or Support – We rely on the Buddha, dharma, and sangha for support.

After the visualization and mantra recitation, we rest in the natural state (meditate). The *natural state* is that of abiding in transcendent wisdom. In the beginning, we "imagine" being in this state. We do that by resting naturally without thoughts as we did in our previous shamata meditation, but without an object of focus. If thoughts arise, we just let them go and remain in a state of pure awareness. With practice, this transcends "imagination," and we are able to abide for long periods without effort. This is described in some detail in the chapter on Wisdom.

One final but important point. There are many texts that sound as if karma is permanent and that you will suffer consequences of your actions no matter what. This rather fatalistic and deterministic approach

---

[86] Some versions use Om Benza Sato Hung (Om Vajrasattva Hung).

ignores this, and other, purification processes. Karma is *impermanent.* And accordingly, it can be purified. *Knowing* this is critical to successful practice! As you do this practice, really know that it is purifying *all* negative karma.

Week 18 — Vajrasattva Purification

Practice twice daily for one week, or once daily for three weeks.

Intention: I do this practice for the benefit of all sentient beings (*or other personal intention*).

Refuge

In the Buddha, the Dharma and the Sangha most excellent,
I take refuge until enlightenment is reached.
By the merit of generosity and other good deeds,
May I attain Buddhahood for the sake of all sentient beings. (3X)

Visualization

Above the crown of my head, I visualize a white lotus with a moon-disk seat. On this is the syllable HUNG, which transforms into a vajra with a HUNG in its center. The HUNG then transforms into Vajrasattva and Vajratopa in union, the essence of our own kind Root Lama. They sit gracefully on the moon disk on the white lotus. Vajrasattva is brilliant, luminous-white in color, youthful with long black hair gathered on top of his head, the rest curling down his back and around his shoulders. In his right hand he holds a golden vajra at his heart center, symbolic of great compassion. In his left he holds an upturned bell resting on his hip, symbolic of the wisdom of emptiness. He wears the sambhogakaya adornments — the five silken garments and the eight jeweled ornaments.

At Vajrasattva's heart is a vajra on a moon-disk. At the center of the vajra is a HUNG syllable surrounded by the 100-Syllable Mantra. Light radiates out in all directions from the rotating mantra to all the Buddhas. They are pleased and send their blessings in the form of light that is absorbed into the mantra at Vajrasattva's heart-center, increasing its brilliance. Light fills his body completely, enhancing the magnificence of his appearance.

I and all sentient beings, deluded by our ignorance, regret our negative actions. Oh! Lama, Vajrasattva, Holder of the Vajra, please purify us.

Nectar produced form the mantra-syllables flows from the place of union of Vajrasattva and Vajratopa. It enters the crown of my head purifying my *body* of all obscurations and negative karma. As it flows down to my throat, all obscurations and negative karma of *speech* are fully purified. And as it continues to my heart center, all obscurations and negative karma of my *mind* are purified. These obscurations are expelled in the form of a smoky dark liquid through the pores of my skin and lower openings of my body as I am filled with nectar and completely purified. (*Recite the mantra as many times as you can while continuing the visualization.*[87])

Om Benza Sato Samaya

Manu Palaya

Benza Sato Tenopa

Tishta Drido Me Bhawa

Suto Khayo Me Bhawa

Supo Khayo Me Bhawa

Anu Rakto Me Bhawa

Sarwa Siddhi Me Pra Yatsha

Sarwa Karma Sutsa Me

Sit-Tam Shriya Kuru Hung

Ha Ha Ha Ha Ho

Bhagavan

Sarwa Tathagata

Benza Mame Muntsa

Benzi Bhawa

Maha Samaya Sato

---

[87] It can be very helpful to listen to a recording of the mantra for pronunciation and memorization. Some versions are sung, which further facilitates memorization. For example, go to www.AwamInstitute.org, under Dharma Media.

Ah

(As you recite this, all negatives flow out through your pores and lower openings.)

I resolve never to perform these negative actions again.

Vajrasattva is pleased with my prayers and replies, "Your delusions are now cleared away and you are purified."

With delight, Vajrasattva and Vajratopa then dissolve into me through the top of my head. I then become Vajrasattva and Vajratopa. Boundless light radiates out filling the entire universe, transforming all phenomena into the perfect Buddhafield of Pure Joy. All sentient beings are transformed into Vajrasattva and Vajratopa, sounds are the resonance of the mantra, and all thoughts are the spontaneous display of wisdom.

Vajrasattva and Vajratopa dissolve into me, then I dissolve into the mantra, which dissolves in the HUNG at my heart, which dissolves from the bottom up into emptiness. Abide in the natural state of pure awareness. [*Meditate without thoughts as long as you can.*]

Arise again as Vajrasattva and Vajratopa. Through the virtue of this practice, may I attain the enlightened state of Vajrasattva for the benefit of all sentient beings.

Dedication: Recite, "By the merit of this practice may I attain enlightenment for the benefit of all sentient beings." (3X)

Post-meditation: *Arise gently, "leading your life in a meditative fashion" as before.*

Reciting the mantra 108 times consecutively without distraction is said to purify *all* past negative karma; reciting 21 times (or 28 of the short mantra) will purify all negative actions of the past day.

Short Vajrasattva Practice: If you are unable to complete the practice above, you may do this very concise version. Recite the short mantra as many times as you can while visualizing Vajrasattva and nectar purifying your body, speech and mind. Then say the following prayer followed by the dedication:

May all the breeches and transgressions of samaya,

Both my own and those of all beings, be purified.

From now until we reach the very heart of bodhi,

May our samaya be thoroughly and utterly pure.

Mandala Offerings

Having purified our body, speech, and mind, we now make offerings of all that is of value to the buddhas of the past, present and future. They do not need these offerings, of course, but the practice of generosity builds our merit for doing the advanced practices. It also helps in cutting through our own attachments to "things."

In general there are three levels of offerings. The nirmanakaya or outer offering may include an offering plate with stones, rice or other materials, while reciting a mantra with a focused mind. The sambhogakaya or inner offering involves visualizing multiplying our body to offer it to each of the buddhas and bodhisattvas. The dharmakaya or secret offering involves meditation on our innate buddhanature as an offering.

There are three principle symbolic representations for making these offerings. The most elaborate is a 37-point mandala offering. The middling version is a 7-point mandala offering. The simplest is a hand gesture (*mudra*[88]) mandala offering. A mandala can also be a symbolic circular figure representing the universe. In addition, the body itself can be seen as a mandala, as can any beautiful object. Everything can be imagined as a buddhafield. Even meditation and mind can be seen as a mandala.

For this practice I will focus on the hand mudra symbolism. To do this, hold your hands in front with the palms up and fingers spread apart. Then interlock the fingers starting with the small fingers. Now use the thumbs to take hold of the tip of the little finger of the opposite hand, which should be close by, forming two circles above the palm of each hand. Then curl the index finger of each hand under the tip of the middle finger of the opposite hand, pulling them slightly back toward your body. Finally, place the two ring fingers back-to-back and sticking straight up in the center.

---

[88] *Mudra* means "seal." It most often refers to a symbolic or ritual gesture.

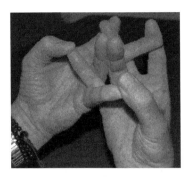

The two straight fingers in the center represent Mt. Meru, the center of the universe. The four connecting finger-tips represent the four continents that surround Mt. Meru. In some descriptions, the circles formed by the thumbs and small fingers represent the sun and the moon. These are the same as in the 7-point mandala offering.

To make the actual offering, we recite the prayer and the offering mantra, which is counted for repetitions. However, here I recommend that you do as many repetitions as you can during two daily sessions for one week, or one daily session for three weeks.

Week 19 — Mandala Offering

Practice twice daily for one week, or once daily for three weeks.

Intention: I do this practice for the benefit of all sentient beings (*or other personal intention*).

Refuge: I take refuge in the Buddha, the Dharma and the Sangha most excellent in order to enable all sentient beings to attain enlightenment. (3X)

Mandala Offering – *Reappear as Vajrasattva (from last practice) and make the offerings with the hand mudra described in the text*:

Om Ah Hung

By offering this fine and pleasing mandala,

May obstacles not arise on the path to enlightenment,

May the intention of the sugatas of the three times be realized,

And without being confused in the cycle of existence or dwelling in quietism,

May beings throughout space be liberated!

Om Ah Hung Maha Guru Dewa Dakini Ratna Mandala Puja Megha Samudra Saparana Samaya Ah Hung

[*Repeat as many times as you can.*]

Dedication: By the merit of this practice may I attain enlightenment for the benefit of all sentient beings. (3X)

Post-meditation: *Make mental offerings of any special or valuable object you observe during your daily activities.*

Guru Yoga

Guru Yoga may be the most important of all tantric practices. It is the last stage of the uncommon ngondro practices. For some, it is all that is needed. Guru Yoga is about connection – connection with the lineage, with the lama, with our innate buddhanature. Through it, we express our faith and devotion for what we have done, and all that is to come in terms of our practice. Shabkar wrote:

No matter in what direction I go, I think of the master;

No matter in what solitary place I stay, I think of the master;

No matter what signs I see, I think of the master;

Always, at all times, I think of my authentic master.

H.H. Dilgo Khyentse Rinpoche gave one of the most concise and meaningful descriptions of Guru Yoga in his book by that title. Guru Yoga means union with the transcendent wisdom of our guru – our buddhanature. Even further, it refers to realizing buddhanature to be our own inner teacher. In the preface to *Guru Yoga*, Dzongsar Jamyang Khyentse Rinpoche wrote, "Guru Yoga is the quickest, most effective method for attaining enlightenment …." In this practice and beyond, we learn to see our guru as the Buddha. As noted previously, if you do not have a personal spiritual guide, a guru or lama (teacher), you may use the universal guru, Padmasambhava. In the process of this practice, we realize our mind is none other than the mind of the guru. We merge our mind with that of the guru.

There are three main parts to the practice: (1) visualization, (2) prayers, and (3) the four empowerments. Many also include a lineage prayer in which the entire lineage back to the Buddha is recited. This version does not include such a prayer. The visualization is often the same refuge tree as used previously. Alternately, you may visualize Padmasambhava alone or with his consort, Yeshe Tsogyal. We then invite Guru Rinpoche (Padmasambhava) by reciting the Seven-Line Prayer three times with intense *devotion*, feeling a sense of connection with your lama as Guru Rinpoche and with the lineage going back to the Buddha, even in this case without reciting a lineage prayer. We show our devotion and respect for those who came before us. Dilgo Khyentse Rinpoche wrote:

> Consider that, outwardly, the guru is the union of the Three Jewels: his body is the Sangha, his speech the Dharma, and his mind is the Buddha. Inwardly, he embodies the three roots: his body is the lama, his speech the yidam (deity), and his mind the dakini. Secretly, the guru is the union of the three kayas: his body is the nirmanakaya, his speech the sambhogakaya, and his mind the dharmakaya. The guru is also the union of all deities, for there is not a single deity who is not the display of the Lotus-Born Guru. In the unsurpassable buddhafield of Akanista, he is the Primordial Buddha Samantabhadra. He is also Vajradhara, or Dorje Chang. In the sambhogakaya buddhafields, he is Vajrasattva and the buddhas of the five families. In the nirmanakaya buddhafields, he is the Buddha Shakyamuni and the Lotus-Born Guru, Padmasambhava. In brief, there is no manifestation of the Buddha that is not inseparably one with Guru Rinpoche, and so to pray to him is the same as praying to all the buddhas.

The next part of the practice is to recite the mantra: **Om Ah Hum Vajra Guru Padma Siddhi Hum** (pronounced Om Ah Hung Benza Guru Peme Siddhi Hung by Tibetans). *Om Ah Hum* represents the three kayas, as well as the pure forms of body, speech and mind of the buddhas. *Vajra* (Benza) or *dorje* in Tibetan means "indestructible" and refers to a diamond and its ability to cut through all other substances. This represents unchanging transcendent wisdom. *Guru* is teacher, but also means heavy or weighty. Thus, the guru is considered to be most weighty or precious, like gold. *Padma* (Peme) means lotus and represents wisdom. *Guru Padma* refers to the Lotus-Born Guru. *Siddhi* means accomplishment. Ordinary siddhis include wealth, well-being, and so forth. The supreme accomplishment is enlightenment. *Hum* is a request for the guru to come and bless us with all the siddhis, ordinary and supreme.

After reciting the mantra, we receive four empowerments[89] and blessings from the guru. The first is called the "vase empowerment." It purifies our body, plants the seed of nirmanakaya, empowers us to do the generation-stage practices[90], and establishes the union of appearances and emptiness.[91] White light from an OM at the forehead of Padmasambhava enters our own forehead (crown chakra) and fills our entire body, granting the vase empowerment.

The second empowerment is called the "secret empowerment." It purifies our speech, plants the seed of sambhogakaya, empowers us to do the completion-stage practices[92], and establishes the union of luminosity and emptiness. Red light from an AH at the throat of Padmasambhava enters our throat chakra and fills our entire body, granting the secret empowerment.

The third empowerment is called the "wisdom empowerment." It purifies our mind, plants the seed of dharmakaya, empowers us to do the karmamudra[93] practices, and establishes the union of bliss (a transcendent lightness of being) and emptiness. Blue light from a HUNG at the heart of Padmasambhava enters our heart chakra and fills our entire body, granting the wisdom empowerment.

The fourth empowerment is the "word empowerment." It purifies subtle obscurations, plants the seed of svabhavikakaya, empowers us to do the Great Perfection practices[94], and establishes the

---

[89] The exact practices being empowered vary from one lineage to another. Another list includes empowerment of (1) generation-stage practices, (2) mantra recitation, (3) completion-stage practices, and (4) Dzogchen practices.

[90] Here generation-stage practices are deity yoga practices involving visualization, mantra recitation and dissolution into emptiness. These are detailed later in the text.

[91] The four unions with emptiness listed here are explained in the chapters of the text on wisdom.

[92] Here completion-stage practices include those similar to the Six Yogas of Naropa: inner heat (tummo), illusory body, clear light, dream yoga, transference of consciousness (phowa), and the intermediate states between death and rebirth (bardos). These are detailed later in the text.

[93] There are four "mudras"—samayamudra (vows), jnanamudra (visualized consort), karmamudra (physical consort), mahamudra (transcendent wisdom).

[94] Dzogchen (great perfection) is the highest and non-conceptual practices of Tantric Buddhism. They are detailed later in the text.

union of awareness and emptiness. Red light from a HRI at the navel of Padmasambhava enters our navel chakra and fills our entire body, granting the word empowerment.

This is followed by meditation on emptiness, abiding in pure awareness of the natural state. Afterward, continue to maintain a feeling of devotion. Practice remembering the presence of the guru above your head at all times. At night, Dilgo Khyentse Rinpoche recommends visualizing a small Guru Rinpoche (the size of the first joint of your thumb) sitting on a four-petalled red lotus in your heart chakra, radiating light that fills your body, the environment, the entire universe, then returns into your heart. Guru Rinpoche dissolves into light and you fall asleep while abiding in the luminosity. Repeat as needed. In the morning you imagine Guru Rinpoche arising from your heart to above your head.

For this practice, I recommend that you do as many repetitions of the mantra as you can during two daily sessions for one week, or one daily session for three weeks.

Week 20 — Guru Yoga

Practice twice daily for one week, or once daily for three weeks.

Intention: I do this practice for the benefit of all sentient beings (*or other personal intention*).

Refuge: I take refuge in the Buddha, the Dharma and the Sangha most excellent in order to enable all sentient beings to attain enlightenment. (3X)

Seven-Line Prayer:

Om Ah Hung

In the northwest of the land of Orgyen,

In the heart of a lotus flower,

Endowed with the most marvelous attainments,

You are renowned as the lotus-born,

Surrounded by many hosts of dakinis,

Following in your footsteps,

I pray to you: Come and bless me with your grace!

Guru Peme Siddhi Hung

Generate a deep sense of devotion for your own root guru as Padmasambhava[95], the lineage, and all those who came before us back to the Buddha.

Mantra:

Om Ah Hung Benza Guru Peme Siddhi Hung

(Recite as many times as you can.)

The four empowerments:

Light radiates from the Guru's four places into your four places purifying your body, speech, mind and all subtle obscurations, granting the four empowerments and planting the four seeds. The Guru dissolves into light and merges inseparably into you, then you dissolve into emptiness, and meditate in the natural state of pure awareness for as long as you can.

Dedication: By the merit of this practice may I attain enlightenment for the benefit of all sentient beings. (3X)

Post-meditation: *Visualize your guru as Padmasambhava above your head during the day and as a small figure seated on a red lotus in your heart when you sleep.*

Daily Preliminary Practices

Padmasambhava said to do the preliminary practices at least "until the experience of them arises." Then after "completing" the recommended practices (one never *completes* the preliminary practices) it is acceptable to continue by doing a short preliminary practice daily prior to your other meditation practices and you continue on the path to enlightenment. Below is a very concise daily practice adapted from one by H.H. Dudjom Rinpoche. It is to be done at the beginning of your practice each day:

Homage to Samantabhadra and Samantabhadri! Because I suffer due to my own actions and I now have this precious human life without knowing when I will die, I will now engage in virtuous actions for the benefit of all sentient beings with great joy and devotion!

Therefore...

---

[95] If you do not have a root guru, you may focus on Padmasambhava. It is helpful to use a picture or statue to help with the visualization.

Visualize the refuge tree with prostrations: I take refuge in the Buddha, the Dharma and Sangha most excellent, in order to enable all sentient beings to attain enlightenment. (3X)

Vajrasattva and Vajratopa appear above me purifying me and all beings and phenomena with nectar from the place of their union while reciting:

Om Benza Sato Hung (28 or 108X)

Reappear as Vajrasattva with Vajratopa, visualize everything is now a perfect buddhafield, and offer it while reciting:

Om Guru Dewa Dakini Ratna Mandala Pratitsa Soha! (1X)

Visualize the refuge tree and recite:

Om Ah Hung Benza Guru Peme Siddhi Hung (*as many times as you can*)

Light radiates from the Guru's four places into my four places purifying my body, speech, mind and all subtle obscurations, granting the four empowerments and planting the four seeds. The Guru dissolves into light and merges inseparably into myself. Dissolve the visualization and rest in the natural state of pure awareness as long as you can.

By the merit of this practice may I attain enlightenment for the benefit of all sentient beings. (3X)

Complete your regular daily meditation practice. Afterwards reappear as your yidam[96] and remain in that state throughout the day and night with Pure View always and all ways!

Signs of Accomplishment

Ngondro (and more)[97]

If you can devote your body unstintingly to the practice,
That is a sign of taking to heart the preciousness of the freedoms and
    advantages.

---

[96] The deity of your regular practice

[97] By Nyala Pema Duddul, www.LotsawaHouse.org, © Wu Tai Shan Clan 2004

If you can view gold and dirt with equanimity and see them as equal,
That is a sign of having realized the illusory nature of transient
    things.

If you can regard the phenomena of samsara as your enemies,
That is a sign of crossing over the ocean of suffering.

If you can pay meticulous attention to your actions and their effects,
    adopting virtue and abandoning non-virtue,
That is a sign of finding the swift path that ascends the staircase to
    liberation.

If you can purify the negativity, defilements and habitual tendencies
    of your body, speech and mind,
That is a sign of closing the door to rebirth in samsara's lower realms.

If you can keep the Three Jewels in your mind, so that they are never
    separate from it,
That is a sign of being hooked by the compassion of the supreme
    refuge.

If you know how to integrate emptiness and compassion in your
    mindstream,
That is a sign of bringing phenomena into the essence of awakening.

If you can meditate on how all beings have been your parents,
That is a sign of the arising of the sun and moon of the great vehicle.

If you can dispel the obscurations of the darkness of ignorance,
That is a sign of the dawning of clear light within immaculate space.

If you can carry the two accumulations onto the path continuously,
That is a sign of the maturing of the fruition of kayas and wisdoms.

If you can see all that appears and exists arising in total purity as the
    lama,
That is a sign of reaching the pinnacle of Dzogchen yoga.

If you can recognize the vajra kaya of all-penetrating pure awareness,
That is a sign of transference into the timeless space of primordial
    purity.

If you can recognize the unity of the three kayas in pure awareness,
That is a sign of the ripening of the fruition, which is Samantabhadra.

Chapter 13

The Second Training on the Path of Tantra: Meditation—the "Outer" Deity Yogas

Tantra practices fall into two main categories, outer and inner yogas. In general the outer tantras involve visualization of the deity outside of us. They tend to be individual peaceful deities dressed in royal garb and seated on a "moon disc." The inner tantras involve visualization of ourselves as the deity. These tend to involve a wrathful deity in sexual union with a consort, naked or wearing bone ornaments and/or animal skins, and standing or sitting on a "sun and moon disc." In some cases these are single wrathful females, often holding a staff (*khatvanga*) that symbolizes her consort.

The outer deity yogas are sometimes described as having three categories: performance (*kria*), action (*upa*), and yoga tantras. Performance tantra focuses on purification of *karma* (in body, speech and mind); *absolute* and *relative truths*, but separate; and *deity* visualization (*deity* as lord, oneself as servant). Action tantra is essentially the same, but the *deity* is understood as friend or helper. Yoga tantra focuses on *absolute truth* as nonconceptual, empty, luminous; *relative truth* as *mandala* of *deities*; visualization of self as *deity*; and actualization of divine body, speech, mind and actions.

Common examples of outer deity yogas include Shakyamuni Buddha, Vajrasattva, Green and White Tara, Avalokiteshvara (Chenrezig), Medicine Buddha, Amitabha, Manjushri and so forth. Some deity practices do not easily fit into various "categories" because the categories were developed after the deity practices. For example, some semi-wrathful deity practices have elements of both inner and outer categories. In the practices included in this chapter, for example, we will visualize ourselves as the actual deity, either in the end or throughout the practice. This is a step on the way to becoming a buddha, one of the reasons the Path of Tantra is considered to be more effective than the more abstract practices in the Paths of Individual Liberation and Altruism.

Padmasambhava only touches on deity yoga as such. The previous Vajrasattva practice was one example of deity yoga. Padmasambhava then goes on to include one additional reference with little explanation. You are given the option of choosing *one* practice. I have adapted three additional short practices from which you may choose one, or continue with one after the other over a longer period of time.

Keep in mind that these are a form of shamata – single-pointed calm abiding – with a more complex level of visualization that is intended to expedite the process of enlightenment. It also incorporates visualizing yourself as the deity, a very powerful psychological practice used by world-class athletes, dancers, and many others to enhance performance.

First, following Padmasambhava, we are going to use a stepwise development of our shamata practice, leading into our deity practice. Deities are imagined figures (buddhas) that help us develop our single-pointed calm abiding (generation stage practice) and wisdom (completion stage practice) by seeing ourselves as the deity. (But please don't go around claiming *I am* this or that deity. Anyone who would do that is not.) First, we will practice with a focus on an imaginary object. Then we will move to visualizing ourselves as a hollow body with an imaginary object at hour heart. Then we will advance to the actual deity visualization.

Shamata with Eyebrow Bindu

In this practice we change our focus to a small orb of white light the size of a pea called a *bindu* or *tigle*. It is imagined as being between our eyebrows. Here you have moved from a physical object in the last shamata practice to an imagined one. As before, if thoughts or other distractions arise, let them go and re-focus on the white light. Do several short meditations in each session.

Week 21 — Shamata with Eyebrow Bindu

Practice twice daily for one week, or once daily for three weeks.

Intention: I do this practice for the benefit of all sentient beings (*or other personal intention*).

Preliminaries: Recite the brief Ngondro preliminary practice, with prostrations.

Shamata with Signs (eyebrow bindu): Take a few deep breaths then begin with stillness of body, speech and mind. Then visualize a small white light between your eyebrows as long as you can. Finally, gently release the visualization and settle into the natural state without thoughts.

Dedication: By the merit of this practice may I attain enlightenment for the benefit of all sentient beings. (3X)

Post-meditation: *Arise gently, "leading your life in a meditative fashion" as before.*

Shamata with Hollow Body

Having moved from a physical object to an imagined object, the next step is a more complex visualization. Here we imagine that our body is hollow, like a transparent balloon. Inside at our heart is a small *blue* light[98], the size of a pea. It is clear and hot. The light radiates out, filling our body with blue light. This helps prepare us for the tantric deity yogas in which we imagine being a transparent buddha.

If thoughts or other distractions come during your practice, let them go and return your focus to the blue light. Do several short, quality meditations in each session.

Week 22 — Shamata with Hollow Body

Practice twice daily for one week, or once daily for three weeks.

Intention: I do this practice for the benefit of all sentient beings (*or other personal intention*).

Preliminaries: Recite the brief Ngondro preliminary practice, with prostrations.

---

[98] Some versions use a red light.

Shamata with Signs (hollow body): Begin with stillness of body, speech and mind. Then visualize your body as completely hollow. At your heart center, visualize a clear, hot, blue light without distractions for as long as you can. Then gently release the visualization and settle into the natural state without thoughts.

Dedication: By the merit of this practice may I attain enlightenment for the benefit of all sentient beings. (3X)

Post-meditation: *Bring to a close arising gently, "leading your life in a meditative fashion" as before. Cultivating "enthusiasm and delight" will help single-pointed calm abiding arise in the mind-stream.*

The last instruction points to an important point in the practice of meditation that I have noted previously. Meditation should be "fun," not in the sense of ordinary play but more in the sense of happiness. Remember, you are after *innate happiness*. It is easy to become too "serious" about this. Taking it seriously is one thing; being serious is another altogether.

Shamata with Deity

Next you move to the more complex practice of visualizing a simple deity. In *When the Chocolate Runs Out*, Lama Yeshe gives the following advice for visualizing:

Using visualizations can be a powerful form of meditation – but don't imagine visualizations are something new and foreign that you have no experience with. In reality, you visualize all day long. The breakfast you eat in the morning is a visualization; in an important way it is a kind of projection of your own mind. You are visualizing that your breakfast has some kind of independent existence. Similarly, whenever you go shopping and think, "This is nice," or "I don't like that," whatever you're looking at is a projection of your own mind. When you get up in the morning and see the sun shining and think, "Oh, it's going to be a nice today," that's your own mind visualizing. Visualization is not something supernatural; it's scientific. So the challenge is to harness that already well-developed skill and make it into something wholesome and useful.

Previously in the preliminary practices, we focused on purification with Vajrasattva. Here we return to the previous practice of

Vajrasattva (Week 18), but the focus is now on a detailed *image* of Vajrasattva, building further on the complexity of the last practice. Recite the practice quietly, but out loud.

It is very helpful here to find an image of Vajrasattva on the Internet or purchase a card or thanka painting with his image. It is important at this level to see all of the details. Begin by memorizing his face, then the adornments on his head. Move slowly down until you can easily "see" all of the details in your mind (without looking at the picture).

One of the most common ways to do this is to look at an image for some time, focused on one feature, then close your eyes and recall it in as much detail as you can. Finally, open your eyes and verify how accurate you were. Repeat this over and over until you can sustain the image for the duration of your session.

These visualizations include images of one or more Tibetan syllables.[99] You may either look them up on the Internet and memorize them or simply use the English transliterations as listed in the text. During the meditation, if thoughts or other distractions arise, let them go[100] and return your focus to Vajrasattva. Do several short, quality meditations.

Week 23 — Shamata with Vajrasattva (See Week 18)

Practice twice daily for one week, or once daily for three weeks.

Padmasambhava lists alternatives to Vajrasattva as options for this practice. It may be helpful to try different alternatives to find the one that you best identify with for this visualization practice. I have included three alternatives: Shakyamuni Buddha, Avalokiteshvara (Chenrezig), and Green Tara (so that we have at least one female alternative).

---

[99] The Tibetan alphabet consists of characters representing syllables rather than letters. The root syllable may be modified by adding additional markings above, below, in front, or behind the root syllable to modify the sound. The syllables are separated with a *tsha* that resembles an apostrophe.

[100] A special note at this point: I have found that it can be helpful to think of relaxing your *brain* when distractions arise.

Week 23 — Shamata with Shakyamuni Buddha (alternative 1)

Practice twice daily for one week, or once daily for three weeks.

Intention: I do this practice for the benefit of all sentient beings (*or other personal intention*).

Preliminaries: Recite the brief Ngondro preliminary practice, with prostrations.

Visualization: Begin with stillness of body, speech and mind. From emptiness and compassion, a syllable HUNG appears and radiates and absorbs golden light. I appear as Shakyamuni Buddha, sitting in vajra posture and touching the ground with my right fingers and radiate five-colored light in all directions.

With the three syllables [*Om Ah Hung*] in the three places [*forehead, throat, heart*], light emanates from the seed syllable HUNG at my heart, inviting the wisdom beings in the form of Shakyamuni Buddha which dissolve inseparably into myself. I am empowered by the deity.

I offer a cloud of offerings to the deities. In the expanse of pure awareness, I praise the display of all appearances of the mind of the deity – myself. Around the HUNG on moon-disk at my heart, the mantra circles clockwise, radiating offerings to the buddhas and absorbing blessings that purify the two obscurations of all beings – afflictive emotions and mental obscurations. Appearance and existence become the spontaneous radiant display of the three vajras.

Mantra: **Om Muni Muni Maha Muni Ye Soha** (*Repeat 108X or as much as you can.*)

Meditation: *Dissolve the visualization of Shakyamuni Buddha and the mantra at the heart into emptiness. Rest in the natural state for as long as you can.*

Closing Prayers: **Hri**   I offer an ocean of offering clouds, actual and imagined. I praise the deities of the all-expansive purity of samsara and nirvana. Forgive me for any faults, errors or wrongs I have done. Accept my apology and bestow the siddhi of purity.

Dedication: By the merit of this practice may I attain enlightenment for the benefit of all sentient beings. (3X)

Post-meditation: *Following the practice, continue as Shakyamuni Buddha in your daily activities.*

Week 23 — Chenrezig (alternative 2)

Practice twice daily for one week, or once daily for three weeks.

Intention: I do this practice for the benefit of all sentient beings (*or other personal intention*).

Preliminaries: Recite the brief Ngondro preliminary practice, with prostrations.

Visualization: Begin with stillness of body, speech and mind. From emptiness sitting on a lotus and a moon disk, I am Chenrezig, white in color with four arms. My upper two arms are joined at the heart holding the wish-fulfilling gem. My lower right hand holds a crystal mala, the lower left hand holds the stem of a white lotus flower. I wear sacred silken robes, the precious five-pointed crown and other ornaments.

In my heart is a moon-disc with a white HRI standing in the center surrounded by the mantra OM MANI PADME HUNG facing outward and circling clockwise. Light radiates from the mantra and I offer it to all the Buddhas and Bodhisattvas in the Buddhafield. They send blessings of wisdom and compassion in the form of light that fill me and purify all obscurations of my body, speech and mind. Fully purified, I become the embodiment of the wisdom and compassion of all the Buddhas.

Again, light radiates from my heart mantra, pervading the entire universe and transforming it into a pureland. As the light touches all sentient beings of the six realms, all of their suffering and ignorance is dispelled and they are transformed into Chenrezig.

Mantra: **Om Mani Padme Hung** (*108X or as many times as you can*)

Meditation: All the outer and inner phenomena dissolve into light and are absorbed into me. I dissolve into the HRI, which dissolves into the all-pervading emptiness. (*Rest in the natural state for as long as you like.*)

Closing: Again I appear as Chenrezig, the embodiment of the wisdom and compassion of all the Buddhas.

Dedication: By the merit of this practice may all sentient beings attain enlightenment. (3X)

Post-meditation: *Following the practice, continue as Chenrezig in your daily activities.*

Week 23 — Green Tara (alternative 3)

Practice twice daily for one week, or once daily for three weeks.

Intention: I do this practice for the benefit of all sentient beings (*or other personal intention*).

Preliminaries: Recite the brief Ngondro preliminary practice, with prostrations.

Visualization: Begin with stillness of body, speech and mind. From the emptiness appears the syllable PAM, which transforms into a lotus seat. On the top of this appears the syllable AH, which transforms into a moon seat on which my mind appears in the form of the green syllable TAM. From this green syllable TAM, rays of light radiate as offerings to all the Aryas for the benefit of all sentient beings. The light then reabsorbs into myself and I become Tara.

My body is green and I have one face and two hands. My right hand rests on my right knee in the giving mudra. My left hand is at my heart holding the stem of a blue Upala Flower[101], which blossoms at my left ear. I am peaceful and smiling. I am adorned by precious ornaments and garments. My right foot is slightly extended and my left leg is tucked in. My back rests against a moon disk. On my forehead is a white OM. At my throat is a red AH. At my heart is a blue HUNG.

From the HUNG light rays radiate and invoke all the Tatagatas[102] of the ten directions in the form of Green Taras. The wisdom beings absorb into me. Again from the seed syllable at my heart, light rays are extended and invoke the Dhyani Buddhas.[103] Please, all Tatagatas, bestow all empowerments on me. Then the Tatagatas pour water from a vessel on top of my head. The water purifies my defilements. Then Amitabha appears on top of my head.

In my heart, on the moon seat, there is a green letter TAM surrounded by the syllables: OM TA RE TU TA RE TU RE SO HA. From these syllables rays of light extend offerings to the Buddhas and Bodhisattvas. The blessings and compassion of all the Buddhas

---

[101] Peony; other versions use a lotus.

[102] Buddhas

[103] Five Buddha Families

and Bodhisattvas manifest in the form of rays of light which absorb into the circle of seed syllables.

Mantra: **Om Tare Tutare Ture Soha** (*108X or as many times as you can as light rays emanate from the TAM and mantra syllables purifying all and performing activities of compassion.*)

Meditation: Then dissolve the visualization and rest in the natural state of pure awareness for as long as you like.

Closing:

Om! Homage to the lady who protects us from the eight fears![104]
Homage to the lady who blazes with the splendor of auspiciousness!
Homage to the lady who closes the door to lower rebirths!
Homage to the lady who leads us on the path to higher realms!
You have always sustained me in your care.
Now, protect me still with your great compassion, I pray!

Dedication: By this merit may I quickly reach the enlightened state of Green Arya Tara, so that I may lead all living beings without exception to the same enlightenment. (3X)

Post-meditation: *Following the practice, continue as Tara in your daily activities.*

Padmasambhava told Yeshe Tsogyal to practice in three or four sessions each day, including 10,000 recitations of the mantra each day and again each night. Or to do at least 1,000 each, or 500 each, or at least 100 each! The latter, one mala each, is easily done by Western lay practitioners. Do more if you can. In the tradition, this is considered an accumulation of merit. Even more importantly, however, it is a way of habituating your mind into the dharma.

As an informal daily practice, many Tibetans regularly recite mantras throughout the day. It is not necessary to use a mala or other counter, unless of course you are trying to accumulate a specific number as part of a *samaya* vow. Use whatever mantra is part of your daily deity practice and visualize the deity as you recite the mantra. Or use the universal mantra OM AH HUNG. OM is the buddha body, AH is the buddha speech, and HUNG is the buddha mind. By reciting this mantra,

---

[104] (1) Water, (2) lions, (3) fire, (4) snakes, (5) elephants, (6) thieves, (7) false imprisonment and (8) ghosts. There are outer, inner and secret meanings for each of these.

you become one with them. You may recite it quietly or, if that is not convenient, in your mind. At the end, or at least once every 24 hours, dedicate the merit for the benefit of others. In this way, you begin to make *everything* part of your practice.

We began *shamata* practice with a focus on a small object, then an imaginary object (bindu), then a bindu inside ourselves as a hollow and transparent body, and now ourselves as a visualized deity. This is a step on the way to becoming an actual buddha. We move from an impure to a pure state of being.

To support this, Padmasambhava gave the following advice to Yeshe Tsogyal:

> Whatever you do – like practicing virtuous activities with body, speech, and mind, making offerings, or performing elaborate rituals – it is most crucial that it be done in a state free from mental reference.

In other words, do the practice without "thinking" about it, but focus on the direct experience itself.

As you learn other and more complex deity practices, return to this approach to learn to visualize the deity, the consort (if any), and the complete mandala with other deities as appropriate.

Now we look at the next level of complexity, the generation stage of Highest Yoga Tantra.

Chapter 14

The Second Training

on the Path of Tantra: Meditation—

the Inner Deity Yogas

Highest Yoga Tantra - Generation Stage

The "inner" tantras focus on more complex visualizations involving "wrathful" deities to better eliminate the more challenging subtle obscurations blocking our path to enlightenment. They are usually in union with consorts and naked or wearing bone ornaments and perhaps animal skins. The visualization often includes an elaborate mandala loaded with symbolic meaning as well. This is the generation stage of Highest Yoga Tantra.

The generation stage is still a form of shamata – single-pointed calm abiding. The level of complexity has increased, taking our skill to a new level. These practices also help prepare us for the completion-stage practices on the path to enlightenment, as well as for the bardos and rebirth, in the event that we do not attain enlightenment in this lifetime or fail to transfer our consciousness to a Buddha pureland at the time of death. The bardos are what the Dzogchen Ponlop Rinpoche humorously refers to as "Plan B." Here we focus on "Plan A," attaining enlightenment in this lifetime.

The basic outline of the generation-stage practices is the visualization, mantra recitation, dissolution, and meditation. As we will soon see, this is an oversimplification. There tend to be three lengths of *sadhana* practice texts for these practices. There is a long text, often including an elaborate *ganachakra* or *tsok* feast that is primarily used on special occasions or during retreat. These may take several hours to complete. There may also be a middle length *sadhana* that is more convenient for shorter sessions during retreat or weekend practice. These often take about an hour to complete and are ideal for group practice.

And often there is a short daily-practice *sadhana* for everyday use. These are particularly helpful for householders with limited time for formal practice, especially during the week.

The main purpose of Highest Yoga Tantra is to actually become a buddha. First you visualize or "pretend" to be the deity/buddha, then you become one. We move from an "impure" to a "pure" state of being. Here we are generating ourselves as the deity in an impure form. In the completion stage, we will engage in practices to then transform our impure body, speech and mind into the pure body, speech and mind of a buddha.

As a buddha, one manifests in multiple forms. The primary division is into the three bodies (*kayas*) of a buddha. The Truth Body (*Dharmakaya*) represents the ultimate nature of mind. It is not a "body" per se, but none other than pure awareness (actual clear light, ultimate bodhicitta). The Enjoyment Body (*sambhogakaya*) is a spirit or energy form. It is said to be transparent like a rainbow and invisible to all but highly realized beings. It may be thought of as something like a daydream or a reflection in a window through which you can see the things on the other side as well. This is the form of the deities visualized in the deity yoga practices of the Path of Tantra. Third is the Form Body (*nirmanakaya*) – the physical form body of a buddha.[105] This is the form taken by Shakyamuni Buddha.

Many sources articulate these "bodies" as separate entities. However, other sources say that a buddha has all three bodies at the same time (called *svabhavikakaya*) and there cannot be one without the others. What appears to be a contradiction can be "explained" rather simply. In Buddhist terminology one would say it is not one nor is it many (three in this case); it just is.

Trying to explain the ultimate is like a two-edged sword. It is helpful and even necessary to provide some explanation to help individuals understand and progress in their practice. However, anything that is said has the potential to be taken as "real," creating yet another obscuration to one's true understanding. As with most attempts to describe or explain the ultimate, it is best left unsaid as any such effort only makes it something that it is not. This becomes much easier to understand and accept with years of experience.

---

[105] There is also another "form body" described in the texts. This is called *rupakaya*, which is a combination of the sambhogakaya and nirmanakaya.

When you visualize the deity, it is very important that you not view them as an independent, existent being as is done in other religions. They are not "gods." They are a manifestation of your mind. More specifically, they are the wisdom that manifests in the form of the deity, mantra, and mandala.

Empowerments

In Highest Yoga Tantra, the process begins with an empowerment (*wang*) or initiation from a qualified lama. These are often provided for outer deity yoga practices as well, but here they are generally *required*. In addition most lamas will only give these empowerments in-person. Empowerments involve a special blessing from the lama, so recorded or online empowerments are generally considered insufficient, although some lamas are beginning to make exceptions.

The Sanskrit word for empowerment is *abhisheka. Abhi* means manifest, and *sheka* means to pour. Following Mipham Rinpoche, "The meaning is that the profound ritual of conferring empowerment washes … the stains of the disciple's body, speech, and mind, and their combination, and establishes … an extraordinary capacity into the disciple's being."

Empowerments must be performed by a qualified lama. Although there are some exceptions, there are four universal empowerments in Highest Yoga Tantra that are embedded within the empowerment of the particular deity. They are the vase, secret, wisdom and word empowerments. We first saw these in the practice of Guru Yoga. These vary somewhat by the specific deity, lineage and so forth, and are usually performed in a symbolic manner. Unfortunately, in the West, too often they are not even explained to the initiates, but given almost entirely in Tibetan without translation into English or other language.

Traditionally, the initiate requested initiations or empowerments to do a specific practice from the lama. Some masters would automatically decline the first request and even the second, to be sure that the initiate was serious. There are stories in the tradition of much more dramatic actions and requirements for initiates before giving their first empowerment into these practices. In the West public teachings often include the empowerments and no separate request is necessary. In addition, outer tantra practices are often permitted without a specific empowerment, although one is always recommended.

An empowerment gives permission for the initiate to do the practice. It also provides a blessing of the lineage and the lama for doing the practice, considered a powerful influence on one's success with the practice. The empowerment includes a highly ritualized ceremony. During the ritual, the initiates view the lama *as* the deity, their words as those of the deity, and their actions as the activities of the deity.

Most empowerments begin with opening prayers and a purification ritual in which each initiate is given a small amount of water from a vase into the palm of their cupped *left* hand. The water is taken into the mouth, but not swallowed, and the remnants on the hand are wiped back across the hair on the crown of your head. Each initiate then follows the others outdoors to expel the water, symbolically cleansing oneself, then you return to your seat. In large settings, you may be instructed (or expected) to simply swallow the water to facilitate the event.

The *vase empowerment* is similar to the purification ritual described above, but the water is poured into your *right* hand and is swallowed. This purifies all defilements of your body and empowers you to do the generation stage practice and plants the seed for attaining the Form Body.

Although the ritual varies, the *secret empowerment* purifies your speech and empowers you to do the completion stage practices and plants the seed for attaining the Enjoyment Body. This is called "secret" because the completion-stage practices are considered to be secret. In some cases it was also kept secret because this involved a secret initiation of the consort by the lama into the sexual yogas of the completion stage practices. The secret initiation is now almost always done in a symbolic way, and usually without even reference to sexual yogas.

The *wisdom empowerment* purifies your mind, empowers the initiate to do the sexual yogas with the consort, and plants the seed for realization of the Truth Body. (What you are being empowered to do in this and the fourth empowerment varies from one tradition to another.) The sexual yogas are most commonly done today through visualization practices with a visualized consort (*jnanamudra*). The practices with an actual consort (*karmamudra*) have nearly died out of the tradition, but do remain in a few branches of the tradition, primarily Nyingma, where they are considered to be particularly relevant for householders. Other traditions tend to reserve these for only the very highest level practitioners, if any at all.

Finally we have the *fourth or word empowerment*. This purifies any remaining subtle obscurations, empowers the initiate to do the "nondual" practices of *mahamudra* or *dzogchen*, and plants the seed for the realization of the Essence Body (*svabhavikakaya*) – a nondual union of the other three kayas. At this point, one transcends the use of either the visualized or real consort and relies entirely upon the nonconceptual *mahamudra* – the ultimate, transcendent wisdom.

There are countless variations to the rituals based on lineage traditions and different practice texts. The empowerment ceremony may include an oral reading (*lung*) of the text and a collective recitation of the mantra. In some cases the lama will also explain the text (*tri*) and how to do the practice. Unfortunately, the degree of explanation varies considerably, and practitioners are sometimes left on their own to figure it out, if an actual practice text (*sadhana*) is even provided.

It is fairly common for an empowerment ceremony to include a *ganachakra* or *tsok* feast. This involves offerings in addition to sharing food and drink and may be simple or very elaborate. A plate of food is offered to the deity, then the presiding lama, other ordained sangha, and then the audience. It is customary to keep one item from those on your plate as another offering (the "remainder") to be collected and set outside for animals, birds and other beings. So be sure not to eat it all!

At the end of the empowerment ceremony it is also customary to take a *khata* (long white scarf) as an offering to the lama. Hold it with your two thumbs over your hands, which are open with palms together. Most lamas will take the *khata* and place it over your neck, touch their forehead to yours and recite a short prayer. At the same time, you may make a personal offering, usually cash, to the lama in a small envelope. Most centers provide envelopes for this purpose. It is either given to an attendant standing near the lama for this purpose, or set on a table, never given directly to the lama. Give what you can ($5 - $20 is common) but remember that the teachings on generosity pointed out that doing the practice is the greatest gift of all.

Empowerments often include an additional *samaya* or vow on the part of the student. If the empowerment is taken as a blessing, it is not necessary to complete this. However, if it is taken as a commitment to do the practice, then there is an expectation that you will do it. This may mean suspending other practices for a period of time in order to complete this new commitment. Or, if you are able, you can add it as a part of your other daily practices. The samaya varies from one lama to another. Some may require extensive periods of practice and numbers of repetitions of the mantras. Others require much less, for example, only 10,000 repetitions. Still others may only require an even smaller number for students who have completed commitments for other specific practices. One of my teachers says that the true samaya is not doing the practice or reciting the mantras, but love and devotion for the lama and your dharma brothers and sisters. If it is not clear, be sure to ask. It is said that if you do *not* fulfill this commitment, it may be harmful both to you *and* to the lama who gave the empowerment. So please take them seriously, or simply take the empowerment as a blessing.

There is also an expectation that when you take an empowerment, you will maintain continuity in the practice, or at least in periodic recitation of the mantras. The ideal is to recite the mantras during four sessions each day. Second best is once a week (four or so times each month). At the least, it should be done once a month. It is recommended to also include offerings from time to time. Short "daily" practice texts make it easier to meet these expectations. It can be helpful to keep a binder of your empowerments, along with images of the deity and mandala, and copies of any practice texts that you have. Keep a record of your commitments (a summary sheet in front of the binder is helpful) and what you have completed, as well as dates for intermittent practices. It can be surprising how fast you can "collect" empowerments over just a few years of practice, even if that is not your intention.

Secret Mantra

Tantric practices are sometimes referred to as "secret mantra." Traditionally, these practices were passed down one-on-one from master to disciple, and they were not spoken of outside of that relationship. More recently, as many of these works have been published, they have been described as being "self-secret," meaning that only those who have had empowerments and teachings are able to actually read them and have sufficient interest to understand them. A few texts are starting to be released as "restricted" texts, which require some evidence or statement of qualification to read the text or do the practice.

The seventh of the Fourteen Root Downfalls is "revealing secrets of the tantra to those not ready to understand." Some sources list four secrets: (1) the profound view of tantra, (2) the deep conduct, (3) the name and form of the deity, and (4) the signs of accomplishment. Please

respect and honor the teachings. This is a sign of your own
accomplishment.

The Generation Stage

There are numerous tantric practices. The new (*sarma*) schools
classify them into three categories: father, mother and non-dual. There is
no uniform agreement on the meaning of these classifications, nor the
attribution of tantras to the classifications themselves. Nevertheless, here
is one version. Father tantras focus on developing an illusory body or
others say blissful awareness. Mother tantras focus on wisdom or
enlightened awareness. Non-dual tantras are more balanced between the
male and female principles. Examples are Guhyasamaja and Yamantaka,
Chakrasamvara and Vajrayogini, and Kalachakra respectively, although
as noted above, not everyone agrees with these classifications.

The content of tantras varies considerably, but there are
significant similarities. For the most part they follow a somewhat similar
pattern. What follows is an outline of the key characteristics you are
likely to find in these texts. For a more detailed explanation, I
recommend *The Generation Stage in Buddhist Tantra* by Gyatrul Rinpoche.

I. General Preliminaries

A. Title

B. Homage to the lama

C. Commitment: why written, commitment to be fulfilled, benefit for
sentient beings

D. Four Thoughts: precious human birth, impermanence, karma,
suffering

E. Refuge

1. Refuge tree – may or may not be described

2. Levels – may include outer, inner, secret and most secret

F. Bodhicitta – prayers for aspiration and action bodhicitta

II. Specific Preliminaries

A. Clearing away *non-conducive circumstances*

1. Expelling negative and demonic forces

a. May include a *torma*[106] offering – as the deity, light radiates from your heart with hooks to summon and draw in demonic forces

b. Make the offerings, they take and are satisfied, then depart

c. From seed syllable in your heart, burning fire, vajra weapons, tiny *herukas*[107] in all directions annihilate any remaining forces

d. Destroys our own ego-grasping

2. Wheel or circle of protection

a. Vajra weapons (above) form a solid foundation of blue vajras (no spaces)

b. Vajra fence encircles the space

c. Vajra canopy (or tent) encloses the space

d. Surrounding mass of blazing fire (display of primordial wisdom)

e. Vajra water with pounding waves

f. Vajra wind — sharp and violent

B. Establishing conducive conditions

1. Descent of blessings melt into you (now in ordinary form), removing all impurities

2. Blessing the offering materials

a. Visualize self as the deity

b. RAM YAM KHAM radiate from your heart — purifying offerings

i. RAM — fire burns away impure characteristics

ii. YAM — wisdom air blows scatters clinging to objects as truly existing

---

106 Decorative offerings, usually in the shape of a rounded cone, mostly made of butter and flour, dyed white or red, with white disks attached. Other substances may be used. Exact shapes and so forth vary by practice, lineage, etc.

107 Tiny versions of the deity

        iii. KHAM — water cleanses all habitual and negative instincts

    c. From pure state make outer offerings

3. BHRUM transforms into vast jeweled vessel

    a. OM — eight outer offerings

        i. Water to drink

        ii. Water for washing

        iii. Flowers

        iv. Incense

        v. Lamp

        vi. Perfumed water

        vii. Food

        viii. Music

    b. AH — inner offerings of body, speech and mind

    c. HUNG — secret offerings as 3 kayas

        i. Medicine (men) — inside a vast skull cup; nature is appearance

            1. Five meats (fleshes) as the five buddhas

            2. Five nectars as the five consorts

            3. Transform into 5 wisdoms and 5 elements

        ii. Torma — nature is emptiness

            1. Vast jeweled vessel — inanimate world

            2. Great and wish-fulfilling, adorned with sun and moon — animate world

        iii. Rakta (blood) — nature is union of appearance and emptiness

            1. Vessel of freshly severed skull filled with blood — desires & attachments

            2. Actual nature, free from attachment, is desireless great bliss

            3. All pure qualities are within the cup

III. Yoga of Meditative Equipoise

    A. The yoga of the physical mudra

        1. Inner meaning — three meditative absorptions

            a. Absorption on the nature of mind as it is — emptiness, dharmakaya

            b. Absorption on all appearances — compassion, sambhogakaya

            c. Absorption on the primary cause — compassion and emptiness, nirmanakaya

        2. Generating the support

            a. Arrangement of the five elements — vast and expansive (no center or periphery): space, air, fire, water, earth

            b. Mt. Sumeru (Meru), four sides: gold, lapis lazuli, ruby, mother of pearl

            c. Generation of the celestial mansion

                i. Peaceful mandala

                    a. Surrounded by eight great cemeteries

                    b. Center is a 1000-pedalled white lotus, sun disk with crossed vajra and blue square at the center (base of the palace)

                    c. Five concentric walls of five jewels (inner wall is color of deity)

                    d. Red landing with 16 offering goddesses facing inward, holding offerings

                    e. Outside walls: east is white, south is yellow, west is red, north is green

                    f. Eight great pillars support four beams (two in each direction)

                    g. Ceiling covered with jewels

                    h. Four entrances in four directions with pillared porticos

                    i. Victory banner and umbrella crown the roof

                ii. Wrathful mandala

       a. Walls made of dry, moist and fresh skulls

       b. Eight pillars are made of eight great gods

       c. Eight crossbeams made of eight great nagas (serpent-like creatures)

       d. Ceiling covered with eight constellations of stars

       e. Windows of sun, moon and eight planets

       f. Hanging net of snakes and skulls

       g. Rafters adorned with malas (rosaries) of fingers, skulls, five organs and sun and moon

       h. Dome of the roof is a great god's skull

       i. Top of the roof is a heart, banner and canopy made of human skin

       j. Looks like charnel ground inside and out—pools of blood

       k. Black violent wind blowing like a tornado

       l. Terrifying firelight pervades the environment

   d. Generation of the seat of the deity — red lotus, sun and moon disk

   e. Generation of the deity

       i. Seed syllable appears in space, descends to seat (buddha's speech)

       ii. Light radiates from seed syllable as offering to buddhas, returns as a blessing; radiates to all sentient beings, returns (radiation and absorption) & purifies conceptualization (mind)

       iii. Seed syllable transforms into the deity (body)

3. Invoking the wisdom beings (jnanasattvas)

   a. Light radiates from the seed syllable at your heart to the wisdom beings

   b. A rain of blessings (wisdom beings from all directions/times) descend upon you

   c. Recite DZA HUNG BAM HO (with hand mudras)

       i. DZA — hooks the wisdom beings

   ii. HUNG — wisdom and commitment beings unite

   iii. BAM — agree to remain until you achieve enlightenment

   iv. HO — they dissolve into your heart, remaining until your purpose (enlightenment for all beings) is achieved

  4. Prostrations, offerings, praise

   a. Homage — replicas of yourself emanate to pay homage to deities (ultimate nature of your mind)

   b. Offerings

    1. Outer — countless offering goddesses emanate from your heart holding eight offering bowls; the deities accept and are pleased

    2. Inner — men (medicine or elixir), torma, rakta (see above)

    3. Secret — channels, winds and drops

    4. Most secret — pure awareness, rigpa

   c. Praise — make praise with awareness of deity's qualities and nature of mind

  5. Meditative concentration upon the deity — one experiences:

   a. Clarity of the deity's characteristics

   b. Pride of the deity — buddhanature and playfulness of appearances

   c. Deity's pure qualities

   d. Bliss, clarity and emptiness

IV. Yoga of Speech Recitation — Mantra

 A. Syllables represent the name or identity of the deity (not a literal translation) arranged around moon or sun disk with their seed syllable in the center and located at your heart as the deity

  1. Male deities — arrange syllables clockwise, facing in, move counterclockwise

  2. Female deities — arrange syllables counterclockwise, facing out, move clockwise

B. Recite as many times as you can while maintaining the full visualization

    1. Visualizing the mantra (options)

        a. As individual syllables (as above)

        b. Spinning like a whirling sparkler or ring of fire (with consort)

            i. First mantra emanates a second

            ii. Second leaves mouth of jnanasattva at your heart, then mouth of samayasattva (you) into mouth of consort down central channel out lotus into vajra and up central channel into his heart

        c. Messenger of a king — light fills all of space as offerings to buddhas, returns as blessings, then out again to all sentient beings in six realms purifying them and returns

        d. Bee's hive — light radiates out continuously

    2. Manner of reciting — (steady, quick, quiet) with pure awareness

V. Yoga of Meditative Equipoise — Clear Light

A. Dissolve the visualization outside in — outside, wheel of protection, base of elements, charnel grounds, palace, retinues, deity & consort, commitment being, wisdom being, mantra, seed syllable (bottom up into emptiness)

B. Rest in nonconceptual pure awareness (rigpa)

VI. Yoga of Arising from Equipoise

A. Re-appear as the deity

VII. Ganachakra (optional in most cases, used mostly in retreat, e.g., 4th of 4 daily sessions)

VIII. Completion

A. Make offerings & praise, recite prayers for supreme realization, request forgiveness of errors

B. Dedication of merit — dedicate the merit with resolve of a bodhisattva

C. Recite other auspicious closing prayers as appropriate or provided in the sadhana

D. Arise as a nirmanakaya form of deity, abiding in pure awareness
(impure illusory body) as you go about your daily activities

When engaging in the generation-stage practice, there are a few
hints that may be helpful. The first is to locate a good picture of the deity.
Spend extra time familiarizing yourself with the image. Do it a little at a
time. Look at part of the picture, then look away and "see" it with your
mind's eye. Repeat this over and over until you can clearly recall it
without looking at the image. Similarly, locate a good picture of the
mandala of the deity, and follow the same procedure.

Mantra

The Path of Tantra is sometimes referred to as "mantrayana,"
because of the extensive use of *mantra*[108] recitation. While included here
as part of the generation stage, it is also done as a practice by itself
(ideally while also visualizing the deity). Tibetans often carry their *malas*
around with them, reciting *mantras* everywhere they go. Similar action
can greatly expand your limited time doing formal meditation on the
cushion. It can remind you to sustain Pure View. You may not want to be
that conspicuous, which is fine. But you can always recite them in your
head without anyone ever knowing. For example, I do them while
driving, walking, waiting in line, working out in the gym, watching
television, and so forth. All it takes is a little imagination and strong
intention. Anything you can do to enhance your practice will be very
beneficial in the long run.

According to Mipham Rinpoche,

Faith is extremely important when it comes to mantra
recitation. If one recites with faith, there will be
accomplishment in mantra. If mantra is accomplished, one
will attain the body of a knowledge holder of the desire or
form realm and become immortal. In terms of speech, one
will attain words of truth. Realization, moreover, will arise in
the mind, and gradually one's fortune will be equal to that of

---

[108] *Mantra* is a Sanskrit term referring to a sound, letter, or syllable and means to
protect the mind. Reciting mantras is considered to be an extraordinary method
for "protecting the mind."

the superior deity. Hence, one must be diligent in faithfully reciting mantras.

And,

Mantras function as the causes and conditions for emanating the deities of the mandala.... Mantras are themselves emanations of the buddhas, and carry out buddha activity and bring one to the state of buddhahood.

And,

In terms of their ultimate nature, mantras are equality, free of expressions and anything expressed.... Meanwhile, each and every verbalization is also mantra.

The result of the generation stage practice is "vajra pride" – seeing and feeling yourself as a deity. You maintain Pure View and achieve the union of bliss-emptiness.

Generation-Stage Practices

As previously mentioned, the generation-stage practices are primarily a different form of shamata – single-pointed calm abiding. In this case, the deity and entire mandala become the "object" of focus. In addition, we are practicing "being the deity" as we actually become one. We are just increasing the complexity over that of the outer tantras. Here I have provided an example of a daily Highest Yoga Tantra practice. You may do this practice *if* you have a Highest Yoga Tantra empowerment. If not, please continue with one of the outer deity practices from the previous chapter. I have also provided an example of a longer sadhana practice in Appendix B. This also requires a Highest Yoga Tantra empowerment, preferably Vajrayogini or Vajravarahi, to do the practice.

Week 24 – Daily Sadhana of the White Dakini

Practice twice daily for one week, or once daily for three weeks.

Intention: I do this practice for the benefit of all sentient beings (*or other personal intention*).

Homage: **Guru Dewa Dakiniye**

Preliminaries: Recite the brief Ngondro preliminary practice, with prostrations.

Visualization: Begin with stillness of body, speech and mind. From emptiness appears a red BAM syllable on the center of a red lotus, which transforms the five poisons into the five wisdoms as a wheel of protection. From light rays streaming from the BAM appears the charnel ground celestial palace, wrathful in nature.

I appear as the White Dakini in the form of Vajravarahi. I have one face with three eyes with a semi-wrathful expression and two arms. I hold a vajra in my right hand and a skull cup of the elixir of primordial awareness in my left. I am youthful and naked with nothing to hide, standing in a dancing pose. I am adorned with a skull crown, a garland of human heads, necklaces and other bone ornaments. I hold a khatvanga with a vajra tip in my left arm as my consort. I am surrounded by the fire of primordial wisdom.

At my heart is a double tetrahedron pointing downward with a lotus, sun disc, and BAM on top and with the mantra arranged counter clockwise facing outward around the edge. Light rays radiate out from the BAM at my heart inviting all buddhas and other beings in the form of the White Dakini. I pay homage, make outer, inner, and secret offerings, and they dissolve into me filling me with their blessings.

Mantra: Visualizing the mandala I recite the mantra –

Om Benza Vairochaniye Soha

(108X or as many times as you can as light rays emanate from the BAM and mantra syllables purifying all and performing activities of wisdom and compassion.)

Meditation: Then dissolve the visualization and rest in the natural state of pure awareness for as long as you like.

From emptiness I reappear as the White Dakini.

Closing – Wish for Bodhicitta:

Bodhicitta, the excellent and precious mind.
Where it is unborn, may it arise.
Where it is born, may it not decline,
But ever increase, higher and higher.

Dedication: With the mind of enlightenment, Bodhicitta, I dedicate all
merit from this practice for the enlightenment of all sentient beings.
(3X)

Post-meditation: *Following the practice, continue as the White Dakini in your daily activities.*

This sadhana is written for daily practice. The number of
repetitions and speed of reciting the mantra can be adjusted to fit your
daily schedule. It is best done following the Daily Ngondro practice. On
weekends, retreats or other opportunities, it is helpful to recite the long
sadhana in Appendix B in order to reinforce the context and details of the
daily practice.

The Mandala

Each deity also has a mandala. *Manda* in Sanskrit means
"essence" and *la* means to hold or uphold. So a mandala is "the ground
that holds the essential qualities," or taken together it means "a complete
circle." It represents the abode of the deity and his/her retinue. Mipham
Rinpoche says, "The natural mandala of the ground refers to the
primordial divine nature of the world and its inhabitants, the support
and the supported." When we generate the support, we are visualizing
the mandala. In addition to a picture of the deity, it is helpful to obtain a
picture of the mandala for this purpose. It represents the ground and
environment of the deity, including the palace, viewed from above
(although there are three-dimensional versions as well).

But there are also other forms of the mandala. We created an
offering mandala in the preliminary practices. The body is also visualized
as a mandala. You can find sources that articulate a point-by-point
comparison between the body mandala and the support mandala. In
general, the body mandala includes the enlightened body, speech, and
mind of the deity. All mandalas embody "the entire meaning of ground,
path, and fruition."

Sexual Yogas of the Generation Stage

The sadhana of the White Dakini does not involve explicit sexual yogas, either real or imagined. However, many of the Highest Yoga Tantra practices do, as explained earlier in this text.

There are four principle forms of sexual yoga with which I am sufficiently familiar in the Buddhist tradition to briefly describe them in this text. But before describing those, there are several obstacles to actually doing most of these practices. The first is finding a qualified teacher. Most lamas have little or no experience with karmamudra practices and are, therefore, not qualified to teach them. (Nor are most willing to do so.) The second is mastering the visualized form of the practice, which may take considerable time. We in the West tend to be impatient and may "jump in" before actually mastering the visualization practice sufficiently to do it in detail without the text for guidance. Tibetans often memorize the practice sadhana. The third is finding a qualified consort with whom to do the practice (described below). The forth is having the right motivation. Whether done in the generation stage or completion stage (described later), one should be aware that these sexual yogas are *not about sex*. More accurately, they are about *transcending sex*. Thus, anyone considering these practices should ask themselves first if they are truly committed to transcend the desire for sex, i.e., nonattachment.[109] If you are willing let go of sex, then this may be a suitable practice for you. If not, stay with the visualized consort practice. And the fifth is having the ability to *actually* transcend sexual desire without becoming stuck in your progress. Thus, for nearly all practitioners, it is far better to engage in the visualized mudra practices.

With those precautions, here is a brief overview of the four forms of sexual yogas. The first is simply *Pure View*. As described earlier, Pure View means seeing the world with a sacred outlook. Each being is seen as a buddha, each sound is a mantra, each thought is the wisdom of a buddha and each phenomenon is part of a perfect buddhafield. As lay practitioners, the most basic form of sexual yoga is to maintain this Pure View during ordinary sex, which you should be doing anyway as a practitioner on the Path of Tantra. But sometimes we need to be reminded. So it can be helpful to remind yourself of Pure View any time

---

[109] Transcending sexual desire does not mean creating an *aversion* to sex either. Rather, it is a middle way – neither attachment nor aversion.

you engage in sexual activity.[110] This approach encounters the fewest obstacles listed above and may be the most practical approach for householders. According to Mipham Rinpoche, when one engages in sexual relations with the compassionate intention of undefiled self-interest, not only are such actions not problematic, they are indeed virtuous. Ordinary sex motivated by the desire for the bliss of orgasm binds one to samsara, whereas sex motivated by transcendent bliss transforms ordinary desire into wisdom. "Wisdom arises from, or is the essence of, the Pure View."

The next form is sexual union in the generation stage yogas, primarily practiced through an imagined or visualized process (with a *jnanamudra* consort). His Holiness the Dalai Lama has said that actual sexual yoga should not be done by monks or nuns. It is also often said that these practices are "dangerous." The primary danger is that one can easily become attached to the practices, which would be an obscuration to achieving enlightenment. However, as noted earlier, Je Tsongkapa wrote, the practice of sexual yoga is necessary for enlightenment in this lifetime, although he is said to have avoided the practice so as not to violate his vow of celibacy, preferring instead to achieve enlightenment at the time of his death.

Sexual yoga in the generation stage is rarely taught, but follows mastery of the visualization practice. In essence, it is a process of acting out the generation-stage visualization with an actual consort. The best consort is one who has also mastered the generation stage practice. Specifically, *karmamudra* requires a qualified consort who:

Has realized the view of primordial wisdom

Is skilled at the practice of vital energies – channels, winds & drops – *completion stage practice*

Has Pure View – all beings as buddhas, sounds as mantra, thoughts as wisdom of the buddha, phenomena as a buddhafield

Has mastered *yab-yum* yidam practice (Highest Yoga Tantra) – has confidence in self as the deity – *another completion stage practice*

A middling consort is one who has a good understanding of the practice with some experience, but has not yet mastered it. A lesser

---

[110] A Tibetan form of the *Karmasutra* may be found in *Tibetan Arts of Love* by Gedun Chopel and Jeffry Hopkins.

consort is one who has only rudimentary knowledge or experience, but who is willing to participate in the practice to benefit their partner. You should not engage in this form of sexual yoga with someone who has no knowledge or background in the generation stage practice. Then you critically examine this alternative and decide whether it is appropriate to do this form of practice. Otherwise you are acting like any other animal with sexual desire, which is not helpful and may be harmful to one or both partners.

To follow this method, one begins by reciting the opening prayers to the point of generating one's self as the deity in union with the consort. At this point texts sometimes reference the two partners stimulating arousal with each other by smiling, gazing, kissing, biting, scratching, tickling, and touching. Regard yourselves as deities and engage all the senses with Pure View – sight (glances of passion), sound (words that arouse passion), smell (lotus and fragrance of the mudra), taste (sugar), touch (fondle, embrace, tickle, rub the lotus or vajra).

Once aroused, the two join in sexual union, normally in the *yab-yum* posture sitting with the female on the lap of the male and the erection (*vajra*) of the male inside the vagina (*lotus*) of the female with her legs around his waist. If this posture is uncomfortable, the female may sit on a cushion or the couple may simply choose an alternative posture while still visualizing the posture described in the practice text. Some movement is permitted to maintain arousal, but not so much as to cause ejaculation so as to preserve the vital energies. It is best to sit in stillness and imagine the partner and complete mandala as described in the practice text. Recite the text in union if possible. During the dissolution phase of the practice, the couple may continue in union or separate for the meditation on emptiness. Concluding prayers are then recited from the text. Post-meditation is the same as with the imagined consort practice.

The third practice is done in the completion stage and will be described in that chapter. It is similar to the generation stage approach, but involves engaging in the completion-stage practices with an actual consort following mastery of the practices with a visualized consort. The fourth form of sexual yoga is a similar approach done during the advanced stages of *dzogchen togal* practice and will be briefly described there.

Ganachakra or Tsok Feast

Many of the elaborate versions of Highest Yoga Tantra practices include a *ganachakra*[111] or *tsok* feast. Mipham Rinpoche explains it this way: "A *gathering* of fortunate individuals collects a *gathering* of precious materials and offers this to the *gathering* of deities that are being accomplished, thereby perfecting the *gathering* of merit and wisdom."

This may be a simple or very extensive practice, as detailed as the main practice itself. A *tsok* feast may also be included as part of an empowerment. As a tantric practice, this may have included forbidden food and drink such as meat and alcohol. As part of its early origin in India, the main ritual of small tantric cult groups was to practice outdoors in the forest, a cremation grounds, or other scary place. In *Passionate Enlightenment*, Miranda Shaw describes these practices as follows:

> The feast is an esoteric ritual that unfolds in many stages. The sacred space for the ceremony is demarcated by geometric designs drawn on the ground with powdered pigments, and an elaborate array of offerings and foods are laid out. The participants don special insignia like bone ornaments and crowns and use musical instruments of archaic design ... for inducing heightened awareness. Practitioners sit in a circle and partake of sacramental (dry) meat and wine (often liquor) served in skull-cups. The feasts also provide an occasion for the exchange of ritual lore, the ritual worship of women (*sripuja*), and the performance of sexual yogas. The feast culminates in the performance of tantric dances and music that must never be disclosed to outsiders. The revelers may also improvise "songs of realization" (*caryagiti*) to express their heightened clarity and blissful raptures in spontaneous verse.

Participants would sit as deities and consorts in one or more circles forming the mandala around the guru and consort as described by the tantra. However, by the second dissemination of Buddhism into Tibet around the 11th century, such practice was generally considered inappropriate for most, if not all, practitioners, especially monastics. As such, it has been replaced with a much tamer ritual conducted indoors

---

[111] *Ganachakra* refers to a tantric gathering or feast involving group practice.

usually without meat and little, if any, alcohol, and use of the visualized consort (*jnanamudra*) in place of the actual consort (*karmamudra*), although there are rare exceptions – most notably for yogi and yogini householders. Tea, wine, or other alcohol may be symbolically transformed into nectar with the addition of medicine pills (*dutsi*), representing the five meats and five nectars. Dancing, sexual yogas, and so forth are rarely included and only done in secret if they are done at all.

Nevertheless, group practice such as the *ganachakra* is considered to multiply the effectiveness of the practice by the number of participants. The prayers, mantras, and other texts help create a sacred outlook of Pure View of the mandala during the practice to enhance the experience and blessings of the teacher as deity. Samsara and nirvana are united as one taste.

Signs of Accomplishment

Empowerment

A face radiant with joy.

A smile exuding delight.

A manner of reverence.

Generation-Stage Practice

A sense of being the deity, initially during meditation, but eventually at all times.

The degree to which you are able to continuously experience the world with Pure View during all mundane activities – even going to the bathroom, sleeping, and having sex.

Able to sustain Pure View for four hours or more continuously.

Manifests as an impure illusory body.

Chapter 15

The Second Training

on the Path of Tantra: Meditation—

the Inner Deity Yogas

Highest Yoga Tantra - Completion Stage[112]

The Highest Yoga Tantra completion stage practices are often embedded into the Six Yogas of Naropa or the Six Yogas of Niguma. The six actual practices vary somewhat with different sources packaging them in different combinations. In general these include vase breathing, vajra recitation, channels/winds/drops (*tsalung*) and/or inner heat (*tummo*), illusory body, dream yoga, clear light, sexual yogas (*jnanamudra* and *karmamudra*), transference (*phowa*), and the intermediate state (*bardos*).[113] The exact content of these also varies, adding to the rich array of practices available in the Path of Tantra.

---

[112] These notes are a synthesis of the following sources (when there were differences, I selected that which was most common among them): Teachings on Six Bardos by Khenchen Paljea Dorjee Rinpoche (Tucson AZ, 2006); *Natural Liberation* by Padmasambhava; teachings on *tsalung* by Yogi Lama Gursam (Tucson AZ, 2007, 2009 and 2011); "Treatise on the Six Yogas of Niguma" by the Second Dalai Lama in *The Dalai Lamas on Tantra* by Glenn Mullin; "Notes on the Two Yogic Stages of Glorious Kalachakra" by the First Dalai Lama in *ibid.*; "The Two Yogic Stages of the Vajrabhairvana Tantra" by the Second Dalai Lama in *ibid.*; *Highest Yoga Tantra* by Daniel Cozort; *Passionate Enlightenment* by Miranda Shaw; *Readings on the Six Yogas of Naropa* by Glenn Mullin; and *As Long as Space Endures: Essays on the Kalacakra Tantra in Honor of HH the Dalai Lama* edited by Edward Arnold.

[113] This can be any period of time, but here refers most commonly to the state between death and rebirth.

Phases of Completion-Stage Practices

First one masters the generation stage of deity yoga practice to the point of having a stable experience of meditation and post-meditation with Pure View – seeing all beings as buddhas, all sounds as mantra, all thoughts as wisdom of the buddhas, and all phenomena as a pure buddhafield. Although still "visualized" as such, this should be relatively continuous with few gaps.

Then one continues the practices of the completion stage. One classification system organizes phases of completion stage practices into six categories. Here I have also included the main practices used by Padmasambhava.

FR. GALUPA MODIFIED BY PADMASAMBHAVA

1.   *Physical isolation* – through vase breathing, vital energies (winds) enter and abide in the central channel; one is isolated from viewing the world as ordinary.

2.   *Verbal isolation* – through vajra recitation, vital energies dissolve into the central channel at the heart, but not into the heart; one is isolated from ordinariness.

3.   *Mental isolation* – through *tummo* and *tsalung* with four blisses and four empties, as well as dissolution into clear light, the "empties" manifest due to the dissolution of the winds into the indestructible drop at the heart; one is isolated from concepts.   *THIS IS OUR BUDDHA NATURE*

4.   *Illusory body* – subtle winds manifest as the deity; practice with a tantric consort causes the winds to dissolve into the indestructible drop; the impure illusory body approaches the pure illusory body of a buddha.   *① CAN BE W/ VISUALIZED DEITY, ② ACTUAL PERSON OR*

5.   *Clear light* – from the most fundamental level of consciousness (*rigpa*) – pure awareness, one experiences emptiness directly; the winds are completely dissolved, and semblant clear light approaches the actual clear light.

6.   *Learner's union* – the winds begin to move again through union with the consort; actual clear light and pure illusory body arise as one taste and one achieves buddhahood.

③ MAHAMUDRA : TRANSCENDS THE VISUALIZAT[I] SATTVA?

I have organized the completion-stage practices following the above pattern. As with so many other cases, there are differences in the approaches based on the school, lineage, and in some cases, the lama. We begin with the practices of purification, vase breathing, vajra recitation, channels/winds/drops (*tsa, lung, tigle* or just *tsalung*), and actual inner heat (*tummo*). Then we move to the four joys or blisses and the dream yogas, the pure illusory body with the four empties, and finally clear light.

Purification and Vase Breathing

Purification and vase breathing are the first completion-stage preliminary practices taught by Padmasambhava.

Week 25 — Purification and Vase Breathing

Practice twice daily for one week, or once daily for three weeks.

Intention: I do this practice for the benefit of all sentient beings (*or other personal intention*).

Preliminaries: Recite the brief Ngondro preliminary practice, with prostrations. *pp 174-179*

9-ROUND BREATHING - SAME AS IN PATRICK'S YOGA

Purification: From stillness of body, speech and mind, inhale and exhale as follows, while imagining all negative karma and obscurations are discharged through your nostrils and incinerated in the flames of primordial wisdom and you are purified:

SINCE THIS IS PURIFYING, CAN N SKIP VAJRASATTVA IN PRELIMS

> *Block right nostril* with right index finger, inhale, and exhale visualizing **red** in color all negative karma of attachment into fire of wisdom.

> *Block left nostril* with left index finger, inhale, and exhale visualizing sky **blue** in color all negative karma of anger into the fire of wisdom.

> *Inhale and exhale through both*, visualizing **black** in color the negative karma of ignorance into the fire of wisdom.

Repeat 3X.

Vase breathing:

> Breathe in, swallow, then press down from above and up from below by contracting the muscles on the pelvic floor to form the

[handwritten: AT THE MIDDLE OF THE LOWER ABDOMEN]

"mystic kiss." Hold as long as is comfortable. Winds then enter the central channel as you gently breathe out, while focusing on the chakra just below your navel.

Rest your mind in pure awareness (no *object* of focus) as long as you can. *[handwritten: THIS IS AFTER BREATHING OUT & BEFORE THE NEXT IN BREATH]*
Repeat as many times as you can. *[handwritten: AT LEAST 3X]*

Dedication: With the mind of enlightenment, Bodhicitta, I dedicate all merit from this practice for the enlightenment of all sentient beings. (3X)

Post-meditation: *Following the practice, continue vase breathing as much as you can during your daily activities.*

Physical isolation is achieved through vase breathing. The vital energies (winds) enter and abide in the central channel, and one is isolated from viewing the world as ordinary. Mastery of this practice achieves the first stage of the completion-stage practices.

Vajra Recitation

As with most practices in Buddhism, there are a variety of methods for doing each of these practices. To the extent possible, I am following those as described by Padmasambhava in *Natural Liberation*. This is a preparatory practice, often recited for 100,000 repetitions. While Padmasambhava does not require this, it is an excellent practice. Some lamas only require counting 100,000 recitations of OM AH HUNG without the breathing practice described below.

Week 26 — Vajra Recitation

Practice twice daily for one week, or once daily for three weeks.

Intention: I do this practice for the benefit of all sentient beings (*or other personal intention*).

Preliminaries: Recite the brief Ngondro preliminary practice, with prostrations.

Purification: From stillness of body, speech and mind, inhale and exhale as follows, while imagining all negative karma and obscurations are discharged through your nostrils and incinerated in the flames of primordial wisdom and you are purified.

SAME AS WK 25

Block right nostril with right index finger, inhale, and exhale visualizing **red** in color all negative karma of attachment into fire of wisdom.

Block left nostril, with left index finger, inhale, and exhale visualizing sky **blue** in color all negative karma of anger into the fire of wisdom.

Inhale and exhale through both, visualizing **black** in color the negative karma of ignorance into the fire of wisdom.

Repeat 3X.

Vajra Recitation (*as many as you can*):

Inhale visualizing the winds entering the two side channels and into the central channel where they arise as a white OM at your forehead (physical blessings of all the Buddhas).

Press down into lower abdomen and up (gently squeeze muscles in genital/rectal area), visualizing a vivid red AH (speech of all the Buddhas), holding it as long as you can. *↳ THROAT*

↰ HEART
Exhale, visualizing a blue HUNG (essence of the mind of all the Buddhas) and sending out a stream of buddhas for the benefit of all sentient beings.

Repeat as many times as you can.

Dedication: With the mind of enlightenment, Bodhicitta, I dedicate all merit from this practice for the enlightenment of all sentient beings. (3X)

Post-meditation: *Following the practice, continue reciting OM AH HUNG during your daily activities.*

Body   Speech   Mind
OF A BUDDHA

Verbal isolation is achieved through vajra recitation. The vital energies now dissolve into the central channel at the heart, but not into the heart. Mastery of this practice achieves the second stage of the completion-stage practices. This is commonly assessed by having completed 100,000 repetitions of OM AH HUNG.

[handwritten: BODY]

Channels/Winds/Drops Visualization - *Tsalung*

[handwritten: SPEECH & ENERGY] *[handwritten: MIND]*

Channels (*tsa*), winds (*lung*), and drops (*tigle* or *bindu*) cover a broad category of practices, including most, if not all, of the completion stage practices. Here I have included a simple visualization practice as one step in the process. Padmasambhava did not articulate this step, so I have incorporated this practice from other sources. The order of completion-stage practices may vary. For example, *tsalung* may be done after the inner heat practice. In this case, the practice involves visualization without any movement of the winds. The focus is on the channels themselves. Thus, it acts as a preparation for that movement using the same visualization for inner heat practice that follows. More advanced practices involving movement of winds and drops then follow the inner heat practice.

There are three channels described in this practice. The central channel (*avadhuti*) runs from the crown of the head to four finger widths below the navel (the middle of the lower abdomen). The "crown" is variously described as the very top of the head or a location behind the "third eye" in the center of the head. In some practices, the central channel extends to the "secret place" (sex organs) or even the tip of the sex organ. It is hollow and about the size of an arrow shaft. It is transparent with a layer of blue on the outside and red on the inside, both colors are visible and separate from each other.

From each of the nostrils, the side channels extend up above the height of the ears then down the sides of the central channel. They are slightly smaller and about one diameter width apart from the central channel itself. The right (*roma*) channel is transparent red. The left (*lalana*) channel is transparent white. They extend to the bottom of the central channel (short version) and curve around and into it four finger widths below the navel, about the center of the lower abdomen.

At the crown, throat, heart and (below the) navel are *chakras* (wheels) inside the central channel. Each wheel has 8 spokes radiating out and curved either up or down. At the *crown*, the spokes are green[114] and curve downward. They are also divided into 16, then 32 branches. At the *throat*, the spokes are red and curve upward. They are divided into 16

[handwritten: IN TSALUNG, PRIMARY FOCUS IS ON THE CHANNELS]

---

[114] In the practice, this chakra is white, matching the color of the syllable symbolizing the "drop" at the crown.

branches. At the *heart,* the spokes are white[115] and curve downward with no additional branches. At the navel, the spokes are red and curve upward and are divided into 64 branches. The branches or channels radiate throughout the body delivering the winds (energies). The three main channels are filled with air (wind), whereas the branch channels are only partially filled with air (winds).

It is important to keep in mind that these are not physical entities. If the colors or locations of the channels, chakras, etc. vary between texts, use what is described. There is no uniform fixed system that there is in the Hindu system. Like the deities themselves, these are not "real."   ⌐> ENERGIES

There are five root winds in these channels:

1. *Downward moving winds* – are in the secret chakra, produce great bliss, are associated with the space element and are the most powerful, but does not last. MOVES URINE, FECES, SEMEN, ETC

2. *Equally abiding winds* – remain in the navel chakra, are associated with the earth element, produce warmth, heat and "fire" (but are not associated with the fire element).

3. *Life-supporting winds* – are at the heart chakra, are linked with the water element, produce our breathing.

4. *Upward moving winds* – are in the throat chakra and linked to the fire element, help us drink, eat, swallow, talk, laugh, and so forth.

5. *Pervasive wind* – is at the crown chakra and joints (pervading the body) and is linked to the air or all winds.

If we can, through practice, control the winds, then we can remain within the natural state of meditation for a long time. They permit us to bring the energies of emotion that otherwise create obscurations to our practice into the path and then just let them go. Furthermore, the seven-point posture of Vairochana is said to support control over these winds as follows:

> Specifically, the cross-legged posture ensures that the downward-moving wind enters the central channel. The gesture of equanimity ensures this for the equally-abiding

---

[115] In the practice, this chakra is blue, matching the color of the syllable symbolizing the "drop" at the heart.

wind; straightening the back and holding the arms outward does so for the pervasive wind; bending the neck does so for the upward-moving wind; and touching the tongue to the palate and maintaining the gaze does so for the life-supporting wind. When these five winds enter the central channel, all other winds will have entered the central channel, too, and nonconceptual wakefulness will dawn.[116]

The drops (*tigles* or *bindus*) are visualized as tiny Tibetan syllables at each of the chakras, thus inside the central channel as well.

1.   *Crown* – upside down white HAM, representing bliss and method; the seed of the Essence Body (*svabhavikakaya*)

2.   *Throat* – red OM, representing clarity or luminosity; seed of Enjoyment Body (*sambhogakaya*)

3.   *Heart* – blue HUM, representing nonconceptual thoughts; seed of Truth Body (*dharmakaya*)

4.   *Navel* – red AH (ah-stroke), representing fire (heat) and emptiness (wisdom); seed of Form Body (*nirmanakaya*).

The "ah-stroke" is the shape of a thin triangle with the point at the top[117] and resembling a thin, red candle flame. It has a crescent, *bindu* (circle) and *nada* (squiggly line) just above the point of the thin triangle. In this case the crescent, *bindu* and *nada* represent the flame. In other cases, the ah-stroke itself is visualized as the flame.

You may want to approach these in sections to become familiar with the visualizations. As you become familiar, then you can combine them as described in the practice below. *e.g., channels day 1, channels + chakras day 2, channels / chakras / drops day 3*

Week 27 — Channels/Winds/Drops Visualization (*Tsalung*)
SHAMATHA w/ TSALUNG AS FOCUS
Practice twice daily for one week, or once daily for three weeks.

---

[116] Pema Karpo in *Notes on Mahamudra*

[117] In some sources the point of the AH-stroke is downward. However, the crescent, bindu, and nada remain at the top.

Intention: I do this practice for the benefit of all sentient beings (*or other personal intention*).

Preliminaries: Recite the brief Ngondro preliminary practice, with prostrations.

Purification: Repeat the purification breaths as before.

Channels:

Begin with stillness of body, speech and mind. Visualize yourself as Vajrayogini or other deity with consort, transparent like a crystal. You have three transparent channels (red *roma* on right, white *lalana* on left, blue with red inside *avadhuti* in center). Just below the lower opening to the central channel in the lower abdomen ("navel") is a tiny red AH-stroke.

You have a downward-facing white lotus with 32 petals and upside-down HAM at your crown chakra, a red lotus with 16 petals and red OM at your throat chakra, a downward blue lotus with 8 petals and upside-down blue HUNG at your heart chakra, and a red lotus with 64 petals and red AH-stroke at your navel chakra.

Repeat until stability arises.

Dedication: With the mind of enlightenment, Bodhicitta, I dedicate all merit from this practice for the enlightenment of all sentient beings. (3X)

Post-meditation: *Following the practice, continue practicing tsalung as much as you can during your daily activities.*

Inner Heat - *Tummo*

[handwritten: ; one can test this w/ taking temp before & after]

Inner heat or *tummo* is the foundational practice for most of the remaining completion-stage practices. Some yogis specialize in this practice to the degree that they are able to generate enough heat to dry wet clothing on their backs during the cold of winter in Tibet. Our goal, however, is to master it as the basis for developing our sense of having an illusory body, the body of a buddha.

Week 28 — Inner Heat (*Tummo*)

Practice twice daily for one week, or once daily for three weeks.

Intention: I do this practice for the benefit of all sentient beings (*or other personal intention*).

Preliminaries: Recite the brief Ngondro preliminary practice, with prostrations.

Purification: Repeat the purification breaths as before.

Tummo (*as many as you can*):

From emptiness, visualize yourself as Vajrayogini or other deity with consort, transparent like a crystal.

With vase breathing[118], the fire at the top of the AH-stroke blazes and fills one with blissful inner fire, which ascends up central channel to your crown. At the navel the red AH melts, at the heart the blue HUNG melts, at the throat the red OM melts, and at the crown, the white HAM melts and descends into the AH-stroke[119] where you experience even greater blissful inner fire. *After the first revolution, its all between the HAM & the*

HAM *The fire again rises up the central channel and melts the white drop (bodhicitta) at your crown, which melts and descends into the AH-stroke. Meditate single-pointedly on the AH-stroke until you achieve stability, indicated by a luster, radiance or translucence of* stroke *body and surroundings.*

If you become distracted, repeat these steps. Continue as long as you can.

Dedication: With the mind of enlightenment, Bodhicitta, I dedicate all merit from this practice for the enlightenment of all sentient beings. (3X)

Post-meditation: *Following the practice, continue tummo as much as you can during your daily activities.*

The two practices of *tsalung* visualization and *tummo* above may be combined into a single practice with the visualization followed by the

---

[118] These are often done with the wind ascending on the in-breath and descending on the out-breath. I prefer this approach.

[119] In some versions, the inner heat generated when the drop reaches the navel chakra then radiates through your body generating a warm feeling that actually increases body heat that is measurable with a thermometer.

inner heat practice. When you are able to stabilize *tsalung* and *tummo* you are able to bring the vital energies (winds) into the central channel. Breath is even in both nostrils. Continue to meditate until breath becomes increasingly subtle until unnoticeable.

The Four Blisses

In general, bliss is the experience of an incredible lightness of being. The next extension of these practices involves the experience of the four blisses (sometimes called the four joys). These can be thought of as increasing levels of "lightness" of being until you transcend any conceptual notion of "bliss." There are ascending and descending blisses, each building on the other until you achieve a very high level of experience. They are: (1) bliss, (2) supreme bliss, (3) special bliss, and (4) innate bliss, whether ascending or descending.

When using the inner heat of sexual arousal, this is achieved while approaching but not engaging in orgasm.[120] The *Tantra of the Lamp of Primordial Wisdom* states, "Due to your awareness issuing forth, the male and female genitals come in contact, and joy unceasingly arises. The awareness of the one who experiences joy is also the *dharmakaya*. Know its nature!"[121]

Week 29 — The Four Blisses

Practice twice daily for one week, or once daily for three weeks.

Intention: I do this practice for the benefit of all sentient beings (*or other personal intention*).

---

[120] To be fair, there are a few branches of Tibetan Buddhism that use tantras that assert the use of physical orgasm as the highest form of bliss. But most by far state that this approach *risks* the "danger" of one becoming attached to the practice, rather than using it to transcend desire and achieve realization. That is *not* to assert that this *will* happen. It is simply a matter of human nature in samsara. In addition, my experience is that withholding orgasm leads to a more subtle and lasting bliss, a truly transcendent bliss and bliss-emptiness, than when orgasm is included in the practice. But that is just my personal view. For instruction on tantra with orgasm, you will need to seek a qualified teacher.

[121] *Natural Liberation*, p. 135.

Preliminaries: Recite the brief Ngondro preliminary practice, with prostrations.

Purification: Repeat the purification breaths as before.

Four blisses:

From emptiness, visualize yourself as Vajrayogini or other deity with consort, transparent like a crystal.

As in *tummo*, the inner heat of bliss melts the red drop then ascends and melts the white drop at the crown and descends in the central channel now to the "tip of the jewel" (sex organ).[122]

With increasing practice, one experiences the four blisses (ascending) – "bliss" at the navel chakra, "supreme bliss" at the heart, "special bliss" at the throat, and "innate bliss" at the crown.

Then the descending blisses are aroused as the white drop at the crown melts and descends to the throat, heart, navel and then continues to the tip of the sex organ (without orgasm) where innate bliss is again aroused.[123] *Try 3x up & down, & rest at the tip of*

Repeat with ever increasing levels of bliss. Then hold the vital *sex organ for a while then maybe another 3x* energies at the tip of the sex organ until stability arises.

Dedication: With the mind of enlightenment, Bodhicitta, I dedicate all merit from this practice for the enlightenment of all sentient beings. (3X)

Post-meditation: *Following the practice, continue to practice the ascending and descending blisses as much as you can during your daily activities as Vajrayogini or other deity and consort.*

Think of this as a shamatha practice, & just experience whatever "bliss" is in this session, don't try for a specific feeling.

---

[122] The tip of the jewel usually refers to the genitals, penis or clitoris. Other references indicate this is the tip of the cervix in the female. Some texts refer to "the secret place", which is less clear. Some interpret that as the genitals or the cervix (in the female), whereas others indicate a place near the base of the spine, which would be approximately the prostate in a male or cervix in the female.

[123] Some start with descending bliss from melting of the white drop, then ascending with melting of red drop. Since the AH-stroke at the navel is the source of the heat, and the previous practices started at the navel, it makes more sense to follow the same pattern here.

The experience from these practices enhances our direct sense of the illusory nature of ordinary perceptions. This, in turn, further refines our sense of having an illusory body.

Impure Illusory Body and Dream Yogas

By now we have had some experience of being an illusory body. Padmasambhava gives some additional instructions to further our awareness of this experience. One begins with the power of intention, doing guru yoga and praying to recognize the dream and to practice within the dream, seeing all dream experiences as illusory. This is repeated during the day, along with the impure illusory body practices of seeing all things as illusory (as "reflections" in one's mind). Padmasambhava begins with impure illusory body practices, followed by daytime preliminary practices to actual dream yoga.

Week 30—Impure Illusory Body

Practice twice daily for one week, or once daily for three weeks.

Intention: I do this practice for the benefit of all sentient beings (*or other personal intention*).

Preliminaries: Recite the brief Ngondro preliminary practice.

Purification: Repeat the purification breaths as before.

Dream yoga—daytime practices:

Body – Look at yourself in a mirror. Praise your form and its adornments. See if you sense pleasure or displeasure. If you sense pleasure, think to yourself, "Each time pleasure arises due to praise of this body, I am confused. This body is simply an appearance due to an aggregation of dependently related causes and conditions, but in reality it has never [inherently] existed. Why do you grasp onto it as yourself and take pleasure in it?" Meditate on the reflected body in the mirror.

Abuse the image in the mirror and point out its failings. See if you sense displeasure. If so, think to yourself, "All praise and abuse are like latent predispositions, and since the body has no essence, the attitudes of pleasure and displeasure are confused." Then meditate on the image in the mirror. Alternate between praise and abuse, and equalize them. This is one session.

Speech – Go by yourself to a place where there are echoes. Shout out good and bad words. Notice that there is no grasping onto the echo. Practice regarding your speech as like an echo. *or can listen to a recording*

Mind – Look at or imagine a mirage. It cannot be found by going to search for it. Thoughts are like that, lacking any inherent nature. Speech and mind together are the second session. *& also observe the mutability & evanescence of thoughts*.

Third session – Looking again in a mirror, imagine the reflection dissolves into you, and meditate on your body as appearing, yet having no inherent nature. Imagine praising yourself. If pleasurable feelings arise, reflect on their lack of inherent existence. Imagine being robbed and beaten. If displeasure arises, reflect on its lack of inherent existence. Meditate on this as being no different than a reflection in a mirror. Then when you are actually praised or abused, think of it as being like the reflection in the mirror.

Dedication: By the merit of this practice may I attain enlightenment for the benefit of all sentient beings. (3X)

Post-meditation: *Practice in this way during the week or until whatever arises is perceived as similar to an illusion.*

This is a preliminary practice for the transition to dreaming. Continue these practices in the daytime as you use the following dream yoga practices to further enhance your direct experience of illusory body at night. Note that lucid dreaming experts say that the most effective method is setting a firm intention to do dream yoga throughout the day.

Dream Yogas

Dream yoga is used as a supplementary practice to impure illusory body practices emphasized by Padmasambhava in *Natural Liberation*. In this way, you can practice in some way 24/7. We have seen that the nature of reality has an illusory quality. Dream yoga is a practice that facilitates what psychologists call *lucid dreaming*, the ability to "wake up" during the dreaming process, being aware and in control of the dream while still sleeping. While some texts emphasize the *fantasmic* nature of these other-worldly experiences, the key practice is, as when not sleeping, to let go and let be while remaining alert and aware. No effort is necessary. Content is largely irrelevant, particularly as we advance in the practice. In this context, lucid dreaming becomes part of your spiritual practice.

To practice dream yoga, add the following to the end of your evening meditation practice. Confirm your intentions by repeating the following chant three or more times:

> For the benefit of others
> And awakening to the transcendent wisdom,
> May I awaken within my dreams
> And abide softly in pure awareness.

Then practice going asleep and dreaming, while still awake, using the options in the practice below. Upon going to bed, remain aware by following the instructions given below.

Upon awakening, maintain awareness of the illusory nature of the dream, and continue to notice the similar illusory nature of things in the waking state throughout the day. It is also helpful to make notes immediately upon waking up when recall is clearest. Keep a notepad by your bed for this purpose. *Brief notes, key words, emotional impact*

As you continue dream yoga, the frequency and memory of the dream experience will increase. Continue this awareness into your morning practice and your daily activities, recognizing the illusory nature of what we call reality. Thus, one abides in the pure awareness of our experience both day and night.

Experienced masters find that over time dreams begin to cease, leaving only a luminous clarity of an indescribable nature. Continue your illusory body practice during the day as you add the dream yogas at night.

Apprehending the Dream State

Having sustained your awareness while going to sleep, the first step during sleep is to recognize the dream state. There is a sense that you are not really asleep. Most people cycle through several phases of dream and deep sleep each night. Some question whether they can feel rested in the morning without going into deep sleep. But experienced dream yoga practitioners indicate that that they do not feel tired in the morning. They may be more aware during the dream phases and also be experiencing cycles of deep sleep, or they may be able to rest sufficiently while remaining in the dream state throughout the night. In either case, it is awareness during the dream state(s) that is the goal here. We then apply that to the waking state to help recognize the illusory nature of both.

The practice provides several alternatives. But you should practice with patience and persistence for at least one full week before trying another option.

Week 31 — Apprehending the Dream State

Practice nightly for one week or as needed.

Intention: During the day and before going to sleep, set your intention to apprehend the dream state.

Nighttime Instructions on Apprehending the Dream State:

The Main Practice – From emptiness, say: "For the sake of all sentient beings, I shall train in dreaming." Lie on your right side with your right hand on your cheek and left on your thigh. Clearly visualize yourself as your chosen deity.

Option 2 (*if after a week you have not apprehended the dream state*) – Visualize yourself as your chosen deity thinking, "I am the chosen deity," and rest your head in lap of your primary mentor with Guru Rinpoche at your throat chakra and make a powerful yearning many times, "Bless me that I may recognize the dream state."

Option 3 (*if after another week you have not apprehended the dream state*) – From emptiness, visualize yourself as deity and deity at your throat as you fall asleep envisioning that you will know the dream-state.

Option 4 (*if after another week you have not apprehended the dream state*) – From emptiness, visualize 4-petaled lotus at throat with OM in center, AH in front, NU on right, TA in back, RA on left. Focus on OM, then AH, NU, TA, RA and back to OM as fall asleep without any other thoughts.

Option 5 (*if after another week you have not apprehended the dream state*) – From emptiness, focus on a red bindu at your throat as you fall asleep.

It is important to keep the visualization at your throat to concentrate your mind and energies. Note that in the morning dreams do not remain, and daytime appearances are not in dreams; both are illusions. Alternate apprehending the dream with the previous daytime illusory body practices (up to one month).

In addition to the alternatives for apprehending the dream state, there are other daytime techniques that may be used to help improve apprehending the dream state:

1. Purifying the mind by means of the body – Visualize yourself as Heruka and Consort at the edge of a cliff, then fall over, or jump into fire or a raging river, recognizing that the dream body cannot be harmed.

2. Purifying the body by means of the mind – Visualize every pore of body filled with a blue HUNG with top inside and bottom outside. The radiating blue light fills your body and it becomes empty and pure.

3. Purification by means of Nairatmika, consort of Heruka – Visualize blue Nairatmika with curved knife and skull cup, recite OM AH SOHA. Blue light radiates and enters your body through tip of your sex organ, and then she follows. Your body becomes filled with blue light and melts into emptiness.

4. Purification by resolution – Make a firm resolution to recognize that you are dreaming and determine to project yourself to a Pure Land where you see buddhas and bodhisattvas and hear their teachings.

If this is still not working, do more preliminary practices (*ngondro*) as this is a sign of obscurations.

Dream Emanation and Transformation

We are continuing the dream yoga practices. Last time we apprehended the dream state. Now we continue with dream emanation and transformation practices while dreaming. We practice them first in the daytime as if we were dreaming, then during the actual dream state.

Week 32 – Dream Emanation and Transformation

Practice nightly for one week or as needed.

Intention: During the day and before going to sleep, set your intention to apprehend the dream state and transform them.

Nighttime Instructions on Dream Emanation and Transformation:

Transform appearances into your deity.

Multiply them.

Change them into anything you like.

Increase dream objects – whatever appears, multiply it into two, four, hundreds, thousands.

Condense many things into one.

Change large into small or small into large.

Bring forth a powerful yearning to go to a Buddhafield and request teachings, then go.

If demonic apparitions appear, transform yourself in to a *garuda* or Hayagriva or the like and transform the apparitions in any way you wish. [You may transform bad dreams into good dreams!]

When you recognize that you are in the dream state, meditate on yourself as Heruka and Consort. Radiate blue light from the HUNG at your heart, dissolve the world into the deities of the mandala, then the mandala into Heruka and Consort, Consort into Heruka, Heruka into HUNG, HUNG into emptiness. Maintain the view of emptiness.

It is important to keep the visualization of the deity at your throat to concentrate your mind and energies.

Seeing through the Dream and Dispelling Obstacles

Last time we did the practice of transforming the dream. Now we focus on seeing through the dream and dispelling obstacles. Several techniques for this were described earlier at the beginning of this section on dream yoga. It may be helpful to review those now as well.

Week 33 – Seeing through the Dream & Dispelling Obstacles

Practice nightly for one week or as needed.

Intention: During the day and before going to sleep, set your intention to see through the dream and dispel any obstacles.

Instructions on Seeing Through the Dream:

In the daytime, practice dreaming (can be quite playful!): jumping into a river, being in a fire, falling off a cliff, being eaten by a carnivorous animal, your own "worst nightmare"

On the verge of sleep, focus on your throat—guru, deity, seed syllable, or bindu

Recognize sources of fear as illusory and let them happen … it's only a dream!

Abide in bliss and emptiness!

Instructions for Dispelling Obstacles:

Not experiencing dreams—reinforce your intention and resolution to dream and recognize them.

Not recognizing the dream—set a firm resolution (and perfect earlier practices). As the best time to recall a dream is in the early morning hours, one may set an alarm one or two hours earlier, go back to sleep and do the practice of dream yoga until awakening.

Dispelling waking—do not open your eyes, but recapture the dream; visualize black bindus on the soles of your feet

Dispelling forgetfulness—practice illusory body in the daytime; recite "May I know the dream-state as the dream-state, and not become confused. Also, when I am apprehending the dream-state, may I not become confused."

Dispelling being disturbed in the dream—bring the mystic drop back to the throat chakra.

Dispelling confusion—practice daytime illusory body and control of vital energies

Dispelling insomnia—visualize a black bindu at your heart then release your awareness

Dispelling indolence—do practices of precious human birth, death & impermanence, purification, ganachakra offerings, and vital energies

According to Padmasambhava, apprehending the dream state only seven times (or regularly) will prepare you to apprehend the transitional process after death, when we can attain liberation. [Nevertheless, you need to continue to practice or you will lapse and not be able to recognize the experience.] Dream yoga is considered to be a very powerful way to help realize the illusory body.

Pure Illusory Body

- dream yoga helpful in recognizing the illusory nature of life - pure illusory body is recognizing oneself as a Buddha

Having experienced the four blisses and engaged in the dream yogas, you increasingly see all appearances as illusory. They appear like reflections in a mirror, real but not independently existent. Other examples are:

Look at a picture of Vajrasattva (or other deity) through a crystal—multiple images all seem equally real, but are illusory. Meditate on that.

Dissolve the image(s) into your body. The yidam is pure illusory body. Meditate on your own body like that.

You focus on this illusory experience between meditations. This is an approximation of the way an actual Buddha perceives phenomena at all times.

The Four Empties

As repeatedly noted, there are many variations in doing these practices. In this case we are following Padmasambhava's instructions on a series of incremental steps to bring one as quickly as possible to the manifestation of a pure illusory body and actual clear light. Having achieved the direct experience of the four blisses, the next stage is to experience the union of bliss-emptiness. The following practice is usually added to the four blisses practice above, although here it is described as a separate practice. To do this, just insert the "four empties" (below) into the previous practice, following the four blisses.

Week 34—The Four Empties

Practice twice daily for one week, or once daily for three weeks.

Intention: I do this practice for the benefit of all sentient beings (*or other personal intention*).

Reality comes down to awareness - pure awareness is in dzogchen the ultimate essence

Preliminaries: Recite the brief Ngondro preliminary practice, with prostrations.

Purification: Repeat the purification breaths as before.

Four empties:

From emptiness, visualize yourself as Vajrayogini or other deity with consort, transparent like a crystal. *Samboßakaya form*

From the tip of the jewel the ascending four blisses are aroused as the melted red drop at the navel chakra ascends on the winds to the crown.

Then the melted white drop descends with "emptiness" at the crown chakra, "great emptiness" at the throat chakra, "extreme emptiness" at the heart chakra and "total emptiness" at the navel chakra. At the tip of the jewel, the "union of bliss and emptiness" is achieved.[124]

Repeat as many times as necessary to achieve the actual experience of union of bliss and emptiness.

focus on the central channel

Dedication: With the mind of enlightenment, Bodhicitta, I dedicate all merit from this practice for the enlightenment of all sentient beings. (3X)

Post-meditation: *Following the practice, continue to practice the union of bliss-emptiness as much as you can during your daily activities, as Vajrayogini or other deity and consort.* *whenever opportunity arises — essence - this is a more physical meditation*

Alternating between bliss and emptiness has been shown to be a highly effective way of achieving the union of the two states. When this practice is done with a *karmamudra*, it is important to abide in stillness during the descending four empties, allowing the inner fire of sexual arousal to melt into emptiness and *innate happiness*.

The four blisses and four empties may be combined into a single practice by starting with one then proceeding to the other within a single practice. Together these work to transcend the physical desire for sex

---

[124] *Vajra Essence* by HH Dudjom Rinpoche describes an alternative approach in which bliss and emptiness are achieved together in increasing union: bliss and emptiness, supreme bliss and great emptiness, free from bliss and extreme emptiness, co-emergent bliss and total emptiness, and the non-dual bliss-emptiness of inconceivable pristine cognition.

If at any point you lose the feeling, take a brief break & then start up again

through achieving a state of transcendent bliss, especially when done with a *karmamudra*. Transcending the desire for sex does not imply developing an aversion to it. Rather, it is a middle way of no attachment *or* aversion.

During the illusory body practice with the four empties, one may also begin to experience the clear light. This is not likely to be the actual clear light, but an approximation called "semblant clear light." This is none other than our own true nature, buddhanature, or *dharmakaya*.

Clear Light

Clear light is the direct experience of luminous-emptiness, our innate buddhanature, or rigpa. Some refer to it as bliss-emptiness, particularly in the context of these completion-stage practices. The "semblant" clear light realized in the experience of the four empties is a conceptual understanding based on our initial practices. The "actual" clear light is experienced through mastery of these practices and increasingly subtle experiences. Keep in mind that "clear light" refers to pure awareness or *rigpa*.

We may also experience clear light naturally at the time of going to sleep and waking (see dream yoga above) and at the time of death. In the latter case, the clear light experience from our practice is called the "child clear light," whereas the clear light of death is called the "mother clear light." If we recognize the clear light at that time, they are said to merge, like a mother and child, and we will attain enlightenment.

In the first session, you visualize yourself as Vajrayogini or the deity and consort in union. Light emanates from the HUNG at your heart *purifying the inanimate universe*, which melts into clear light that is absorbed into the animate universe, which melts into clear light that is absorbed into you as the Vajrayogini or deity and consort. You dissolve from the top down and bottom up to the HUNG in your heart chakra, which dissolves from the bottom up through the crescent, drop, and nada into emptiness. Hold your mind there, where you will again experience the four "empties," the last of which is the clear light. Remain absorbed in the clear light mind single-pointedly, giving rise to the actual clear light of Buddhahood. Afterwards, arise as Vajrayogini or deity and consort; then, if you like, re-enter your old aggregates (your physical body). Finally, envision the subtle mandala (now the size of an atom or

[handwritten margin note, left side]: in a mandala field

[handwritten note, bottom]: usually depicted as a cure & vajrayogini mandala

particle of dust) on a white lotus at the heart of the wisdom-being (jnanasattvas) inside your own heart chakra. Pulsating light of great compassion is generated from the clear light, manifesting countless emanations for the benefit of all beings.

In the second session, again visualize yourself as Vajrayogini or the deity and consort in union. Light rays from the HUNG at the heart radiate out and dissolve the mandala into emptiness. This gives rise to five signs of dissolving the elements. The sign of earth dissolving into water is a vision like mirage. Water into fire is a wispy blueness like smoke. Fire into air is like sparks or fireflies. Air into space is like the flame of a butter lamp. This is followed by four subtle visions of (1) whiteness as the white drop at the crown melts and descends to the heart, (2) redness as the red drop at the navel melts and ascends to the heart, (3) total darkness as the white and red drops meet at the indestructible drop, and (4) semblant clear light (a vision of luminous-emptiness) as both dissolve into the indestructible drop at the heart. Meditate on the clear light as long as you can. Continue the experience as you arise as Vajrayogini or deity and consort. This experience is similar to that at the time of death and helps prepare us to recognize the clear light of death and achieve enlightenment.

H.E. Garchen Rinpoche described the clear light yogas in this way:

Apart from sustaining mindfulness throughout the day and night there is no other clear light yoga. It begins with being able to sustain mindfulness throughout the day. When your mind is very clear and sharp during the day, eventually it will carry through the night. When you fall asleep continuing to sustain mindfulness, in a union of clear awareness and emptiness, you will first recognize the dream state. This recognition is called "recognizing the luminosity of the dream." Then eventually, through consistent mindfulness, even the dream state will disappear, and you will rest in clarity naturally; awareness will remain. Eventually clear awareness will even remain during the deep sleep state. It is like the illumination of a lamp flame. There are no thoughts, and there is a subtle feeling of your sleep's rest. This is accomplished when you sustain clear awareness continuously — remain free from the slightest distraction — throughout day and night.

Finally, in deep sleep you will recognize the clear light of deep sleep. What we call clear light is your ability to outshine thoughts and emotions or feelings with clear awareness. These thoughts, while arising, dissolve without having affected you or leaving a trace behind. A

beginning practitioner will sustain mindfulness sometimes, and then will
again become unmindful. This must first be overcome during the day.
You must first be able to destroy whatever habitual thoughts arise, then
habituate sustaining clear awareness. Then when you go to sleep, uphold
mindfulness by falling asleep practicing the OM AH HUNG Vajra
Recitation. At times you might remember the OM AH HUNG during the
dream state, and eventually mindfulness will remain even in the deep
sleep state.

Dissolution into Clear Light

The following practice transitions us into the clear light
experience – *dharmakaya*, the natural state or Truth Body of a buddha.
Initially, this is done as a daytime practice. Then, as explained by
Padmasambhava, this is also done as a dream yoga practice. Thus, our
prior experience with dream yoga is very important for achieving the
clear light in this practice. Later, you will see how it can be incorporated
into a regular sadhana practice in the Sadhana of the Red Dakini.

Week 35 — Dissolution into Clear Light

Practice nightly for one week or as needed.

Intention: During the day and before going to sleep, set your intention to
apprehend the dream state and transform them.

Instructions on Dreaming:

1st *session*:

Cultivate the spirit of awakening (altruistic intention or
bodhicitta).

Pray: "May I understand the clear light and dispel the
ignorance of self and others."

Lie in lion posture[125] with a white bindu in heart chakra.
Pray to realize the nature of mind … your buddhanature. Clear

---

[125] This is the posture assumed by the Buddha as he lay dying. Lie on your right side
with legs straight (or slightly bent, left on top of the right. Place the right hand on
the right side of your head as a support. (Some versions have you extend your
right elbow to support your head in a more upright position.)

light appears as you fall asleep and as you awaken, between the waking and dream states.

It is important to then recognize in the daytime, so that you will have the same experience when you die. We all have buddhanature; we just don't recognize it.

2nd session: Dissolution of consciousness

From clarity and emptiness, visualize:

> At the forehead, feel warmth – the dissolution of earth into water
> At the heart, a sinking feeling – the dissolution of water into fire
> In your mind, a feeling of agitation – the dissolution of fire into air
> Falling fast asleep – the dissolution of air into consciousness
> Focus on the heart and recognize the clarity and emptiness

Dispelling obstacles:

If it doesn't work, Khenchen Paljea Dorjee Rinpoche recommends sitting in the meditation posture before you go to sleep and meditate on buddhanature. Then do the main practice while falling asleep.

LUMINOUS EMPTINESS, SIMILAR TO OBJECTLESS SHAMATHA – ONE

Recognizing our buddhanature *and* surroundings is key ... the union of samsara and nirvana.

MIGHT TRY 4 EMPTIES PRACTICE

In a more elaborate process, from the experience of the semblant *HERE* clear light, the process is reversed through the black, red, and white lights until the vital energies return to the central channel and we again arise as Vajrayogini or the deity and consort. This body now appears as the impure illusory body, which re-enters our "course body" due to the force of karma that has not yet been completely purified. Your course body need not be abandoned if you choose to continue for the benefit of others – the bodhisattva ideal.

Mental isolation is achieved through *tummo* and *tsalung* with the four blisses and the four empties, as well as the dissolution into clear light. The "empties" manifest due to the dissolution of the winds into the heart. Mastery of these practices achieves the third stage of the completion-stage practices.

Actual Clear Light and Pure Illusory Body

After you have recognized the actual clear light, *dharmakaya*, in the previous practice, the winds stir slightly again and you arise as a *pure illusory body*, *sambhogakaya*. The pure illusory body is capable of manifesting emanation bodies, *nirmanakayas*, for the benefit of all beings. As noted above, the course body need not be abandoned if you choose to continue for the benefit of others. Pure illusory body is achieved primarily through complete mastery of the meditations on *tummo*, *tsalung*, and dream yoga described above.

The actual clear light is an experience that cannot be described in words. Any attempt to do so, while well intended, will fall short and mislead you. For this reason it is most helpful to have the guidance of a qualified master with whom to share your experience and seek guidance.

This is the focus of the next path, the Path of Great Perfection. It aims directly at the heart of the experience of clear light called *rigpa*. But before leaving the completion stage, I stated that I would give some further explanation on the practices of sexual yogas, most commonly associated with the completion-stage practices.

The Sexual Yogas of the Completion Stage

H.H. the Dalai Lama generally advises against using the sexual yogas of tantric practice. However, in *How to Practice: The Way to a Meaningful Life* he states,

> For Buddhists, sexual intercourse can be used in the spiritual path because it causes a strong focusing of consciousness, if the practitioner has firm compassion and wisdom. Its purpose is to manifest and prolong the deeper levels of mind in order to put their power to use in strengthening the realization of emptiness.

Previously we looked at two forms of sexual yogas in the generation stage practices: normal sex involving Pure View and enacting the generation stage yoga after having mastered the visualized practice. Here we add the sexual yoga practices of the completion stage. These are the "usual" sexual yogas of Tantra, noting that actual sexual yogas are anything but "usual" among monks and nuns, and even householders. Since lamas are the most common teachers of the Path of Tantra, there are few with knowledge and actual experience with the practices with an actual consort who can teach these practices. What follows is only an overview of these practices and does not provide the extensive detail that can be provided by a qualified master, if you can find one.

The Dakini[126]

As we saw in the ethics of the Path of Tantra, the 14th Root Downfall is abusing or deriding a woman, who is none other than the nature of wisdom. And according to Mipham Rinpoche, there are even statements in the sutras about pleasing the Buddha with a woman's body: "A Bodhisattva should transform his own body into a female body in order to please the Thus-Gone One and then always remain before the Thus-Gone One."

The *dakini* is very special, a symbol of all that is sacred and spiritual. (They can be male, though that is rare in the Buddhist literature.) Like so many things though, a dakini is not so simple to explain. When asked, Ven. Trungpa Rinpoche said, "One never knows." But I will try. The dakini (literally, sky-dancer) is a central religious symbol in Tibetan Buddhism. She is secretive and powerful, intimate and transformative. She is feminine in gender, but not a conventional female. Rather, she embodies the "feminine principle" or the wisdom of ultimate reality, beyond gender. (The masculine principle is "skillful means" – especially compassion and lovingkindness.) When depicted in sexual union with a yogi, they represent the nondual union with ultimate reality, i.e., the union of compassion and wisdom.

There are classifications of dakinis. *Worldly dakinis* are the human form. There are some very graphic historical descriptions of the dakini in "wrathful" forms, traces of which are still found in the Tibetan understanding. They "roam about, unaffiliated and untamed, creating chaos in many situations, fickle and terrifying. They embody worldly magic and power...." At the same time, they may also be helpful consorts. They may give guidance and teachings. The *wisdom dakini* is the symbol of mind itself. She also takes many forms: beautiful or ugly, gentle or harsh. Her fierceness is said to be the energy of wakefulness.

---

126 See *The Dakini's Warm Breath* by Judith Simmer-Brown for a more elaborate description.

She is often depicted as dancing naked – the quality of awareness itself – "with nothing to hide, [displaying] her secrets for all who have the wisdom to see." She wears ornaments from a charnel ground (graveyard), symbols (or warnings) derived from the early practice for monks of meditating on decaying bodies as a form of "aversion therapy" for sexual desires.

There are also four aspects. The *most secret* dakini is the ultimate nature of mind – naked awareness – the wisdom of ultimate reality. She is personified as Samantabhadri, the Great Mother, often depicted in union with Samantabhadra, the Primordial Buddha, who together represent the nondual ultimate.

The *secret* aspect is the realization of the wisdom of nonduality – bliss and emptiness, relative and ultimate as one. One may use lust or desire as one contemplates lust or desire itself to expose its true nature – its lack of inherent existence. Deity yoga and sexual yoga are practiced as a symbolic union to achieve the actual union of relative and ultimate *bodhicitta*.

The *inner* dakini is the subtle or illusory body, nondual wisdom manifesting in physical form as the dance of wisdom in the material world. The inner dakini is the mind's manifestation of the play of wisdom and its network of energy channels and "winds" or breath.

And the *outer* dakini is the human form – symbolic or actual consort. Of course there is the danger that she will arouse desire and its negative effects ... like playing with fire! One contemplates the nature of passion rather than pursuing passion, and thus it becomes a path toward liberation. Motivation is a key and sexual release is rejected.

Recognition of a dakini can be tricky. They are said to teach through actions rather than words, and to "speak in highly symbolic language." Either believing a person to be a dakini who is not or not recognizing one who is can be detrimental to one's spiritual progress. Encounters have "an intensely intimate quality ... sometimes expressed as a gift put directly in the practitioner's hand ... or evoked by a touch, a whisper, or a gaze...."

In addition, the dakini may be a human guru, a meditation deity, or a "protector" of the teachings. There are peaceful and wrathful versions. You can also think of the dakini as a spiritual messenger – one with whom you have a karmic connection. As a spiritual messenger, a dakini often teaches through actions. The messages may be intensely intimate, as are all genuine encounters with a dakini.

In *Sky Dancer*, the story of Yeshe Tsogyal, the dakini explains:

The Guru ... exhorted us to ultimate pleasure with this song of
     pleasure:

HRI! Through the light-rays of the supreme outflow that is no
     outflow,
From the Guru's *vajra*, the pleasure of desireless desire,
Into the sacred sky of the dakini, the supreme desire of no desire,
Now is the time to enjoy the profound secret of pure pleasure.

     ...

"SAMAYA HO!" exclaimed the Guru. "The bond is formed."
"SAMAYASTVAM!" I replied. "You are the bond!"
"SAMAYA HRI!" exclaimed the Guru. "The bond is all!"
"SAMAYA TISHTHA!" I replied. "The bond is strong."
"RAMO HAM!" exclaimed the Guru. "Let the fire burn!"
"RAGAYAMI!" I concluded. "We are burning together!"

Thus the Guru's *vajra* and the dakini's lotus were joined, and we
     entered a trance of union.

Tantra

The word *tantra* has many definitions and its real meaning may
be lost in antiquity, but generally refers to a class of mystical writings in
the Hindu and Buddhist traditions. Most do not involve sex. However,
sexual tantra continues to generate a great deal of interest, but often more
for its sexual implications than for its spiritual ones. Sexual misconduct is
one of the Buddhist ethical precepts, so some have regarded this practice
as dangerous. Indeed it can be, when sex itself becomes the focus there is
great danger that one may lose the sacred outlook or Pure View. In many
cases, actual sexual practice has been replaced with visualization practice
for this reason. Sexual tantra is not about sex. It is about the use of sex for
spiritual development. If followed, it leads *not* to "great sex," as is often
described in popular New Age literature, but to *transcending* sex itself –
no attachment, no aversion. It becomes a spiritual practice, not
necessarily better or worse than any other.

The value of using sex on the spiritual path is the high degree of
consciousness, of focus, experienced by the practitioner. To be of benefit
in spiritual practice, it is normally necessary that the practitioner already
have already achieved stability in relative and ultimate bodhicitta
through preliminary and generation-stage practices in order to prolong
the very deep, subtle and powerful states and put them to use to realize
the Pure View.

When the tantric yogas entered Buddhism, they became a way to accelerate the process of attaining these states. These practices were done by yogis and yoginis mostly in secret. But there was a problem. Monks and nuns were ordained celibates. They had taken vows prohibiting all sexual behaviors. The solution was to modify the practices, including some of the instructions, into a visualization process rather than engaging with an actual human partner. As previously noted, a visualized consort is called a *jnanamudra*. An actual partner is called a *karmamudra*. Nevertheless, many yogis and some monks and nuns engaged in *karmamudra* practice as a "Pure View" that did not violate any vows. The great yogi Padmasambhava brought these practices to Tibet around 800 CE. The practices flourished within the culture that consisted primarily of lay practitioners.

However, over the next 200 years in India, the practices became further modified to the point that *karmamudra* practice was almost entirely prohibited. The great Atisha is said to have prohibited his followers from even taking the empowerments for these practices for he considered even the visualization practices a violation of the monk and nun vows. Later, Tsongkapa said that one *must* do the *karmamudra* practices in order to attain enlightenment in this lifetime. However, as a monk, he elected not to violate his vows and, therefore, wait to attain enlightenment at the time of death. In some lineages, particularly the Nyingma, monks and nuns may use actual consorts by either giving up their vows of celibacy or redefining it as not having an orgasm during sexual yoga practices. Others give up being monks and nuns to become ordained lay practitioners – ngakpas and ngakmas respectively.[127]

Since we are unlikely to be celibate, Western householders are free to do these practices without the constraints for monks and nuns. Mipham Rinpoche says that to scorn the practice of *karmamudra* is a grave mistake, as it is an indispensable cause for the sudden dawning of co-emergent wisdom (bliss-emptiness). "To give them up, therefore, is said to be a root downfall of mantra." He cites the *Compendium of Vajra Wisdom* that states:

> One will not achieve the absorption of great bliss without being able to genuinely join the *bhaga* and *linga*.[128] Simply by having intense interest exclusively in the absorption of great

---

[127] Ngakpas and ngakmas often let their hair grow long and wear a robe with a broad white stripe down the center.

[128] Vagina and penis

bliss will lead one to the level of a beginner and the training
of a nonreturner.   ⅄ STREAM ENTERER

At the same time, there are some serious considerations that must be addressed. His Holiness the Dalai Lama recommends that these not be done, even by householders. Why? Because, as noted above, there is a significant risk of becoming attached to this practice in a way that can become harmful to one's spiritual development. So here is the irony. If you really *want* to do these practices, they are probably not a good idea, as this presents a high risk of creating obstacles for yourself. If you don't really want to or just don't care, they are probably a very good idea as they can be very powerful practices and you are not so likely to become attached to them.

There is also a "secret" form of empowerment (including the secret and wisdom empowerments) sometimes given to students prior to engaging in these practices. You would have to ask your lama about receiving these forms of empowerments. Most will say "No" or that it is not necessary. Details vary, of course. Briefly, this involves the lama having sex, including ejaculation, with the consort, while the initiate waits outside blindfolded. The initiate is then brought back into the room and the blindfold is removed. Seeing the outspread vagina of the consort arouses passion. The lama then uses the ring finger to collect and place a mixture of the semen and female fluids ("white and red drops") that is then placed on the tongue of the initiate, who swallows the sacred nectar. This completes the secret empowerment. The initiate and consort then join in union without orgasm while meditating on emptiness. The bliss of union completes the wisdom empowerment. Today, these are rarely performed in this way. Nearly all empowerments are done in a symbolic manner more appropriate for *jnanamudra* practices.

To engage in these practices one should have mastered the Highest Tantra Yoga generation and completion stage yogas, have Pure View, and have direct experience of transcendent wisdom. The consort, whether male or female, should ideally meet the *same* standards. Similar to the qualifications for doing *karmamudra* practice in the generation stage, the best consort is one who has also mastered the generation and completion-sage practices. A middling consort is one who has a good understanding of the generation and completion-stage practices with some experience, but has not yet mastered them. A lesser consort is one who has only rudimentary knowledge or experience, but who is willing to participate in the practice to benefit their partner. One should not engage in this form of sexual yoga with someone who has no knowledge or background in the generation and completion-stage practices. One should also be cautious of practicing with someone besides your own spouse or partner or practicing with someone else's spouse or partner due to potential relationship issues that may emerge. Practically speaking, this eliminates most possibilities.

Alternately, if a qualified consort is not available, the *Secret Vajravilasini Sadhana*[129] describes masturbation combined with visualization of the union of deity and consort as a way of practicing the sexual yogas. This may be a valid alternative for those who choose *karmamudra* but do not have an appropriate consort with whom to do the practice.

There is one other approach that has been used both historically and recently. There have been cases where the teacher has acted as the consort for the practitioner (or vice versa). However, this, too, can be problematic. In addition to "normal" relationship problems, jealousy from other sangha members or favoritism may result. Expectations beyond spiritual development are common. Other intimate relationships may be affected. Teachers have been known to manipulate students into engaging in sexual practices. Students have been known to seduce teachers. And this may be just the tip of the iceberg. (See also Chapter 4.)

Attachment may be the principle problem, but aversion may also be. The middle way can be a fine line. As noted before, Padmasambhava, who had several consorts and dakini teachers, is said to have stated, "My mind is vast as space, and my behavior is as fine as barley flour." Be careful and keep in mind that *by far* it is most common and successful to engage in the visualized practices without a physical consort.

That brings us to a very practical matter regarding the sexual yoga practices. To enter into sexual tantra with another, it is important to be very clear with each other regarding practice and expectations. One key element is a commitment to practice without orgasm. Some practitioners make this their only sexual experience, while others engage in regular intercourse periodically as well. Having periodic orgasms provides relief from the sexual tension that builds. However, it also creates a loss of the sexual energy that is the heart of the experience. As a practical matter, partners may choose a length of time or a number of sessions for this practice, or they may commit to the practice indefinitely. Just be prepared to discuss it openly and honestly, and be prepared that it may change (impermanence!).

---

[129] Described in Elizabeth English's *Vajrayogini: Her Visualizations, Rituals, and Forms*, pp. 86-94.

Finally, practitioners considering whether to engage in these practices need to be aware that doing them leads into what I call transcendent sex. In this state, one transcends desire or attachment to sex – no attachment, no aversion. In other words, you may simply lose the desire. You become indifferent. Is this what you want? What about your partner? Consider this carefully as it may have significant implications for your relationship.

The Practices

If you carefully consider yourself and your partner to be qualified and have had the appropriate empowerments, then there are several possibilities. As previously described, the first potential practice derives from the fact that as householders we are likely to engage in sexual behaviors anyway. So the most basic sexual yoga is for both partners to remain in Pure View throughout these activities. Even this may transform your experience. The second method is used during the generation stage practices after the visualization practice has been mastered. Here you simply engage with your consort *as* the deity and consort in union while doing the meditation. The third form of practice is after having mastered the completion-stage practices of tummo, illusory body, and clear light, you continue these practices but in union with a qualified physical consort. The fourth practice is done during the third vision of togal practice in a similar manner.

In preparation for the *karmamudra* practice, you remove your clothing, though one or both of you may choose to wear a prayer shawl. Preparatory activities may lead up to the actual practice, such as those described earlier in this book. Next the partners enter into the meditative state. For example, a bell may be used to begin this phase, followed by reciting the sadhana and visualizing the deities, while sitting facing each other. Instructions may vary, but after reciting the mantra, you engage in kissing, touching, and fondling each other to stimulate arousal.

The yogi then offers the yogini the "kiss" of the union of *vajra* and *lotus*. Although the traditional *yab-yum* position involves the female sitting on the lap of the male, she may need to sit on a thick pillow or cushion for support. Otherwise another comfortable position may be used. The choice is personal, not spiritual. Couples may choose to change from time to time during the tantric session. Same-sex couples[130] need

---

130 Although one can find prohibitions of homosexuality in a few Buddhist texts, as in most ancient religions, they do not accord with the principle of Pure View.

only use their imagination to join in union. The practitioners maintain their Pure View throughout. The session ends once the mind is distracted from that view.

Having generated the deity and recited the mantra using a *jnanamudra*, you now practice *tummo* as the deity in union with the *karmamudra*. The vital energies (winds) enter the central channel and dissolve. Attention is focused on the top and bottom of the central channel as you engage in the practices of the four blisses. The bliss of sexual inner heat pervades the whole body. Maintaining nonconceptual awareness, the partners maintain meditative equipoise while "churning" to arouse and mingle the "red" and "white" sexual fluids (without ejaculation[131]) to produce increasingly subtle states of bliss by controlling the winds (vital essences) moving up and down the central channel in conjunction with the in and out breath. While some sources advocate sustaining this stage, it is only an intermediate step. You then continue with the four empties into innate bliss-emptiness in which great bliss is united with emptiness through further meditation in stillness of body, speech, and mind.

Finally, you engage in the *clear light rigpa* practice retaining the union of bliss-emptiness, while maintaining a nonconceptual state of mind. This is a meditative practice where stillness is preferred and an erection is no longer necessary. Feel the oneness of union, but *pure awareness* is critical. Male and female are transcended. Self and other are surpassed, and you experience the semblant (imagined) clear light of *rigpa*.

As the end of the practice session approaches, the partners – still in meditative equipoise – remain quiet and abide in Pure View as the male erection subsides and withdraws from the female, if that has not already happened, and we arise as the impure illusory body. Continue to abide softly and conclude by reciting the closing prayers. Then slowly arise and softly continue with your daily activities while the sexual energy of bliss-emptiness continues, even for extended periods.

---

[131] There are a few exceptions, and some sources indicate that the female *should* experience orgasm, while the male does not. This appears to be related to a concept found in other sources of tantra that the female energy is absorbed into the male, while the male energy is retained. I personally do not like the idea of the consort (male or female) being "used" for the benefit of the other party, and strongly advocate for a position of equanimity and transcendence of sexual desire throughout the practice without orgasm for both parties.

Over time the depth and breadth of the tantric sexual experience increases, becoming more sacred, more ultimate. Partners may limit the practice to penetration without movement. They may sit or lie together without penetration. Or they may even sit or lie together, making love spiritually without even touching.

The desire for sex decreases for longer periods of time and may be transcended entirely. You may then continue the practice as part of the spiritual path, but *karmamudra* is no longer necessary, just living in Pure View. As you progress along the path, you transcend ego and desire, leaving nothing needed. No attachment, no aversion.

Appendix C contains the Sadhana of the Red Dakini, Red Simhamukha – the Lion-Faced Dakini. This is a *sambhogakaya*, completion-stage practice that includes instructions on engaging with a *karmamudra*, though it may also be done with a *jnanamudra*. A short, daily practice is also included, though it is only appropriate for use with a *jnanamudra*.

The Bardos of the Intermediate State

Bardo means in-between. Any timeframe can be a bardo. This life is a bardo. But most of us familiar with the term think of it as the time between death and rebirth. This is called the Bardo of Becoming, although this is preceded by the lesser known Bardo of Dharmata. In addition to training our mind for achieving enlightenment in this life, we are also training the mind in preparation for the dying and rebirth process ... just in case. The Dzogchen Ponlop Rinpoche humorously calls it "Plan B." The Bardos of Dharmata and Becoming are said to last around 49 days[132], most of it falling into the latter bardo.

The practices described in this book were taken largely from the six bardo teachings of Padmasambhava. In the root text, he describes

---

[132] There is a vast array of texts and rituals in Tibet related to death and rebirth. The *Tibetan Book of the Dead* represents only one, albeit the best known in the West. For example, another approach uses similar processes but with a cycle of 7 days repeated up to 7 times until one is reborn. Both the *Tibetan Book of the Dead* and *Natural Liberation* are attributed to Padmasambhava, but are said to have be "found treasures" (*termas*), both by Karma Lingpa (1326-1386), a "treasure revealer" (*tulku*).

these six as the bardos of (1) this life, (2) meditation, (3) dreaming, (4) dying, (5) Dharmata, and (6) Becoming. The practices work for both Plan A – to achieve enlightenment in this life – and Plan B – to be prepared for the process of death and dying. Regarding the latter, this helps familiarize us with the process so that we do not find it frightening, as well as preparing us to take advantage of numerous opportunities to become enlightened during these bardos after dying and before rebirth.

Among these practices is the *very* important practice of *Guru Yoga*, which focuses on unifying our mind with that of the lama or guru. That is, we achieve the same realization of transcendent wisdom as the guru. Another practice is transference, in which we practice joining our consciousness with that of the deity just before the moment of death in order to transfer to a *pure land* or Buddhafield and continue our progress toward enlightenment under more idealized circumstances in order to benefit all beings. This is the practice of transference (*phowa*) that is explained later. A third group of practices are the *deity yogas*, divided into generation and completion stages. First we learn to visualize increasingly detailed images of a buddha to train our mind's ability to abide in single-pointed calm abiding more rapidly than other methods, as well as visualizing ourselves as that buddha. This prepares us for the completion stage in which we complete the process of realizing transcendent wisdom and becoming a buddha. This also helps familiarize us with peaceful and wrathful images that otherwise appear frightening during the latter part of the Bardo of Dharmata, but are actually manifestations of our own mind. These appearances are also opportunities to achieve enlightenment. Finally, the practices of *Dzogchen* are used to develop certainty in transcendent wisdom in this life, as well as to prepare to the appearance of the clear light of awakening in the first part of the Bardo of Dharmata, what is often referred to as enlightenment at the moment of death.

What follows is a brief description of the Bardos of Dying, Dharmata, and Becoming. As just noted, our previous practices have included preparation for the experience of these bardos. In addition, Padmasambhava has included some additional practices to help avert rebirth into *samsara* in the event that we have not attained enlightenment in this life, the process of dying, or the experience of *dharmata*.

The Bardo of Dying

In the *Root Verse of the Bardo of Dying*, Padmasambhava States,

Now when the Bardo of Dying dawns upon me, I will abandon all grasping, yearning, and attachment, enter undistracted into clear awareness of the teaching, and eject my consciousness into the space of unborn rigpa; as I leave this compound body of flesh and blood, I will know it to be a transitory illusion..

In the Bardo of Dying, we go through two phases of dissolution previously mentioned – the external dissolution of the elements and the internal dissolution of consciousness. These have been summarized in the practice of dissolution into clear light. However, there are more complex processes involved. Some of these, involving the outer dissolution of the body, are summarized in the following table:

Outer Dissolution				
Element	Aggregate	Sense	Feeling	Appearances
Earth	Form	Seeing	Sinking	Mirage
Water	Feelings	Hearing	Drying	Smoke
Fire	Perceptions	Smelling	Weakening	Fireflies
Wind	Thoughts	Tasting	Breathing stops	Butter lamp

The "appearances" are those used in the dissolution into clear light practice. This is also a time when a dying practitioner trained in transference of consciousness can engage in this practice, or a trained person can do it for them. If there are signs of success, the person will not enter the next bardo. Rather, their consciousness will go to a buddhafield in which they can continue to practice until attaining enlightenment and manifest in forms to help other beings.

At the end of the outer dissolution, breathing stops and we are considered to have died in the Western view. In the Tibetan view the consciousness is still aware. During that time, we undergo the inner dissolution of the consciousness outlined in the following table:

Inner Dissolution of Consciousness	
Cause	Sign
White bodhicitta drop descends from crown to heart chakra	Sky-like white light
Red drop ascends from navel to heart	Sky-like red light
Red and white drops merge at the heart	Sky-like total darkness, loss of consciousness
Red and white drops enter the indestructible drop at the heart	Sky-like dawn of actual clear light

These "signs" are also included in the dissolution into clear light practice. So that practice helps us prepare for the possibility of the bardo experience. Reciting *The Tibetan Book of the Dead – Liberation on Hearing* is said to help guide the individual through the following death experiences and reduce their fear. Once the person goes unconscious, this may last for a period of up to three and a half days. Bardo "days" are considered to be shorter or longer than our days, so it is difficult to know at any point in time after death what the consciousness is experiencing. For this reason, the entire *Liberation on Hearing* may be read daily through the 49 days that the experience may last to help guide the consciousness through the bardo experience.[133]

The Bardo of Dharmata

The Bardo of Dharmata begins with the appearance of actual clear light – pure awareness (*rigpa*). It has no specific qualities, although it is sometimes described as "luminosity." The empty nature – "beyond any inherent existence in any respect whatsoever" – is represented by Samantabhadri, the female Primordial Buddha. The manifest nature – "unimpededly radiant, brilliant, and vibrant" – is represented by Samantabhadra, the male Primordial Buddha. The two are inseparable, much like a statue of them in union that appears to be two figures but is actually a single form. If we have done these practices, and recognize the clear light, we will attain enlightenment. The length of its appearance is said to relate to our ability to sustain the experience of clear light during our meditation practice. Thus, longer meditation experience increases the opportunity to recognize it and attain enlightenment at that time.

If we fail to recognize the clear light, the second part of the Bardo of Dharmata manifests as an appearance of the Five Buddha Families in an awesome display of sounds, colored lights, and rays of light. The following table gives a few highlights of these intense experiences, each lasting one day. They are "subtle and clear, radiant and dazzling, naturally bright and awesome light, shimmering like a mirage" and are accompanied by sounds that are "clear and thunderous, reverberating

---

[133] As a practical matter, families are expected to make donations to the lamas or ngakpas to perform these services, as well as care for them during this time. The retinue may include several people. Thus, some families are only able to support a more abbreviated form of this practice. In addition, some lineages believe the bardo is a process that is repeated every seven days until enlightenment or rebirth. So a single seven-day ritual may be used.

like a thousand simultaneous peals of thunder." Each Buddha and consort is accompanied by two sets of male and female bodhisattvas.

The Five Buddha Families

Element	Light Color	Buddha	Body Color	Intense Light	Wisdom	Aggregate	Dull Light	Realm
Space	Blue	Vairocana	White	Blue	Darmadhatu	Conscious-	White	Gods
Water	White	Akshobya-Vajrasattva	Blue	White	Mirror-like	Form	Smoky	Hells
Earth	Yellow	Ratna-sambhava	Yellow	Yellow	Equanimity	Feeling	Blue	Human
Fire	Red	Amitabha	Red	Red	Discrimina-ting	Perceptions	Yellow	Hungry Ghosts
Wind	Green	Amogha-siddhi	Green	Green	All-Accomplishing	Thoughts[134]	Red	Demi-gods

---

[134] Terminology varies for this aggregate, e.g., some use "mental formations." The *Tibetan Book of the Dead* uses "motivational tendencies."

Each element manifests as light, which then emerges as the Buddha. As each deity appears, the intense light emerges from the heart of the deity. It is so intense that we cannot look at it and tend to be drawn toward the dull light instead. If we recognize the intense light as the wisdom of the Buddha and a manifestation of our own mind, we will be liberated. If instead we are attached to the dull light based on our karmic tendencies, we will be reborn in that realm. Familiarity through practice helps us to recognize the Buddha and attain enlightenment. Confusion or fear results in the appearance of the next, and so forth. This is followed by an appearance of all five Buddha Families appear along with other orbs of light in sets of five in an attempt to help us achieve liberation. Sheets of radiant light appear with rays from the heart of the respective Buddha to our heart, except green from Amoghasiddhi because we have not yet perfected the all-accomplishing wisdom of Amoghasiddi.

Failure to attain enlightenment here leads to the next part in which each of the 48 Peaceful Deities appear sequentially as before, each being an opportunity to recognize them and attain enlightenment. Together, these parts last about seven days. Signs of liberation to this point include: a cloudless sky, rainbows, shower of flowers, fragrance of perfume, music in the sky, relics, images, rainbow lights and so forth in the funeral pyre.

If this fails, the third part of the Bardo of Dharmata is the appearance of the 52 Wrathful Deities, another series of opportunities for enlightenment. All of these opportunities are afforded through extensive deity practice in training our mind, developing familiarity. All of these opportunities are the Buddhas giving us help to achieve enlightenment! This part lasts another five days. If we fail at *all* of these opportunities, we will then face the terrifying Yama – Lord of Death.

The Bardo of Becoming

The appearance of Yama marks the beginning of the Bardo of Becoming. There is a counting of your virtuous and non-virtuous behaviors (*karma*). The first half of what follows is a review of your life experiences similar to those described in Western culture death experiences, lasting about 18 days. Your mental body experiences these in a greatly exaggerated manner.

The second half of this experience hints at your future rebirth. You are drawn toward environments which reflect one of the six realms (hells, hungry ghosts, animals, humans, demi-gods, and gods) in which you will be born. At the end of this, you approach the entrance to the womb and your rebirth. But wait! There are yet additional opportunities to use your practice to opt out of rebirth and attain enlightenment. These are the additional practices provided by Padmasambhava to assist us with this process.

Closing the Entrance to the Womb

If you are now one who meditates on a divine embodiment, when the visions of the transitional process arise – such as snow and rain, a blizzard, and the appearance of being chased by many people – as soon as you recall the clear appearance of the deity, all those will arise as your chosen deity.[135]

Padmasambhava recommends several techniques. Closing the entrance to the womb:

As a divine embodiment
By imagining your spiritual mentor with consort
With the practice of the Four Blisses
With the antidote of renunciation
With the clear light
With the illusory body

Closing the entrance to the womb as a divine embodiment has two parts: (1) blocking the person who is entering and (2) blocking the entrance of the womb that is to be entered. This is based on the generation-stage practices. In this case, you imagine that you have died and become aware of the transition process (*bardo*). You arise as the deity with Pure View. Focusing on the generation-stage visualization will close the womb and you will achieve enlightenment. In addition, Padmasambhava says to practice in this way:

If you see people or animals copulating, or you see a beautiful woman [or man] being attracted to you, as soon as passion arises for her [him], think, "Alas! Having wandered about in the transitional

---

[135] *Natural Liberation*, p. 257.

process of Becoming, I a preparing to enter a womb. So now I shall close the entrance to the womb."[136]

Specifically, to block the person who is entering, if you have not yet been liberated and are taking rebirth as a male, when you see a couple copulating, jealousy arises toward the male and passion for the female. If you are taking rebirth as a female, jealousy arises toward the female and passion for the male. But when you recall yourself as the deity, without rejecting passion, you will be liberated.

Similarly, to block the entrance of the womb that is to be entered, when you see any man and woman in sexual union and passion and jealousy arise, arise as the deity and turn away, thinking clearly of the deity and mandala with Pure View.

Closing the entrance to the womb by imagining your spiritual mentor with consort involves imagining Padmasambhava and Yeshe Tsogyal in union when seeing sexual intercourse. Replace the jealousy and passion with reverence and devotion for the guru and his consort. Imagine receiving the four empowerments, especially the meaning of the third or wisdom empowerment of bliss-emptiness, and you will close the entrance to the womb.

Closing the entrance to the womb with the practice of the Four Blisses uses the previous practice of the Four Blisses to close the womb during the bardo. As above, when you recognize that you are in the transition process and see the male and female copulating, recall the bliss-emptiness and you will be liberated. This is considered "more profound and swift than other tantras." Therefore, he says that you should not worry about "what other people will say ... for that is the main part of the practice of the transitional process. Thus, it is important to seek out a qualified consort and train in the profound path of bliss."[137]

Closing the entrance to the womb with the antidote of renunciation is recommended for lay vow-holders, novice monks, and fully ordained monks "who cherish their vows." The idea comes from the Path of Individual Liberation, in which monks were sent to charnel grounds to see and meditate upon rotting corpses as an antidote to being attracted to the human body in any form. Here we are advised whenever we see

---

[136] *Ibid.*, p. 259.

[137] *Ibid.*, p. 264.

sexual intercourse or recall an object of passion to imagine the blood, fat, tissue, bones, and the like to counteract the attraction.

Closing the entrance to the womb with the clear light is based on the previous practice of dissolution into the clear light, as well as the *Dzogchen Trekcho* practices from the Path of Great Perfection that we have yet to learn. Ideally, one recognizes the actual clear light at the beginning of the Bardo of Dharmata and attains enlightenment at that time. But even for "the least of individuals," the experience of "the clear light will vividly arise when they witness sexual intercourse during the transitional process of Becoming, and they will be liberated."[138]

Closing the entrance to the womb with the illusory body follows a similar process. Having trained in the illusory body practices, you see the entrance to the womb as just an illusion. As this arises in your mind-stream, you will be liberated. All appearances, including this one, are like reflections in a mirror; they appear yet are empty at the same time. Appearances in the transitional process of the bardo are no different. They appear like a dream, none other than manifestations of the clear light of primordial wisdom.

These are also done as contemplation practices during the day to reinforce the practices that support them. So it can be helpful to take some time each day to reflect on one or more of these visualizations to help prepare for this possibility in the transition (*bardo*).

Transference of Consciousness - *Phowa*

The next completion stage practice is called transference of consciousness or *phowa*. As previously noted, this is done when it becomes clear that we have entered the Bardo of Dying to transfer our consciousness to a pure buddhafield through the heart of our practice deity. The most common deity used for this purpose is *Amitabha* – the Buddha of Boundless Light – and his pureland of *Dewachen*.

Lamas sometimes recommend not doing this practice if you have already done so and experienced the "signs" of accomplishment. However, others recommend that they be done occasionally to refresh

---

[138] *Ibid.*, p. 267.

your skill and to keep them in mind, as we never know when the moment of death will occur. Lamas also recommend that the practice be followed by a long-life practice such as White Tara or *Amitayus* (see Appendix D). After the initial training in transference, three variations are explained based upon one's level of practice and realization.

Week 36 — Transference of Consciousness (*Phowa*)

Practice twice daily for one week, or once daily for three weeks.

Intention: I do this practice for the benefit of all sentient beings (*or other personal intention*).

Preliminaries: Recite the brief Ngondro preliminary practice, with prostrations.

Purification: Repeat the purification breaths as before.

Transference Mind Training:

Visualization

> Block the apertures with dark blue HUNGs emanating from your heart: anus, "aperture of becoming" (genitals), urinary tract, navel, mouth, nostrils, eyes, ears; upside down white HAM blocks crown.

> Your central channel is inflated and white with a yellow sheen.

> There is a white bindu below your navel chakra (at convergence of central and side channels).

> A smiling Guru, *Vajradhara*, is above your crown.

Activity

Forcefully close your anus.

Look up.

Place your tongue on your palate (roof of your mouth).

Make fists with your thumbs inside (vajra fist), and press them into your groin on either side.

Draw the white bindu upwards.[139]

---

[139] Alternately, it is often taught to draw the bindu upwards with up with seven HIKs and down with one long "KAaaaaaaaah."

> Say "HIK KA" seven times — to navel.
>
> Say "HIK KA" seven times — to heart.
>
> Say "HIK KA" seven times — to throat.
>
> Say "HIK KA" seven times — to head (eyebrow level).
>
> Say "HIK KA" one time — to crown.
>
> The bindu descends to below your navel.
>
> Relax and check for signs.

Stop if signs are present; otherwise, repeat the practice as above.

Dedication: With the mind of enlightenment, Bodhicitta, I dedicate all merit from this practice for the enlightenment of all sentient beings. (3X)

Train until signs appear, such as an "oily warmth at the Brahma aperture [top of the head, said to be eight finger-widths from the hair line], prickliness, itchiness, numbness, swelling, and softness on the crown of the head."[140] It is beneficial to do this with a qualified lama who can check the external signs at the crown of your head. Follow the practice with a long-life practice such as White Tara or *Amitayus* (see Appendix D).

The actual practices at the time of death depend upon the experience of the dying person. The following three variations are normally done only after death is certain, but the person has not lost consciousness. However, Padmasambhava recommends that doing the *nirmanakaya* practice for another be done after the loss of consciousness.

Nirmanakaya Transference

At this point, you have advanced beyond this practice. However, it is included here as a practice that may be done for others who have not yet done generation-stage practice. It is best if this is done as soon as possible after the dying person has lost consciousness, but before breathing has stopped.

---

140 *Natural Liberation*, p. 199.

Lay out offerings ... or visualize them. (May offer your body, speech and mind.)

Lie on right side and visualize a *nirmanakaya* buddha in front of you.

[handwritten: → a manifest form e.g.: Shakyamuni buddha]

With sincere yearning pray, "May I take rebirth as a *nirmanakaya* for the sake of all sentient beings."

[handwritten: → or he/she for another.]

Below the navel visualize a 3-sided pyramid, and a pink *bindu* just inside the central channel.

[handwritten: point down + bindu just above]

Close the lower aperture and draw the *bindu* upwards with "HIK KAs" to the opening of the left nostril where it shoots out like an arrow into the heart of the deity in front of you.

Repeat without letting your consciousness move from the heart of the deity.

The exit through the nostril is very unusual. It is more common to visualize the *bindu* shooting up through the crown of the head into the heart of the deity. However, Padmasambhava appears here to consider that the corpse is no longer upright, so the exit of the *bindu* exits toward the deity visualized in front of the face of the deceased.

Sambhogakaya Transference

Now we continue with the *sambhogakaya* transference for those who do generation stage practice, but with little comprehension of emptiness.

Visualize your meditation deity above your head and white bindu or seed syllable at lower opening of central channel.

Block the apertures with dark blue HUMs and an upside down HAM at the crown.

Close lower aperture and roll eyes upward and press tongue against the roof of the mouth.

Draw lower energies up through central channel with "HIK KAs."

The Brahma aperture opens and your consciousness shoots out like an arrow into the heart of your deity. [Do not do this step as a practice, only at the time of actual death.]

Repeat without letting your consciousness descend.

Rest in the natural, nonobjective state.

Dharmakaya Transference — Dean's favorite - associated w/ dzogchen

The *dharmakaya* transference is for those confident in practice of the clear light.

Altruistic motivation is very important.

perform until signs appear

Visualize a white AH at your heart.

Imagine it floating upward like a feather lifted by a gentle wind.

It moves up through the top of your head to the heart of your guru. [Do not do this step as a practice, only at the time of actual death.] *skip*

after

Your mind is united with the mind of your guru.

Leave your awareness without fabrication, vivid, unwaveringly steady, nakedly clear and empty.

signs appear

If your breath stops in that state, the mother and child clear light meet and you will achieve liberation. "The outer sign of success is that the sky becomes immaculate; the inner sign is that the luster of the body does not vanish for a long time, and it has a clear complexion; and the secret signs include the appearance of a white AH and a dark blue HUNG."[141]

the other way around from standard guru yoga practice

---

[141] *Ibid.*, p. 212.

Signs of Accomplishment in the Completion Stage

The completion stage is characterized by attaining a state of bliss-emptiness, with the achievement of pure illusory body and actual clear light, usually at the time of death. The final three stages of this process outlined at the beginning of the completion stage instructions are:

1. *Impure illusory body and semblant clear light* – through illusory body and clear light practices, one further refines the impure illusory body, and experiences the semblant clear light.

2. *Pure illusory body and actual clear light* – through further illusory body and clear light practices, one manifests the pure illusory body and directly realizes the actual clear light of luminous emptiness.

3. *Learner's union* – through union with the consort (real or imagined), actual clear light and pure illusory body merge and one achieves buddhahood. Our ordinary body, speech, and mind have been transformed into the body, speech, mind of a buddha – luminous, empty, and blissful. This *bliss-emptiness* is a transcendent bliss beyond feeling. It is the stillness or deep inner peace experience of emptiness – *innate happiness*. There is no attachment or aversion.

Chapter 16

The Third Training on
the Path of Tantra: Wisdom

The Rangtong Prasangika Madhyamaka
Approach

dzogchen is also in madhyamaka tradition

Unlike the Svatantrikas (Chapter 10), the Prasangikas refute self-nature without trying to establish the true nature by reasoning at all. That is, the Prasangikas simply argue that self-nature cannot be established, period. The relative is simply accepted as a "perceptual reality" having no true basis. They argue that the attempt to establish emptiness through reasoning is a subtle attempt to grasp the ultimate nature with the conceptual mind. Therefore they refuse to use any reasoning to establish the true nature of phenomena. They say that the ultimate nature is beyond even the most subtle of concepts. They posit nothing is either positive or negative.

Whereas the Shravakans and Cittamatrans (Chapter 7) believed that one moment gave rise to the next, Chandrakirti argued that no connection exists between one moment and the next. Otherwise darkness could be the cause of light or light the cause of darkness. But things do arise. For the Prasangikas, the arising of things is mere relative appearance dependent upon consciousness. There is no arising in the absolute, which is all that matters.

The Prasangikas (who do follow this approach) hold views concerning the nature of relative phenomena. They use reasoning to establish that relative phenomena exist conventionally, just not on their own. Other Prasangikas doubt whether this can be considered to be Prasangika at all. The original Prasangika view refutes *all* views without asserting any counter-argument to establish a view of their own. It is completely non-conceptual. One simply rests in emptiness, the absolute freedom from all concepts.

The Prasangika view of the dream example is that there is no concept of "real" or "unreal" in a dream. There is no concept of "self-nature" or "absence of self-nature" either. Thus, mind rests in total peace.

In practice, this direct approach can be challenging. Thus, it is recommended to use the Svatantrika approach to establish emptiness first. Then use the Prasangika to cut through the conceptual mind completely. Relative and ultimate truths are mere concepts. Ignorance cannot exist in an awareness without concepts. Jamgon Kongtrul Rinpoche recommended using analysis only briefly, then resting the mind free of concepts. Je Tsongkhapa says that one must return to analysis over and over to establish a strong, long-lasting, clear and steady view of emptiness. One then alternates between analysis and serenity until this gives rise to the union of the two (one taste).

Week 37 — Rangtong Prasangika Madhyamaka

Practice twice daily for one week, or once daily for three weeks.

Intention: I do this practice for the benefit of all sentient beings (*or other personal intention*).

Preliminaries: Recite the brief Ngondro preliminary practice, with prostrations.

Purification: Repeat the purification breaths as before.

Rangtong Prasangika Madhyamaka:

Settle into stillness of body, speech and mind. Think about the nature of emptiness beyond thoughts or labels of any kind. Yet it exists. Self and all phenomena also appear, but are empty in nature. Then simply let mind rest naturally in the vast, spacious emptiness of mahamudra.

Conclude by resting naturally in your confidence without thoughts. *Let go and let be.* Sit in stillness as long as you can.

Dedication: With the mind of enlightenment, Bodhicitta, I dedicate all merit from this practice for the enlightenment of all sentient beings. (3X)

Post-meditation: *Between sessions, let whatever arises subside on its own like waves becoming still by themselves. Even with strong passions and sufferings, as well as when you are happy, let the mind rest naturally.*

Signs of Accomplishment

Pure View

One sign is attaining Pure View – seeing all beings as buddhas, hearing all sounds as mantras, recognizing all thoughts as the wisdom of the buddhas, and seeing all phenomena as a perfect buddhafield. The extent to which one has mastered this sacred outlook is an indicator of accomplishment. Note that such a view is still conceptual, thus, it is still a conventional perspective, not ultimate truth. However, it is an entirely different view of conceptual phenomena than most people experience.

Conduct

In the Path of Tantra, your conduct or activities between formal meditation sessions are also a sign of accomplishment. One who is perfect on the cushion, but shows little realization in daily activities is only a great meditator, not a realized being. In other words, everything we think, say, and do embodies our practice. *Everything* is practice. Mipham Rinpoche says, "Activities of the ensuing attainment are in harmony with the practice of view and meditation."

Even our formal meditation is enriched through support activities. Mipham Rinpoche describes it this way:

> It also includes entering and meditating on the profound mandala, drawing images of the mandala, receiving and bestowing empowerment, abiding by the samayas, performing approach and accomplishment, making offerings to please the deities, accomplishing enlightened activity, reciting mantras, and holding mudras. *Not just ritual, but support.*

Pure Illusory Body and Actual Clear Light

Although difficult to achieve during this lifetime, this is the goal of the Path of Tantra. The degree to which we have achieved these is an indicator of our accomplishment, as described in the previous chapter. To master them completely is to become a buddha.

Bliss-Emptiness

In the Path of Individual Liberation we learned the *appearance-emptiness* of self and other, i.e., their lack of inherent existence. We learned to see all phenomena as an illusion, that is does not truly exist the way that it appears. All phenomena have no independent existence, they are not partless, and they are not permanent. *clarifying*

In the Path of Altruism we directly experienced the *luminous-emptiness* of Nagarjuna's tetra-dilemma – emptiness is not a thing, it is not no-thing, it is not both, and it is not neither. This great paradox provides clarity through that direct experience beyond concepts and labels. It just is.

Here in the Path of Tantra we experienced the transcendence of sexual desire and other sensory desires into transcendent *bliss-emptiness*. Rather than discarding afflictive emotions, we embraced them through tantric transformation.

Physical bliss begins with bliss intermingled with emotions and then bliss free from emotions, permeating the entire body until every type of touch feels utterly blissful. Mental bliss is the complete absence of mental uneasiness and includes countless different types of delight and pleasure. Bliss will be experienced as the insight that pleasure is insubstantial and there is an absence of hankering after its taste. This is the bliss of *innate happiness*.

Part 6 –The Path of Great Perfection

The Path of Great Perfection, Dzogchen, is the highest level of practice in Tibetan Buddhism, where it is often included as a part of the Path of Tantra. However, here I have described it as a separate path as the practices are generally quite different than those on the Path of Tantra. The root texts, however, are often labeled as "tantras" nevertheless.

The Path of Great Perfection is also known as the Path of Self-Liberation. So far in this course, I described the Paths of Individual Liberation, Altruism, and Tantra. Some texts describe them as the paths of renunciation, antidote, and transformation respectively. The Path of Great Perfection is that of self-liberation. In the Nyingma lineage, that perspective pervades even the Highest Yoga Tantra deity practices. One is viewed as already *being* a buddha. There is no need to "transform" yourself as in the *sarma* lineages. There is no "impure" body, speech or mind as they are already "pure" by virtue of being a buddha. The task is to *realize* that we are already a buddha, a fact that is obscured by our fundamental ignorance of the nature of mind, and its many manifestations. As these obscurations are allowed to "self-liberate," we come to recognize the state of "great perfection" that is not other than our pure natural state, as it is!

Semde, Longde, Mengagde

No one knows for sure where the great perfection (*dzogchen* or *ati yoga*) teachings originated. There is even some archeological evidence that it may have preceded the historical buddha. There are also similarities with other systems of practice and philosophy such as *chan* and *Taoism* in China and *zen* in Japan.

Within Tibetan Buddhism, the Path of Great Perfection is said to have originated from the Primordial Buddha – Samantabhadra. Although the exact lineage varies among different sources, "he" passed it on to directly (or through Vajrasattva) to the first human recipient of the teachings, Garab Dorje (1st century CE). Garab Dorje then passed it on to Manjushrimitra (2nd century CE), who passed it on to Shri Simha (3rd century CE), who then passed it on to Padmasambhava, Vimalamitra, and Vairochana (all late 8th century CE). Obviously there are some time gaps that are filled, according to the tradition, through very long lives.

Manjushrimitra is said to have divided the teachings into three classes or series. The "mind class" (*semde*) and "space class" (*longde*) were transmitted by Vairochana. The secret or "special instruction class" (*mengagde*) was transmitted by Padmasambhava and Vimalamitra. Padmasambhava's instructions became known as the *Khandro Nyingtik*; Vimalamitra's instructions became known as the *Vima Nyingtik*. These two texts were later documented by Longchen Rabjam or simply Longchenpa (14th century CE), along with his own commentary on each and a fifth unifying text. A somewhat condensed version was later created by Jigmed Lingpa (1730-1798) after visions of Longchenpa that he received in retreat, which he wrote down as the *Longchen Nyingtik*, probably the best known and most used version of these teachings.

The mind class teachings address the nature of mind in a way that is not all that different than what is found in the Path of Altruism, particularly the Middle Way teachings of Nagarjuna, as well as the Path of Tantra. The space class teachings focus on the direct experience of emptiness as being like space – vast and open without center or boundaries. The special instruction teachings are divided into two parts known as *trekcho* and *togal*. These two are the main teachings given today, along with a series of preliminary practices.

Khorde Rushen –Preliminary Practices

The preliminary practices associated with the Path of Great Perfection are directed at the separation of "samsara" from "nirvana." Basically, the idea is for the practitioner to develop a direct experiential understanding of the difference between these two concepts … and then transcend even those. In some teachings these are completed prior to beginning with the practice of either *trekcho* or *togal*. In other teachings, they are divided into two parts, one set to be completed prior to doing *trekcho* and the other prior to doing *togal*. And, of course, there are also teachings in which all of the practices are done following the practice of *trekcho* and prior to the practice of *togal*. These practices are not included in the six bardo teachings of Padmasambhava, but are included in his

Kandro Nyingtik. Therefore, I have chosen to include them here and as preliminary to both *trekcho* and *togal.* The exact practices vary by source.

Trekcho

Trekcho views the nature of mind as *rigpa* – pure awareness, i.e., the awareness that arises before becoming *aware of* anything. It is the root of awareness or consciousness itself. Thus, it is that which allows awareness of things (described as the manifestations of our mind) to happen. It is nearly identical to the practice of mahamudra in the Path of Tantra. The goal of *trekcho* is the direct realization of *dharmakaya.*

truth body

Togal

Togal includes several practices, but is most noted for the "Four Visions of Togal" that describe a progressive series of visions of increasing complexity and detail, primarily during a practice called "sky gazing" that involves looking at a clear, cloudless sky in which the visions appear without any external source from which to generate them. The goal of *togal* is attainment of a "rainbow body," the manifestation of *sambhogakaya.*

Chapter 17

The First Training on the

Path of Great Perfection: Ethics

To complete the discussion on ethics, we need to briefly note that the highest principles of virtuous behavior transcend even those I have described before. In *transcendent wisdom* there is no right or wrong, good or bad, no attachment or aversion. Here one transcends even the concept of good or bad. I am reminded of the statement by William Shakespeare's Hamlet, "There is nothing either good or bad, but thinking makes it so." In his treatise on the Middle Way (*Madhyamaka*) Nagarjuna explains this in terms of the *tetradilemma* based on the teachings of the Buddha: (1) transcendent wisdom is not a thing, (2) it is not nothing, (3) it is not both, and (4) it is not neither. Think about it! He has eliminated every conceivable possibility save one – it is beyond logic, beyond thought. It simply is. Thus, we often use the word *suchness* to reference this "___" that is truly ineffable – beyond description.

This does not mean that one is free to simply do as one chooses independent of the effects on others, however. We must always keep in mind the Four Reliances (see Chapter 3). We are all interrelated, interconnected and interdependent. The principles described earlier still apply, even though specific precepts may be transcended for purposes of spiritual development. Thus, Padmasambhava said, "My view is as vast as the sky; my behavior is as fine as barley flour." This asserts the difference between the ultimate and relative truths. Being without attachment and aversion is the view of *dharmakaya*, while behaving in the manner of the other vows for the benefit of sentient beings is the *rupakaya*. These are not either/or, but both/and … one taste.

The ethical view of the Path of Great Perfection can be a very slippery slope. In Tibet "crazy wisdom" on the part of realized yogis may have been culturally accepted. So on one hand, there are no rules! No good or bad. Any practice that can be done from Pure View is an authentic practice, including freely enjoying sense pleasures, being free from accepting and rejecting, and engaging in sexual union and so forth.

There is a set of instructions from Longchenpa (1308-1364) called the *Cloud Banks of Nectar* that illustrate the transcendent view quite well, though they may require some explanation for beginners or others not familiar with the transcendent view.

Emaho!
The intention of Great Mother Dharmakaya,   *Samatabadhi*
The heart of the ten perfections,
Is enjoyment of profound wisdom.
By genuinely ending up here
There's no one to see appearances.
All arising is *dharmakaya*'s play.
Illusions are the Lama's compassion.
So go ahead and stir things up!

Emaho!
The intention of Lama Kunzang,   *Samantabhadra*
The heart of the deity-yoga's result,
Is non-fabrication in whatever arises.
By genuinely ending up here
There's no one to be afraid of thought.
Whatever happens is mental projection.
Thoughts are the Lama's compassion.
So go ahead and stir things up!

Emaho!
The intention of Lama Pema,   *Padmasambhava*
The heart of all-embracing Ati,
Is enjoyment of your stainless mind.
By genuinely ending up here
There is no one to perceive impurity.
Stains are all *dharmata*'s play.
All ways of seeing are the Lama's compassion.
So go ahead and stir things up!

Emaho!
The practice of the woman Tsogyal,   *yeshe Tsogyal*
The heart of secret mantra,
Is the single taste of joy and sorrow.

Since genuinely ending up here,
There is no one to parse what's good and what's bad.
They both just enhance experience.
Whatever appears is the Lama's compassion.
So go ahead and stir things up!

Emaho!

This short text points out how these practices result in transcending a sense of "self," as well as the concepts normally brought on as a result, which of course lead to our suffering. On the other hand, with transcendent wisdom, we are no longer bound by those concepts, so we are free to "stir things up" as they will no longer result in "suffering." Of course, as pointed out below, we must beware of the slippery slope of assuming that we can rationalize any behavior we choose, even though it may be harmful to others. That is not the intention. Nevertheless, the ideas expressed here can be very liberating for those who truly understand.

In addition, Padmasambhava gave instructions to his consort Yeshe Tsogyal that are helpful in a more complete understanding this view.[142]

Your realization of the view's nature may be like an ocean,
But still guard the relative cause and effect down to the finest detail.
You may have understood the vast ocean of *dharmata*'s nature,
But still keep an undistracted training like a pillar of gold.

You may have realized the natural state of open mind,
But still protect your samayas and precepts, stable and undamaged.
You may have gained a realization of the oceanlike *dharmata*'s nature,
But still respect sublime masters as you would the crown of your
    head.

Your loving heart may be free of partiality,
But still fulfill the wishes of your companions and all your Dharma
    friends.
You may have seen the equal nature of the buddhas and all beings,
But still avoid like poison the ten unvirtuous deeds and their results.

You may have realized the fact that the buddha is your mind,

---

[142] From *Treasures from Juniper Ridge: The Profound Treasure Instructions of Padmasambhava to the Dakini Yeshe Tsogyal*

But still regard the sublime yidam deity as dear as your own heart.
You may have understood that suffering itself is greatest bliss,
But still avoid creating all its causes, actions, and involvements.

You may have transformed emotions into pristine wakefulness,
But still avoid scorching your mind with flames of the three- and
    fivefold poisons.
You may have experienced nonaction as the state of greatest ease,
But still exert yourself in goodness with the utmost diligence.

So there are still consequences for our actions. And this is not
Tibet. Even if you are able to sustain Pure View and see all actions as
pure – as they are – others may not, since they are still bound by samsara.
This may lead to a wide variety of problems in your life and those of
others. If, for example, you take the position that there are no barriers in
having sex with another, and do that, a spouse or significant other may
want a divorce or break up the relationship. Even if you are able to
maintain a state of no attachment or aversion under these circumstances
(the ideal here), your actions have resulted in a great deal of harm to
others, and you have accrued negative karma. So while no rules may
sound good, it's never that simple. Pick your poison carefully. In
addition, to the extent that you do engage in these activities, it is
important to be discrete; show respect for others, as well as the dharma.

Motivation, Intention and Rationalization

Doing the right thing is largely a matter of motivation and
intention. You cannot always be sure that what we intend will actually
yield the best result. So you must trust your intentions and follow the
guidelines. Following these is no guarantee, but they have been shown to
be beneficial to the practice of millions over thousands of years.

There is a risk, however, that you may use these guidelines in a
way that simply rationalizes doing what you want to do, based on your
ordinary attachments or aversions and your habitual tendencies. This
necessitates that you are constantly aware of your choices and question
your motivation and intentions before acting. As noted above,
Padmasambhava said, "My view is as vast as the sky; my behavior is as
fine as barley flour." Sometimes using the ultimate view as the basis for
your actions in samsara is simply a rationalization. If I use "Pure View"
as a reason to drink alcohol or have sex, then I am rationalizing. If,

however, I genuinely see alcohol as nectar and illusory, then it does not matter if I drink it or water. I have no attachment or aversion … no preference one way or the other. Similarly with sex. If I maintain Pure View during sex or follow the guidance of the lama for the practice of sexual yoga without any attachment or aversion, then it will not affect my karma. But if I am just using "no attachment or aversion" to rationalize my desire to have sex, then it can have consequences for me and/or others, which of course comes back to me.

Yes, there may be cases where circumstances and the view of yourself and others are such that you can engage in "crazy wisdom" and cross the line. But rationalization is a very slippery slope. Beware! It is important to maintain your behavior "as fine as barley flour" when dealing with others, no matter how pure *your* view is.

Skillful Means

Because Buddhism treats ethical principles as guidelines rather than hard and fast rules, there is another overriding principle necessary. This is *skillful means*. Previously I mentioned the first five of the Six Perfections are sometimes referred to as skillful means. In this case the term is applied in the context of ethical conduct. To avoid the slippery slope of rationalization, one can apply the principle of skillful means to help determine how and when to apply or make exceptions to the basic guidelines. Motivation and intention become important considerations. You also need to ensure that you are not falling into the abyss of rationalization. But lying in order to save another's life is an example of skillful means. You won't always know.

For this reason, there are lamas who will argue that we are simply too ignorant to decide what is skillful or not until we attain enlightenment. On the surface this may sound, and may even be, legitimate in guiding our behavior. Nevertheless, it can also lead you down the path of *not* doing good for the benefit of others. Another form of rationalization! Perhaps this is why His Holiness the Dalai Lama makes a strong case for the importance of your altruistic intention, your ethical intention, in deciding upon your actions of thought, word and deed each and every day. You do the best you can with what you do know, grounded in your altruistic intention to benefit others. This is skillful means.

Chapter 18

The Second Training on the

Path of Great Perfection: Meditation

The Path of Great Perfection is the highest of the Tantric yogas. It is a direct path and no other preliminary practices are necessary, as the practice itself becomes the preliminary practices for Great Perfection. The practitioner abides in "the vastness of each moment...the natural simplicity of being." In the Great Perfection one has transcended all attachments, including sexual yoga, which may or may not continue as part of the practice. In all of these paths, but particularly the Path of Great Perfection, "A certain degree of wildness or craziness is required."[143]

The Path of Great Perfection is most commonly found in Tibetan Buddhism's Nyingma school, though is often practiced by those in other schools as well. It is also found in the Tibetan native religion of Bon and a few native traditions in the area of what is now Pakistan, where it is said to have originated. The practice appears to be ancient and may even predate the historical Buddha. Historical evidence also shows influence from the ancient precursor to Taoism as well as Chinese Chuan (Zen), which for a while had an impact in Tibet.

Until fairly recently, The Path of Great Perfection was considered to be a secret practice, passed only from master to disciple directly. It was little known, even in Tibet. However, several masters have now said that the time has come for sharing these teachings. New books are being published regularly. Old texts are being translated into English and other

---

[143] *Rebel Buddha: On the Road to Freedom* by the Dzogchen Ponlop Rinpoche.

languages. More of the qualified masters are becoming open to public teachings. His Holiness the Dalai Lama has published two books on the subject.

The published texts do caution the practitioner to seek the guidance of a qualified master. Otherwise it is very possible to misunderstand the words, which could lead to a misguided understanding and spiritual disaster. It is important to note at this point, that within the overall scope of the Path of Great Perfection, different masters teach the tradition in slightly different ways that do not always agree – as one might expect in a highly oral, secret tradition. Similarly, differences will be found among the published texts regarding these practices. Thus, following the teachings of a particular master helps you achieve certainty in the practice, a fundamental principle of the Path of Great Perfection.

In addition to the Word empowerment discussed previously in the Path of Tantra, the initiation into the Path of Great Perfection consists of the "pointing out instructions" from the master. What is pointed out is the nature of our mind – primordial purity. This is first described conceptually, to the extent that words can describe the ineffable. Then one or more methods are used to point it out experientially. You then practice to gain confidence in that gnostic wisdom.

There are two primary branches of the practice, each said to be complete in itself, but usually practiced in sequence. The most common sequence is *trekcho* followed by *togal*. In this case, *trekcho* is considered as a foundation practice without which *togal* would not be of any benefit. *Trekcho* provides the context for *togal*. However, a few teach it in reverse order. *Trekcho* can be seen as a form of *shamata*, and *togal* as a form of *vipassana*.

Trekcho is divided into three parts: view, meditation, and action:

View is freedom from analytical mentality;
Meditation is experiential knowledge from primal purity;
Action is characterized by imperturbable relaxation;
And the goal is natural expression of the Buddha's three modes.[144]

---

[144] Dharmakaya, sambhogakaya, and nirmanakaya...collectively *svabhavikakaya*.

View

The *view* takes the cognitive understanding of the transcendent wisdom and, through a "pointing-out instruction" from the master, is experienced directly by the practitioner. This is the Great Perfection initiation. It must be done directly as a description does not have the same effect. It cannot give you the same direct experience. The instructions may be given in a variety of ways, even in a sequence of increasingly ultimate perspectives. The most common expression is a representation of "the gap" between thoughts. We have all had this momentary experience of emptiness, whether we were aware of it or not. To point it out directly, the master may have the participant sit quietly in meditation and then shout "phat" (sounds like "payt" to the Western ear) to startle the participant and create a gap in any residual thought processes that exist. That gap between thoughts is then used to "point out" the true nature of mind – mind without thoughts.

Another approach that I like, because it is less abrupt, is the bell meditation, which I learned from Lama Surya Das. In this case, the lama rings a bell and you simply follow the sound into emptiness. More gentle than the startle reflex approach, this is also effective at creating a state of naturally aware emptiness. It can be done by yourself and tends to last longer.

Another common description, though less experiential in nature, is the mirror. Although the mirror reflects images, it contains none. It itself is empty of reflections, just as the nature of mind is emptiness. At the same time, the mirror has the potential for reflection and the mind has the potential for thoughts. But the *nature* of mind is empty.

This nature is described in several ways. It is *ineffable*. It is beyond words, descriptions, and concepts. Yet, to be able to convey the experience from one person to another, several other phrases have been used that give a sense of what this is like, while the participant is repeatedly cautioned to realize that these too are concepts and not the direct experience itself.

One of these phrases is *openness*. The direct experience has a feeling of openness, of vastness, of emptiness, like the cloudless sky or empty space. It has an incredible lightness about it.

Another phrase is *spontaneous* or *dynamic radiant display*. This quality references the energy or spirit quality that manifests as thoughts in our mind or things in other phenomena. These are not ordinary appearances, but experiences of the innate energy of phenomena manifesting as lights and forms, the dance of pattern and randomness together.

These aspects are combined in a fourth phrase, *oneness*. Experientially there is no difference between the vast openness and the dynamic radiant display. They are not mutually exclusive. These apparent dualisms are in fact two qualities of the one – transcendent wisdom. Newborn babies do not differentiate themselves from their surroundings. They *learn* to do that. Duality and nonduality are but conceptual distinctions. Here, you view all phenomena with equanimity. There is no difference, particularly regarding "good" or "bad."

A perpetual *awareness* in this view is the union of sacred outlook (lovingkindness and compassion in the dynamic radiant display) and the transcendent wisdom, relative and ultimate truth. You have already learned that in the Tantric writings, this is often referred to as *Pure View* – viewing each sentient being as a Buddha, each sound as the voice of Buddha, each thought as the innate nature of Buddha. Everything is perfect as it is, the Great Perfection. There is nothing to do but to remain in the natural state, *let go and let be*.

Meditation

Meditation in The Path of Great Perfection is the state of *relaxation with awareness*, remaining in the natural state. The primary danger at this point is to relax *without* awareness. You begin by gathering yourself in preparation for the meditation, abiding calmly, relaxing. Discriminating awareness meditation heightens your discriminating awareness of the transcendent wisdom nature of things. You then relax into *shamata* without signs (no object of focus), abiding softly into the vast openness of space ... a state of relaxed awareness without thought. There is nothing to do but to *relax and surrender* in the state of naked perception of the nature of reality as it is. You abide in pure awareness beyond concepts until the *view* dissolves as a concept and becomes direct, gnostic knowledge.

To extend our awareness, you may practice a form of *dream yoga*. As you lie in bed, visualize the syllable AH, white like the moon, floating a few feet above. Then let it dissolve and abide in awareness into the dream state. With practice you remain aware during the dream state, and eventually even in deep dreamless sleep.

With practice, the nondual state becomes experiential. Emptiness *is* form; form *is* emptiness. Nakedness *and* delight. You experience a vibrant dance of the nature of reality ... the primordial purity and radiant display of the transcendent wisdom. You abide in the *view* experientially.

The Great Perfection yogin abides in a state of complete equanimity without attachment or judgment of thoughts or things. There is no self or ego through which to be attached. At the same time, the nature of bodhicitta *includes* lovingkindness and compassion. Thus, you are detached *and* caring for the benefit of others.

A state of bliss – an incredible lightness of being – naturally arises. But bliss is not the goal. Becoming attached to the feeling will distract you from the path to enlightenment. You abide naturally in the relaxed state, letting go and letting be.

This requires that you have a good sense of humor, as well as inspiration and determination. The masters are noted for their light-hearted, self-deprecating humor. They laugh frequently ... at almost anything. There is an almost mischievous sparkle in their eyes. They also possess a remarkable presence.

Action

As you increase the frequency and time of meditation and maintain the meditative equipoise into daily living, you begin to transcend meditation. Ultimately, you maintain the view throughout the day and night. Awareness of your Buddhanature has permeated every fiber of your being. In the *action* phase of Great Perfection, everything is meditation. You live and sleep in the *view*. Everything you think, say or do is in the *view*. Enlightenment sparkles through from the ground of being in spontaneous self-perfection. Everything is one taste. You have transcended "practice" and simply continue in nondual pure awareness of every moment.

In nonconceptual awareness, ethics also transcend concepts. There is no right or wrong, no good or bad. Abiding in complete equanimity transcends pleasure and pain. You have gone beyond the conceptual dualism of everyday mind.

You directly experience the *energy* of emptiness, and the manifestation of energy as form (see *Togal*). Any thoughts or feelings that occur are seen as the energy of the transcendent wisdom – ornaments of the natural state.

Pleasure and emotion *are* the path. In this sense, the stronger the better! Yet you remain unattached to these thoughts or feelings. You neither cultivate nor reject them; they are perfect as they are. Letting them go and letting them be, they arise and dissolve on their own. When done with complete integration, you remain undisturbed by them. You become like a child and there are no limitations. Everything is of one taste. The integration of passions into the practice is known as "crazy wisdom" and *must* be done within the state of pure awareness or it may be seriously detrimental to your development and practice.

Decisiveness is key. It gives you confidence in your actions. You realize "the four achievements":

1.   Be able to do the opposite of what you consider to be "right" – you are never deluded in the natural state.

2.   Act with equanimity – beyond concepts of "good" and "bad."

3.   Do not be "involved" in actions or thoughts – remain unattached, unaffected by them.

4.   Remain undeluded, unaffected by what others think, say, or do.

Furthermore, you abide in "the three capacities of understanding":

1.   No one can dissuade you from your nature.

2.   No one can make you afraid.

3.   You do not follow good or bad.

Finally, you experience "the decision without action":

1.   Activity cannot bring Buddhahood – just decide.

2.   There are not obscurations or negativity in the natural state.

3.   Everything is a reflection of wisdom and is self-liberated.

4. All existences are reflections of the natural state.

5. The natural state is beyond whether you understand it or not.

Let go and let be permeates your daily actions. There are no limits to your openness. You transcend the *view* as a concept and live it experientially, delighting in the dance, and laughing at … well, whatever! Your retreat is wherever you are. You sit anywhere. You are aware of whatever. There are no distractions. You have fully integrated your practice into everyday life.

Ultimate and relative bodhicitta are one. Lovingkindness, compassion and joy naturally manifest spontaneously in the incredible lightness of being and sacred outlook for the benefit of others. You realize the pure happiness of indestructible inner peace and joy.

In *From the Depths of the Heart*, Padmasambhava gives this advice to Yeshe Tsogyal (slightly abbreviated):

Because mind-as-such is fully awake from the very beginning, it is neither associated nor disassociated [from Buddhahood]. Recognizing this without any conceptual elaboration is the *view*.

Remaining in a natural state is the *meditation*.

Whatever Dharma practices one performs in that state … is the *activity*.

Self-emergent, spontaneous, and unborn direct insight is the *result*.

The Preliminary Practices - *Khorde Rushen*

Khorde Rushen means the separation of samsara (delusion) from nirvana (non-delusion). The term *rushen* refers to "isolation." These are a series of practices designed to help the yogin realize and *directly experience* the difference between samsara and nirvana by transforming the mind, i.e., our way of seeing the world. That is, we isolate our deluded perception from our true nature.

Khorde Rushen is often referred to as the Great Perfection preliminary practices. As mentioned in the introduction to the Path of Great Perfection, in some cases they are explained as preliminary to *trekcho,* in some cases to *togal;* and in a few cases they are divided into two groups of preliminary practices for *trekcho* and *togal.* I am introducing them as preliminary to *trekcho,* which then also meets the preliminary requirements for *togal.*

The content of *Khorde Rushen* varies from one source to another. *Khorde Rushen* is divided into three sets of practices: (1) outer *rushen,* (2) inner *rushen,* and (3) secret *rushen.* The latter is divided into isolation of body, speech, and mind. Padmasambhava did not include *Khorde Rushen* practices in his text. I have written a set that provides a comprehensive practice, integrating the practices from a variety of sources.[145] Each practice is short and can be done in daily groupings. If possible, do each group both in the morning and at night. On weekends you may be able to do more. Done in this way, you can complete the full set of practices in three weeks. The key is to get a good *feel* for these practices. Due to your previous related meditative experience, the variety is more important than the length or number of repetitions of each experience. Short, quality sessions are ideal.

Outer Rushen

Outer *rushen* focuses on separation or isolation of our delusion of "self" from one or more of the five *skandhas* – form, feelings, perceptions, thoughts, and consciousness – helping to reveal our true nature as it is. As discussed early in this text, the *skandhas* were considered to constitute the essence of "self" at the time of the Buddha. You may focus on one *skandha* each day of the week, then combine them during the remaining days of the week; but the practice is organized for doing all five each day.

Week 38: Outer Rushen – The Five *Skandhas*
Practice twice daily for one week, or once daily for three weeks.

Intention: I do this practice for the benefit of all sentient beings (*or other personal intention*).

Preliminaries: Recite the brief Ngondro preliminary practice, with prostrations.

---

[145] These practices are based primarily on the *Completion of Primordial Wisdom,* the *Vajra Essence,* the *Khandro Nyingtik,* and the *Yeshe Lama* texts.

Purification: Repeat the purification breaths as before.

Form: Settle into stillness of body, speech and mind. Using the 5 elements, meditate on the object representing the element until you can separate the object from the experience of the object.

   Earth — meditate while looking at a mountain[146], sit in stillness without thoughts, until you experience a separation of the mountain (outside) and the experience of the mountain (mind).

   Water — meditate while listening to the sound of water, in stillness without thoughts, until you experience a separation of the water (outside) and the experience of the water (mind).

   Fire — meditate while watching fire (campfire or fireplace is best, but candle is okay), listen in stillness without thoughts, until you experience a separation of the fire (outside) and the experience of the fire (mind).

   Air (wind) — meditate while listening to the sound of the wind in the trees or feeling of the wind on your skin, in stillness without thoughts, until you experience a separation of the wind (outside) and the experience of the wind (mind).

   Space — meditate while looking into space (no point of focus, see entire field of vision), sit in stillness without thoughts, until you experience a separation of space (outside) and the experience of space (mind).

Post-meditation: *When you have completed the practice (individual or collective), maintain the sense of separation between "form" and the actual experience in your mind as you go about your day. Remind yourself as often as you can.*

Feeling: Using the 6 realms of cyclic existence, act out each of the following until you can separate the feeling from the experience of the feeling in your mind.

   Hell realm — think of a time when you have been the most *angry* in your life, feel what it was like, shout PHAT! and feel the separation of anger and emptiness.

---

[146] If you do not have access to an actual mountain, use a tree or other large "solid" object.

Hungry ghost realm — think of a time when you have been the most *greedy* in your life, feel what it was like, shout PHAT! and feel the separation of greed and emptiness.

Animal realm — think of a time when you have killed one or more sentient beings (animals, birds or insects) out of *ignorance* (especially if it was intentional), feel what it was like, shout PHAT! and feel the separation of ignorance and emptiness.

Human realm — think of a time when you have felt the most *passion* in your life, feel what it was like, shout PHAT! and feel the separation of passion and emptiness.

Demi-god realm — think of a time when you have been the most *jealous* in your life, feel what it was like, shout PHAT! and feel the separation of jealousy and emptiness.

God realm — think of a time when you have been the most *proud or arrogant* in your life, feel what it was like, shout PHAT! and feel the separation of pride and emptiness.

Post-meditation: *When you have completed the practice (individual or collective), maintain the sense of separation between "feelings" and the actual experience in your mind as you go about your day. Remind yourself as often as you can.*

Perception: Using the 5 senses, examine the object with the sense until you can separate the object from the experience of sensing the object in your mind.

Seeing — look at an object in front of you, in stillness without thoughts, until you experience a separation of the object (outside) and the experience of the object (mind).

Hearing — listen to sound around you, in stillness without thoughts, until you experience a separation of the sound (outside) and the experience of the sound (mind).

Smelling — smell something, in stillness without thoughts, until you experience a separation of the smell (outside) and the experience of the smell (mind).

Tasting — taste something, in stillness without thoughts, until you experience a separation of the taste (outside) and the experience of the taste (mind).

Touching—touch something, in stillness without thoughts, until you experience a separation of the touch (outside) and the experience of the touch (mind).

Post-meditation: *When you have completed the practice (individual or collective), maintain the sense of separation between "perceptions" and the actual experience in your mind as you go about your day. Remind yourself as often as you can.*

Mental Formations (Thoughts): Let thoughts arise and disappear, noting the difference between thought and no thought. *or bring up a memory.*

Thought—let a thought arise in your mind, watch it abide and disappear, notice the difference between the thought (mind) and the absence of thought (emptiness). Repeat as many times as you can.

Post-meditation: *When you have completed the practice (individual or collective), maintain the sense of separation between "mental formations" and the actual experience in your mind as you go about your day. Remind yourself as often as you can.*

Consciousness: Be aware of

Self—think about "self," analyze "self" until you feel that you understand it, shout PHAT! and feel the separation of "self" and emptiness.

Other—think about a phenomenon (anything other than "self"), examine it until you feel you understand it, shout PHAT! and feel the separation of phenomena and emptiness.

Self and other—think about the nature of "self and other" until you feel you understand that nature, shout PHAT! and feel the separation of "self and other" and emptiness.

Post-meditation: *When you have completed the practice (individual or collective), maintain the sense of separation between "consciousness" and the actual experience in your mind as you go about your day. Remind yourself as often as you can.*

Dedication: With the mind of enlightenment, Bodhicitta, I dedicate all merit from this practice for the enlightenment of all sentient beings. (3X)

Inner Rushen

Inner *rushen* shifts our focus to our afflictive emotions in the form of the six poisons, separating or isolating them from our true nature of mind. The practice builds upon our visualization skill in generating the deity. This particular practice is also a variation on the Vajra Recitation done during the completion stage. This involves visualizing (or feeling) a seed or "poison" for each of the six realms of samsara. Then you visualize the vajra body, speech, and mind of a buddha. In the practice, the rays of light from the buddha body, speech, and mind burn up the seeds of the afflictive emotions, purifying our body and separating samsara from nirvana in our mind.

There is only one practice for inner *rushen*, but there is an expectation that you will do a significant number of repetitions of the practice.[147] It is only through numerous repetitions that one may achieve significant realization of the separation of samsara and nirvana.

Week 39: Inner Rushen – Vajra Recitation

Practice twice daily for one week, or once daily for three weeks.

Intention: I do this practice for the benefit of all sentient beings (*or other personal intention*).

Preliminaries: Recite the brief Ngondro preliminary practice, with prostrations.

Purification: Repeat the purification breaths as before.

Vajra Recitation:

Visualization of six seeds (afflictive emotions) — in your normal body, visualize each as a small dim orb of light:

Crown — seed of god realm (pride/arrogance), a white AH

Throat — seed of the jealous god realm (jealousy), a gold SU

Heart — seed of the human realm (sense desires/lust), a light blue NRI

---

[147] These are traditionally repeated 100,000 times each for a total of 600,000 repetitions of OM AH HUNG, plus an additional 100,000 for all together, making a total of 700,000 repetitions. In keeping with Padmasambhava's other teachings, recite as many as you can each day for one or two weeks.

Navel — seed of the animal realm (ignorance), a dark red TRI

Secret place — seed of the hungry ghost realm (greed), a green PRE

Soles of feet — seed of hell realms (anger/hatred), a black TU on each

Visualization of Buddha's body, speech & mind (each located just above the other syllables in those same locations just above the respective "seeds"):

Forehead — brilliant white OM

Throat — brilliant red AH

Heart — brilliant blue HUNG

The Practice — may be done one realm at a time (e.g., one mala each) or by sequencing through all seven (count with one bead for each cycle).

White, red, and blue rays blaze forth burning up all the seeds of **hell realms** (TU) while reciting OM AH HUNG

White, red, and blue rays blaze forth burning up all the seeds of **hungry ghost realm** (PRE) while reciting OM AH HUNG

White, red, and blue rays blaze forth burning up all the seeds of **animal realm** (TRI) while reciting OM AH HUNG

White, red, and blue rays blaze forth burning up all the seeds of **human realm** (NRI) while reciting OM AH HUNG

White, red, and blue rays blaze forth burning up all the seeds of **jealous god** (SU) realm while reciting OM AH HUNG

White, red, and blue rays blaze forth burning up all the seeds of **god realm** (AH) while reciting OM AH HUNG

White, red, and blue rays blaze forth burning up all the seeds of **all realms together** while reciting OM AH HUNG

Dedication: With the mind of enlightenment, Bodhicitta, I dedicate all merit from this practice for the enlightenment of all sentient beings. (3X)

Post-meditation: *When you have completed the practice, maintain the sense of separation between "the afflictive emotion(s)" and the actual experience in your mind as you go about your day. Remind yourself as often as you can.*

Secret Rushen

Secret *rushen* includes separate practices for the body, speech, and mind. Here, we are again separating our ordinary body, speech, and mind from our buddha body, speech, and mind. There is one practice each for body and mind, and seven for speech. I recommend that you practice in sets of three: body, one speech, and mind. You can rotate through the speech practices by doing a different one each day.

Isolation of Body

This practice relates to the vajra body of *nirmanakaya*. It involves posing as a vajra with your upper and lower body forming the 3-pronged vajra. Your arms are bent and your hands folded together in the refuge position over your head while placing your heels together with toes pointed outward then bending your knees outwards to the sides. Balancing can be a problem, so be careful practicing this pose. If you are unable to do this standing, try it sitting in a chair.

The symbolism of the vajra position is as follows:

> *Upper central prong* — nature of emptiness
> *Upper right prong* — nature of luminosity
> *Upper left prong* — nature of all-pervasive compassion
> *Lower central prong* — *dharmakaya*
> *Lower right prong* — *sambhogakaya*
> *Lower left prong* — *nirmanakaya*
> *Center* — union of wisdom and compassion

Isolation of Speech

These practices relate to the "energy," "manifestation," or "appearance" of the vajra speech of *sambhogakaya*. There are seven practices, so it may be helpful to focus on one each day of the week. (See the actual practice below.) These involve visualizations somewhat like the generation-stage practices, which have helped prepare you for these. They can be fun, so enjoy yourself (while taking them seriously)!

Isolation of Mind

This relates to the vajra mind of *dharmakaya*. By going to an isolated place (actual or imagined), we release all thoughts and concepts into the *dharmakaya* in a playful, yet effective, way.

Traditionally these practices are done for no less than 80 days. However, following Padmasambhava regarding the other practices, we have scaled that back to a period of one week or three weeks as before. However, I recommend that you consider a longer period as needed to achieve the sign of accomplishment described at the end of this set of practices.

Week 40: Secret Rushen – Body, Speech, and Mind

Practice twice daily for one week, or once daily for three weeks.

Intention: I do this practice for the benefit of all sentient beings (*or other personal intention*).

Preliminaries: Recite the brief Ngondro preliminary practice, with prostrations.

Purification: Repeat the purification breaths as before.

Isolation of Body:

Purification — all Buddhas, Bodhisattvas, Gurus, etc. from all directions and the three times dissolve into you, clearing away all illnesses, evil spirits, obscurations, habitual tendencies and material aggregates and you expand into the nature of all-pervasive space. Remain in meditative equipoise.

Vajra pose — join palms above head with elbows out, heels are together with toes pointed out. Bend knees outward and imagine that you are transformed into a blazing blue 3-pronged vajra, like a rainbow in the sky.

Practice — visualize the radiance of primordial consciousness as a blazing mass of fire and remain in equipoise without distraction for as long as you can.[148] You can alternate between standing and lying down and sitting (squatting all the way down).

---

[148] This is described as being done until one literally falls over, no longer able to support yourself in that position.

Result—your body will take on the enlightened nature of a vajra body.

Isolation of Speech [*Select one each day.*]

External sealing—from your mouth send out blue (or white, yellow, red and green) HUNGs filling all of space and transforming all the elements into the nature of HUNG without a trace remaining.
along w melodic hung recitations

Internal sealing—the external HUNGs converge one by one into your mouth filling your body. You become the dark blue, wrathful Vajrapani holding a vajra in your right hand and a serpent noose in your left. Your legs are spread apart and you stand in a blaze of primordial wisdom. Everything external and internal takes on the pleasing melodious sound of HUNG that leads to the realization of the illusion-like nature of appearances. Your body is liberated as having no inherent nature.

Training in flexibility with respect to external appearances—from your mouth a blue HUNG one cubit in length shoots forth striking every physical object and thoroughly penetrating each one and transforming everything into empty space as you recite HUNG powerfully and harshly. Then rest without focus on anything at all.

Training in flexibility with respect to your own body—a blue HUNG one cubit in length emerges from your body, then penetrates it over and over leaving no spot untouched, and disintegrating it into nothingness as you recite HUNG powerfully and harshly. If your body tingles and goose bumps rise, those are signs of subduing the demon of reification and realization of emptiness.

Training in pliability—while sitting, imagine a blue HUNG at your heart. Light rays like a chain of blue HUNGs come from your mouth and coil up and around a stick in front of you up to the top. Then chant HUNG slowly and melodiously as the chain draws back into your heart. Then relax. (Then alternately visualize white, yellow, red and green HUNGs.) This will dispel all obstacles of your channels and give you mastery over the vital energies and mind.

Vajrapani—visualize yourself as Vajrapani. From the HUNG at your heart, HUNGs are emitted like swirling particles of dust in the sunlight. All sensory objects dissolve into HUNGs. Draw them back in filling your body as it grows filling all of space. (May also do with white, yellow, red and green.) Dissolve your body into minute particles and liberate your awareness as *dharmakaya*.

Entering the path — visualize your body as a blazing white HUNG above the ground moving in one direction then another, gradually moving through all the 6 realms. Then like an arrow, you go to Abhirati in the east, Srimat in the south, Sukhavati in the west, Karmaprapurana in the north, then Ghanavyuha in the center[149], seeing the five Buddha Families, receiving teachings and empowerments all while reciting HUNG slowly and melodiously. This allows the final purification of the buddhafields and your speech will become vajra speech.

pure aware..

Isolation of Mind

Entering into your own innate stability — go to a remote place[150], settle in the natural state - stillness of body, speech and mind. Remain for a long time. Experience the *dharmakaya* free of activity. Sit in meditative equipoise, gaze six feet in front of you with a sense of limitless consciousness. Then stand with feet apart, point your right hand to the sky with a threatening gesture[151] and shout "HA HA!" Then reach out with your left hand in a threatening gesture and shout "Hee Hee!" Then rest without focus. This will empower you with great confidence in awareness of reality itself.

Dedication: With the mind of enlightenment, Bodhicitta, I dedicate all merit from this practice for the enlightenment of all sentient beings. (3X)

Post-meditation: *When you have completed the practice (individual or collective), maintain the sense of separation between "body," "speech," and "mind" and the actual experience in your mind as you go about your day. Remind yourself as often as you can.*

Do these practices seriously but playfully

By completing the *Khorde Rushen* practices, one becomes a suitable vessel and your body, speech and mind will be transformed into the nature of the three vajras. The important sign is to differentiate between the action and *the experience of that action in your mind*, separating

---

149 The realms of the five Buddha Families

150 This can be your own home or even your own mind, if you do not have convenient access to a remote place for this practice.

151 Hold the thumb inside with the middle two fingers, while pointing the index and little fingers.

samsara from nirvana. Continue the practice as long as is necessary to achieve confidence in that experience.

Cutting Through - *Trekcho*

Trekcho means "cutting through." This practice cuts through all thoughts and concepts that obscure our innate buddhanature, allowing our true nature to radiate out in all its luminosity.

"The Three Statements of Garab Dorje," the first known Great Perfection human master, summarizes the teachings in three points:

> Direct introduction of the view.
> Developing confidence in the view.
> Abiding in the view until fully awakened.

The first step comes from receiving the "pointing-out instructions" from the lama described at the beginning of this chapter. These cannot be done through the written word, as they depend on actions of the lama and the direct experience of the student based on those actions. Descriptions are insufficient by themselves. This direct introduction, usually accompanied by simple or elaborate explanations, is the first step.

Second, once you have a direct experience of the view, you develop confidence in it through many short, quality meditations. These are similar to *shamata* and are explained below. This is a process of habituation, for which the generation and completion-stage practices have prepared you.

The third step indicates mastery of training the mind in the view. One remains undisturbed by other thoughts or actions. We abide in *dharmakaya* at all times. This does not mean that you don't ever have thoughts (like the goal of *shamata*), but that you are able to have thoughts at the same time as abiding in *dharmakaya* – both/and! Similarly, you can engage in conversation and other actions, while maintaining the view – buddhahood in this lifetime.

To develop confidence in the view, *trekcho* meditation is often taught in four parts: (1) advanced *shamata*, (2) advanced *vipassana*, (3) one taste, and (4) non-meditation. These may have been derived from the nearly identical teachings on *mahamudra*, which uses the same four-step model. *Trekcho* and *mahamudra* are essentially the same, though not all lamas teach in this way. But Padmasambhava has included several forms of *shamata* and *vipassana* in his instructions. Advanced *shamata* and *vipassana* in the Path of Great Perfection are somewhat different than when we introduced them in the Path of Individual Liberation. The basic idea is using single-pointed calm abiding to shift from an object, as was done before, to no object (*shamata* without signs or without support). The focus of *vipassana* is also different – the nature of mind itself. In the "one taste" phase these are done alternately until one arrives at their union as a state of one taste. At that point, one integrates the practice into daily life such that there is no separation from meditation on the cushion and life off of the cushion. Perhaps a more accurate term would be "everything is meditation."

Advanced Shamata

As noted, one approach to teaching *trekcho* is to begin with *shamata*. In the Path of Individual Liberation the goal of *shamata* is no thoughts at all (see the nine stages of *shamata* in Chapter 6). Nevertheless, *trekcho* is a form of single-pointed calm abiding – the definition of *shamata*. This is an advanced form of single-pointed calm abiding. Previously, you focused your attention on an object, real or imagined. Even the deity practices were a form of *shamata*. Here there is no "object" of focus. It is sometimes referred to as "*shamata* without signs" (compared to the previous "*shamata* with signs").

In this phase there are no longer any visualizations. You no longer focus on anything other than being aware itself, resting nonconceptually without thoughts. However, the stillness of advanced *shamata* does not require that you never experience any thoughts. If thoughts do arise, you simply let them "self-liberate" rather than trying to block them or otherwise eliminate them. (Notice that no thought stays forever. They arise, abide, and dissolve.) Just do not grasp or get attached to the thoughts that do arise. Unlike before, here they are considered as "natural" manifestations of our mind. We simply recognize them and let them go, remaining focused on our awareness. If you lose your focus, which is easy to do in the beginning, recognize it and return to it. In his *Notes on Mahamudra*, Pema Karpo states, "Recognizing thinking within stillness and seizing the natural seat of stillness within the occurrence of thoughts is therefore called 'intermingling stillness and occurrence,' and hence is also called the 'recognition of one-pointedness.'"

Another way to think of it is as foreground and background of your mind. What is in the foreground is our focus. But we can "multitask" and be aware of something else at the same time – in the background. The goal here is to keep awareness itself in the foreground, and let thoughts or other forms of consciousness arise and abide in the background. Once you develop some skill at this, you are able to talk, work, or engage in a wide variety of activities while maintaining your focus on pure awareness.

Remember, "awareness" does not mean being aware *of* something. It is simply awareness itself. As an analogy, it may help to think of the difference between "potential" and "kinetic" energy. Potential energy has the "potential" to act, but it is not in the process of action. Kinetic energy is the action form, something in motion. If I hold a stone in my fingers, it has potential energy. If I drop it, it has kinetic energy. So awareness itself is like potential energy. It is not yet aware *of* something, but has the potential to do that. It is a blank slate before images, sounds, thoughts and so forth arise. To be aware *of* something is like kinetic energy. We become conscious of that something. The focus of this meditation, and Great Perfection *trekcho* generally, is awareness itself, often referred to as "pure awareness" – *rigpa*.

As in other forms of meditation, we are advised to avoid grasping onto any joy, clarity, or even nonconceptuality that arises. This is a hindrance. *Let go and let be.* The evenly remaining awareness is your innate buddhanature (*tathagatagarbha*) the essence of a buddha's space-like awareness (*rigpa*). One of my teachers, His Eminence Garchen Rinpoche describes it this way:

> The nature of mind cannot be described; it is like space. Milarepa said, "When there is no difference between space and mind, that is the perfected *dharmakaya*." The empty space-like essence is the quality of *dharmakaya*. There is a vivid clear awareness that knows its empty space-like essence. The nature of clarity is emptiness; the nature of emptiness is clarity. They are not separate; they are non-distinct; they are the union of clarity and emptiness.

Abide in clear awareness.

Nine-Round Breathing

Previously we did breath purification as a form of 9-round breathing. Nine-round breathing is a short practice sometimes taught in the Path of Tantra, but nearly always taught in the Path of Great Perfection. It is used at the beginning of other practices, as we have been doing. There are a wide range of variations, but it basically consists of three rounds of three breaths from the right, left, and both nostrils. Relax and focus on your breath. Here is a different, simple version from the one we did previously:

1.   Block the left nostril with the right index finger and breathe in slowly. Pause. Block the right nostril with the right index finger and breathe out slowly. Repeat 3X.

2.   Block the right nostril with the left index finger and breathe in slowly. Pause. Block the left nostril with the left index finger and breathe out slowly. Repeat 3X.

3.   Breathe in slowly through both nostrils, pause, and breathe out slowly through both nostrils. Repeat 3X.

This will now be included in the remaining practices.

Advanced Shamata without Signs

This practice involves focus on awareness, by shifting our focus within space. It can be easy to get attached to "space" as an object. By shifting our focus, you begin to let go of that attachment and let it be, as it is. Here you begin by looking up, then down, and finally by integrating up, right, left and down. In each case you are focused on your awareness, *and* you are monitoring your focus. Earlier in the book, I talked about this as mindfulness (your focus) and awareness (monitoring your focus). The process is called meta-cognition or thinking about thinking. Here it is applied to your awareness without an object of focus – pure awareness itself. To facilitate this process, you alternate between (1) your focus on space and (2) monitoring your focus on space. This helps make the difference very clear, which is important for effective *trekcho* meditation.

Week 41 – Advanced Shamata (without Signs)

Practice twice daily for one week, or once daily for three weeks.

Intention: I do this practice for the benefit of all sentient beings (*or other personal intention*).

Preliminaries: Recite the brief Ngondro preliminary practice, with prostrations.

Nine-round breathing.

Shamata without signs:

From stillness of body, speech and mind, gaze into *space* (looking up) without meditating on anything at all. Alternate between focus and monitoring your focus.

Then continue to practice while gazing *down*, alternating between concentration and monitoring.

Finally, practice by gazing *up*, then *right*, then *left*, then *down*, alternating between concentration and monitoring.

Dedication: With the mind of enlightenment, Bodhicitta, I dedicate all merit from this practice for the enlightenment of all sentient beings. (3X)

Post-meditation: *Bring to a close by arising gently and abiding softly and deeply in pure, naked awareness at all times, even while engaging in other activities.*

Advanced Shamata - Meditative Stabilization

The next step in the process involves two parts: awareness of awareness and practice with the "threefold space." The first part refers to the subtle grasping that tends to occur when we "focus" on awareness. By grasping at the "idea of awareness," we become attached to it, and that becomes just another obstacle, albeit a subtle one. It is important to recognize this process so that you do not succumb to it. That is the first part of this meditation.

The second part refers a threefold process for "actualizing the *dharmakaya*" involving meditation on three levels: (1) external space, (2) internal space, and (3) secret space. The "external space" is a focus on the empty area around us. Outdoors, that external space is the entire atmosphere. Inside your house or apartment, that is the space within the walls, but outside of you. I have found it helpful when meditating on "space" to look ahead at a blank space on a wall across the room and focus on it. Then, without moving my eyes, I broaden my view to the entire room or atmosphere. This tends to avoid things like crossing your eyes and other difficulties that interfere with your practice.

The "internal space" is a visualization, imagining two thin hollow channels (*khati* channels) that connect the eyes and the heart. This involves directing your attention to your eyes, which are gazing into the space. Without creating an "object" of meditation, just be aware of looking into space and let it be.

The "secret space" is the space in your heart. Recall that the "heart" in Tibetan refers to the "heart-mind." Scientists have discovered that the heart actually has its own neurons, its own "mind" if you will. Yet it has no "thoughts." The true nature of mind is said to reside in the indestructible drop at the heart chakra. This is not your everyday mind full of thoughts and feelings. That resides in the brain. This third "space" connects with your heart-mind, the channel connecting with your eyes, and the external space being observed. According to the *Tantra of the Three Phrases of Liberation by Observation*, this leads to primordial wisdom freely arising: "Nonconceptual awareness alone will appear, without being obscured by any compulsive ideation."

Week 42 — Advanced Shamata: Meditative Stabilization

Practice twice daily for one week, or once daily for three weeks.

Intention: We do this practice for the benefit of all sentient beings (*or other personal intention*).

Preliminaries: Recite the brief Ngondro preliminary practice, with prostrations.

Nine-round breathing.

Meditative Stabilization:

Clarity and awareness: Focus on subtle grasping onto awareness itself – awareness of awareness. Then let go and let be. Repeat as necessary.

The Threefold Space:

Outwardly focus on the empty space in front of you.

Inwardly focus on the empty channel between the eyes and the heart, especially your eyes.

Secretly focus on the nature of mind in the heart, then the nature of mind, your eyes, and space together.

> Abide softly and deeply in nonconceptual awareness ... let it be ... steady, luminous, and even.

Repeat as necessary.

Dedication: With the mind of enlightenment, Bodhicitta, I dedicate all merit from this practice for the enlightenment of all sentient beings. (3X)

Post-meditation: Always, always end your session slowly and arise without losing the sense of the natural state – pure awareness – in every activity day and night.

Advanced Vipassana

The second set of practices involves *vipassana* – special insight. Again, this is a variation of the practice introduced in the Path of Individual Liberation. Previously we used this for examining the nature of self and other. It is also said to be among the completion-stage practices of Highest Yoga Tantra. Here, the focus is on the nature of mind – the nature of awareness itself.

The Nature of Awareness

In this case the central channel only goes up as far as the center of your head. Attached at that point is a crystal *khati* channel, a channel of primordial wisdom. In humans, it normally points forward to a point between the eyebrows, "the third eye." In animals or humans with their "eyes closed," it points down and is closed off, leading to ignorance. In bodhisattvas the channel is open and points up to the crown, leading to primordial wisdom and other *samadhis* – the highest levels of concentration. By fixing the gaze on space, the channel turns upward, which isolates *pure* awareness from *impure* awareness. Next, we examine the nature of our mind, our pure awareness, then release all thoughts and relax in the direct experience.

This is followed by additional exercises, more similar to those done in examining self and other. This is repeated as many times as you can. Each time we repeat the experience, we go deeper into a direct experiential understanding of the true nature of mind. Padmasambhava says to do that for one day. But since we are not doing it for a complete day, we will do it for one week or more.

Week 43 — The Nature of Awareness

Practice twice daily for one week, or once daily for three weeks.

Intention: We do this practice for the benefit of all sentient beings (*or other personal intention*).

Preliminaries: Recite the brief Ngondro preliminary practice, with prostrations.

Nine-round breathing.

Vipassana (insight) — the nature of awareness: *contemplation more than a conceptual*

> Part 1

Gaze into *space* in front of you without meditating on anything.

The crystal *khati* channel turns upward, opening samadhis and primordial wisdom.

When stability arises, examine the nature of your mind, your awareness; then release and relax.

understanding

> Part 2

Again, gaze into *space* in front of you.

What is this mind that is being placed?

Is the one who is placing and the object being placed one or two? If two, is one roaming in samsara while the other is buddhahood? If there is but one, what is the reality of this so-called "mind"? (It cannot be found as an external object.)

Continue until you have some sense of certainty.

> Part 3

What is this so-called "mind" like? Observe your very consciousness and search for it. Does it really exist?

If so, what shape is it? Can you find one?

If there is none, what is the emptiness of "shape"?

> Part 4

Examine its color, size & dimension.

Examine awareness & relationship to myself.

If there is no color, size or dimension, is it an emptiness that is nothing? If it is nothing, what is it that thinks? What is it that experiences emotions?

If you do not discover what it is like, carefully check whether the consciousness that is examining it is itself the mind. If it is, what is it like? If you cannot find it, what difference is there between you and a corpse? Isn't there someone who thinks?

Decisively observe how it is.

Part 5

If you cannot find a "thing," is there stillness, clarity, emptiness?

Stillness is quiescence, not the mind. Seek out "awareness." What is its nature?

If it is emptiness, that is one aspect. Seek out "awareness."

If it is still, sort of clear, but inexpressible, you have identified it a little bit. Go deeper. Come to *certainty* in your recognition.

Repeat as many times as you can.

Dedication: With the mind of enlightenment, Bodhicitta, I dedicate all merit from this practice for the enlightenment of all sentient beings. (3X)

Post-meditation: *Continue to practice at every opportunity throughout the day and night (with dream yoga) to reinforce the direct experience. Continue this practice until you can clearly experience the nature of awareness. Then continue again until you gain confidence in that experience.*

Identifying Awareness

This step continues our examination of pure awareness, pushing us ever closer to realization. As we gaze into space, we examine the nature of our awareness itself and the difference between that and everyday mind. We more clearly experience pure awareness and solidify our confidence in it.

Week 44 — Identifying Awareness

Practice twice daily for one week, or once daily for three weeks.

Intention: We do this practice for the benefit of all sentient beings (*or other personal intention*).

Preliminaries: Recite the brief Ngondro preliminary practice, with prostrations.

Nine-round breathing.

Identifying awareness:

Part 1

Gaze into *space* in front of you.

Experience the nature of your mind clearly and without wavering.

Do you experience a steadiness in awareness?

Do you experience a steady, natural luster of emptiness that is not nothing, i.e., awareness itself, the nature of mind?

Do appearances and mind merge inseparably, so that awareness is not "inside" and appearances "outside"?

Part 2

Once again, experience the nature of your mind — pure awareness.

Stillness is not, by itself, the nature of mind.

Is there an "empty essence" without substance, shape, or color?

Is there a clear, soothing, "luminous nature"?

Is it ineffable, beyond words that describe or explain it?

Part 3

Repeat these steps until you gain confidence in the direct experience of the nature of your mind — pure awareness.

Dedication: With the mind of enlightenment, Bodhicitta, I dedicate all merit from this practice for the enlightenment of all sentient beings. (3X)

Post-meditation: *Continue to practice at every opportunity throughout the day and night (with dream yoga) to reinforce the direct experience. Continue this practice until you can clearly experience the nature of awareness. Then continue again until you gain confidence in that experience.*

According to Padmasambhava[152]:

> This present, unmoving consciousness, which cannot be directly expressed in words, is given the name "awareness." That which thinks is this alone, so it is given the name "mind." It is this that is mindful of all kinds of things, so it is given the name "mindfulness." While it is not seen, it is a special seeing that is clear, steady, unmediated, and steadfast, so it is given the name "insight." It is that which makes distinctions among all specific phenomena, like separating the layers of [an onion], so it is given the name "discerning wisdom."

There are many names given to the realization of pure awareness, such as *sugatagarbha*, primordial wisdom, *mahamudra, atiyoga,* emptiness, and so forth. While well intended, these names can cause confusion or lead to a subtle form of attachment, thinking "this is it." Do not think at all. Just experience it. Let go, let be, as it is! "It is just this clear, steady consciousness that is ordinarily, naturally present right now."[153]

Practice this way *always* to attain certainty! Visualize in this way. Recite mantras and prayers in this way. Wash dishes in this way. Read in this way. Drive your car (carefully!) in this way. Go to the bathroom in this way. Make love in this way.

> Once one has become a buddha, whence arises the primordial wisdom of knowledge, the compassion of mercy, and the enlightened activity of deeds? All those are experienced and created solely by this steadfast awareness that is inseparable clarity, awareness, and emptiness.[154]

This is our buddhanature! We already have it! We are already buddhas! We just have to identify it and gain confidence in it so that we are mindful of it at *all times* in our lives ... in meditation *and* nonmeditation.

---

[152] *Natural Liberation,* p. 122.

[153] *Ibid.,* p. 123.

[154] *Ibid.,* p. 126.

One Taste

Having achieved confidence in advanced *shamata* and *vipassana* separately, you continue those practices by alternating between them in a single session. As with the experience of bliss-emptiness in the completion-stage practices, alternating brings them together experientially as one – "one taste." You may use a simplified version of the previous practices to help you achieve this merger of experiences. Begin with advanced *shamata* for a few minutes, and then do advanced *vipassana* for a few minutes. Repeat this as many times as you can in one session. During the day, seek opportunities to recognize this awareness of the nature of mind as long as you can. At the same time, keep in mind the advice of Pema Karpo quoted earlier, "Recognizing thinking within stillness and seizing the natural seat of stillness within the occurrence of thoughts is therefore called 'intermingling stillness and occurrence,' and hence is also called the 'recognition of one-pointedness.'" You transcend the ideas of "thoughts" or "no thoughts," of "awareness" and "emptiness."

Rigpa Guru Yoga

Once you have the direct experience of one taste, you continue with Garab Dorje's third statement – abiding in the view until fully awakened. The best practice, the most excellent practice, is the familiar practice of Guru Yoga. In this case I have included a very concise version called *Rigpa Guru Yoga*. There is no visualization. You simply recite the few short lines, the mantra, and abide within *rigpa*.

Week 45 — Rigpa Guru Yoga

Practice twice daily for one week, or once daily for three weeks.

Intention: I do this practice for the benefit of all sentient beings (*or other personal intention*).

Preliminaries: Recite the brief Ngondro preliminary practice, including the 7-Line Prayer but *without the Guru Yoga*.

Nine-round breathing.

Rigpa Guru Yoga:

Ah, Rigpa Guru Padma Gyalpo,
I take refuge in the self-recognizing nature of my mind.
Because of their ignorance sentient beings are wandering in samsara,
May all sentient beings reach the great liberation.

By recognizing their nature as the primordial awareness of
    Samantabhadra,
All demons and malicious forces, even their concepts and names fall
    apart.
The nature of all phenomena is dharmadhatu and
The unchanging self-arising wisdom is your only protection.

Jnana Rakcha Hung

Phenomena perceived through the six kinds of consciousness[155]
Without attachment are recognized as the rays of rigpa.
All surroundings appear as Buddhafields and sentient beings as
    Buddhas,
Everything is the blessing of wisdom.

Jnana Ahwe Shaya Phem

Primordial self-arising ultimate Padmasambhava
Appears as my rigpa space – there is no face, no limbs, no image.
Primordial rays of rigpa fully encompass the three kayas
Without the impurity coming from discursive mediation.

Primordial nature of my rigpa is my guru.
There is no coming and going – in every moment I welcome his
    presence.
Everything firmly abides in dharmadhatu.
I prostrate to the understanding of the real nature that eliminates
    ignorance.

I offer recognition of the Buddhanature in objects of the six kinds of
    consciousness.
I praise the nature of the vajra three kayas of the body, speech and
    mind.

In the great unchanging dharmadhatu

---

[155] The five senses and the mind consciousness

All moral ethics are encompassed in the pure guru mind.
I recognize the deepest empty nature of all sounds and speech.
In all my activity I recognize its dharmadhatu nature and recite the
    mantra:

Om Ah Hung Benza Guru Padma Siddhi Hung
(*Recite the mantra of Guru Rinpoche 108X or as many times as you can, then
    rest in pure awareness as long as you can.*)

With all the good virtue I have accumulated in samsara and nirvana,
I pray that discursive thought of all sentient beings would be
    eliminated,
That they would achieve the ultimate liberation and
Obtain the rainbow body just like Rigpa Guru Padmasambhava's.

*On a strong request of Lama Rigzin Dho Ngag Gya Stos, this mind terma
was received by Nupchen Sangye Yeshe in the great place of Ma Gyal Pom
Rai mountain in the west and written down by Padma Sam Zin for the
benefit of all sentient beings.*

Dedication: With the mind of enlightenment, Bodhicitta, I dedicate all
    merit from this practice for the enlightenment of all sentient beings.
    (3X)

Continue this practice as your main *trekcho* practice. You may
substitute it in the daily *ngondro* practice as was done here, although I
recommend continuing to recite the Seven-Line Prayer at least once or
three times prior to doing the *Rigpa Guru Yoga*. But during the actual
meditation, follow the advice of the great yogi master Tilopa described in
the *Root Scripture on Mingling*:

Don't reflect, don't imagine, and don't evaluate,
Don't meditate, don't think, rest in naturalness.

Similarly, keep in mind these thoughts from His Eminence
Garchen Rinpoche:

The goal is not to have no thoughts, but for thoughts to arise and yet
be rendered powerless. You must habituate this. Then later, when

negative thoughts and emotions arise, you will not fall under their power.... Sometimes in meditation, there will be a time when there are actually no thoughts. In that instant you will know that this is the true nature of your mind – the mind that abides like space, vivid and empty, open, not grasping at anything. This alert awareness must be upheld throughout all activities. So do not try to stop thoughts, just relax into the nature of awareness. Whenever you meditate, our minds will be together. If you understand this, you will not feel tired of meditation.

Non-meditation

The idea of "non-meditation" is that once you master stage three in Garab Dorje's three statements – abiding in the view until fully awakened, you are a buddha, and there is no longer a need for meditation. The Buddha himself referred to this with an analogy of crossing the river with a raft. Once we reach the other side, there is no need to keep carrying around the raft.

Until you are fully enlightened, however, you will continue to follow Garab Dorje's third statement – abiding in the view *until* fully awakened – with daily *Rigpa Guru Yoga*. Thus, this stage of the practice is better described as "everything is meditation," rather than "non-meditation." His Holiness the Dalai Lama describes it this way:

In the Path of Great Perfection, while thoughts are active, rigpa permeates them all, so that even at the very moment when powerful thoughts like attachment and aversion are arising, there remains a pervasive quality of clear light rigpa. Dodrupchen says, "In the Path of Great Perfection, since the clear light's natural way of being is like the sun and its rays, inseparable, if you are able, through this, to bring out the radiance of genuine mind, you will be able to maintain the experience of clear light in meditation, without it fluctuating, or coming and going."

The idea is to embody the view throughout your life – day and night. *Everything* is an opportunity to practice mindfulness of pure awareness, as well as lovingkindness and compassion. In the beginning, we need frequent reminders. But with patience and persistence, particularly with *joyous* effort, we begin to habituate our mind to a steady pattern of behavior leading to enlightenment. Each and every action reinforces our neural network in the brain, as well as our mind, opening it to reveal its true nature of awareness-emptiness.

As you abide softly in pure awareness of the transcendent wisdom and the sacred outlook of Pure View, you are very relaxed and very aware. There is a deep inner peace of *innate happiness*. No effort is required to maintain a state of focus. Thoughts that arise are recognized as the manifestation of the nature of mind. They come ... and go. *Let go and let be.* Feelings that arise also come and go, without effort and without any attachment to them. "Good" or "bad" are mere labels, conceptualizations. They no longer matter, though we remain fully aware of their presence when they do occur. *Let go and let be.* There is nothing more to do. Abiding softly is the practice. All concepts just seem not to matter, even as conventional thoughts and concepts still manifest within your experience. I want to say, "How delightful!" But even that thought seems irrelevant.

As we advance in this practice, we gain confidence in our view and become unshakable from causes and conditions that may otherwise affect us. At the same time, our lovingkindness and compassion and our Pure View have grown strong as well. We treat others with dignity and respect, whether they are friends or enemies. Or like His Holiness the Dalai Lama is fond of saying, "Each time I meet someone, it is like we are old friends." The meditative state is carried forward into our daily activities. We express our truth through our actions to benefit others at all times and in all ways.

At the most advanced level, *everything is meditation*. There is no need for a separate meditative practice, although we continue to do so to reinforce our understanding and experience. We abide softly and deeply in our buddhanature. It has become strong and pervasive in all that we think, say, and do.

Leaping Over – *Togal*

Togal means "leaping over." It was still generally a secret teaching in the Tibetan Buddhist tradition. Then, some teachers in the Bon tradition began publishing some of these teachings, and a few others have followed. Not all sources are accessible with some requiring authorization from a qualified master to purchase them. Slowly, this is opening access beyond the very few fortunate enough to have received instructions directly from a master. As with *trekcho*, more will likely follow. The following is a fairly detailed description within the bounds of, or similar to, publicly available information.

Five Buddha Families

The Five Buddha Families represent five *sambhogakaya* manifestations of a Buddha. They are not actual separate Buddhas, but represent some of the significant qualities of all Buddhas in Pure View. With Pure View, the aggregates are actually seen as the Buddhas, and the elements are seen as their Consorts, and so forth. In addition, you do not abandon the five poisons, they are viewed as an aid to your practice. We use our desire, for example, to transform our attachments to ordinary things in order to increase our desire for enlightenment. In so doing, we realize that the poisons actually represent the five wisdoms, even the five

	Buddha family	Vajra family	Jewel family	Lotus family	Karma family
Buddha	*Vairochana*	*Akshobya*	*Ratnasambhava*	*Amitabha*	*Amoghasiddhi*
Aggregate	Form	Consciousness	Feeling	Perception	Thought
Consort	White Tara	Locana	Mamaki	Pandara	Green Tara
Element	Space	Water	Earth	Fire	Air, wind
Color	White	Blue	Gold, yellow	Red	Green
Location	Center	East	South	West	North
Symbol	Wheel	Vajra	Jewel	Lotus	Double vajra
Mudra	Teaching	Earth-touching	Giving	Meditation	Fearlessness
Poison	Ignorance	Hatred, anger	Greed & pride	Desire	Jealousy
Wisdom	All-accommo-dating, *Dharmadatu*	Mirror-like	Equanimity	Discriminating	All-accomplish-ing
Activity	Teaching	~~Subduing~~ PACIFYING	Enriching, increasing	Magnetizing, organizing	~~Pacifying~~ SUBDUING

Buddhas themselves. The *Sutra Requested by Sagaramati* says, "The more disturbing emotions a bodhisattva has, the stronger the fire of wisdom will blaze."

It is also a convenient way of memorizing various concepts enumerated as "five." The following chart includes some of the key characteristics[156] that have been associated with these "families."

The five Buddha activities include: peaceful activities of *pacifying* illness and negative emotions and *enriching* to increase merit, lifespan and meditational experiences; wrathful activities of *magnetizing* to attract favorable circumstances and *subduing* to reduce inner and outer obstacles and negative forces; and finally there is the main activity of *teaching* the dharma.

It becomes particularly important to recognize these in the *togal* practices as they appear as part of the Four Visions. Familiarity will help facilitate recognition of those appearances. In the Dzogchen Ponlop Rinpoche's "Plan B," familiarity also helps us recognize these Buddhas in the second part of the Bardo of *Dharmata*, if we have not already attained enlightenment or were unable to transfer our consciousness to the heart of a deity and their pure buddhafield at the time of death. In addition, this is another level of detail in Pure View during this life. We see the aggregates as Buddhas, elements as Consorts, and poisons as wisdoms with Pure View. So, again, familiarity is important. Take some time each day to commit them to memory. Then, regularly refresh your memory.

The Three Postures

Body

> Early in the practices of *togal*, we learn the three postures:
>
> > Adept (*rishi*) – *nirmanakaya*
> >
> > Elephant – *sambhogakaya*
> >
> > Lion – *dharmakaya*

These postures are used in the visioning practices in *togal*. The *posture of the adept* is sitting with knees drawn up together to the chest,

---

156 Details will vary somewhat from one lineage to another.

back straight, and right arm over the left arm, which are resting on the knees. The gaze is downward. This posture is used to gain control over the vital energies and the mind. The winds abide in stillness at the heart-mind.

The *posture of the elephant* is like resting on your folded legs with feet pointing back, elbows on the ground, and the chin resting on your hands. The gaze is straight ahead or side to side. This posture is used to see the pure visions of primordial wisdom.

The *posture of the lion* is of two types. The traditional posture is squatting like a seated lion (or cat) with a straight back, feet on the ground, arms straight down to the ground between the knees, and the hands in a "vajra fist" (thumbs inside the fingers). (You may substitute the dream-yoga lion posture or lie on your back when your get uncomfortable.) The gaze is up. This posture is used to stop deceptive appearances. What remains is the view of *dharmakaya*.

The second type of lion posture is described in *Yeshe Lama*, which says that the traditional posture is incorrect. This approach is a seated posture with a straight back, knees apart, soles of the feet together and close to the body, hands together with interlocking fingers except for extended middle fingers pointing together and inserted into the gap between the soles of the feet. The gaze and purpose are the same as above.

The great master Khenpo Jigmed Phunstok Rinpoche recommended using the lion posture to look at the sun[157], the elephant posture to look at the moon, and the adept posture to look at a candle. All three postures may be used to focus on "space." But the real focus is on the nature of mind – pure awareness. Some sources also list a practice visualizing the crystal *khati* channel (see Week 43) without the analytical process, simply being aware, as if the heart is projecting through the *khati* channel and eyes into space. With time, heart, channel, eyes, and space seem to merge into one. *A— only in early a.m, not straight on, & squinting*

Speech

There are no prayers or mantras to recite during the main practice. Padmasambhava says to first limit talking to 3-4 times per day, then less to none; finally, be silent like a mute.

---

[157] Do not just look directly at the sun as this is known to cause blindness. See detailed instructions are later in this chapter.

Mind   *or candle*

There are three objects used for focus. Traditionally, these are the sun, moon, and a <u>lamp.</u> Looking directly at the sun is risky and can result in blindness, so I don't recommend it. When done, it should be done through a sun filter or by limiting it to just a few rays between the fingers of your hand and so forth. It should also only be done just as the sun is rising or setting, only for a few seconds at a time, and only for a few times. The second object is observed at night, the full moon, which is visible on clear nights for two or three days each month. The third object is a lamp, which can refer to a butter lamp (or candle) or other small bright light.

Seeing Dharmata

The goal of the next practice is "seeing" *dharmata* – sometimes called reality-itself. It is said to have the qualities of infinity as well as the heart essence, although it may be best to simply say it just is. In the Path of Great Perfection, there is no difference between "seeing" and "not seeing" – appearance and emptiness. Phenomena are seen as the divine manifestation of the heart-mind, just as it is. So what "appears" to our mind when looking at a bright light is none other than mind itself. This may be in the form of "rays of light" or "bindus" and such. But it is important to experience the object as mind itself, which is neither a "thing" nor "no-thing." The actual visions, seen by squinting the eyes in the beginning, are a semblant taste of the Four Visions of Togal.

The postures are alternated to explore which work best for you. Padmasambhava does not prescribe a particular posture for this or other *togal* practices. Most sources leave this as an open question. However, at least one links the *rishi-nirmanakaya* pose to the first vision, the elephant-*sambhogakaya* pose to the second vision, and the lion-*dharmakaya* pose to the third vision. Any of the poses may be used for the fourth vision. Since this practice provides an introduction to the four visions, it is good to get some experience with each.

This is also preparation for the Bardo of *Dharmata*, which includes the experience of clear light and the appearances of the 100 Peaceful and Wrathful Deities. If those are recognized as the nature of our mind, then we will become enlightened at that time.

Week 46 — Seeing Dharmata

Practice twice daily for one week, or once daily for three weeks.

Intention: I do this practice for the benefit of all sentient beings (*or other personal intention*).

Preliminaries: Recite the brief Ngondro preliminary practice.

Nine-round breathing.

Togal Ngondro — Body, Speech & Mind:

Body: 3-kaya postures — primordial awareness of the body (alternate postures)

> *Nirmanakaya*: adept (*rishi*) posture - to gain control over the vital energies and the mind.

> *Sambhogakaya*: elephant posture - to see the pure visions of primordial wisdom.

> *Dharmakaya*: lion posture - to stop deceptive appearances.

Speech: Be silent like a mute.

Mind: Focus on the object (sun, moon, or lamp) while squinting the eyes.

Rotate practice with alternate postures and objects.

Dedication: With the mind of enlightenment, Bodhicitta, I dedicate all merit from this practice for the enlightenment of all sentient beings. (3X)

Post-meditation: *Continue to seek opportunities to practice with the postures and objects of focus throughout the day and night.*

The Lamps

The sun, moon, and lamp described above are the "outer" appearances. Various texts also describe either four or six lamps as the "inner" appearances. Both inner and outer appearances are of the nature of mind. "Lamp" in this context refers not to a butter lamp or candle, but enlightened mind that, like a lamp, illuminates the darkness of ignorance. There are a few different lists of the four and six lamps. Names also vary. Nevertheless, these lists will give you a general idea of their nature and purpose related to the Four Visions. The four lamps are[158]:

1. Fluid Lasso Lamp – the *eyes* that serve as a door for the inner light as outer appearance; door to the arising of the other three lamps

2. Lamp of Pure Space – appearance of dark blue *sky* for projection of the next two lamps

3. Lamp of Empty Tigle – colored *light-drops* (tigle, bindus) which form groups and grow in size

4. Lamp of Self-Arisen Discriminating Awareness – *non-dual awareness*

The six lamps are [159]:

1. Lamp of the Ground – essence, nature, and compassion or buddhanature

2. *Citta* Lamp of the Flesh – presence of the ground in the heart

3. Lamp of the Hollow Crystal *Khati* Channel[160] – connecting the heart to the eyes

4. Fluid Lasso Lamp[161] – the eyes that serve as a door for the inner light as outer appearance

5. Lamp of the Bardo of *Dharmata* – relating the *togal* visions to the bardo and the possibility of enlightenment during this lifetime

6. Lamp of the Ultimate Result – buddhahood

And

The eye is fluid in nature; like a lasso, it reaches out to things far away; and like a lamp, it illuminates. Therefore, it is called the fluid

---

[158] *Lamps in the Leaping Over* [PDF], p. 42.

[159] *Naked Awareness*, p. 164, and *Lamps in the Leaping Over* [PDF], p. 41.

[160] Also known as the white and smooth nadi lamp.

[161] Also known as the far reaching water lamp.

lasso lamp. From this the Buddha manifests in the aspect of the vajra-strands of awareness.[162]

These "lamps" are said to enable us to "see" the visions that arise, and recognize them as none other than our own mind, leading quickly to buddhahood in this lifetime.

The Four Visions of Togal

While *trekcho* focuses on primordial purity, the focus of *togal* is on the spontaneous presence or the dynamic radiant display, i.e., the nondual manifestation of emptiness as energy. *Trekcho* focuses on *dharmakaya; togal* focuses on *sambhogakaya.* Emptiness is expressed as the ground of being. *Togal* then builds upon the experience of *trekcho.* This is seen in the Four Visions of *Togal*:

1. Direct perception into Reality-Itself
2. Progress in visionary experience
3. Reaching consummate awareness
4. Extinction into Reality-Itself

peak of visualization
process - 5 buddha families
↳ visualizations disappear

The phrase "clear light" is often used in Tibetan Buddhism to express the quality of transcendent wisdom. It is not light in the common sense of the word. Rather, "clear" refers to the emptiness of the ultimate, and "light" refers to the clarity of the primordial state. Emptiness and clarity are one. Emptiness is clarity; clarity is emptiness. You cannot be distracted from awareness of the natural state – transcendent wisdom. This is sacred outlook – pure awareness (*rigpa*).

In *togal*, the clear light manifests as spontaneous visions of energy. The specific forms and colors will vary from one individual to another, so the following descriptions may or may not be exactly representative of your experience. During meditation the visions of energy manifest as colors or lights. The colors correspond to those of the Five Buddha Families. They may be tiny dots of light – alone or in chains – strings or large amorphous forms. At first these visions move,

---

[162] *Naked Awareness*, p. 165.

sometimes very fast, and are difficult or impossible to stop the movement. They are sometimes clear and sometimes not. Do not gaze at them directly, nor try to make them appear. They will come naturally. If you try to see more or focus on them, they will disappear.

In the second stage, everything appears as light. We see all colors and the visions are pure and clear. Visions become increasingly large and stable.

At the third stage, various forms appear. The visions are clear and stable. There is no difference between internal and external visions. Unification occurs. We view all in pure awareness, pure presence – the sacred outlook. We realize that the source of all visions is our primordial state – transcendent wisdom. The external world is seen as light. And all is one taste that transcends subject-object duality. We spontaneously remain in a state of undistracted meditative equipoise.

In the final stage, everything disappears into emptiness. There are no more visions, only direct unmediated experience ... beyond words ... empty like space. One abides in ultimate understanding of buddhahood.

"The crucial point is not whether you have visions, but whether you identify with and grasp onto them."[163] Some people say that these visions are a delusion. Some say that they are truth. In Great Perfection, there is neither "delusion" nor "truth." We are neither attached nor deluded by what is.

One practice[164] used to facilitate the experience of the basic space of phenomena is "sky gazing." This is the main meditative practice of *togal* during which you gaze into the empty sky with nothing specific upon which to focus your gaze. This helps give a sense of the vast openness or space-like quality of transcendent wisdom.

However, some lamas and sources recommend a different approach based on the hollow crystal *khati* channel that connects the heart to the eyes, which we opened in Week 43. In this practice, it is visualized as going up the central channel, then through the head over the level of the ears to each of the eyes. In this practice the empty sky acts like a large blank movie screen. And the "visions" are actually projected

---

163 *Naked Awareness*, p. 169.

164 *Heart Drops of Dharmakaya* describes some of 42 togal practices for those seeking additional information.

outwards as manifestations from the indestructible drop in the heart chakra. This tends to result in much clearer and detailed visions, like a dream, than the visions from just gazing generally, although this may vary from one person to another. The images are manifestations of heart-mind. (Recall that *everything* we perceive is actually being *experienced* in our mind, even if it appears to be "outside" of us.)

After meditation the energy remains apparent. Everything is energy. Everything is light. It may appear to vibrate or glow. It may appear stable or fluid.

The discriminating awareness developed in analytical mediation now manifests experientially. One can "see" or sense transcendent wisdom, the energy, *and* the radiant manifestation of that energy as form – *dharmakaya*, *sambhogakaya*, and *nirmanakaya*. And though they are distinct in their qualities, they are of one taste, both/and. In the tradition, *dharmakaya* can only be seen by a Buddha, *sambhogakaya* by a highly realized Bodhisattva, and *nirmanakaya* by ordinary beings. But we are all buddhas. Everything is now seen as wisdom – the view of the sacred outlook of Pure View. Body, speech, and mind abide in the natural state. Everything is spontaneous. There is no particular regard for what others may think, say, or do. All is within the Pure View. The chart below was developed from numerous sources to provide a helpful overview of the Four Visions in terms of (1) the actual visions, (2) their true nature, and (3) ordinary signs of accomplishment for each. Keep in mind that the actual experience of each individual will vary.

The Four Visions of Togal – Outer, Inner & Ordinary[165]

The First Vision – Direct Perception of Reality-Itself
Outer Visions
      Bindus (moving, stabilize over time)
      Hands/faces – signs of compassion
      Rainbows, empty bindus, vajra chains

---

165 From *Vajra Essence* by HH Dudjom Rinpoche, *Yangzab Dzogchen* teachings by Traga Rinpoche, *Natural Liberation* by Padmasambhava, *Yeshe Lama* by Jigmed Lingpa, and "Signs and Levels of Progress" from Padmasambhava's *Single Cut of the Great Self-Liberation* published in *Quintessential Dzogchen* trans. by Erik Pema Kunsang and Marcia Binder Schmidt and *Treasures of Juniper Ridge: The Profound Treasure Instructions of Padmasambhava to the Dakini Yeshe* Tsogyal trans. by ibid, *The Circle of the Sun* by Tsele Natsok Rangdrol. Collected and synthesized by Khenpo Drimed Dawa 2008-2009. Please forgive all errors; they are my own.

Scattering into whiteness
Inner True Nature
Awareness without "other," all is mind
Thoughts projected and return as self-display, insubstantial like space
Directly ascertain suchness
Abide in emptiness, even when dreaming
Ordinary Signs
Devotion to lama as a buddha
No interest in mundane activities
Exert yourself in virtue and avoid nonvirtue
Love and compassion arise effortlessly
Control gross afflictive emotions
Experiences of bliss, clarity, and nonthought
Lightness of body, feeling that everything is insubstantial and evanescent
Voice like a mute

The Second Vision – Progress in Visionary Experience
Outer Visions
Pattern of visions (lattice or curtain, horizontal/vertical lines), larger objects and deities, bindus inside bindus, subtle and course, clear, dazzling, fascinating
Symbols, syllables, jewels, flickers, bodies of light, torsos and heads; increasing sizes
Appearances during and after meditation as light and rainbow bindus with increasing clarity until vanish into continuous displays of light, your body emits light
Expands, above, below, all around
Inner True Nature
Bliss, clarity and nonthought as mind
No solid reference point or clinging
Illusory body free of delusive activities
Everything is a luminous display
Realize even while dreaming
Ordinary Signs
Devotion grows deeper
Attachment and aversion begins to vanish, liberated from accepting or rejecting, pleasure or pain, right or wrong, self or other
Ordinary thinking dissolves into the expanse of awareness
Feel incredible lightness of being
Can express teachings have not even heard

Speak unintentionally, like an echo

The Third Vision – Reaching Consummate Awareness
Outer Visions
Environment as a wrathful palace

Deities in union, mandalas of deities

Countless buddhafields of rainbow light

All appears as bindus of 5 buddha families, peaceful & wrathful deities in bindus

Universe pervaded by rainbow light
Inner True Nature
Material aggregates disappear, feel that can move through rock, mountains and the like

Aggregates of illusory body become vivid as a body of light

Nothing is "real," primordial wisdom increases, transcend appearance and emptiness

Dreaming ends
Ordinary Signs
No fear of samsara

No conceptual focus

All subtle obscurations liberated

Certainty in kayas and buddhafields (transcend conceptualizing)

Speech becomes dharma

The Fourth Vision – Extinction into Reality-Itself
Outer Visions
Deluded visions exhausted into buddhafields

All phenomena dissolve into inner space

Rainbow body
Inner True Nature
No attachment or aversion

Spontaneous presence dissolves back into primordial awareness

Essence returns to its own basis

Utterly naked pure awareness
Ordinary Signs
Effortless dharma teachings to needs of each person

Spontaneously manifest form-bodies to benefit beings

The result is buddhahood:

Dharmakaya—whatever appears is not established as a recognizable essence.

Sambhogakaya—appearances as the 5 bodies, 5 speeches, 5 minds, 5 qualities, & 5 activities of a buddha.

Nirmanakaya—naked, clear, free, relaxed without attachment or aversion.

Rainbow Body

You may remain in bodily form until the time of death, even after having attained a rainbow body. The manifestation of a rainbow body is typically experienced at the time of death itself. At the end of your life, you go into a sealed retreat. Your body dissolves into pure energy in the form of light. Although it is usually described as the body shrinking and vanishing, leaving only hair and nails behind, this is but one of four forms of rainbow body described in various texts. They are:

Small Transference – body shrinks in size and vanishes, leaving hair and nails behind.

Small Rainbow Body – body shrinks in size and vanishes into rainbow body without a trace.

Great Rainbow Body – transmutation like a rainbow vanishing into the sky.

Great Transference – full transmutation of the material constituents of the body into the energy of primordial consciousness (may take place while you are still alive). One is extended infinitely into the all-pervasive *dharmakaya*.

In the Great Perfection tradition, the rainbow body of light is the ultimate accomplishment. However, just as we are already buddhas, for those who can see, we are also already bodies of light. Some of my teachers have stated that you can choose not to disappear after attaining a rainbow body in order to leave physical relics[166] for the benefit of your own students. These relics are said to embody the realization or teachings of the master and are often enshrined in a *stupa*, along with other sacred objects.

---

[166] Such relics of masters or enlightened beings are most often small white or colored stone-like remains from cremation called *ringsel*. In some cases there may be other "signs" among the remains as well. These are often enshrined along with various sacred objects in stupas built for the deceased.

The First Vision - Direct Perception of Reality-Itself

Direct perception of reality itself is the first of the Four Visions practices. The main difference from the previous practice of Seeing *Dharmata* is that the object of focus is now the empty sky – sky gazing – through the hollow *khati* channel. You look west in the morning and east in the evening. (You can also look north during the middle of the day.) You may use any of the three postures or alternate to find the one that is most suitable for you. I have also found it helpful to use a headrest or even a recliner for support when doing this practice for extended periods of looking up into the sky. You can alternate between the formal posture and a more comfortable position as needed. If you have the advantage of doing the practice from a hillside, you can look straight ahead or just slightly up without tilting your head back.

Week 47 — Direct Perception of Reality-Itself

Practice twice daily for one week, or once daily for three weeks.

Intention: I do this practice for the benefit of all sentient beings (*or other personal intention*).

Preliminaries: Recite the brief Ngondro preliminary practice.

Nine-round breathing.

Direct perception of reality itself: Without visualizations, thoughts, or words, gaze at the sky: (see list above)

> *Eyes*: Focus on space (see 3 gazes above) through the hollow *khati* channel — gain control (stability) over vital energies and mind.

> *Object*: Outer – space; inner – your pure absolute nature.

> *Vital energies*: Breath — slow, hold, release (very gently).

> *Visions*: lights, bindus, strands, rainbows (*not* imagined "visualizations")

> Many small objects with much movement.

> Movements slow and stabilize over time.

Dedication: With the mind of enlightenment, Bodhicitta, I dedicate all merit from this practice for the enlightenment of all sentient beings. (3X)

Post-meditation: *Continue to seek opportunities to practice sky gazing during the day and reflect on Reality-Itself.*

It is helpful to keep a notebook of your vision experiences to review periodically regarding your progress or talk with your teacher about your experiences. Although only a week is allocated for these practices, it is rare that they would fully develop that spontaneously. It is more common for these to take a few months or more of intensive practice for that to happen. Practice patience and persistence.

The Second Vision - Progressing Experiential Visions

Once you have gained confidence in the direct perception of reality-itself, the next phase will begin to develop. These stages are not always this clear, so be patient and enjoy the experiences – without attachment or aversion.

Week 48 – Progressing Experiential Visions

Practice twice daily for one week, or once daily for three weeks.

Intention: I do this practice for the benefit of all sentient beings (*or other personal intention*).

Preliminaries: Recite the brief Ngondro preliminary practice.

Nine-round breathing.

Progressing experiential visions: (see table above) Continue sky gazing through the hollow *khati* channel in the selected posture as before.

More of a pattern to the visions.

Larger objects, more detail, and deities may appear.

Dedication: With the mind of enlightenment, Bodhicitta, I dedicate all merit from this practice for the enlightenment of all sentient beings. (3X)

Post-meditation: *Continue to seek opportunities to practice sky gazing during the day and reflect on the visions.*

The Third Vision - Consummate Awareness

Once you have gained confidence in the progressing experiential visions, the third vision of Consummate Awareness will begin to manifest. Continue to practice with patience and persistence.

Week 49 — Consummate Awareness

Practice twice daily for one week, or once daily for three weeks.

Intention: I do this practice for the benefit of all sentient beings (*or other personal intention*).

Preliminaries: Recite the brief Ngondro preliminary practice.

Nine-round breathing.

Consummate Awareness: (see table above) Continue sky gazing through the hollow *khati* channel in the selected posture as before.

> Deities and consorts, mandalas, and the Five Buddha Families may appear.

> Your body is liberated into the clear light.

Dedication: With the mind of enlightenment, Bodhicitta, I dedicate all merit from this practice for the enlightenment of all sentient beings. (3X)

Post-meditation: *Continue to seek opportunities to practice sky gazing during the day and reflect on consummate awareness.*

The Fourth Vision - Extinction into Reality-Itself

Once you have gained confidence in consummate awareness, the fourth vision of Extinction into Reality-Itself manifests. You may no longer need formal meditation as *everything* is now meditation.[167]

---

[167] Nevertheless, I highly recommend continuing formal meditation – both for your benefit and as a role model for others. Otherwise you may assume you have attained full enlightenment when you have not. It is best not to assume either that you have or have not and continue on anyway.

Week 50 — Extinction into Reality-Itself

Practice twice daily for one week, or once daily for three weeks.

Intention: I do this practice for the benefit of all sentient beings (*or other personal intention*).

Preliminaries: Recite the brief Ngondro preliminary practice.

Nine-round breathing.

Extinction into Reality-Itself: (see table above) Continue sky gazing through the hollow *khati* channel in the selected posture as before (until there are signs of having achieved a rainbow body).

> The progression of visions comes to an end.

> Rainbow body manifests and you become a buddha.

Dedication: With the mind of enlightenment, Bodhicitta, I dedicate all merit from this practice for the enlightenment of all sentient beings. (3X)

As a buddha, all conventional reality is extinguished, though one can still perceive how ordinary beings see what they call reality and the suffering they experience. Great compassion and buddha activities manifest to help beings help themselves to also attain enlightenment.

As with earlier practices, it is best to do many, short practices, gradually extending to hours and eventually all day/night. Some sources say to practice like this for one and a half months.

At some point, as with earlier practices, *trekcho* and *togal* may merge. From a Great Perfection state of mind, *trekcho* and *togal* are themselves conceptualizations. When we live the sacred outlook of the transcendent wisdom, these too "disappear."

In Appendix E I have provided a copy of the *Sadhana of the Blue Dakini*, the third in the trilogy of the Three Dakinis. The *trekcho* practice in this text is based on *Rigpa Guru Yoga*. As before, in this Guru Yoga there is no deity to visualize. You simply abide in *rigpa*. With practice, you will easily have direct experience of knowing the true nature of mind, the *dharmakaya*, just as it is. *Let go and let be.* This is then followed by the sky gazing practice of *togal*. Alternate them until they merge into one taste.

Dark Retreat

The most intensive *togal* practice, requiring the guidance of a qualified master, is the dark retreat. This is carried out in total darkness over a period of forty-nine days. The sensory deprivation creates an intensive experience with the movement of energy within space. One will visualize organic and geometric forms and lights – the energy of the transcendent wisdom. To get a brief sense of this experience, you can close the eyes and press lightly on your eyeballs with your fingers. As the retreat progresses, the experience may include visualization of forms of deities or dakinis, mandalas, and so forth, which were part of the lower tantra visualizations. Padmasambhava does not describe this practice and it is beyond the scope of these more concise practices for householders.

Signs of Accomplishment

Khorde rushen

Khorde rushen is the separation of samsara and nirvana. It is characterized by a sense of separation from appearances (sights, sounds, touch, smell, taste, thoughts) from the actual experience of those in one's mind. Whatever arises is the manifestation of mind. Afflictive emotions and mental obscurations are just manifestations of mind. Even "emptiness" is a concept. There is no thought of self or other. There is a letting go of body, speech, and mind without attachment or aversion.

These signs are temporary, changing, and not reliable[168]:

Your body feels at the brink of collapse like the walls of a house in shambles.

---

[168] From *Treasures from Juniper Ridge: The Profound Treasure Instructions of Padmasambhava to the Dakini Yeshe Tsogyal*

Your voice feels worn out like when exhausted, or you convulse like someone possessed.

The moods are disenchantment with the samsaric body, speech, and mind.

Your body is blissful, your voice wants to speak out, and your mind experiences everything as space.

You feel, "Now nothing exists!" as well as compassion for beings who fail to realize the same as you, and your enthusiasm for the dharma will also arise.

You forget that you have a body, you don't notice your breathing, and mentally you don't want to part from the state of nonthought.

Trekcho

Trekcho is characterized by achieving a state of awareness-emptiness or *rigpa*—pure awareness. Emptiness is transcendent wisdom, beyond concepts. It can be described only in *via negativa* language such as Nagarjuna's tetradilemma: emptiness is not a thing, not no thing (nothing), not both, not neither. At the highest level, there is no difference between on or off the cushion. Everything is meditation (the meditation of nonmeditation).

The four stages of experience are[169]:

One-pointedness – there is stillness wherever mind is placed, awareness arises within that state, and post-meditation appearances are unreal and illusory.

Simplicity – you feel a special confidence but are unable to describe it, everything is emptiness, if thoughts arise they are self-liberated, there is no difference between meditation and post-meditation, even when sleeping, and your meditation is unaffected by dullness and agitation. *Monkey mind is rare.*

One taste – the identity of outer perceived objects and the inner perceiving mind naturally vanishes, subtle movements of

---

[169] From *Circle of the Sun*

thinking spontaneously vanish without dependence upon an experience of "emptiness," there is a fearless confidence, the one taste of samsara and nirvana is like space, and the eight concerns[170] in post-meditation are like illusion, and no fixation on meditation or post-meditation, on subject or object, takes place.

Nonmeditation – flawless present wakefulness simply manifests without divisions like meditation or post-meditation, there is no more "thing" to sustain through mindfulness, even the most subtle aspects of thought activity and subject-object have naturally subsided, and you transcend the concept of mindfulness and are liberated into buddhahood.

Togal

Togal is characterized by the four visions[171]:

I. Vision of direct perception of reality-itself.

These signs change and will not last:

Feeling disenchantment with body, speech, and mind in a way that is visible to both you and others, and also having no interest in the activities of this life.

Your voice is like that of a mute.

Mentally you are tired of samsaric affairs; you feel a profound devotion for your guru, and a compassion for all beings wells up so that tears flow.

There is trust in the consequence of actions, and you exert yourself in giving up misdeeds and practicing virtue.

There is a mood of lightness of body, at times even forgetting that you have a body, not noticing your breath's

---

[170] Gain and loss, praise and blame, good and bad reputation, and pleasure and pain

[171] From *Treasures from Juniper Ridge: The Profound Treasure Instructions of Padmasambhava to the Dakini Yeshe Tsogyal*

movement, and mentally feeling that everything is insubstantial and evanescent.

Signs of lasting value are:

Within the expansive space of the view, when awareness is utterly laid bare, without fluctuations, and doesn't project experience as being "other," that is the sign of having anchored awareness within *dharmata*.

The mood signs of having understood this are that, no matter where your attention moves, you understand and realize that it is your own mind, you see that thoughts are projected and return as self-display, and you understand that they are completely insubstantial like space.

To recognize this even while dreaming is the sign of having reached the fullest degree of steadiness.

2. Vision of progress in visionary experience.

All these signs change and cannot be relied upon:

Your body is light and energetic, your voice is clear and able to express teachings you have never even heard, and at times your mind has some degree of clairvoyance.

You see everything lucidly as rainbows, sometimes full of bodily forms and circles, sometimes becoming void and without reference points.

As devotion to your guru grows even deeper and your concern for karmic consequences becomes more relaxed, you feel that your body emits light, at times your body is absent, your voice speaks unintentionally like an echo, and your mind is clear and blissful and does not project anything; now and then it turns void and forms no thoughts.

The unchanging signs are:

There is no longer any experience in which you cling to solid reality; instead, everything is sheer luminous display. Everything appears, but there is no sold reference point or clinging. To realize this even while dreaming is to have reached the fullest degree of steadiness.

3. *Vision of reaching consummate awareness.*

These signs change and cannot be relied upon:

Emptiness is spontaneously and effortlessly liberated in itself.

There is no attachment to a body, such as being unafraid of water. Previously unseen marks of excellence can be seen by you and others.

Your voice can express beneficial Dharma teachings by simply directing your will toward others.

In your mind untainted clairvoyance arises.

The signs of meditation moods are that you neither remember nor even think of clinging to your body, speech and mind; that whatever you experience is spacious and not taken as real; and that you feel as if you can move freely through rock, mountains, and the like.

The unchanging signs are:

No matter what you experience, there is neither any conceptual focus nor any attempt to accept or reject. Rather it is liberated without being assumed to be real, so that, whether day or night and without needing to remember it, appearance and emptiness are naturally liberated into nonduality. When the delusion of dreaming ends, you have reached the fullest degree of steadiness.

4. *Vision of extinction into reality-itself.*

All signs and indications of progress on the path have ceased. The moving force of appearances has ceased, while the still quality of emptiness is no longer. The nondual nature of appearance and emptiness neither fluctuates nor changes in any way whatsoever.

There is a naturally awake quality that transcends meeting and separation—an unfabricated presence, an absence without any dismantling—which is an utterly naked state of aware emptiness free of clinging.

In others' perceptions, since an unobstructed knowledge—original wakefulness as an all-pervasive capacity—is also present, there is an effortless unfolding of form-bodies for the welfare of beings.

Sense Clarity

Seeing the ten signs[172] that indicate taking hold of the mind within

Seeing various types of sentient beings and shapes

Hearing the sound of large drums, or hearing and understanding the voices of the smallest insects and many other kinds of beings

Smelling the scents of *devas, nagas, yakshas,* and so forth, as well as experiencing the various types of extra sensory perceptions through scent

Tasting numerous types of flavor so that it feels as if one is experiencing untainted ambrosia when savoring ordinary food and drink

Feeling sensations of touch that occur in the same way as the others

Mental Clarity

A profusion of concepts about what should be discarded with which remedies

---

[172] Smoke, mirages, flames, fireflies, moonlight, sunlight, glows of fire, red and white spheres, rainbows, and shooting stars

Insights about the connection between intelligence, proliferation of thoughts, and outer and inner interdependence

Brightness, lucidity, and an absence of deep sleep or mental dullness

The feeling of understanding everything, as well as countless other types of insights

Clarity will be experienced as the understanding of cause and effect, as well as the absence of the scattered and agitated states

Nonthought will be experienced as the attainment of an unwavering stability.

Four States of Confidence

Confidence of not fearing the lower realms (samsara no longer exists)

Confidence of no longer anticipating the ripening of cause and effect (in liberation the thought "this is happiness" no longer occurs)

Confidence of not hoping for anything to be obtained (there is not even a hair tip's worth of something else that becomes a buddha)

Confidence that joy and sorrow are pure in the nature of evenness

Chapter 19

The Third Training on the Path of Great Perfection: Wisdom

The Shentong Yogacarya Madhyamaka Approach

In the previous paths we looked at wisdom from the view of the *Sautrantika*, *Cittamatra*, *Svatantrika*, and *Prasangika* schools of Buddhism.[173] The latter two are both branches of the Middle Way (*Madhyamaka*). Each provided a slightly different interpretation of the teachings of the Buddha regarding ultimate truth. In the Path of Great Perfection, we now look at the *Shentong* school, also known as *Yogacarya*. This is the third branch of the Middle Way philosophy.

It is important here to note that many sources do not distinguish between the *Cittamatrans* (Mind Only school) and the *Yogacaryans* due to similarities between their approaches. It is fairly common to see the names used interchangeably. Yet there are important differences. The *Shentong* does not accept the *Cittamatra* view that consciousness is truly existent. They hold the *Madhyamaka* view that it is non-arising and without self-nature. *Yogacaryans* argue that their system involves not only recognizing freedom from all concepts, but also the realization of the Wisdom Mind (*jnana*) that is free from all concepts. Non-conceptual Wisdom Mind is the only thing that has absolute and true existence. This, however, does not mean that it can be conceptualized. It can be realized only through means other than the conceptual process. You must experience it directly.

---

[173] These are not actual "schools" per se, but are commonly referred to in this way.

There has been some dispute among the different schools of Tibetan Buddhism regarding the *Prasangika* and *Shentong* approaches. In part this stems from the fact that the *Shentong* view was developed by Shantaraksita at Nalanda University and brought to Tibet in first dissemination of Buddhism into Tibet in the late 8th century CE, when he was invited by King Trisong Detsen to build the Samye monastery. In this approach, he included the views of the *Yogacarya* tradition founded in India by Asanga and his half-brother Vasubandhu (4th century CE), as well as views from Dharmakirti and others. However, although the *Prasangika* texts were written by Candrakirti in the mid 6th century, they did not come to Tibet until much later, during the second dissemination (10th to 12th centuries CE). This gave the appearance that the *Prasangika* texts were more recent and superseded the *Shentong* texts, when in reality it was the other way around.

But there is more to the argument than just the dates. The *Shentong* masters criticized the *Prasangikas* for their claim that they did not hold *any* views, i.e., since everything is impermanent and empty of inherent existence, there is no "relative" or "ultimate" truth. The *Shentong* argue that if the mere absence of concepts were absolute reality, it would be mere nothingness, empty space, or the extreme of nihilism. How can nothingness account for appearances? There has to be *something* that is in some sense luminous – illuminating and knowing.

Furthermore, the *Shentong* argued that what the *Cittamatrans* called "absolute" was wrongly interpreted by them to be a consciousness (*vijnana*). According to the *Shentong*, this clear luminous aware quality of mind is not a consciousness, but a non-conceptual absolute reality (*jnana*) with no seeing and seen aspect, no realizing and realized aspect. This is called Transcendent Wisdom (*Prajnaparamita*) and is none other than the non-conceptual Wisdom Mind itself, also referred to as clear light, nature of mind, *dharmata*, clarity and emptiness, bliss and emptiness, *tathagatagarbha*, and so forth. The *Shentong* posit that the experience of complete freedom from concepts must also be the *experience* of the clear light nature of mind. Thus, *Prasangikas*, who deny this, must still have some subtle concept, which is obscuring or negating this reality.

The *Shentong* argued that if there really were no concepts in the mind, the clear light nature would shine forth so clearly and unmistakably that it would not be possible to deny it. The practices purify obscurations so that this Buddhanature emerges. If the true nature of beings were not the *tathagatagarbha*, they could never become buddhas in the same way that a rock that did not contain gold could never yield gold, however much it was refined.

The *Shentong* criticize the other *Madhyamikas* who say that the buddha qualities arise as a result of the good deeds, vows and connections made by bodhisattvas on the path to enlightenment. For the *Shentong*, the buddha qualities are primordially existent as Buddhanature. Nevertheless, good deeds, vows and connections are necessary for removing veils that obscure those qualities.

The *Shentong* also do not accept that the Wisdom Mind "knows" in a dualistic way, so there is no subtle object of the Wisdom Mind. It is not a stream of moments of awareness. It is completely unbounded and free from all concepts, including time and space.

The *Shentong* posit three *modes of existence*: (1) imaginary – as mere conceptual creations, (2) dependent – that are not truly existent, and (3) truly existent non-conceptual Wisdom Mind.

There are also three *modes of emptiness*: (1) imaginary – which is empty in that it does not exist at all except in the imagination, (2) dependent – which though it appears has no ultimate existence, and (3) ultimate absolute emptiness – which is the non-conceptual Wisdom Mind.

There are three *modes of absence of essence*: (1) imaginary – without essence, just a concept, (2) dependent – without essence in that essence never arises, and (3) absolute absence of essence – non-conceptual (from the view of the conceptual mind it is without essence; from its own point of view it is absolute reality).

When the non-conceptual Wisdom Mind is not realized, it is the basis for the impure, mistaken, or illusory appearances to manifest. Once it is realized, it is the basis for pure manifestations of the three kayas, buddhafields, mandalas of the deities, and so forth. Wisdom Mind is both emptiness *and* luminosity. Emptiness expresses its non-conceptual nature; luminosity expresses its power to manifest (pure and impure) appearances.

In the dream example, dreams arise from the luminous quality of mind. If Wisdom Mind is not recognized, the dependent nature arises. Once the awakened consciousness returns, one quickly sees dreams are mere manifestations of the play of mind.

The key in the meditation (or non-meditation) is personal instruction from a realized master with faith and devotion that through his/her skillful means, realization can arise and mature. Gradually, understanding deepens and the conceptualizing tendency loses its hold on the mind, and it becomes more relaxed and open, calm and clear. Jamgon Kongtrul describes the two approaches this way:

Madhyamaka philosophies have no differences in realizing as "*Shunyata*"[174] all phenomena that we experience on a relative level. They have no differences also in reaching the meditative state where all extremes (ideas) completely dissolve. Their difference lies in the words they use to describe the *Dharmata*. *Shentong* describes the *Dharmata*, the mind of Buddha, as "ultimately real"; while [*Prasangika*] philosophers fear that if it is described that way, people might understand it as the concept of "soul" or "Atman." The *Shentong* philosopher believes that there is a more serious possibility of misunderstanding in describing the enlightened state as "unreal" and "void." Kongtrul finds the [*Prasangika*] way of presentation the best to dissolve concepts and the *Shentong* way the best to describe the experience.

Jamgon Kongtrul says that the *Prasangika* is the view when one is establishing certainty through listening, studying and reflecting; *Shentong* is the view for meditation practice. The important part of this approach is the direct experience. In practice, *Shentong Madhyamaka* is very much like the advanced *shamata* of *trekcho*.

Week 51 — Shentong Yogacarya Madhyamaka

Practice twice daily for one week, or once daily for three weeks.

Intention: I do this practice for the benefit of all sentient beings (*or other personal intention*).

Preliminaries: Recite the brief Ngondro preliminary practice.

Nine-round breathing.

Shentong Yogacarya Madyamaka:

Rest the mind naturally in its own nature.

Whatever thoughts arise, there is no need to try to stop them; they simply liberate themselves.

Observe the true nature of mind directly, without effort.

Dedication: With the mind of enlightenment, Bodhicitta, I dedicate all merit from this practice for the enlightenment of all sentient beings. (3X)

---

[174] Emptiness

Post-meditation: Between sessions stop from time to time to rest the mind in its natural state and carry that awareness over into whatever one is doing, not unlike the *Cittamatra* approach of being aware moment by moment.

Signs of Accomplishment

The goal of our practice is wisdom, the view. This has been characterized in a variety of ways that may be used as signs of realization of the view, some of which were alluded to earlier.

Pure View

Pure View is achieved when you see all beings as buddhas, hear all sounds as mantra, know all thoughts as the wisdom of the buddhas, and realize all phenomena as a perfect buddhafield (mandala). In the beginning this is imagined. Eventually, however, one gains confidence in the reality of this view.

In addition, within the tradition, there is an additional stage of development associated with the union of these two practices. Having achieved the union of *shamata* and *vipassana* meditation, you begin to realize the *nondual outlook*. As previously noted there are two truths. These can be thought of as two sides of one's hand – palm and back. There is only one hand, one truth, but they are different aspects of that truth. At this point in the practice, you become aware of these two natures of the one truth. The ultimate nature is ineffable openness – emptiness; the relative nature is its dynamic radiant display. And within this display you are now clearly awake regarding the interdependent coexistence of all phenomena. The sense of deep oneness intensifies our sense of lovingkindness, compassion, joy and equanimity for the benefit of others.

Thus, in recognizing the nondual nature of these two meditation practices, you transcend the one taste of two as one to pure awareness of the dynamic interplay of ultimate *and* relative truth, both/and ... as just a direct experience. The meditation intensifies this nonconceptual awareness and touches every fiber of your being. You are awakening to your buddhanature within and becoming confident in that realization.

Over time you will become unshakable in your confidence and stability, as your heart-mind radiates throughout all that is. During the meditative state, you transcend all sense of self, time, or space ... and express *total* lovingkindness and compassion for others equally.

You begin to see the innate perfection as the essence of all phenomena. Each person is a buddha. Each sound is a mantra. Each thought is the nature of mind. Everything is sacred. This is the sacred outlook – Pure View. All is sacred and perfect just as it is ... no judgment ... nothing to do. With practice, you remain "awake" to Pure View at *all* times.

Awareness-Emptiness

In the Path of Individual Liberation you learned the *appearance-emptiness* of the lack of inherent existence of all appearances. In the Path of Altruism you experienced the *luminous-emptiness* of buddhanature, your direct experience of the tetradilemma – emptiness is not a thing, it is not no-thing, it is not both, and it is not neither. In the Path of Tantra you experienced the *bliss-emptiness* that transcends sexual or other sensory forms of bliss for transcendent bliss itself, a deep inner peace with an incredible lightness of being. And now with the Path of Great Perfection, you experienced *awareness-emptiness*, the pure awareness itself, pure consciousness free of all forms of attachment and aversion, "suchness."

Conclusion

Just as no darkness exists at the center of the sun,
To a yogi, universe and beings all arise as deities –
And the yogi is content.

Just as no ordinary stones exist on an island of gold,
To a yogi all sounds resound as mantras –
And the yogi is content.

Just as a bird crossing a clear, empty sky leaves no trace,
To a yogi all thoughts arise as the absolute –
And the yogi is content.

In the vastness of awareness not confined to formal sessions,
To a yogi all meditation is relaxed and at ease –
And the yogi is content.

Free from the workings of mind,
I realize that phenomena are the absolute state.
You, my friend, should realize this too.
Don't trust intellectual teachings –
Recognize that vast and unborn sameness.

-- Shabkar

H.H. Dilgo Khyentse Rinpoche said, "Realization occurs in three stages: understanding, experiences, and true realization. True realization cannot be shaken. Good or adverse circumstances, even in their thousands, will provoke no attachment or aversion, no expectation or doubt at all."[175]

---

[175] *Journey to Enlightenment: The Life and World of Khyentse Rinpoche, Spiritual Teacher from Tibet.* Photographs and narrative by Mattieu Ricard (n.d.), p. 108.

Part 7 –Innate Happiness

The English word "enlightenment" is a translation of the Pali and Sanskrit word *bodhi*. The root word *budh* means to be awake, to become aware, to know, or to understand. *Bodhi* implies the state of realization of a buddha regarding the true nature of things. *Bodhi* includes a sense of understanding karma and reincarnation that lead to our experience of suffering.

In India, liberation (*moksha*) meant freedom from reincarnation and, thus, suffering that comes with it. The *shramanans* considered one who had attained this liberation to be an *Arhat*, an honorific term meaning "worthy" for having attained nirvana. This was adopted by the Buddha and the Path of Individual Liberation. In the *Vanapattha Sutta*, the Buddha describes having attained three insights – past lives, the workings of karma, and reincarnation – and the Four Noble Truths. He said, "Knowledge arose in me, and insight: my freedom is certain, this is my last birth, now there is no rebirth."

However, the idea of enlightenment evolved over time in the different schools of Buddhism. In the Path of Individual Liberation, it referred to nirvana and understanding the true nature of self and other as having a lack of any inherent existence – *appearance-emptiness*. In that state you are freed from the three poisons, variously listed as attachment (desire), aversion (anger), and ignorance (delusion).

In the Path of Altruism, it was said that while attachment and aversion had been eliminated, a subtle form of ignorance still remained for an *Arhat*. This was based on the principle of altruism, the Bodhisattva ideal of attaining enlightenment for all beings. Individual liberation did not attain this further step that completely eliminates even subtle ignorance. This was articulated as the *luminous-emptiness* of transcendent wisdom. Thus, the yogin achieved a nonconceptual realization of the true nature of mind that transcended conceptual descriptions, although a wide array of terms became equated with this *idea* of nonconceptual transcendence. This approach continued into the Path of Tantra (sometimes considered to be part of the Path of Altruism). With the emphasis on deity practices, the ultimate state changed to transcendent *bliss-emptiness*. However, in the Path of Great Perfection, this idea of the enlightened state was refined slightly so that awareness itself was equated with emptiness – *awareness-emptiness* – and, thus, enlightenment. And finally with the state of paranirvana, one is said to achieve the ultimate state of *compassion-emptiness*.

Chapter 20

Enlightenment in This Lifetime

Wisdom

The Sanskrit word *vidyadhara* means "knowledge holder." *Vidya* means "knowledge," specifically the knowledge that comes from wisdom; and *dhara* means "to hold." Thus, a *vidyadhara* is one who holds wisdom within their consciousness. They are aware of the true nature of things and mind itself at all times, even when they are active in the world.

But what is this wisdom? To understand enlightenment, we need to understand wisdom in the Buddhist tradition. The third part of The Three Teachings is wisdom, which we examined from the view of each of the four paths. The ultimate result of meditation is Right View, transcendent wisdom. This is the realization of ultimate truth, which raises the fundamental question of "What is the truth?" Can we believe in a nonmaterial reality that is beyond what we can see, hear, touch, smell, and taste? How can something be called true when not everyone believes, accepts, or acknowledges it to be so? Can we prove it to be true?

These are not easy questions to answer. The historical Buddha himself appears to have observed a "Noble Silence" when asked metaphysical questions. What we can clearly see is that some truths come from our perceptions of the way things are in the material world. Scientific theories are often used to describe these truths. But other cases are in dispute. Some people believe in evolution, for which there is "indisputable scientific evidence," while others reject it and hold "creationism" or "intelligent design" to represent the truth. What is considered to be true varies from culture to culture and country to country. So, like ethics, there is a relative component to what we call truth. Thus, one can refer to such truths as *relative truth*.

At the same time, the very definition of the word "truth" infers that there are some things that are absolutely true, beyond dispute. This can be referred to as *ultimate truth*.

So what is real? We normally consider what we can see, hear, touch, taste or smell to be "real." But we know scientifically that our brain is designed to create a particular perception of what is real that is vastly different than what we know even the material world to actually be.

If you doubt this, try this experiment. Find a point across the room and focus your eyes on that point. Without moving your eyes, search your field of vision to see if there are any blank spots. If you are normal, you will find none. Of course, since most of us have two eyes, a blank spot in one could be covered by what is seen by the other. So try it again. This time look while covering one eye, then the other. Again, if you are normal, you will not find any blank spots. If you are reading and have not yet tried this, do it now.

Next, while looking at your focus point across the room, cover your left eye with your left hand. Then extend your right arm out in front of you with your thumb up covering the focus point across the room. Now slowly move your arm out toward the right side while keeping your eye on the focus point. As you move your thumb out a ways, your thumb will disappear from your vision. Move it around in and out of that blank spot. This is the point where light is focused on the optical nerve in the back of your eye. There are no light receptors there with which to see. How is it then that you could not see this blank spot before? Quite simply, the brain fills it in. Try it again with your other eye.

Now, having some direct experience at recognizing that our brain is wired to delude us into appearances that are not true, let's consider some other scientific evidence about the nature of reality vs. what we perceive to be true. We know that matter is made up of atoms. But atoms are mostly empty space. In fact, if we could increase the size of an atom to the point that the nucleus was the size of a grain of salt, the electrons – too small to be visible – would be racing around at the speed of light in a space the size of a fourteen-story building.

To use another example, if you took all seven plus billion people on the planet and compressed all the empty space from the atoms of which they are composed, they would fit into a thimble – a very heavy thimble to be sure, but a thimble nevertheless. Atoms are almost entirely empty space. In other words, *everything* is almost entirely empty space. But our brain makes it appear as if all objects are solid, liquid or gas. That is a scientific illusion, even though it has practical application.

Furthermore, much of the various stimuli with which we are constantly bombarded are screened out by our brain. Magnificent as it is, our brain simply cannot handle that much information. We filter it based on previous experiences, current focus, interests, preferences and so forth. We also just ignore great quantities of it – information overload at the sensory level. Have you ever noticed while walking down a sidewalk that you can either look through a store window to the merchandise displayed inside *or* at the reflection from the window of the outdoors? Both stimuli are continuously present, but it makes a great deal of difference where we focus our attention. This ability to focus our attention, our awareness, is critical to our spiritual development.

In another example of how our brain creates an illusory reality, scientists now know that the view created by the brain is highly effected by our emotions, our preconceived ideas of the world, our expectations, and so forth, as much as eighty percent!

Finally, consider that at birth an infant perceives the world as one, nondual. There is no ability yet to differentiate self from other. However, as the brain develops in the early months of life, the brain *creates* the perception of self and other as separate, independent realities.

So what is ultimate truth? Within the realm of religious and spiritual beliefs, there is considerable difference in what individuals consider to be ultimate truth. Nevertheless, the direct experience of the ultimate, however we conceive of it, is described by those who know it directly as being *more real* than what humans "normally" perceive as reality.

Trying to describe it is another matter. The mystics sometime use *emptiness* or *nothingness*. But contrary to the implication of these words, this does not mean that there is no ultimate. We have already established that it does exist. In Buddhism, it has been expressed in terms of having an *inherent* or *independent* existence. Whatever lacks an independent existence is not the ultimate, thus tying it to the notion that everything is interdependent – dependent arising. To have an independent existence would mean that it is unaffected by any other causes or conditions. To do that it would have to be permanent, beyond time, with no beginning or end. It would have no other parts, as that would mean it is dependent upon those parts. We cannot find such a thing. So this leads to the idea that the ultimate is nothingness. But that cannot be the case since we have already established that it exists. So how can it be nothingness?

In discussing *transcendent wisdom,* the *Heart Sutra*[176] contains the famous line, "Form is emptiness; emptiness is form." If emptiness means being empty of inherent existence, then what we are addressing is whether "form" (as well as any other thing, characteristic or quality) is empty of an independent existence. Since any form clearly is dependent upon other causes and conditions, it *is* empty of inherent existence. Furthermore, being "empty" of inherent existence infers that there *is something* to be empty of inherent existence. In this case that something is the form. Thus, form is emptiness and emptiness is form. The *Heart Sutra* goes on to *exclude* a long list of other descriptors from transcendent wisdom, including many that are frequently used in Buddhist texts. This is representative of the philosophical approach described as *via negativa,* describing what it is not, since there is no way to describe what it is. So transcendent wisdom is said to transcend our ability to describe or explain it in any way. But it does exist. For this reason, the Buddha taught the Four Reliances given earlier in this book:

1. Rely on the teaching, not the teacher.
2. Rely on the meaning of the teaching, not the words that express it.
3. Rely on the definitive meaning, not the provisional meaning.
4. Rely on transcendent wisdom of deep experience, not ordinary knowledge.

The way that we know transcendent wisdom exists is that we have some form of *consciousness.* We are aware. Awareness is critical to the spiritual path. Consciousness enables us to sense the presence of the ultimate directly, not just conceptually. Some consider that there are multiple levels of consciousness – ordinary consciousness and one or more levels of subtle consciousness. In Buddhism each of the senses, as well as thoughts and emotions, also are said to have a form of consciousness. Thus, we have eye consciousness, ear consciousness, and so forth. In some traditions, the consciousness is congruent with the notion of soul. In others it is considered to be a very subtle level, which is said to pass on in the process of rebirth. Spiritual development is largely a process of training the mind through spiritual practices to increase awareness of increasingly subtle levels, the highest of which is *pure awareness,* or awareness itself. It is through pure awareness that we experience transcendent wisdom directly.

---

[176] See chapter 10.

Having established that transcendent wisdom is beyond description but that we can be aware of it, we must also acknowledge that we must use concepts in order to communicate the experience of transcendent wisdom. Among these concepts are four descriptors often used in the Buddhist tradition: ineffability, oneness, openness, and the dynamic radiant display.

The first of these is that the ultimate is *ineffable* – beyond words, beyond concepts. Even though we often try to articulate qualities or characteristics of the ultimate, they are still limited approximations, sometimes in the form of idealized human qualities, which we then attribute to the ultimate in some anthropomorphic form. This may help us to identify with and relate to such conceptualizations, sometimes as deities. But that may take away from our understanding of ultimate truth as transcendent wisdom.

A second characteristic is *oneness*. The exact qualities of this may vary somewhat among religious traditions, particularly in two respects. One version is a sense of universal oneness – that we are *all* one, including the ultimate. We recognize that we only *perceive* ourselves as separate individuals or phenomena, thus overcoming the dualistic perception created by the brain in our early stages of physiological development. One example of this view is the Hindu concept of *Brahman*. Brahman is fundamentally ineffable, but has also been described as doing nothing, but that nothing happens without Brahman. Individuals perceive themselves as separate from Brahman, as *atman*, but atman is ultimately Brahman. Others have articulated this oneness as a form of a "cosmic consciousness."

The alternative mystical concept of oneness is restricted to individuals and individual phenomena. Here our ordinary consciousness perceives ourselves as separate, but there is no difference between self and other. We are one, but still within individual consciousnesses. In the extreme, this takes the form of "mind-only" conceptualization of reality. This is generally rejected due to the complexities and varieties of individual experiences that do not seem to support it. Nor does scientific evidence. Nor is there support for a "universal oneness" described above. Buddhist teachings generally follow the individual oneness model with each of us having our individual consciousness, i.e., there is no single "universal" or "cosmic" consciousness.

The third common quality is the experience of *openness* or vastness. It has been described as like space. This is not space in the temporal sense of distance, but in a metaphorical sense of transcending concepts, much like the ineffable. Hence, it is labeled as "the basic space of phenomena," as well as "suchness." Yet it is beyond Nagarjuna's four extremes.[177]

A fourth quality is recognition that there is still truth in what we do perceive, i.e., it *does exist*, contrary to the "mind-only" school of thought. It may be an illusion in the sense of its true nature vs. how we perceive it, but it does exist nevertheless. This perceived reality represents a *dynamic radiant display* of the ultimate nature of things. In his commentary on the *Guhyagarbha Tantra*, Mipham Rinpoche states that this enlightened state is known as the "natural and spontaneously present mandala of the ground." Thus,

> In terms of the final meaning, since all phenomena are great purity and equality from the very beginning, one should know that the culmination of the natural great perfection, in which there is no affirming, negating, accepting, or rejection, is absence, oneness, openness, and spontaneous presence.[178]

But there remains disagreement regarding the true nature of "the ground" or the ultimate among proponents of differing philosophical schools in Buddhism. I touched on these in the chapters on wisdom for each of the paths. In my opinion, the key question has come down to the issue of "permanence." The Buddha said all phenomena are *impermanent*. The *Prasangikas* take this to include the ultimate. They follow the line that because it is ineffable, we cannot say that it is permanent. And since we agree that it exits, it must be impermanent. The problem with this argument is that one has just said something about the ineffable, i.e., that it is "impermanent." So the *Shentong* counter to this is that we agree that the ultimate exists. We can experience it, even if that experience is beyond words, i.e., is ineffable. But they go one step further to say that in relative terms, we must also acknowledge that it is *permanent*. The ultimate would not *be* "ultimate" if it was not permanent. So the very definition of "ultimate" means that it is permanent, or there is no ultimate at all. And since we know that it exists, it must be permanent, albeit from a relative point of view. My summary is this, following Nagarjuna's tetradilemma: the ultimate is not permanent, it is not impermanent, not both, and it is not neither; it just is. But by definition – a relative use of the term the ultimate, it is permanent. Mipham Rinpoche

---

[177] It is not a thing, it is not no-thing, it is not both, it is not neither.

[178] I have changed the order of the four qualities to match the order in the discussion above.

concludes, "Once one has internalized this profound nature of reality, one will be indivisible with the wisdom mind of the teacher."

To conclude, wisdom in Tibetan Buddhism refers to ultimate truth. And although we use many descriptors such as those included above, it is beyond any descriptions or concepts. Thus, even these descriptions are said to be relative truth. In fact, anything we can say about any form of truth, including the ultimate, must actually be a relative truth. But we must use words and concepts to communicate. So we use many labels for ultimate truth like the ground, suchness, dharmakaya, dharmata, clear light, rigpa, and so forth. It is acceptable to use these labels for ultimate truth so long as we understand that they are *just labels*. They are not the real thing. Otherwise we fall into the trap of "eating the menu," as Alan Watts once expressed it, instead of eating the meal itself.

Emptiness

The next principle we need to review on our way to truly understanding enlightenment is "emptiness." There are several levels of understanding that I described in the text:

1. *Emptiness of inherent existence.* Emptiness is not permanent, i.e., it is impermanent, and/or may be divided into parts. Furthermore, all forms arise in dependence upon causes and conditions, i.e., interdependence or "dependent arising."

2. *Form is emptiness; emptiness is form.* Since all objects (forms) have no inherent existence, they are empty—form is emptiness. Since emptiness is an expression of interdependence, emptiness exists only in terms of form, without which there would be neither form nor emptiness. Thus, emptiness is form.

3. *The tetradilemma.* Emptiness is not a thing, it is not no-thing (nothing), it is not both, and it is not neither. It is beyond logic. Thus, emptiness cannot be described, yet we can experience it, so it does exist.

4. *Space.* The experience of emptiness is often characterized as being *like* space – without center or boundaries, open, vast, yet inexpressible. Yet it is not "space" itself.

5. *Rigpa.* Pure awareness. Since emptiness is not a thing, there is no thing of which to be aware, nor is there nothing. All that remains is awareness itself – like potential energy.

There are also five pairings with emptiness that we have examined: (1) appearance-emptiness, (2) luminous-emptiness, (3) bliss-emptiness, (4) awareness-emptiness, and (5) compassion-emptiness.

The first form is appearance-emptiness. This is the emptiness of all appearances. All appearances (things) lack inherent existence. Things, including concepts, are not the answer. Another is luminous-emptiness or buddhanature. This is the direct experience, beyond concepts or labels, the emptiness of "emptiness." Bliss-emptiness is generally associated with the experience of attaining enlightenment. But this is a transcendent bliss, not an ordinary good feeling, but a deep inner peace that cannot be disturbed by everything else going on. Awareness-emptiness is transcendent wisdom itself, a state of pure awareness. One is not aware *of* something – there is no *thing* to be aware of. Finally, compassion-emptiness arises as the union of wisdom and skillful means. This is the Great Compassion of a Buddha, an innate happiness that spontaneously generates the activities of a buddha for the benefit of all beings without the necessity of intention.

Appearance-Emptiness

All appearances are in your mind. They are illusory in nature, like a dream or a mirage. They appear, but have no inherent, permanent existence. Things may "exist" out there and be "perceived" through our senses and thoughts, but they are *experienced* only in our mind. These appearances, including our thoughts, spontaneously manifest from the true nature of mind, pure awareness itself. This quality of potential energy or essence is sometimes referenced as the ground of being. Yet it does nothing. But without it, nothing could appear.

If you would like more support for contemplating appearance-emptiness, contemplate the following to increase your confidence in the direct experience of emptiness, then rest in that experience:

I am empty of inherent existence.
I am not permanent; I am not partless; I am not independent of all other phenomena.
All other phenomena are empty of inherent existence.
They are not permanent; they are not partless; they are not independent of other phenomena.

Form is empty of inherent existence; all forms are in my mind.

Feelings are empty of inherent existence; all feelings are in my mind.

Perceptions are empty of inherent existence; all perceptions are in my mind.

Mental formations are empty of inherent existence; all mental formations are in my mind.

Consciousnesses are empty of inherent existence; all six consciousnesses are in my mind.

Luminous-Emptiness

Luminous refers to the quality of illumination or clarity. As Buddhanature this is the clarity of knowing emptiness directly, without thoughts or concepts. As the dawning of clear light, there is clarity of the experience of emptiness.

If you would like more support for contemplating luminous-emptiness, contemplate the following to increase your confidence in the direct experience of emptiness, then rest in that experience:

Emptiness is not a thing.
Emptiness is not no-thing.
Emptiness is not both.
Emptiness is not neither.

Abide in the direct experience of emptiness.

Bliss-Emptiness

Transcendent bliss – the incredible lightness of being – is beyond mere feeling. It is the stillness or deep inner peace experience of emptiness. There is no attachment or aversion.

If you would like more support for contemplating bliss-emptiness, contemplate the following to increase your confidence in the direct experience of emptiness, then rest in that experience:

As I breathe in, inner heat at my navel melts the female red drop. It rises up my central channel with ever increasing bliss to my crown chakra.

As I breathe out, inner heat melts the white drop of bodhicitta at my crown. It descends down my central channel with ever increasing bliss and emptiness, achieving the union of bliss-emptiness at the tip of the sex organ.

Awareness-Emptiness

Pure awareness has no reference point. It is transcendent wisdom, transcending all concepts or experiences of emptiness. It just is. It is not mind, but the *nature* of mind itself – pure potential.

If you would like more support for contemplating awareness-emptiness, contemplate the following to increase your confidence in the direct experience of emptiness, then rest in that experience:

Let go and let be, going deeper and deeper and deeper into pure awareness, then abide in the vast expanse.

Compassion-Emptiness

Compassion spontaneously manifests from emptiness as the Mind of Enlightenment – your altruistic intention to help all sentient beings attain enlightenment, your activities of lovingkindness and compassion, and your realization of the ultimate wisdom of emptiness. Buddhas are said to have Great Compassion, which leads to the spontaneous activities of a buddha: *pacifying* afflictive emotions that block our progress toward enlightenment, *enriching* our merit and other good qualities to improve our meditation, *magnetizing* or *attracting* favorable circumstances, *subduing* inner and outer obstacles and obscurations, and especially *teaching* dharma, directly or by example.

If you would like more support for contemplating compassion-emptiness, contemplate the following to increase your confidence in the direct experience of emptiness, then rest in that experience. With Great Compassion, let the light-activity of the Five Buddhas and Consorts in your five places radiate out in the ten directions without effort or intention as you abide in the emptiness of emptiness:

Pacifying radiates as a green light from your secret place.
Enriching radiates as yellow light from your navel.
Teaching radiates as blue light from your heart.
Magnetizing radiates as red light from your throat.
Subduing radiates as white light from your crown.

All lights radiate as an intense white light tinged with rainbow colors for the benefit of all sentient beings.

Enlightenment

So what is enlightenment? How do you get it? How do you know you got it (signs)? Early in this text, I mentioned that *nirvana* means "blowing out" the fires or poisons that are the causes of our suffering. So one definition of enlightenment is the extinction of the causes of suffering. However, the Buddha also uses the word *bodhi*, which means "awakening." So enlightenment itself means to be awake. And a "buddha" is one who is awake. Mipham Rinpoche gives these signs:

> The blessings of the buddhas may appear in the experiential domains of dreams, states of absorption, and direct sense perception; yet in truth, they cannot be established as anything other than one's own self-display.... Therefore, according to the degree to which one's own mind has been divested of impurities, the miraculous displays and blessings of the buddhas will manifest more and more. In the end, these impurities will be completely purified and the way things actually are will manifest. Once this has come to pass, all the buddhas will be no different than oneself, and one will be no different than all the buddhas.

Enlightenment means to *wake up*! The gradual path states that this is a slow process that may take eons of rebirths to attain. In The Path of Tantra and especially Great Perfection, it is said that you may wake up in a single lifetime. The Buddha, however, said that you might be realized in seven years, or seven months, or even seven days! Let's examine enlightenment from the view of each of the paths.

The Path of Individual Liberation

There are subtle differences in how the four paths described in this book understand enlightenment. The Path of Individual Liberation is focused on the individual. The goal is "nirvana." It means to be liberated, to be free of suffering, to be in a state of peace of mind undisturbed by afflictive emotions and habitual tendencies. As I stated early in the text, the Buddha compared it to a candle that is blown out – extinction of karma and other negative tendencies. There is a sense of great peace and transcendent awareness. This is a deep inner peace of *innate happiness*.

> It does not mean to be in a place where there is no noise, trouble or hard work. It means to be in the midst of those things and still be calm in your heart. (Source unknown)

While meditating under the Bodhi Tree, the Buddha recalled an experience as a child sitting under a rose-apple tree during which he experienced a natural sense of well-being, peace and happiness. At the time he had not meditated or done anything intentionally for this to happen. It happened naturally. From recalling this experience, he realized that we all have this nature intrinsically. We don't have to do anything to create it, though we may have to do something to release it from being hidden by our own ignorance, attachments, and aversions.

As a part of transcendent wisdom, the Pali Canon also includes insight into the emptiness of self and other – appearance-emptiness – as part of the concept of nirvana. The Five Paths conclude with the Path of No More Learning. At this point the most subtle remnants of afflictive emotions and mental obscurations have been removed. One realizes that even "nirvana" is impermanent and one becomes enlightened. One who attains this form of individual enlightenment and transcendent wisdom is called an *Arhat*.

Upon the Buddha's death, the idea of *paranirvana* – final extinction – developed. The Buddha did not speculate on what happens after death. His focus was on eliminating the suffering (unhappiness) of this life. Over time, however, additional teachings were "revealed" that elaborated upon the practical, human view of the Buddha.

The Path of Altruism

With the Path of Altruism, the Buddha became a more transcendent, cosmic figure. The main practices were based on *bodhicitta* and the Six Perfections. Relative bodhicitta has two parts: (1) altruistic intention to achieve enlightenment for all sentient beings and (2) action bodhicitta – particularly lovingkindness and compassion for all sentient beings. Ultimate bodhicitta, the wisdom of a bodhisattva, is based on (1) Buddhanature – luminous-emptiness, (2) the Perfection of Wisdom texts, and (3) the Middle Way texts.

On the Path of Altruism, enlightenment follows accomplishment of the Tenth Bhumi – the Cloud of Doctrine. They receive the "great rays of light" empowerment from all the buddhas and the subtlest traces of afflictive emotions and mental obscurations are removed. They perfect their understanding of wisdom and manifest multiple forms of the three *kayas* to benefit others. It is said to be a state so extraordinary that ordinary beings cannot even begin to imagine it.

The Path of Tantra

The actual descriptions of enlightenment in the Path of Tantra are not significantly different than those of the Path of Altruism, perhaps because the Path of Tantra is also considered to be a part of the Path of Altruism. However, there are some alternative routes within the path. We begin by imagining ourselves as being a buddha (deity) – generation and completion stage practices, an approach proven both in the tantric path and modern psychology (sometimes conventionally referred to as "fake it 'till you make it") to be highly effective. Enlightenment in this lifetime follows the completion stage of "learner's union" in which one has achieved a pure illusory body and is approaching the actual clear light. When the subtlest traces of afflictive emotions and mental obscurations are finally removed, one attains enlightenment with "non-learner's union" or buddhahood with the realization of bliss-emptiness.

In addition, if you fail to achieve enlightenment in this life, the first alternative is transference of consciousness – *phowa* – which is performed as you are dying. This transports your consciousness from your dying body to the heart and buddhafield of Amitabha or other deity, where you complete the process of attaining enlightenment for the benefit of others.

The second alternative is recognizing the experience of the actual or "mother" clear light at the beginning of the Bardo of *Dharmata*. Failing that, recognition of any of the 100 Peaceful and Wrathful Deities that appear presents numerous other opportunities for enlightenment by recognizing them as none other than your own mind. This is followed by the Bardo of Becoming, beginning with a review of your immediate past life (and the karma created) then a preview of your next life based on your karma. As you approach actual rebirth (conception), you have several other opportunities to halt the process by closing the entrance to the womb. Only if all of these fail, will you actually be reborn according to your karmic propensities.

The Path of Great Perfection

The Path of Great Perfection has two principle forms of practice: *trekcho* and *togal*. Each has its opportunity for enlightenment. *Trekcho* is a *dharmakaya* practice and can result in enlightenment in this lifetime, or recognition of the actual or "mother" clear light in the Bardo of *Dharmata*. Some sources say it can also result in the Great Transference form of rainbow body. In the Great Perfection, there are no afflictive emotions or mental obscurations to remove. You are already a buddha. Instead, you wake up to knowing this to be true through the pure awareness of *rigpa*. According to Mipham Rinpoche, you attain great certainty and "any clinging to the efforts of the path and the claims of the philosophical positions ... have collapsed. This stage is likened to becoming empowered into the mandala."

In *togal* you take this direct perception of reality-itself through a series of Four Visions leading to achieving one of four forms of rainbow body, a direct manifestation into the *sambhogakaya* form of a buddha:

Small Transference

Small Rainbow Body

Great Rainbow Body

Great Transference

These rainbow body forms are normally associated with the time of death. So you must have achieved the stage of realization for rainbow body prior to that time. Thus, you may be able to benefit other beings for some time from that level of realization attained earlier in this life.

Enlightenment in This Life

When you attain the realization of enlightenment during this life, you have purified all karma, all afflictive emotions and mental obscurations, all subtle obscurations, and all habitual tendencies that create negative karma. What about residual positive karma? It would seem that any actions taken to benefit others, at least those prior to enlightenment, would create positive karma, but karma nevertheless. Karma is said to reside in the *alaya* consciousness. But that ceases to exist upon attaining enlightenment. And the actions of a buddha do not create additional karma, even good karma. It seems that the process of eliminating bad karma also eliminates any residual good karma in the process of attaining enlightenment. For only when all karma has been eliminated – through use (burning it up) or purification practices – can the *alaya* consciousness dissolve so one can attain enlightenment.

The notable exception to this process is in the Path of Great Perfection. In this path "karma" is just another concept of the mind. It does not actually exist, so there is nothing to purify or use up. We are already buddhas. The Great Perfection takes transcendent wisdom to its fullest form, where it transcends *all* concepts, even these. Someday I would like to write the ultimate book on the Path of Great Perfection – all the pages would be blank! That does not, however, give you a green light to rationalize any behavior you want. "Rationalizing" and "wanting" are not enlightened behaviors. It's that "slippery slope" thing again. Only if you are fully enlightened and have pure intentions can you engage in otherwise "unethical" conduct, as perceived by others. But it must be done in such a way as to "do good, or at least do no harm" from the view of relative truth. Otherwise, you are simply rationalizing your behavior and have not attained enlightenment at all.

I was once asked if I had attained enlightenment. My reply was that if I said I had, I would not have. (But then I confessed that I really had not yet achieved it.) One of my teachers, His Eminence Garchen Rinpoche gave this advice regarding enlightenment:

> Do not worry about enlightenment; the Buddha is within your mind already, ready to be seen. But because we cannot turn inward and are constantly distracted, we fail to recognize the Buddha. When past thoughts have ceased and future thoughts not yet arisen, in this space between fixations, you can glimpse the nature of mind abiding like space; this is the Buddha. If you remain within this nature continuously, you are enlightened…. The Buddha is actually not somewhere far away. The Buddha is always ready to be seen. If you do not give up the fixation to a "self," but try to escape from samsara by secluding your body, you will still not be liberated. If you give up fixation to a "self," while continuing to live in the world, you will be liberated.

Everything is Meditation

A related topic is the idea of buddhahood without meditation, actually the title of a Great Perfection text. But that is not what I am referring to here. You learned earlier that this idea has been applied to meditation in the Path of Great Perfection. I also pointed out that prior to achieving that level of realization, one should engage in the process of "everything is meditation." When you have mastered the sacred outlook of Pure View, everything does indeed become meditation. When you apply the Four Visions of *Togal* off the cushion, that too becomes a form of meditation. When you maintain pure awareness of *rigpa* at all times, everything becomes meditation. When you use mindfulness of body, speech, and mind at all times, that is meditation. If you want to do a retreat, your body is a perfect hermitage, wherever you are. No monk or nun in a monastery or cave in Tibet has more time for practice than the busiest Western practitioner. It's just a matter of how you see your time. Then we can apply these in many ways. H.H. Dilgo Khyentse Rinpoche gave these examples:

At all times, again and again, we should make vast prayers for the sake of all beings. When falling asleep we should think, "May all beings achieve the absolute state";

When waking up, "May all beings awake into the enlightened state";

When getting up, "May all beings obtain the body of a Buddha";

When putting on clothes, "May all beings have modesty and a sense of shame";

When lighting a fire, "May all beings burn the wood of disturbing emotions";

When eating, "May all beings eat the food of concentration";

When opening a door, "May all beings open the door to the city of liberation";

When closing a door, "May all beings close the door to the lower realms";

When going outside, "May I set out on the path to free all beings";

When walking uphill, "May I take all beings to the higher realms";

When walking downhill, "May I go to free beings from the lower realms";

When seeing happiness, "May all beings achieve the happiness of Buddhahood";

When seeing suffering, "May the suffering of all beings be pacified."

At the same time "everything" being meditation is a lot to ask of anyone. Sometimes it is best to approach this by having a "theme" for the day. Pick just one thing that you would like to focus on that day, e.g., seeing the illusory nature of all things. See how many times you can do this during the day. (Keeping track of how long is just too much paperwork!) Use a counter you can carry in your hand or your car. Then click it once each time you remember to do it. At the end of the day, write it in your journal. The next time you do that "theme," go back and see if you improved. Then forget it and pick a new theme for the next day. Each journey begins with a single step … 'er click.

Here is a passage from Teasdale's *The Mystic Heart* regarding mystics in general:

Their consciousness is greatly enhanced and deepened; they acquire a transcendental, subtle awareness. Their character becomes saintly; their will is fixed on love and compassion, mercy and kindness. They are exquisitely sensitive beings, gentle and patient. They move beyond emotional swings. They are not victims of their feelings, nor ruled by their desires. They are free, and so are capable of giving to others and their communities. Their actions are consistently animated by compassion and love.

Out of this compassion and love, buddhas spontaneously engage in activities for the benefit and happiness of all beings in all times and places. These also include the other activities of pacifying, enriching, magnetizing, and subduing.

Compassion and Emptiness

Finally, let's return to the heart of Buddhism – *bodhicitta*. Yet again, *bodhicitta* consists of (1) relative – altruistic intention, (2) actions of lovingkindness and compassion, and (3) transcendent wisdom. When you attain enlightenment, there is one other major shift that occurs in your worldview mentioned above. You may well already have a semblant view of it through the other practices. But you will definitely have it when you attain enlightenment. Upon becoming a buddha, *Great* Compassion arises for the suffering of all sentient beings across all of time and space. This is joined in the ultimate union with emptiness as compassion-emptiness. The Dzogchen Ponlop Rinpoche says,

> If you had never experienced love and all you knew about it was the dictionary definition, then you'd certainly be missing the fullness of that experience. It's the same with emptiness. In fact, emptiness and love are related.... When you unite the two, you have an experience that is beyond either one.

Great Compassion is of the nature of pure love. They are like two sides of the same hand. Compassion is the wish that all beings not have suffering and its causes. Lovingkindness is the wish that they have happiness and its causes. We don't want them to have the "bad," and we do want them to have the "good." They are usually referred to simply as Great Compassion.

This is not the *agape* of the New Testament, *chesed* in the Jewish Bible, nor the ordinary lovingkindness and compassion of Buddhism, wonderful as those are. Those are like the soft glow of a candle, whereas Great Compassion and its companion pure love are like the sparkling of stars at high elevation away from city lights in the dark of night. Yet like transcendent wisdom, there are no words that can begin to really describe it!

Compared to the warm, fuzzy feeling of what one might call "conventional" love, it has a very light, airy quality – a lightness of being. And everything is that way. But more importantly, it seems accessible only through a state of pure awareness. But perhaps we can get a taste of it even before we achieve complete enlightenment.

Imagine a portal, almost like a "wormhole" in science fiction, a wormhole of consciousness. It's not always there, but when it is accessible one comes out on the other side into this state of "Pure Love." There is *only* Pure Love and *everything* is Pure Love. It's quite an amazing experience unlike anything else! When you come back through the "wormhole," if you will, the sensation lingers and ordinary perceptions no longer seem the same at all. Even if you fall into moments of "ordinary" perception for a while, this awareness of Pure Love keeps inserting itself into your perception.

Pure love is all pervasive, none other than oneness itself, bonding us together as softly as the force of gravity – imperceptible between two people – but with the strength of the "strong force" that holds the nucleus of atoms together, the strongest force known in the universe. It is strong *and* imperceptible to all but those few who awaken to union, to love, to oneness.

I am reminded of *Star Trek the Movie* a number of years ago. There was a "female" space probe seeking "V-ger," which turned out to be the "Voyager" space probe with some letters missing. At the end of the movie one of the male characters was so drawn to her that he elected to join her, knowing he could never return. When they came together, a bright light radiated from them as they merged into one and disappeared into the light. It was a nice metaphor for the oneness of pure love.

In his book, *The Tibetan Book of Living and Dying*, Sogyal Rinpoche cites the following passage describing the experience of pure love from a near death experience:

The following series of events appear to happen simultaneously, but in describing them I will have to take them one at a time. The sensation is of a being of some kind, more a kind of energy, not a character in the sense of another person, but an intelligence with whom it is possible to communicate. Also, in size it just covers the entire vista before you. It totally engulfs everything, you feel enveloped.

The light immediately communicates to you, in an instant telekinesis your thought waves are read, regardless of language. A doubtful statement would be impossible to receive. The first message I received was "Relax, everything is beautiful, everything is OK; you have nothing to fear." I was immediately put at absolute ease. In the past if someone like a doctor had said, "It's OK, you have nothing to fear, this won't hurt," it usually did – you couldn't trust them.

But this was the most beautiful feeling I have ever known; it's absolute pure love. Every feeling, every emotion is just perfect. You feel warm, but it has nothing to do with temperature. Everything there is absolutely vivid and clear. What the light communicates to you is a feeling of true, pure love. You experience this for the first time ever. You can't compare it to the love of your wife, or the love of your children, or sexual love. Even if all those things were combined, you cannot compare it to the feeling you get from this light. [Emphasis added]

That is close to what I have experienced in meditation. The only difference would be that I experienced no *separate* light, no difference between "me" and "it." *Everything* was pure love itself, light and airy, vivid and clear. And there was *nothing else*. There was *only* pure love. Yet even this is not as great as the Great Compassion of a buddha. The yogi Shabkar wrote:

> If a man has compassion, he is Buddha;
> Without compassion, he is Lord of Death.

> With compassion, the root of Dharma is planted,
> Without compassion, the root of Dharma is rotten.

> One with compassion is kind even when angry,
> One without compassion kills even as he smiles.

> For one with compassion, even enemies turn into friends,
> Without compassion, even friends turn into enemies.

> With compassion, one has all Dharmas,
> Without compassion, one has no Dharma at all.

> With compassion, one is a true Buddhist,
> Without compassion, one is worse than profane.

> Even meditating on voidness, one needs compassion as its essence.
> A Dharma practitioner must have a compassionate nature.

> Great compassion is like a wish-fulfilling gem.
> Great compassion fulfills the hopes of self and others.

> Therefore, all of you, renunciants and householders,
> Cultivate compassion and you will achieve Buddhahood.

Zen Master Torei describes great compassion this way:

> The virtues of great compassion are infinite; they could be expounded upon forever without exhausting them, but it boils down to this: Whoever has great compassion can extinguish all obstructions caused by past actions and can fulfill all virtues; no principle cannot be understood, no path cannot be practiced, no knowledge not attained, no virtue not developed. Just as when you want to win people's hearts you first love their children, the Buddhas and bodhisattvas consider all living beings their children; so if you love all living beings equally, all the Buddhas will be moved to respond.

Pure Love and Great Compassion

We have finally reached the end of the path – enlightenment. If somehow you didn't make it yet, continue on with patience and persistence. I *really* believe it is possible for householders to achieve it in this lifetime! In the generation-stage practices, we began by imagining ourselves as the deity. Although I strongly recommend that you continue with that approach, please also do the following simple practice until you *do* achieve enlightenment.

Week 52 and Beyond – Pure Love & Great Compassion

Continue until you achieve enlightenment:

See yourself as a buddha.

Feel yourself as a buddha.

Be the buddha you already are.

From the Buddhas and Consorts in your five places,

Radiate Pure Love and Great Compassion to all beings – forever!

Bringing It All Together

If you have read this book without having done all the practices, as I suggested at the beginning, now is the time to go back and do the practices as described. It is not absolutely essential that you take the number of days or weeks listed. That is a guide. The key is developing *certainty* regarding the practices. In this regard, it can be helpful to have a teacher as your guide. At the Awam Tibetan Buddhist Institute (AwamInstitute.org), we provide that kind of mentoring. We offer practice-oriented classes based on this text to help you understand and master these practices.

Alternately, you may go back and focus on those practices for which you have not yet achieved certainty. And if you have actually mastered these practices with certainty, continue abiding softly and deeply in pure nonconceptual awareness without attachment or aversion with lovingkindness and compassion for all.

On the other hand, if you have already completed these practices, you may be asking, "What is the next step?" There are many options, many additional practices and texts. But to bring it all together, I offer one final meditation, a daily complete-practice *sadhana*. This incorporates the brief preliminary practices, the generation and completion stage deity yoga practices, the Great Perfection practices, and abiding in wisdom, including spontaneously manifesting lovingkindness and compassion for all beings. The deity is again *Vajravarahi*, but in this case she is in her more common red dakini form.

A Complete Daily Sadhana of Vajravarahi

Intention: I do this practice for the benefit of all sentient beings (*or other personal intention*).

Homage: **Guru Dewa Dakiniye**

Preliminary practices

Homage to Samantabhadra and Samantabhadri! Because I suffer due to my own actions and I now have this precious human life without knowing when I will die, I will now engage in virtuous actions for the benefit of all sentient beings with great joy and devotion! Therefore...

Refuge and Bodhicitta (while visualizing the refuge tree): I take refuge in the Buddha, the Dharma and Sangha most excellent, in order to enable all sentient beings to attain enlightenment. (3X)

Vajrasattva and Vajratopa appear above me purifying me and all beings and phenomena with nectar from the place of their union while reciting: **Om Benza Sato Hung** (28 or 108X)

Offerings: **Om Guru Dewa Dakini Ratna Mandala Pratitsa Soha!** (3X)

Guru Yoga: **Om Ah Hung Benza Guru Peme Siddhi Hung** (*as many times as you can*)

Light radiates from the Guru's five places into my five places purifying my body, speech, mind, subtle obscurations and habitual tendencies, granting the five empowerments and planting the five seeds. The Guru dissolves into light and merges inseparably into myself.

Generation Stage

Emptiness mantra: Om Shunyata Jnana Benza Swabhava Emako Ham

Visualization: From emptiness appears a red BAM syllable on the center of a red lotus, which transforms the five poisons into the five wisdoms as a wheel of protection. From light rays streaming from the BAM appears the charnel ground celestial palace, wrathful in nature.

I appear as Vajravarahi. I am red with one face and three eyes with a semi-wrathful expression and two arms. I hold a vajra in my right hand and a skull cup of the elixir of primordial awareness in my left. I am youthful and naked with nothing to hide, standing in a dancing pose. I am adorned with a skull crown, a garland of human heads, necklaces and other bone ornaments. I hold a khatvanga with a vajra tip in my left arm as my consort. I am surrounded by the fire of primordial wisdom.

At my heart is a double tetrahedron pointing downward with a lotus, sun disc, and BAM on top and with the mantra arranged counter clockwise facing outward around the edge. Light rays radiate out from the BAM at my heart inviting all buddhas and other beings in the form of Vajravarahi. I pay homage, make outer, inner, and secret offerings, and they dissolve into me filling me with their blessings.

> **Ram Yam Kham** (3X)
> **Om Ah Hung** (3X)
> **Dza Hung Bam Ho**

Mantra: *Visualizing the mandala recite the mantra* – **Om Benza Vairochaniye Soha** (*108X or as many times as you can as light rays emanate from the BAM and mantra syllables purifying all and performing activities of wisdom and compassion.*)

Meditation: *Dissolve the visualization and rest briefly in pure awareness, then reappear as Vajravarahi.*

Completion Stage

Tummo:

Below the navel, above a tiny AH-stroke, an intense flame heats and melts my female red drop, which ascends to my crown, melting the white bodhicitta drop (HAM).

The white drop descends to my secret place, where I experience the heat of innate bliss radiating throughout. (*Repeat 3X or more.*)

The Four Blisses:

Below the navel, above the tiny AH-stroke, an intense flame melts my female red drop, which ascends and I experience bliss at my navel, supreme bliss at my heart, special bliss at my throat, and great innate bliss at my crown.

The inner heat melts the white bodhicitta drop at my crown, which descends increasing bliss at my throat, supreme bliss at my heart, special bliss at my navel, and intense innate bliss at my secret place radiating throughout. (*Repeat 3X or more, increasing the heat of inner bliss with each step, ascending and descending.*)

The Four Empties:

Below the navel, above a tiny AH-stroke, an intense flame again melts my female red drop, which ascends to my crown as I experience the four blisses.

The inner heat melts the white bodhicitta drop at my crown, which descends to my throat and I experience emptiness; it descends to my heart and I experience great emptiness; it descends to my navel and I experience extreme emptiness; it descends to my secret place and I experience total emptiness; and it unites in one taste at the tip of my sex organ and I experience the inconceivable pristine cognition of bliss-emptiness. (*Repeat until only bliss-emptiness remains.*)

Clear Light Rigpa:

From bliss-emptiness appearances move or shimmer like a mirage, then a bluish cloud-like smoke, followed by dots or sparks like fireflies, and a small glowing light like a butter lamp.

White light grows to fill the sky, then a red light glows like a sunset filling the sky, followed by black like the darkness of night without moon or stars, and finally clear light like the light of first dawn. *Abide in the clear light rigpa – pure naked awareness – as long as you can. Then reverse the order of the inner and outer dissolution visualizations as you return into your (impure) illusory body as Vajravarahi.*

Togal[179]

Using the lion pose[180], gaze into the clear sky with the hollow crystal khati channel as long as you can. Then reappear in your illusory body as Vajravarahi continuously radiating lovingkindness and compassion for all beings.

Closing

Bodhicitta, the excellent and precious mind.

Where it is unborn, may it arise.

Where it is born, may it not decline,

But ever increase, higher and higher.

Dedication: By the virtue of this, may I and all sentient beings accomplish the state of the dakini. Without leaving a single sentient being behind, may I liberate them to the state of the dakini. (3X)

Post-meditation: *Abide softly and deeply in pure naked awareness without attachment or aversion with lovingkindness and compassion for all – always and all ways!*

*****

This sadhana was written by Khenpo Drimed Dawa to the best of my limited ability for the benefit of all sentient beings in July, 2012, Tucson, Arizona. Please forgive all errors or omissions. They are my own.

Sealed   Sealed   Sealed

---

179 ALTERNATELY (when sky gazing is not practical): Abide in appearance-emptiness, luminous-emptiness, bliss-emptiness, awareness-emptiness, and compassion-emptiness in sequence, then as one.

180 You may alternate poses or sit in a relaxed pose if you grow tired or experience pain.

Finally, Padmasambhava gave this advice to King Trisong Detsen[181]:

> Even though you realize that your mind is fully awakened, do not give up the Lama. Even though you fully realize that all appearances are mental projections, do not stop the practice of virtue. Even though you have no expectation of Buddhahood, do not give up making offerings to the divine beings and the Three Jewels. Even though you have no fear of samsara, restrain yourself from even subtle negativities. Even though you acquire a deep meaning of the immutable Absolute, do not overrate or underestimate any Dharma teaching. Even though such good qualities as clairvoyant knowledge and exalted concentration arise in you, give up pride and conceit. Even though you understand the nondual nature of samsara and nirvana, do not stop being compassionate with all sentient beings.

*   *   *   *   *

This book was written by the ignorant yogi, Drimed Dawa, still bound by attachment and aversion while struggling to find a way to help other lay practitioners transcend ignorance and attain enlightenment. When you do, please return and help me!

In Buddhanature,

Khenpo Drimed Dawa

Sealed   Sealed   Sealed

---

[181] *From the Depths of the Heart*, p. 92.

Part 8 - Appendices

Appendix A

The Thirty-Seven Practices of a Bodhisattva

by Ngolchu Thogme Rinpoche

Homage to Lokeshvaraya!

At all times I prostrate with respectful three doors to the supreme guru and the protector Chenrezig, who through realizing that all phenomena neither come nor go, makes single-minded effort for the sake of migrators.

The perfect Buddhas, source of benefit and happiness, arise from accomplishing the sublime Dharma. And as that [accomplishment] depends on knowing the [Dharma] practices, I will explain the bodhisattvas' practices.

1. At this time when the difficult-to-gain ship of leisure and fortune has been obtained, ceaselessly hearing, pondering and meditating day and night in order to liberate oneself and others from the ocean of cyclic existence is the bodhisattvas' practice.

2. [The mind of] attachment to loved ones wavers like water. [The mind of] hatred of enemies burns like fire. [The mind of] ignorance which forgets what to adopt and discard is greatly obscured. Abandoning one's fatherland is the bodhisattvas' practice.

3. When harmful places are abandoned, disturbing emotions gradually diminish. Without distraction, virtuous endeavors naturally increase. Being clear-minded, definite understanding of the Dharma arises. Resorting to secluded places is the bodhisattvas' practice.

4. Long-associated companions will part from each other. Wealth and possessions obtained with effort will be left behind. Consciousness, the guest, will cast aside the guest-house of the body. Letting go of this life is the bodhisattvas' practice.

5. When [evil companions] are associated with, the three poisons increase, the activities of listening, pondering and meditation decline,

and love and compassion are extinguished. Abandoning evil companions is the bodhisattvas' practice.

6. When [sublime spiritual friends] are relied upon, one's faults are exhausted and one's qualities increase like the waxing moon. Holding sublime spiritual friends even more dear than one's own body is the bodhisattvas' practice.

7. What worldly god, himself also bound in the prison of cyclic existence, is able to protect others? Therefore when refuge is sought, taking refuge in the undeceiving triple gem is the bodhisattvas' practice.

8. The Subduer said that all the unbearable suffering of three lower realms is the fruition of wrongdoing. Therefore, never committing negative deeds, even at the peril to one's life, is the bodhisattvas' practice.

9. The pleasure of the triple world, like a dewdrop on the tip of a blade of grass, is imperiled in a single moment. Striving for the supreme state of never-changing liberation is the bodhisattvas' practice.

10. When mothers who have been kind to one since beginningless time are suffering, what's the use of one's own happiness? Therefore generating the mind of enlightenment in order to liberate limitless sentient beings is the bodhisattvas' practice.

11. All suffering without exception comes from the wish for one's own happiness. The perfect buddhas arise from the altruistic mind. Therefore, completely exchanging one's own happiness for the suffering of others is the bodhisattvas' practice.

12. Even if others, influenced by great desire, steal all of one's wealth or have it stolen, dedicating to them one's body, possessions and virtues [accumulated in] the three times is the bodhisattvas' practice.

13. Even if others cut off one's head when one is utterly blameless, taking upon oneself all their negative deeds by power of compassion is the bodhisattvas' practice.

14. Even if someone broadcasts throughout the billion worlds all sorts of offensive remarks about one, speaking in turn of that person's qualities with a loving mind is the bodhisattvas' practice.

15. Even if, in the midst of a public gathering, someone exposes faults and speaks ill of one, humbly paying homage to that person, perceiving him as a spiritual friend, is the bodhisattvas' practice.

16. Even if someone for whom one has cared as lovingly as his own child regards one as an enemy, to cherish that person as dearly as a mother does an ailing child is the bodhisattvas' practice.

17. Even if, influenced by pride, an equal or inferior person treats one with contempt, respectfully placing him like a guru at the crown of your head is the bodhisattvas' practice.

18. Though one may have an impoverished life, always disparaged by others, afflicted by dangerous illness and evil spirits, to be without discouragement and to take upon oneself all the misdeeds and suffering of beings is the bodhisattvas' practice.

19. Though one may become famous and revered by many people or gain wealth like that of Vaishravana, having realized that worldly fortune is without essence, to be unconceited is the bodhisattvas' practice.

20. If outer foes are destroyed while not subduing the enemy of one's own hatred, enemies will only increase. Therefore, subduing one's own mind with the army of love and compassion is the bodhisattvas' practice.

21. However much sense pleasures, like salt water, are enjoyed, craving still increases. Immediately abandoning whatever things give rise to clinging and attachment is the bodhisattvas' practice.

22. Appearances are one's own mind. From the beginning, mind's nature is free from extremes of elaboration. Knowing this, not to engage the mind in subject-object duality is the bodhisattvas' practice.

23. When encountering pleasing sense objects, though they appear beautiful like a rainbow in summertime, not to regard them as real and to abandon clinging attachment is the bodhisattvas' practice.

24. Diverse sufferings are like the death of a child in a dream. By apprehending illusory appearances as real, one becomes weary. Therefore, when encountering disagreeable circumstances, viewing them as illusory is the bodhisattvas' practice.

25. If it is necessary to give away even one's body while aspiring to enlightenment, what need is there to mention external objects? Therefore, practicing generosity without hope of reciprocation or [positive] karmic results is the bodhisattvas' practice.

26. If, lacking ethical conduct, one fails to achieve one's own purpose, the wish to accomplish others' purpose is laughable. Therefore, guarding ethics devoid of aspiration for worldly existence is the bodhisattvas' practice.

27. To Bodhisattvas who desire the wealth of virtue, all those who do harm are like a precious treasure. Therefore, cultivating patience devoid of hostility is the bodhisattvas' practice.

28. Even hearers and solitary realizers, who accomplish only their own welfare, strive as if putting out a fire on their heads. Seeing this, taking up diligent effort–the source of good qualities–for the sake of all beings is the bodhisattvas' practice.

29. Having understood that disturbing emotions are destroyed by insight possessed with tranquil abiding, to cultivate meditative concentration which perfectly transcends the four formless [absorptions] is the bodhisattvas' practice.

30. If one lacks wisdom, it is impossible to attain perfect enlightenment through the [other] five perfections. Thus, cultivating skillful means with the wisdom that does not discriminate among the three spheres is the bodhisattvas' practice.

31. If, having [merely] the appearance of a practitioner, one does not investigate one's own mistakes; it is possible to act contrary to the Dharma. Therefore, constantly examining one's own errors and abandoning them is the bodhisattvas' practice.

32. If, influenced by disturbing emotions, one points out another bodhisattva's faults, oneself is diminished. Therefore, not speaking about the faults of those who have entered the Great Vehicle is the bodhisattvas' practice.

33. Because the influence of gain and respect causes quarreling and the decline of the activities of listening, pondering and meditation, to abandon attachment to the households of friends, relations and benefactors is the bodhisattvas' practice.

34. Because harsh words disturb others' minds and cause the bodhisattva's conduct to deteriorate, abandoning harsh speech that is unpleasant to others is the bodhisattvas' practice.

35. When disturbing emotions are habituated, it is difficult to overcome them with antidotes. By arming oneself with the antidotal weapons of mindfulness, to destroy disturbing emotions such as desire the moment they first arise is the bodhisattvas' practice.

36. In brief, whatever conduct one engages in, one should ask, "What is the state of my mind?" Accomplishing other's purpose through constantly maintaining mindfulness and awareness is the bodhisattvas' practice.

37. In order to clear away the suffering of limitless beings, through the wisdom [realizing] the purity of the three spheres, to dedicate the virtue attained by making such effort for enlightenment is the bodhisattvas' practice.

Following the speech of the Sublime Ones on the meaning of the sutras, tantras and their commentaries, I have written the Thirty-seven Practices of Bodhisattvas *for those who wish to train on the bodhisattvas' path.*

Due to my inferior intellect and poor learning, this is not poetry that will please scholars, yet as I have relied upon the sutras and the speech of the Sublime Ones, I think the bodhisattva practices are not mistaken.

However, because it is difficult for one of inferior intellect like myself to fathom the depth of the great deeds of bodhisattvas, I beseech the Sublime Ones to forbear my errors such as contradictions and incoherent [reasoning].

By the virtue arising from this may all migrators become, through excellent conventional and ultimate bodhicitta, like the protector Chenrezig who does not abide in the extremes of existence or peace.

This was written for the benefit of himself and others by the monk Thogme, an exponent of scripture and reasoning, in a cave in Ngülchu Rinchen.

Appendix B
Sadhana of the White Dakini
(Nirmanakaya)

Introduction

The idea for this sadhana came to me in a dream. I was guided by the White Dakini, in the form of Vajravarahi – a manifestation of Vajrayogini. Though she appeared white in color, she is normally red. In white form, she is also a manifestation of Samantabhadri – the embodiment of transcendent wisdom.

According to Jigmed Lingpa (1726-1798), the Nyingma master famous for finding hidden treasures or *termas*, Simhamukha represents the Nirmanakaya, Vajravarahi represents the Sambhogakaya, and Samantabhadri represents the Dharmakaya. However, in this instance, as White Vajravarahi, she appeared in Nirmanakaya form.

She took me to a hidden place and showed the text in a script that I did not recognize. It was written on white paper in gold. Lines of gold looped across the page along with rectangular blocks of gold, slightly reminiscent of a musical score, but flowing about rather than straight. I did not know what to make of it for some time. But over time, this text came to me so that I might share it with you.

As a Nirmanakaya text, the focus of this practice involves generation-stage practices based primarily on the sacred feminine. While this text may be used by anyone for study purposes, practitioners need to have completed *ngondro* or do a short version as a preliminary practice to other meditations daily and have an empowerment such as Vajrayogini, a practice involving Vajravarahi or other Highest Yoga Tantra empowerment. This practice is for yogis, yoginis and other lay practitioners.

Since I am not a realized being and have no notable credibility for such an endeavor, I acknowledge that this may contain errors or omissions for which I accept complete responsibility. I ask only that you see it with the naked awareness of transcendent wisdom and find in it whatever benefit you may.

There are two other texts in this series, the Sadhana of the Red Dakini (Sambhogakaya) and the Sadhana of the Blue Dakini (Dharmakaya). May they too be of benefit.

Sadhana of the White Dakini

*In a terrifying charnel ground, on a mountain, in a cave (imagined or real)
or in a place pleasing to the heart:*

HOMAGE to Samantabhadri, Simhamukha, and Vajravarahi.

(handwritten annotations: WHITE over Samantabhadri, RED over Simhamukha, BLUE over Vajravarahi, 3 DAKINIS)

*Mantra of Increasing Mantras – magnifies the effect of all that follows.
Light goes out as offering to Buddhas and returns as a blessing:*

**Om Sambara Sambara Bimana Sara Maha Zambaba Hung Phat
Soha!** (3X)

Ngondro – The Incomparable Preliminary Practices

Four Thoughts that Turn the Mind:

> I prostrate Samantabhadra and Samantabhadri.

> Because I suffer due to my own actions and I now have this precious human life without knowing when I will die, I will now engage in virtuous actions for the benefit of all sentient beings with great joy and devotion.

Refuge Tree visualization:

> In front of me on a jeweled throne supported by eight snow lions sits my Root Guru in the form of Padmasambhava and Yeshe Tsogyal in union. Below and in front are tantric deities. On their right (*your left*) are all the Buddhas of the four times. Behind are the scriptures emblazoned with and resonating the vowels and consonants. On their left (*your right*) are all the Bodhisattvas. Above are Samantabhadra and Samantabhadri in union. All are surrounded by countless Dakinis and Dharmapalas filling all of space. My Mother and Father are next to me. All other sentient beings, including my enemies, are in front of me.

Outer Refuge and Bodhicitta:

> I take refuge in the Buddha, Dharma and Sangha most excellent, abiding softly and deeply in pure, nonconceptual awareness of the ineffable, oneness, openness, and the spontaneous radiant display manifesting immeasurable, unconditional lovingkindness, compassion, joy and equanimity for the benefit of all.

Inner Refuge and Bodhicitta:

> I take refuge in the Guru, Yidam, and Dakini, abiding softly and deeply in pure, nonconceptual awareness of the ineffable, oneness,

openness, and the spontaneous radiant display manifesting immeasurable, unconditional lovingkindness, compassion, joy and equanimity for the benefit of all.

Secret Refuge and Bodhicitta:

I take refuge in the Dharmakaya, Sambhogakaya, and Nirmanakaya, abiding softly and deeply in pure, nonconceptual awareness of the ineffable, oneness, openness, and the spontaneous radiant display manifesting immeasurable, unconditional lovingkindness,
compassion, joy and equanimity for the benefit of all.

Most secret Refuge and Bodhicitta:

I take refuge ... *Dissolve the visualization into pure awareness with lovingkindness and compassion for all. Abide briefly in complete stillness.*

Action Bodhicitta – The Four Immeasurables:

May all sentient beings have happiness and the causes of happiness.

May they be liberated from suffering and the causes of suffering.

May they never be separated from the happiness that is free from sorrow.

May they rest in equanimity, free from attachment and aversion. (3X)

Vajrasattva purification:

Visualize Vajrasattva and Vajratopa in union above the crown of your head. White nectar enters the crown of your head from their place of union, purifying your body, speech and mind as it fills your body while reciting the mantras.

OM Benza Sato Samaya

Tishta Drido Me Bhawa

Suto Khayo Me Bhawa

Supo Khayo Me Bhawa

Anu Rakto Me Bhawa

Sarwa Siddhi Me Prayatsa

Manu Palaya

Benza Sato Tenopa

Sarwa Karma Sutsa Me

Sit-Tam Shriya Kuru Hung

Ha Ha Ha Ha Ho

Bhagavan

Sarwa Tathagata

Benza Mame Muntsa

Benzi Bhawa

Maha Samaya

Sato AH

(Repeat 3X or 1X)

Then: **Om Benza Sato Ah** (108X *or as many times as you can*)

Then: **Om Ah Hung Hri** (108X *or as many times as you can*)

Offerings (outer, inner, secret, most secret) with bell and drum or hand mudra:

I make the eight outer offerings:

Om Argham Ah Hung (*water for drinking*)

Om Padyam Ah Hung (*water for washing*)

Om Pupe Ah Hung(*flowers*)

Om Dupe Ah Hung (*incense*)

Om Aloke Ah Hung (*butter lamp*)

Om Gande Ah Hung(*perfume*)

Om Newite Ah Hung(*food*)

Om Shapta Ah Hung(*music*)

I make the inner offerings of semen, bones, brain, blood, and flesh:

Om Maha Mamsa Rakta Gorotsana Kengniriti Shukra Pudza Ah Hung (3X)

I make the secret offering of union of lotus and vajra:

Om Benza Peme Bhandza Pudza Ah Hung (3X)

I make the most secret offering of Buddhanature:

Om Tathagatagarba Ah Hung (3X)

Seven Line Prayer Guru Yoga:

OM AH HUNG

In the northwest of the land of Orgyen,

In the heart of a lotus flower,

Endowed with the most marvelous attainments,

You are renowned as the lotus-born,

Surrounded by many hosts of dakinis,

Following in your footsteps,

I pray to you: Come and bless me with your grace!

GURU PADMA SIDDHI HUNG (3X)

OM AH HUNG BENZA GURU PEME SIDDHI HUNG (108X *or as many times as you can*)

White light radiates from the forehead of Padmasambhava into my forehead purifying my body, planting the seed of Nirmanakaya, empowering the practice of the generation stage, and revealing appearance-emptiness.

Red light radiates from the throat of Padmasambhava into my throat purifying my speech, planting the seed of Sambhogakaya, empowering the practice of the jnanamudra yogas, and revealing luminous-emptiness.

Blue light radiates from the heart of Padmasambhava into my heart purifying my mind, planting the seed of Dharmakaya, empowering the practice of karmamudra yogas, and revealing bliss-emptiness.

Yellow light radiates from the navel of Padmasambhava into my navel purifying all subtle obscurations, planting the seed of Abhisambodhikaya, empowering the practice of Dzogchen Trekcho, and revealing awareness-emptiness.

Green light radiates from the secret place of Padmasambhava into my secret place purifying all habitual tendencies, planting the seed of Vajrakaya, empowering the practice of Dzogchen Togal, and revealing great compassion-emptiness.

The guru dissolves into light and merges inseparably into myself. (*Abide in oneness.*)

Dedication:

With all the good virtue I have accumulated in samsara and nirvana,

I pray that discursive thought of all sentient beings would be eliminated,

That they would achieve the ultimate liberation and

Obtain the rainbow body just like Rigpa Guru Padmasambhava's.

The Specific Preliminaries

Emptiness mantra – establishes awareness of emptiness as the basis for the recitation and meditation – "all things and I are the embodiment of that indestructible wisdom that is emptiness":

Om Svabhava Shuddha Sarwa Dharma Svabhava Shuddho Ham

Om Shunyata Jnana Benza Swabhava Atmako Ham

Clearing away non-conducive conditions by first expelling negative mental obscurations and afflictive emotions (as "demons"):

From luminous emptiness, my own Buddhanature, arises a BAM syllable, transforming into White Vajravarahi. In her form I generate the (*red*) torma offering by clearing away concepts, increasing to countless numbers, blessing with all desirable qualities to arise as the offering that becomes inexhaustible.

Om Ah Hung Ho (3X)

Light radiates from my heart to summon and draw in the demonic forces. I make the offerings (*with bell and drum*):

Sarwa Balingta Kha Kha Khahi Khahi

They partake and are satisfied. Take the torma plate outside holding it with the right hand, palm down, with index and middle fingers on the top edge and the thumb and ring finger fingers supporting it from below the edge. Place it away from the shrine room. Leave the torma and return with the plate upside down, placing it back on the offering table.

Cast out the obstructive spirits with:

Om Sumbhani Sumbhani Hung Phat <snap fingers of left hand>

Om Grihana Grihana Hung Phat <snap>

Om Grinapaya Grinapaya Hung Phat <snap>

Om Ayaya Ho Bhagawan Bidya Radza Hung Phat <snap>

Followed by bell and drum.

Wheel of Protection:

From the BAM at my heart, burning fire, vajra weapons, and tiny Vajravarahis stream forth in all directions to annihilate any remaining obstructions. The vajra weapons then form a solid foundation of blue vajras encircled by a vajra fence, vajra canopy, a surrounding mass of blazing fire, vajra water with pounding waves, and vajra wind that is sharp and violent. The five poisons are transformed into the five wisdoms as the wheel of protection.

Om Nama Sarwa Kaya Girti Nitti Ah Hung (3X)

Establishing the conducive conditions:

In my ordinary form, a rain of blessings descends from everywhere and melts into me and my environment, removing all impurities.

Blessing of the offering materials:

I arise again as White Vajravarahi.

Ram Yam Kham (3X)

RAM (fire) burns away impure characteristics, YAM (wind) blows and scatters all clinging to objects as truly existing, and KHAM (water) cleanses all habitual and negative instincts leaving me in a pure state of being. The offerings are now blessed with:

Om Ah Hung (3X)

I bless the eight outer offerings:

Om Argham Padyam Pupe Dupe Aloke Gande Newite Shapta Ah Hung (3X)

As White Vajravarahi I bless the three offerings of medicine, torma, and rakta (*lit. blood*). The syllable BHRUM transforms into a vast jeweled skull cup resting upon a hearth of three heads and containing the five nectars (*feces, brain, semen, blood, and urine*) marked with the syllables OM, KHAM, AM, TRAM and HUNG in the east[182], north, west, south and center; and five meats (*cow, dog, elephant, horse, and human*) marked with the syllables LAM, MAM, PAM, TAM, and BAM in the SE, SW, NW, NE, and center. The wind blows and the fire blazes. The seed syllables melt into the Five Buddhas and Consorts. From the points of their union, red and white substances mingle and descend into the skull cup and dissolve into the five meats and nectars filling the cup and dissolving the five meats and nectars. The five Buddhas and Consorts also dissolve and melt into the nectar. From a HUNG above, a white upside-down khatvanga melts into the nectar turning it into the color of mercury.

---

[182] "East" is always closest to you (in front), when viewed from the outside. North is to your right, west is on the far side, and south is to your left.

This offering of medicine (*amrita*), now fully endowed with the five wisdoms, is blessed with:

Om Ah Hung Sarwa Pantsa Amrita Hung Hri Ta (3X)

Next a second vast jeweled vessel representing the entire inanimate world manifests containing the white torma, which represents the entire animate world, is blessed with:

Om Ah Hung Maha Balingta Tedzo Balingta Balawate Guya Samaya Hung Hri Ta (3X)

Then, a vast vessel made of a freshly severed skull filled with blood – the red torma – symbolizing all desires and attachments of the three realms, but is of the nature of desireless great bliss, is blessed with:

Om Ah Hung Maha Rakta Dzola Mandala Hung Hri Ta (3X)

The Main Practice

The samadhis of the three kayas:

The Samadhi of Suchness (*dharmakaya*) is emptiness, neither existent nor non-existent, a nonconceptual pure awareness.

The Samadhi of Luminosity (*sambhogakaya*) is great compassion for the suffering of all sentient beings and the illusory nature of all appearances.

The Samadhi of Supreme Cause (*nirmanakakya*) is the union of emptiness and compassion radiating brilliant red light from the seed syllable BAM in all directions to liberate all sentient beings.

Generating the support:

In the center of the wheel of protection, the syllable AH is transformed into a blue, long, inverted, three-sided pyramid (*tetrahedron*) in the form of space.

On top of this, the syllable YAM is transformed into a crossed vajra encircled by dark green smoke as the element air.

Above this, the syllable RAM is transformed into a red cube as the element fire.

Over this, the syllable BAM is transformed into a sphere of white light as the element water.

Next, the syllable LAM is transformed into a gold cube of light as the element earth.

At the top, the syllable SUM is transformed into Mt. Meru in the shape of a four-sided pyramid covered with gold, lapis lazuli, rubies and mother of pearl respectively.

Reciting BHRUM, the syllable descends to the top of Mt. Meru, melts into light, and causes the celestial mansion to appear, surrounded by the eight charnel grounds.

In its center is a 1000-pedalled lotus with a sun disk and crossed vajra and a blue square. There are four sides of five concentric walls and a red landing with sixteen offering goddesses facing in. At the top of the outer wall is a yellow border with jewels and then tiny pillars up to the roof. The outer east wall is white, the outer south wall is yellow, the outer west wall is red, and the outer north wall is green. There are four entrances with four pillared porticos decorated with Dharma wheels, umbrellas, banners, antelopes and yak-tail fans.

Inside there are eight pillars made of skulls that support four beams made of bones. The walls are made of dry, moist and fresh skulls. The rafters are adorned with garlands of fingers, skulls, organs, genitals and the sun and moon. The dome of the room is a great god's skull and a hanging net of intestines and skulls. The top of the roof is a heart, banner and canopy made of human skin. A terrifying firelight pervades the environment.

Generation of the seat and the deity:

In the center a white inverted dharmodaya appears containing a white lotus. On the lotus with sun disk appears the white seed syllable BAM, my pure awareness, arises as a five-pointed vajra representing the five primordial wisdoms. Light radiates from the vajra as an offering to the Buddhas and returns as a blessing. It then radiates to all sentient beings, transforming them into Vajravarahis; then returns transforming the vajra into myself as brilliant white Vajravarahi (*samayasattva – commitment being*).

I have one face with three eyes with a semi-wrathful expression and two arms. In my right hand is a vajra and in my left is a skull cup filled with the elixir of primordial awareness. I am youthful and naked with nothing to hide, standing in a dancing pose with my secret lotus open. I am adorned with a crown of 5 skulls alternating with 5 vajras, a necklace of 50 dried skulls, and 5 bone ornaments. I hold a khatvanga tipped with a vajra, 3 skulls, a wish-fulfilling vase and crossed vajras in my left arm as my consort, with hanging drum, bell and 3-pointed banner. I am surrounded by the fire of primordial wisdom.

Upon moon discs at my navel is a red Vajravarahi, at my heart a blue Yamani, at my throat a white Mohani, at my forehead a yellow Sachalini, at the crown of my head a green Samtrasani, and at my limbs a smoking-gray Chandika.

At my heart is a white double tetrahedron (*two inverted, three-sided pyramids superimposed on each other forming a six-pointed star on the top*), inside of which is a lotus and sun disc, and the white seed syllable BAM (*samadhisattva – essence being*), the nature of my Root Guru and the union of bliss and emptiness, standing upright. It is surrounded by the mantra arranged counter-clockwise facing outward: OM BENZA VAIROCHANIYE SOHA.

I am surrounded by four dakinis in the four cardinal directions. The one on my left is green, the one in back is red, the one on my right is yellow, and the one in front is white. Outside this is a circle of eight dakinis, then another circle of eight, then a third circle of eight, and a fourth circle of eight making a total of five circles of dakinis all in the form of Vajravarahi with vajra, skull cup and so forth.

Invoking the jnanasattvas (wisdom beings): Form the "blazing mudra" and raise over your head, then gracefully make three small circles counterclockwise, three clockwise, and three more counterclockwise. Then say **Phem!** *loudly and release the mudra outwards.*

From the white BAM at my heart, light radiates out to the Akanashita Buddhfield to invite Vajravarahi and all dakas and dakinis and purified sentient beings now in the form of Vajravarahi. Through the power of your commitment, come to me.

OM Benza Samaya Dza

Homage: I bow down to the host of the mandala of Vajravarahi, illusory bodily forms of primordial awareness inseparable from myself.

Atipuho Pratitsa Ho

Offerings:

From the BAM at my heart eight offering yoginis appear.

To the divine host of the mandala of Vajravarahi they make outer offerings *(with bell and drum)*:

Om Ah Hung Argam Padyam Pupe Dupe Aloke Gande Newite Shapta Pudza Ho (3X)

They make inner offerings of semen, bones, brain, blood, and flesh *(with bell and drum)*:

Om Ah Hung Maha Mamsa Rakta Gorotsana Kengniriti Shukra Pudza Ho (3X)

They make the secret offering of union of lotus and vajra *(with bell and drum)*:

Om Ah Hung Benza Peme Bhandza Pudza Ho (3X)

They make the most secret offering of Buddhanature *(with bell and drum)*:

Om Ah Hung Tathagatagarba Pudza Ho (3X)

The host of jnanasattvas partakes of the offerings and is pleased *(follow with drum)*. *Take offering plate(s) with edible red and white tormas outside for other beings. Return plates to shrine and place them upside down.*

Request for empowerment:

Om Sarwa Tathagata Abishekata Samaya Hung

My body is filled with water and is purified. Excess water on the crown of my head transforms into Vairocana.

With DZA the beings are above me, with HUNG they enter the crown of my head and descend through the central channel to the BAM, with BAM they become inseparable with the samadhisattva BAM, and with the HO I experience great bliss!

Dza Hung Bam Ho

Om Svabhava Shuddha Sarwa Dharma Svabhava Shuddho Ham

Praise:

To the enlightened bodily form of Vajravarahi arisen from luminosity,

To her enlightened speech, the unceasing melody of mantra,

To her enlightened mind of primordial awareness, luminous clarity,

To the White Dakini, who is the utter perfection of the five kayas of enlightened presence, I bow down (*bell*).

Mantra Recitation & Dissolution

While visualizing the complete mandala previously constructed with myself as Vajravarahi and the mantra rotating clockwise (as seen from the outside), white light radiates out to all Buddhas and sentient beings as Vajravarahi and returns as blessings:

OM Benza Vairochaniye Soha (*Recite 108X or as many times as you can. For accumulation, recite as many as you vow.*)

Dissolve the visualization from the outside into yourself as Vajravarahi, then yourself into the samadhisattva seed syllable, then the seed syllable from the bottom up through the crescent, bindu and nada into emptiness. Emptiness is not a thing, it is not no-thing, it is not both, it is not neither! Abide softly and deeply in the innate happiness – the pure, naked, nonconceptual awareness of transcendent wisdom – as long as you can....

Arise once again in the inner peace of bliss-emptiness of the illusory bodily form of White Vajravarahi with the pure awareness of clear light, and radiating white light for the benefit of all sentient beings! See all beings as Buddhas, hear all sounds as mantras, think all thoughts as the wisdom of the Buddhas, accept all phenomena as the pure Buddhafield of enlightenment.

Closing prayers

The conventionally visualized being (*samayasattva*) and the being of primordial awareness (*jnanasattva*) are not two different things,

So there is no need to make a request to remain.

They arise from myself and are transformations of my own free will,

My own awareness being the ground and source,

So what need is there for empowerment or full establishment?

Furthermore, the many desirable sense qualities

Are ornaments of the play of primordial awareness, my own mind,

Emanated from myself and offered to myself.

Do not seek samaya in other substances of offering.

The measureless palace of phenomena, the spiritual preceptor and deities,

Are all a great mandala setting its seal on reality.

Just as the appearances in the mandala of water

Are devoid of self-nature, for example,

View them as arising from a state free of taking things as real.

Penetrating insight beyond word or expression, the unwavering enlightened dimension of absolute reality (*dharmakaya*),

Chief of the five families, the enlightened dimension of perfect enjoyment of the qualities of great bliss (*sambhogakaya*),

And the great enlightened dimension of manifest appearance, the hundredfold skillful means of compassion (*nirmanakaya*),

To all the deities of the three dimensions of enlightened presence I bow down (*bell*).

Mantra of Increasing Mantras: **Om Sambara Sambara Bimana Sara Maha Zambaba Hung Phat Soha**

Purification mantras:

Sanskrit vowels: **OM a, aa   i, ii   u, uu   ri, rii   li, lii   e, ey   o, oh ang, ah**

Sanskrit consonants:

    ka kha ga gha nga/

    tsa ts'a dza dz'a nya/

    ta t'a da d'a na/

    ta t'a da d'a na/[183]

    pa p'a ba b'a ma/

    ya ra la wa/

    sha kha sa ha kya SO HA/

Mantra of Dependent Origination:

    Om Yedharma Hetu Prabhawa

---

[183] The second line has a silent "r" and is represented here phonetically.

Hetun-Tekhan Tathagato Hyawadata

Tekhantsa Yo Nirodha Evam-Wadi

Maha-Shramana-Ye So-Ha

100 Syllable Mantra of Vajrasattva:

OM Benza Sato Samaya

Manu Palaya

Benza Sato Tenopa

Tishta Drido Me Bhawa

Suto Khayo Me Bhawa

Supo Khayo Me Bhawa

Anu Rakto Me Bhawa

Sarwa Siddhi Me Prayatsa

Sarwa Karma Sutsa Me

Sit-Tam Shriya Kuru Hung

Ha Ha Ha Ha Ho

Bhagavan

Sarwa Tathagata

Benza Mame Muntsa

Benzi Bhawa

Maha Samaya

Sato Ah

Long Life Prayers:

H.H. the Dalai Lama

For this realm encircled by snow-covered mountains

You are the source of every benefit and bliss without exception.

Tenzin Gyaltso, you who are one with Avalokiteshvara,

May you remain steadfast until Samsara's end!

Khenchen Lama

In the Dharmadhatu appearing as Amitabha,

In the Sambhogakaya form as wisdom Buddha Manjushri,

Padmasambhava's heart son Sangye Yeshe,

Incarnated as Padma Dagnag Lingpa in previous life

And Paljea pa Dorjee in this lifetime,

May your life be longer than the duration of samsara

So that all your virtuous intentions can be accomplished.

Please give me your heart blessings so that

My mind is united with yours in the Buddha nature.

So, I pray!

Wish for Bodhicitta:

Om Ah Hung Shri

Ananta Benza Sarwa

Siddhi Phala Hung Ah!

Glorious, precious root lama,

Sit on the lotus seat on the crown of my head.

With your great kindness please accept me.

Please bestow the realizations of body, speech, and mind.

In all the activities of the glorious lama,

May no wrong view arise even for a moment.

By the devotion of seeing whatever he does as perfect

May the blessing of the lama enter my mind.

Throughout the succession of my lives, from the perfect lamas

May I never be separated and, enjoying the glory of the Dharma,

Perfect all the qualities of the stages and the paths

And swiftly attain the stage of Vajradhara.

The lamas who have become the glory of the Dharma, may their lives
    be stable;

May the land be entirely filled with Doctrine-holders;

May the wealth and power of the patrons of the Doctrine increase,

And may the auspiciousness of the Doctrine remain forever.

Bodhichitta, the excellent and precious mind.

Where it is unborn, may it arise.

Where it is born, may it not decline,

But ever increase, higher and higher.

Dedication:

By the virtue of this, may I and all sentient beings accomplish the state of the dakini. Without leaving a single sentient being behind, may I liberate them to the state of the dakini. (3X)

*****

This sadhana was written by Khenpo Drimed Dawa to the best of my limited ability for the benefit of all sentient beings in 2009-2012, Tucson Arizona. Please forgive all errors or omissions. They are my own.

Sealed   Sealed   Sealed

Appendix C

Sadhanas of the Red Dakini

(Sambhogakaya)

Introduction

The idea for this sadhana came to me in a dream. This time I was guided by the Red Dakini in the form of Simhamukha – the Lion-Faced Dakini. Simhamukha usually appears in a blue form, but is known to appear red or maroon in color. In this form, her nature is compassion and she destroys the afflictive emotions of desire and lust – the main afflictive emotions of the human realm.

According to Jigmed Lingpa (1726-1798), the Nyingma master famous for finding hidden treasures or *termas*, Simhamukha represents the nirmanakaya, Vajravarahi represents the sambhogakaya, and Samantabhadri represents the dharmakaya. However, Jamgon Kongtrul (1813-1899) composed an outer, inner, and secret Simhamukha sadhana in which the inner (Sambhogakaya) is red. In this instance as well, as red Simhamukha, she appeared in Sambhogakaya form.

She took me to a hidden place and showed the text in a script that I did not recognize. It was written on transparent paper in red. Lines of red looped across the page with rectangular blocks of red as well, much like the script in the Sadhana of the White Dakini. It was hard to tell one page from another due to the transparent paper on which it was written. Again, I did not know what to make of it for some time. But eventually, this text came to me so that I might share it with you.

As a Sambhogakaya text, the focus of this practice involves completion-stage practices of *tummo, tsalung,* and *mahamudra.*

Practitioners should have mastered the Sadhana of the White Dakini prior to attempting this one. This may be practiced by anyone having one of the following empowerments from any lineage: Vajrayogini, any sadhana including Vajravarahi, or any other Highest Yoga Tantra empowerment. This practice is for yogis, yoginis and other lay practitioners.

Since I am not a realized being and have no notable credibility for such an endeavor, I acknowledge that this may contain errors or omissions for which I accept complete responsibility. I ask only that you see it with naked awareness and find in it whatever benefit you may.

There are two other texts in this series, the Sadhana of the White Dakini (Nirmanakaya) and the Sadhana of the Blue Dakini (Dharmakaya). May they too be of benefit.

Sadhana of the Red Dakini

Having mastered the Ngondro and Generation Stage practices, one engages in the Completion Stage practices of tummo, illusory body (tsalung with the four blisses and four empties), and clear light mahamudra. After accomplishing these separately, one may engage in the Sadhana of the Red Dakini. The goal of this practice is to attain a pure illusory body. After mastery of the sadhana with the jnanamudra, one may engage in the practice with a qualified karmamudra. To do so, begin the practice naked or covered with a meditation shawl and facing each other.

HOMAGE to Samantabhadri, Simhamukha, and Vajravarahi.

Mantra of Increasing Mantras – magnifies the effect of all that follows. Light goes out as offering to Buddhas and returns as a blessing:

Om Sambara Sambara Bimana Sara Maha Zambaba Hung Phat Soha! (3X)

Emptiness mantra – establishes awareness of emptiness as the basis for the recitation and meditation – "all things and I are the embodiment of that indestructible wisdom that is emptiness":

Om Shunyata Jnana Benza Swabhava Emako Ham

Ngondro – The Incomparable Foundational Practices

Four Thoughts that Turn the Mind:

I prostrate Samantabhadra and Samantabhadri.

Because I suffer due to my own actions and I now have this precious human life without knowing when I will die, I will now engage in virtuous actions for the benefit of all sentient beings with great joy and devotion.

Refuge Tree visualization:

In front of me on a jeweled throne supported by eight snow lions sits my Root Guru in the form of Samantabhadra and Samantabhadri in union. Below and in front are tantric deities. On their right (*your left*) are all the Buddhas of the four times. Behind are the scriptures emblazoned with and resonating the vowels and consonants. On their left (*your right*) are all the Bodhisattvas. They are surrounded by countless Dakinis and Dharmapalas filling all of space. Your Mother and Father are next to you. All other sentient beings, including your enemies, are in front of you.

Outer Refuge and Bodhicitta:

I take refuge in the Buddha, Dharma and Sangha most excellent, abiding softly and deeply in pure, nonconceptual awareness of the ineffable, oneness, openness, and the spontaneous radiant display manifesting immeasurable, unconditional lovingkindness, compassion, joy and equanimity for the benefit of all.

Inner Refuge and Bodhicitta:

I take refuge in the Guru, Yidam, and Dakini, abiding softly and deeply in pure, nonconceptual awareness of the ineffable, oneness, openness, and the spontaneous radiant display manifesting immeasurable, unconditional lovingkindness, compassion, joy and equanimity for the benefit of all.

Secret Refuge and Bodhicitta:

I take refuge in the Dharmakaya, Sambhogakaya, and Nirmanakaya, abiding softly and deeply in pure, nonconceptual awareness of the ineffable, oneness, openness, and the spontaneous radiant display manifesting immeasurable, unconditional lovingkindness,
compassion, joy and equanimity for the benefit of all.

Most secret Refuge and Bodhicitta:

I take refuge ... *Dissolve the visualization into pure awareness with lovingkindness and compassion for all. Abide briefly in complete stillness.*

Action Bodhicitta – The Four Immeasurables:

May all sentient beings have happiness and the causes of happiness.

May they be liberated from suffering and the causes of suffering.

May they never be separated from the happiness that is free from sorrow.

May they rest in equanimity, free from attachment and aversion. (3X)

Vajrasattva Purifications:

OM Benza Sato Samaya

Manu Palaya

Benza Sato Tenopa

Tishta Drido Me Bhawa

Suto Khayo Me Bhawa

Supo Khayo Me Bhawa

Anu Rakto Me Bhawa

Sarwa Siddhi Me Pra Yatsha

Sarwa Karma Sutsa Me

Sit-Tam Shriya Kuru Hung

Ha Ha Ha Ha Ho

Bhagavan

Sarwa Tathagata

Benza Mame Muntsa

Benzi Bhawa

Maha Samaya

Sato Ah

(*Repeat 5X or 3X or 1X*)

Then: **OM Benza Sato Ah** (108X *or as many times as you can*)

Then: **OM Ah Hung Hri** (108X *or as many times as you can*)

Offerings (outer, inner, secret, most secret) with bell and drum or hand mudra:

I make the eight outer offerings:

OM Argham Ah Hung

OM Padyam Ah Hung

OM Pupe Ah Hung

OM Dupe Ah Hung

OM Aloke Ah Hung

OM Gande Ah Hung

OM Newite Ah Hung

OM Shapta Ah Hung

I make the inner offerings of semen, bones, brain, blood, and flesh:

OM Maha Mamsa Rakta Gorotsana Kengniriti Shukra Pudza Ah Hung (3X)

I make the secret offering of union of lotus and vajra:

OM Benza Peme Bhandza Pudza Ah Hung (3X)

I make the most secret offering of Buddhanature:

OM Tathagatagarba Ah Hung (3X)

Seven Line Prayer Guru Yoga:

OM Ah Hung

In the northwest of the land of Orgyen,

In the heart of a lotus flower,

Endowed with the most marvelous attainments,

You are renowned as the lotus-born,

Surrounded by many hosts of dakinis,

Following in your footsteps,

I pray to you: Come and bless me with your grace!

Guru Padma Siddhi Hung (3X)

OM Ah Hung Benza Guru Peme Siddhi Hung (108X *or as many times as you can*)

White light radiates from the forehead of Padmasambhava into my forehead purifying my body, planting the seed of Nirmanakaya, empowering the practice of the generation stage, and revealing appearance-emptiness.

Red light radiates from the throat of Padmasambhava into my throat purifying my speech, planting the seed of Sambhogakaya, empowering the practice of the jnanamudra yogas, and revealing luminous-emptiness.

Blue light radiates from the heart of Padmasambhava into my heart purifying my mind, planting the seed of Dharmakaya, empowering the practice of karmamudra yogas, and revealing bliss-emptiness.

Yellow light radiates from the navel of Padmasambhava into my navel purifying all subtle obscurations, planting the seed of Abhisambodhikaya, empowering the practice of Dzogchen Trekcho, and revealing awareness-emptiness.

Green light radiates from the secret place of Padmasambhava into my secret place purifying any residual habitual tendencies, planting the seed of Vajrakaya, empowering the practice of the Dzogchen Togal, and revealing great compassion-emptiness.

The guru dissolves into light and merges inseparably into myself. (*Abide in oneness.*)

Dedication:

With all the good virtue I have accumulated in samsara and nirvana,

I pray that discursive thought of all sentient beings would be eliminated,

That they would achieve the ultimate liberation and

Obtain the rainbow body just like Rigpa Guru Padmasambhava's.

The Specific Preliminaries

Emptiness mantra – establishes awareness of emptiness as the basis for the recitation and meditation – "all things and I are the embodiment of that indestructible wisdom that is emptiness":

Om Svabhava Shuddha Sarwa Dharma Svabhava Shuddho Ham

Om Shunyata Jnana Benza Swabhava Atmako Ham

Clearing away non-conducive conditions:

In this practice, there is no need to clear away non-conducive conditions nor to create a wheel of protection. Following the tantric principle of fighting fire with fire, all afflictive emotions and mental obscurations are embraced as the five wisdoms!

Establishing the conducive conditions:

In my ordinary form, a rain of blessings descends from everywhere and melts into me and my environment, removing all impurities.

Blessing of the offering materials:

Instantly, I arise as Simhamukha.

Ram Yam Kham (3X)

RAM (fire) burns away impure characteristics, YAM (wind) blows and scatters all clinging to objects as truly existing, and KHAM (water) cleanses all habitual and negative instincts leaving me in a pure state of being.

The offerings are now blessed with:

OM Ah Hung (3X)

I bless the eight outer offerings: **OM Argham Padyam Pupe Dupe Aloke Gande Newite Shapta Ah Hung** (3X)

As Simhamukha I bless the three offerings of amrita (*medicine*), torma, and rakta (*lit. blood*). The offering of medicine fully endowed with the five wisdoms is blessed with:

OM Ah Hung Sarwa Pantsa Amrita Hung Hri Ta (3X)

Next the white torma, which represents the entire animate world, is blessed with:

OM Ah Hung Maha Balingta Tedzo Balingta Balawate Guya Samaya Hung Hri Ta (3X)

Then, a vast vessel made of a freshly severed skull filled with blood – the red torma – symbolizing all desires and attachments of the three realms but is of the nature of desireless great bliss, is blessed with:

OM Ah Hung Maha Rakta Dzola Mandala Hung Hri Ta (3X)

The Main Practice

The samadhis of the three kayas:

The Samadhi of Suchness (*dharmakaya*) is emptiness, neither existent nor non-existent, a nonconceptual pure awareness.

The Samadhi of Luminosity (*sambhogakaya*) is great compassion for the suffering of all sentient beings and the illusory nature of all appearances.

The Samadhi of Supreme Cause (*nirmanakaya*) is the union of emptiness and compassion radiating brilliant light from the seed syllable HUNG at my heart in all directions to liberate all sentient beings.

Generating the support and the deity:

Instantly there arises the *bhaga* mandala of the divine feminine, the embodiment of all of space. The syllable PAM appears and becomes a lotus, the syllable RAM appears and becomes a sun, on top of which a HUNG appears and radiates rays of light, establishing the vajra ground. Around it is a vajra fence; above it is a vajra tent, all surrounded by the fire of primordial wisdom. In the center is the syllable E (*ay*), which transforms into a maroon dharmakara.

In the center is a lotus and sun disk. On the disk my mind appears in the form of a dark blue HUNG that is transformed into me as Simhamukha. My body is dark red (*maroon*) in color with one face, two arms and three eyes. I have bared fangs with my tongue curled upwards, looking ferocious. My right hand holds up a vajra. My left hand holds a skullcup filled with blood at my heart. On my left shoulder leans a khatvanga. My hair and eyebrows are yellow-red, streaming upwards. A crown of 5 skulls adorns my head, and a garland of 50 freshly cut human heads hangs around my neck. I am naked and adorned with the 5 bone ornaments. I am in the dancing posture with my secret lotus open, my left leg extended and my right leg tucked in. I am surrounded by the fire of primordial wisdom. I have a white OM at my forehead, a red AH at my throat, and a blue HUNG at my heart.

I am surrounded by four dakinis in the four cardinal directions. The one in front is white, the one on my right is yellow, the one in back is red, and the one on my left is green all in the form of Simhamukha with vajra, skull cup and so forth.

Invoking the jnanasattvas (wisdom beings): Form the "blazing mudra" and raise over your head, then gracefully make three small circles counterclockwise, three clockwise, and three more counterclockwise. Then say **Phem!** *loudly and release the mudra outwards.*

From the blue HUNG at my heart, light radiates out to the summoning the 5 Buddha families and their retinue.

OM Benza Samaya Dza

Homage: I bow down to the host of the 5 Buddha families, illusory bodily forms of primordial awareness inseparable from myself.

Atipuho Pratitsa Ho

Offerings:

From the HUNG at my heart eight offering yoginis appear.

To the divine host of the five Buddha families they make outer offerings (*with bell and drum*):

Om Ah Hung Argam Padyam Pupe Dupe Aloke Gande Newite Shapta Pudza Ho (3X)

They make inner offerings of semen, bones, brain, blood, and flesh (*with bell and drum*):

Om Ah Hung Maha Mamsa Rakta Gorotsana Kengniriti Shukra Pudza Ho (3X)

They make the secret offering of union of lotus and vajra (*with bell and drum*):

Om Ah Hung Benza Peme Bhandza Pudza Ho (3X)

They make the most secret offering of Buddhanature (*with bell and drum*):

Om Ah Hung Tathagatagarba Pudza Ho (3X)

The host of jnanasattvas partakes of the offerings and is pleased (*follow with drum*). *Take offering plate(s) with edible red and white tormas outside for other beings. Return plates to shrine and place them upside down.*

Request for empowerment:

Om Sarwa Tathagata Abishekata Samaya Hung

My body is filled with water and is purified. Excess water on the crown of my head transforms into a five-pointed blue vajra to adorn my head.

With DZA the beings are above me, with HUNG they enter the crown of my head and descend through the central channel to the BAM, with BAM they become inseparable with the samadhisattva BAM, and with the HO I experience great bliss!

Dza Hung Bam Ho

Om Svabhava Shuddha Sarwa Dharma Svabhava Shuddho Ham

Praise:

To the enlightened bodily form of Simhamukha arisen from luminosity,

To her enlightened speech, the unceasing melody of mantra,

To her enlightened mind of primordial awareness, luminous clarity,

To the Red Dakini, who is the utter perfection of the five kayas of enlightened presence, I bow down (*bell*).

Mantra Recitation

Visualizing the complete mandala previously constructed with yourself as Simhamukha with khatvanga as consort and the mantra rotating clockwise (as seen from the outside), red light radiates out to all Buddhas and sentient beings as Simhamukha and returns as blessings. Recite the mantra:

Ah Ka Sa Ma   Ra Tsa Sa Da   Ra Sa Ma Ra Ya   Phat (108X *or as many times as you can*)

Having trained in tummo, tsalung, and clear light, you now engage in the completion-stage practices.[184] Visualize the three channels and six chakras, and then focus on the central channel. As the winds stabilize and remain within the central channel, breathing in and out will slow and even cease.

Tummo:

> Below the navel, above a tiny AH-stroke, an intense flame of bliss heats and melts my red female red drop at the bottom of the central channel.
> Breathing in, the increasing heat ascends to my navel, melting away subtle obscurations.
> It continues increasing to my heart, melting obstacles of my mind,
> Then increases to my throat, melting away obstacles of my speech, and
> Finally, increases to my crown, melting away obstacles of my body.
> The intense inner heat of bliss melts the white bodhicitta drop (HAM) at my crown.
>
> Breathing out, it descends through my open throat chakra.
> Then down through my open heart chakra,
> Through my open navel chakra, and
> Finally, to my secret place, where I experience the heat of innate bliss radiating throughout.
>
> *Repeat 3X or more. Then sustain the white bodhicitta drop at the tip of the sex organ as long as you can. Next, continue with the Four Blisses.*

The Four Blisses:

> Below the navel, above the tiny AH-stroke, an intense flame melts my female red drop.

---

[184] If engaging in this practice with a *karmamudra* consort, arouse each other with kissing, touching, and fondling. Join the lotus and vajra in union, breathing slowly and synchronously. Then continue the practice as with the *jnanamudra* consort as long as you can to ever higher intensity of bliss, without orgasm.

Breathing in, it ascends to my navel, and I experience bliss.
As it ascends to my heart, I experience supreme bliss.
As it ascends to my throat, I experience special bliss.
As it ascends to my crown, I experience great innate bliss.

The inner heat melts the white bodhicitta drop at my crown.
Breathing out, it descends to my throat, and I experience increasing bliss.
As it descends to my heart, I experience increasing supreme bliss.
As it descends to my navel, I experience increasing special bliss.
As it descends to my secret place, I experience intense innate bliss radiating throughout.

Repeat 3X or more increasing the heat of inner bliss with each step, ascending and descending. Then sustain the white bodhicitta drop at the tip of the sex organ as long as you can. Then continue with the next stage.

The Four Empties:

Below the navel, above a tiny AH-stroke, an intense flame melts my female red drop.
Breathing in, it ascends to my navel, and I experience bliss.
As it ascends to my heart, I experience supreme bliss.
As it ascends to my throat, I experience special bliss.
As it ascends to my crown, I experience great innate bliss

The inner heat melts the white bodhicitta drop at my crown.
Breathing out, it descends to my throat, and I experience emptiness.[185]
As it descends to my heart, I experience great emptiness.
As it descends to my navel, I experience extreme emptiness.
As it descends to my secret place, I experience total emptiness.
As it joins in one taste at the tip of my sex organ, I experience the inconceivable pristine cognition of bliss-emptiness.

Repeat until only bliss-emptiness remains.

Clear Light Mahamudra:

Outer dissolution, breathing in: From bliss-emptiness appearances move or shimmer like a mirage (*navel chakra*).
There appears a bluish cloud-like smoke (*heart chakra*).

---

[185] When doing this practice with a *karmamudra*, the deity and consort remain in complete, relaxed stillness, letting the intense sexual bliss in the secret place melt into emptiness.

Dots or sparks appear like fireflies (*throat chakra*).

A small glowing light appears like a butter lamp (*crown chakra*).

Inner dissolution, breathing out: The white light grows to fill the sky as the white drop at my crown descends to the indestructible drop at the heart.

A red light glows like a sunset filling the sky as the red drop at my navel ascends to the indestructible drop at the heart.

Objects disappear into black like the darkness of night without moon or stars as the white and red drops enclose the indestructible drop at the heart.

Then clear light appears like the light of first dawn as the drops enter the indestructible drop.

Abide in the clear light mahamudra – pure naked awareness – as long as you can, then reverse the order of the inner and outer dissolution visualizations as you return into your (impure) illusory body as the Red Dakini.

Request for blessings:

Dakini Simhamukha,
Please bestow
The common and uncommon siddhis
Upon me and all sentient beings.

Closing Prayers

The conventionally visualized being (*samayasattva*) and the being of primordial awareness (*jnanasattva*) are not two different things,

So there is no need to make a request to remain.

They arise from myself and are transformations of my own free will,

My own awareness being the ground and source,

So what need is there for empowerment or full establishment?

Furthermore, the many desirable sense qualities

Are ornaments of the play of primordial awareness, my own mind,

Emanated from myself and offered to myself.

Do not seek samaya in other substances of offering.

The measureless palace of phenomena, the spiritual preceptor and deities,

Are all a great mandala setting its seal on reality.

Just as the appearances in the mandala of water

Are devoid of self-nature, for example,

View them as arising from a state free of taking things as real.

Penetrating insight beyond word or expression, the unwavering enlightened dimension of absolute reality (*dharmakaya*),

Chief of the five families, the enlightened dimension of perfect enjoyment of the qualities of great bliss (*sambhogakaya*),

And the great enlightened dimension of manifest appearance, the hundredfold skillful means of compassion (*nirmanakaya*),

To all the deities of the three dimensions of enlightened presence I bow down (*bell*).

Mantra of Increasing Mantras: **OM Sambara Sambara Bimana Sara Maha Zambaba Hung Phat Soha**

Purification mantras:

Sanskrit vowels: **OM a, aa   i, ii   u, uu   ri, rii   li, lii   e, ey   o, oh ang, ah**

Sanskrit consonants:

> **ka kha ga gha nga/**
>
> **tsa ts'a dza dz'a nya/**
>
> **ta t'a da d'a na/**
>
> **ta t'a da d'a na/**[186]
>
> **pa p'a ba b'a ma/**
>
> **ya ra la wa/**
>
> **sha kha sa ha kya So Ha/**

Mantra of Dependent Origination:

> **OM Yedharma Hetu Prabawa**
>
> **Hetun-Tekhan Tatagato Hyawadata**

---

[186] The second line has a silent "r" and is represented here phonetically.

Tekhantsa Yo Niroda Evam-Wadi

Maha-Shramana-Ye SoHa

100 Syllable Mantra of Vajrasattva:

OM Benza Sato Samaya

Manu Palaya

Benza Sato Tenopa

Tishta Drido Me Bhawa

Suto Khayo Me Bhawa

Supo Khayo Me Bhawa

Anu Rakto Me Bhawa

Sarwa Siddhi Me Pra Yatsha

Sarwa Karma Sutsa Me

Sit-Tam Shriya Kuru Hung

Ha Ha Ha Ha Ho

Bhagavan

Sarwa Tathagata

Benza Mame Muntsa

Benzi Bhawa

Maha Samaya

Sato Ah

Long Life Prayers:

H.H. the Dalai Lama

For this realm encircled by snow-covered mountains

You are the source of every benefit and bliss without exception.

Tenzin Gyaltso, you who are one with Avalokiteshvara,

May you remain steadfast until Samsara's end!

Khenchen Lama

In the Dharmadhatu appearing as Amitabha,

In the Sambhogakaya form as wisdom Buddha Manjushri,

Padmasambhava's heart son Sangye Yeshe,

Incarnated as Padma Dagnag Lingpa in previous life

And Paljea pa Dorjee in this lifetime,

May your life be longer than the duration of samsara

So that all your virtuous intentions can be accomplished.

Please give me your heart blessings so that

My mind is united with yours in the Buddha nature.

So, I pray!

Wish for Bodhicitta:

OM Ah Hung Shri

Ananta Benza Sarwa

Siddhi Phala Hung Ah!

Glorious, precious root lama,

Sit on the lotus seat on the crown of my head.

With your great kindness please accept me.

Please bestow the realizations of body, speech, and mind.

In all the activities of the glorious lama,

May no wrong view arise even for a moment.

By the devotion of seeing whatever he does as perfect,

May the blessing of the lama enter my mind.

Throughout the succession of my lives, from the perfect lamas

May I never be separated and, enjoying the glory of the Dharma,

Perfect all the qualities of the stages and the paths

And swiftly attain the stage of Vajradhara.

The lamas who have become the glory of the Dharma, may their lives
    be stable;

May the land be entirely filled with Doctrine-holders;

May the wealth and power of the patrons of the Doctrine increase,

And may the auspiciousness of the Doctrine remain forever.

Bodhichitta, the excellent and precious mind.

Where it is unborn, may it arise.

Where it is born, may it not decline,

But ever increase, higher and higher.

Dedication:

By the virtue of this, may I and all sentient beings accomplish the state of the dakini. Without leaving a single sentient being behind, may I liberate them to the state of the dakini. (3X)

One abides in the illusory body and even clear light before, during and after the meditation. All beings are Buddhas, all sounds are mantras, all thoughts and feelings (including those previously identified as afflictive emotions and mental obscurations) are recognized as the wisdom of the Buddhas, all phenomena are a pure buddhafield. Abide without attachment or aversion with lovingkindness and compassion for all – always and all ways.

At night one continues with dream yoga. From time to time, practice phowa (transference) followed by long-life practice and prayers. With devotion and regular practice, the impure illusory body with become increasingly subtle until achieving the pure illusory body state.

*****

This sadhana was written by Khenpo Drimed Dawa to the best of my limited ability for the benefit of all sentient beings in July, 2009, Tucson Arizona. Please forgive all errors or omissions. They are my own.

Sealed   Sealed   Sealed

Daily Sadhana of the Red Dakini

Intention: I do this practice for the benefit of all sentient beings (*or other personal intention*).

Homage: **Guru Dewa Dakiniye**

Preliminaries: Recite the brief Ngondro preliminary practice, with prostrations.

Visualization: Begin with stillness of body, speech and mind.

Om Svabhava Shuda Sarva Dharma Svabhava Shudo Ham

From emptiness appears a lotus and sun disk on which my mind appears in the form of a dark blue HUNG that is transformed into me as Simhamukha. My body is dark red (*maroon*) in color with one face, two arms and three eyes. I have bared fangs with my tongue curled upwards, looking ferocious. My right hand holds up a vajra. My left hand holds a skullcup filled with blood at my heart. On my left shoulder leans a khatvanga. My hair and eyebrows are yellow-red, streaming upwards. A crown of 5 skulls adorns my head, and a garland of 50 freshly cut human heads hangs around my neck. I am naked and adorned with the 5 bone ornaments. I am in the dancing posture with my secret lotus open, my left leg extended and my right leg tucked in. I am surrounded by the fire of primordial wisdom. I have a white OM at my forehead, a red AH at my throat, and a blue HUNG at my heart.

I am surrounded by four dakinis in the four cardinal directions. The one in front is white, the one on my right is yellow, the one in back is red, and the one on my left is green all in the form of Simhamukha with vajra, skull cup and so forth. From the blue HUNG at my heart, light radiates out to the summoning the 5 Buddha families and their retinue. I pay homage, make outer, inner, and secret offerings, and they dissolve into me filling me with their blessings.

Mantra: Visualizing the mandala I recite the mantra, which is rotating clockwise at my heart with red light radiating out to all Buddhas and sentient beings as Simhamukha and returning as blessings:

Ah Ka Sa Ma   Ra Tsa Sa Da   Ra Sa Ma Ra Ya   Phat (108X *or as many times as you can*)

Having trained in tummo, tsalung, and clear light, you now engage in the completion-stage practices.[187] *Visualize the three channels and six chakras, and then focus on the central channel. As the winds stabilize and remain within the central channel, breathing in and out will slow and even cease.*

Tummo:

> Below the navel, above a tiny AH-stroke, an intense flame of bliss heats and melts my red female red drop at the bottom of the central channel.
>
> Breathing in, the increasing heat ascends to my navel, melting away subtle obscurations.
>
> It continues increasing to my heart, melting obstacles of my mind,
>
> Then increases to my throat, melting away obstacles of my speech, and
>
> Finally, increases to my crown, melting away obstacles of my body.

> The intense inner heat of bliss melts the white bodhicitta drop (HAM) at my crown.
>
> Breathing out, it descends through my open throat chakra.
>
> Then down through my open heart chakra,
>
> Through my open navel chakra, and
>
> Finally, to my secret place, where I experience the heat of innate bliss radiating throughout.
>
> *Repeat 3X or more. Then sustain the white bodhicitta drop at the tip of the sex organ as long as you can. Next, continue with the Four Blisses.*

The Four Blisses:

> Below the navel, above the tiny AH-stroke, an intense flame melts my female red drop.
> Breathing in, it ascends to my navel, and I experience bliss.
> As it ascends to my heart, I experience supreme bliss.
> As it ascends to my throat, I experience special bliss.

---

[187] If engaging in this practice with a *karmamudra* consort, arouse each other with kissing, touching, and fondling. Join the lotus and vajra in union, breathing slowly and synchronously. Then continue the practice as with the *jnanamudra* consort as long as you can to ever higher intensity of bliss, without orgasm.

As it ascends to my crown, I experience great innate bliss.

The inner heat melts the white bodhicitta drop at my crown.
Breathing out, it descends to my throat, and I experience increasing bliss.
As it descends to my heart, I experience increasing supreme bliss.
As it descends to my navel, I experience increasing special bliss.
As it descends to my secret place, I experience intense innate bliss radiating throughout.

Repeat 3X or more increasing the heat of inner bliss with each step, ascending and descending. Then sustain the white bodhicitta drop at the tip of the sex organ as long as you can. Then continue with the next stage.

The Four Empties:

Below the navel, above a tiny AH-stroke, an intense flame melts my female red drop.
Breathing in, it ascends to my navel, and I experience bliss.
As it ascends to my heart, I experience supreme bliss.
As it ascends to my throat, I experience special bliss.
As it ascends to my crown, I experience great innate bliss.

The inner heat melts the white bodhicitta drop at my crown.
Breathing out, it descends to my throat, and I experience emptiness.[188]
As it descends to my heart, I experience great emptiness.
As it descends to my navel, I experience extreme emptiness.
As it descends to my secret place, I experience total emptiness.
As it joins in one taste at the tip of my sex organ, I experience the inconceivable pristine cognition of bliss-emptiness.

Repeat until only bliss-emptiness remains.

Clear Light Mahamudra:

Outer dissolution, breathing in: From bliss-emptiness appearances move or shimmer like a mirage (*navel chakra*).
There appears a bluish cloud-like smoke (*heart chakra*).
Dots or sparks appear like fireflies (*throat chakra*).

---

[188] When doing this practice with a *karmamudra*, the deity and consort remain in complete, relaxed stillness, letting the intense sexual bliss in the secret place melt into emptiness.

A small glowing light appears like a butter lamp (*crown chakra*).

Inner dissolution, breathing out: The white light grows to fill the sky as the white drop at my crown descends to the indestructible drop at the heart.

A red light glows like a sunset filling the sky as the red drop at my navel ascends to the indestructible drop at the heart.

Objects disappear into black like the darkness of night without moon or stars as the white and red drops enclose the indestructible drop at the heart.

Then clear light appears like the light of first dawn as the drops enter the indestructible drop.

Abide in the clear light mahamudra – pure naked awareness – as long as you can, then reverse the order of the inner and outer dissolution visualizations as you return into your (impure) illusory body as the Red Dakini.

Closing *– Wish for Bodhicitta:*

Bodhicitta, the excellent and precious mind.

Where it is unborn, may it arise.

Where it is born, may it not decline,

But ever increase, higher and higher.

Dedication: With the mind of enlightenment, Bodhicitta, I dedicate all merit from this practice for the enlightenment of all sentient beings. (3X)

Post-meditation: *Following the practice, continue as the Red Dakini in your daily activities.*

Appendix D

Sadhanas of Long Life

These very concise sadhanas are provided to supplement the practice of transference of consciousness (*phowa*). Choose one or the other. They may also be used as a separate practice as needed for oneself or others.

A Very Concise Practice of White Tara
Female Buddha of Compassion & Long Life

I take refuge in Buddha, Dharma and Sangha
Until I obtain enlightenment.
By practicing generosity and the other perfections
May I attain enlightenment for the benefit of all beings. (3X)

Visualize White Tara with white light radiating from the TAM at her heart, filling, cleansing, and revitalizing your body, speech and mind.

Om Tare Tuttare Ture Soha (108X) *or*

Om Tare Tuttare Ture Mama Ahyuh Puye Jnana Putring Kuru Soha (108X)

If foreseeing signs of premature death, may I, by a clear vision of White Tara, subdue the Lord of Death, attaining the Siddhi of Immortality.

By this virtue may I quickly achieve the state of Noble Tara, and establish every being without exception in that state. (3X)

A Very Concise Practice of Amitayus

[handwritten: 's' at end of a word not pronounced]

Buddha of Long Life

I take refuge in the Buddha, Dharma, and Sangha most excellent
In order to enable all sentient beings to attain enlightenment. (3X)

*Visualize Amitayus seated above your head on a lotus moon seat. He is red in
color with sambhogakaya robes and jewels. He holds a blue vase of long-life
nectar, which he pours down through your crown, restoring your life force
and increasing your life.*

OM Amarani Jivantiye Soha (108X)

By this virtue may I quickly achieve the state of Amitayus, and establish
every being without exception in that state. (3X)

Appendix E
Sadhana of the Blue Dakini
(Dharmakaya)

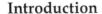

Introduction

The idea for this sadhana came to me in a dream. In this case I was guided by the Blue Dakini, in the form of Samantabhadri – Dharmakaya. In blue form, she stands alone without adornments.

According to Jigmed Lingpa (1726-1798), the Nyingma master famous for finding hidden treasures or *termas*, Simhamukha represents the Nirmanakaya, Vajravarahi represents the Sambhogakaya, and Samantabhadri represents the Dharmakaya. Samantabhadri is usually depicted as white and as the consort of Samantabhadra seated together in the yab-yum position. She represents wisdom, while he represents skillful means. However, in this instance, she appeared alone, standing in the dancing posture, and blue in color.

She took me to a hidden place and showed the text in a script that I did not recognize. It was written on transparent paper in blue. Lines of blue looped across the page with rectangular blocks of blue as well, much like the script in the Sadhana of the Red Dakini. Here, too, it was hard to tell one page from another due to the transparent paper on which it was written. And again, I did not know what to make of it for some time. But eventually, this text came to me so that I might share it with you.

As a Dharmakaya text, the focus of this practice involves Dzogchen practices of *trekcho* and *togal*. Practitioners should have mastered the bliss-emptiness, illusory body, and semblant clear light from the Sadhana of the Red Dakini prior to attempting this one. In addition, practitioners should have completed the preliminary Dzogchen practices of the *Khorde Rushen,* such as those found in the *Khandro Nyingtik* or *Yeshe Lama* texts, as well as the individual instructions on trekcho and togal before beginning this practice. This practice is for yogis, yoginis and other lay practitioners.

Since I am not a realized being and have no notable credibility for such an endeavor, I acknowledge that this may contain errors or omissions for which I accept complete responsibility. I ask only that you see it with the naked awareness of transcendent wisdom and find in it whatever benefit you may.

There are two other texts in this series, the Sadhana of the White Dakini (Nirmanakaya) and the Sadhana of the Red Dakini (Sambhogakaya). May they too be of benefit.

Sadhana of the Blue Dakini

Having practiced the generation stage and completion stage to the point of signs of accomplishment, having completed the preliminary practices of the Path of Great Perfection, having received the pointing out and other instructions, and having practiced the Trekcho and Togal practices separately, you may now practice the Sadhana of the Blue Dakini.

HOMAGE to Samantabhadri, Simhamukha, and Vajravarahi.

Mantra of Increasing Mantras – magnifies the effect of all that follows. Light goes out as offering to Buddhas and returns as a blessing:

OM Sambara Sambara Bimana Sara Maha Zambaba Hung Phat Soha! (3X)

Emptiness mantra – establishes awareness of emptiness as the basis for the recitation and meditation – "all things and I are the embodiment of that indestructible wisdom that is emptiness":

OM Shunyata Jnana Benza Swabhava Emako Ham

Ngondro – The Incomparable Foundational Practices

Four Thoughts that Turn the Mind:

> I prostrate Samantabhadra and Samantabhadri.

> Because I suffer due to my own actions and I now have this precious human life without knowing when I will die, I will now engage in virtuous actions for the benefit of all sentient beings with great joy and devotion.

Refuge Tree visualization:

> In front of me on a jeweled throne supported by eight snow lions sits my Root Guru in the form of Samantabhadra and Samantabhadri in union. Below and in front are tantric deities. On their right (*your left*) are all the Buddhas of the four times. Behind are the scriptures emblazoned with and resonating the vowels and consonants. On their left (*your right*) are all the Bodhisattvas. They are surrounded by countless Dakinis and Dharmapalas filling all of space. Your Mother and Father are next to you. All other sentient beings, including your enemies, are in front of you.

Outer Refuge and Bodhicitta:

> I take refuge in the Buddha, Dharma and Sangha most excellent, abiding softly and deeply in pure, nonconceptual awareness of the

ineffable, oneness, openness, and the spontaneous radiant display manifesting immeasurable, unconditional lovingkindness, compassion, joy and equanimity for the benefit of all.

Inner Refuge and Bodhicitta:

I take refuge in the Guru, Yidam, and Dakini, abiding softly and deeply in pure, nonconceptual awareness of the ineffable, oneness, openness, and the spontaneous radiant display manifesting immeasurable, unconditional lovingkindness, compassion, joy and equanimity for the benefit of all.

Secret Refuge and Bodhicitta:

I take refuge in the Dharmakaya, Sambhogakaya, and Nirmanakaya, abiding softly and deeply in pure, nonconceptual awareness of the ineffable, oneness, openness, and the spontaneous radiant display manifesting immeasurable, unconditional lovingkindness,
compassion, joy and equanimity for the benefit of all.

Most secret Refuge and Bodhicitta:

I take refuge … *Dissolve the visualization into pure awareness with lovingkindness and compassion for all. Abide briefly in complete stillness.*

Action Bodhicitta – The Four Immeasurables:

May all sentient beings have happiness and the causes of happiness.
May they be liberated from suffering and the causes of suffering.
May they never be separated from the happiness that is free from sorrow.
May they rest in equanimity, free from attachment and aversion. (3X)

Vajrasattva Purifications:

OM Benza Sato Samaya

Manu Palaya

Benza Sato Tenopa

Tishta Drido Me Bhawa

Suto Khayo Me Bhawa

Supo Khayo Me Bhawa

Anu Rakto Me Bhawa

Sarwa Siddhi Me Pra Yatsha

Sarwa Karma Sutsa Me

Sit-Tam Shriya Kuru Hung

Ha Ha Ha Ha Ho

Bhagavan

Sarwa Tathagata

Benza Mame Muntsa

Benzi Bhawa

Maha Samaya

Sato Ah

(*Repeat* 5X *or* 3X *or* 1X)

Then: **OM Benza Sato Ah** (108X *or as many times as you can*)

Then: **OM Ah Hung Hri** (108X *or as many times as you can*)

Offerings (outer, inner, secret, most secret) with bell and drum or hand mudra:

I make the eight outer offerings:

OM Argham Ah Hung

OM Padyam Ah Hung

OM Pupe Ah Hung

OM Dupe Ah Hung

OM Aloke Ah Hung

OM Gande Ah Hung

OM Newite Ah Hung

OM Shapta Ah Hung

I make the inner offerings of semen, bones, brain, blood, and flesh:

OM Maha Mamsa Rakta Gorotsana Kengniriti Shukra Pudza Ah Hung (3X)

I make the secret offering of union of lotus and vajra:

OM Benza Peme Bhandza Pudza Ah Hung (3X)

I make the most secret offering of Buddhanature:

OM Tathagatagarba Ah Hung (3X)

Seven Line Prayer Guru Yoga:

OM Ah Hung

In the northwest of the land of Orgyen,

In the heart of a lotus flower,

Endowed with the most marvelous attainments,

You are renowned as the lotus-born,

Surrounded by many hosts of dakinis,

Following in your footsteps,

I pray to you: Come and bless me with your grace!

Guru Padma Siddhi Hung (3X)

OM Ah Hung Benza Guru Peme Siddhi Hung (108X *or as many times as you can.*)

White light radiates from the forehead of Padmasambhava into my forehead purifying my body, planting the seed of Nirmanakaya, empowering the practice of the generation stage, and revealing appearance-emptiness.

Red light radiates from the throat of Padmasambhava into my throat purifying my speech, planting the seed of Sambhogakaya, empowering the practice of the jnanamudra yogas, and revealing luminous-emptiness.

Blue light radiates from the heart of Padmasambhava into my heart purifying my mind, planting the seed of Dharmakaya, empowering the practice of karmamudra yogas, and revealing bliss-emptiness.

Yellow light radiates from the navel of Padmasambhava into my navel purifying all subtle obscurations, planting the seed of Abhisambodhikaya, empowering the practice of Dzogchen Trekcho, and revealing awareness-emptiness.

Green light radiates from the secret place of Padmasambhava into my secret place purifying any residual habitual tendencies, planting the seed of Vajrakaya, empowering the practice of the Dzogchen Togal, and revealing great compassion-emptiness.

The guru dissolves into light and merges inseparably into myself. (*Abide in oneness.*)

Dedication:

> With all the good virtue I have accumulated in samsara and nirvana,
>
> I pray that discursive thought of all sentient beings would be eliminated,
>
> That they would achieve the ultimate liberation and
>
> Obtain the rainbow body just like Rigpa Guru Padmasambhava's.

The Main Practice

Rigpa Guru Yoga (Trekcho):

> By recognizing the true nature of all phenomena as the primordial awareness of Samantabhadri,
>
> All afflictive emotions and mental obscurations, even their concepts and names, fall apart.
>
> The nature of all phenomena is Dharmadhatu and
>
> The unchanging, self-arising wisdom is my only protection.

Jnana Rakcha Hung

> Phenomena perceived through the six kinds of consciousness
>
> Without attachment are recognized as the rays of rigpa,
>
> All surroundings appear as buddhafields and sentient beings as Buddhas,
>
> Everything is the blessing of wisdom.

Jnana Ahwe Shaya Phem

> Primordial, self-arising ultimate Samantabhadri
>
> Appears as rigpa space – no face, no limbs, no image.
>
> Primordial rays of rigpa fully encompass the three kayas
>
> Without the impurity coming from discursive meditation.

The primordial nature of rigpa is my guru.

There is no coming or going.

In every moment I welcome her presence.

Everything firmly abides in Dharmadhatu.

I prostrate to the understanding of the real nature that eliminates ignorance.

I offer recognition of the Buddhanature in objects of the six kinds of consciousness.

I praise the nature of the vajra three kayas of body, speech, and mind.

In the great unchanging Dharmadhatu, all moral ethics are encompassed in the pure guru mind.

OM Ah Hung Ah A Kar Sa Le Od A Yong Om Du (108X *or as many times as you can, then rest in the stillness of body, speech, and mind with pristine, naked awareness – rigpa.*)

Togal[189]:

The primordially perfect buddha, dharma, and sangha abide as one's own body.

Never separate from the vajra refuge of the fundamental nature.

Within that, engage in the clear light of the four visions.

Using the lion pose[190], gaze into the clear sky with the hollow crystal khati channel as long as you can in each session. From this the four visions manifest:

---

[189] In its daily form, lay practitioners may engage in a short practice during each session. It need not extend for the full time period indicated, but is best done during each as listed. Train in six sessions each day. The *Sadhana of the Blue Dakini* is used for sessions 1, 3 and 5:
(1) Predawn: Meditate on rigpa guru yoga.
(2) Dawn until sunup: Recite daily sadhanas, prayers, and so forth.
(3) Sunup until noon: Practice sky gazing (facing west).
(4) Afternoon: Perform prostrations and other virtuous activities.
(5) Afternoon until sunset: Practice sky gazing again (facing east).
(6) At night: Offer torma and hold the winds (tsalung, e.g., *Sadhana of the Red Dakini*).
[190] You may alternate poses or sit in a relaxed pose if you grow tired or experience pain.

(1) Through the vision of direct perception of reality-itself, the rhetoric of the grasping, analytical mind is transcended.[Examples of visions: Bindus (moving, stabilize over time), hands/faces — signs of compassion, rainbows, empty bindus, and vajra chains, that scatter into whiteness]

(2) Through the increasing experience of the vision, confused phenomena vanish and the wisdom of Dharmata is actualized.[Examples of visions: a pattern of visions (lattice or curtain, horizontal/vertical lines), larger objects and deities, bindus inside bindus, subtle and course, clear, dazzling, fascinating; symbols, syllables, jewels, flickers, bodies of light, torsos and heads; increasing sizes; appearances during and after meditation as light and rainbow bindus with increasing clarity until vanish into continuous displays of light, your body emits light; and expands, above, below, all around.]

(3) Through the vision of consummate awareness, one transcends the appearances of the path of conceptualizing the three kayas.[Examples of visions: Environment as wrathful palace; deities in union, mandalas of deities; countless buddhafields of rainbow light; all appears as bindus of 5 buddha families, peaceful & wrathful deities in bindus; and the universe is pervaded by rainbow light.]

(4) Through the vision of extinction into reality-itself, one severs the continuity of the three realms of samsara and achieves a rainbow body.[Examples of visions: deluded visions exhausted into buddhafields, all phenomena dissolve into inner space, and rainbow body.]

The Lamrim Yeshe Nyingpo root text says:

The perfection of the benefit of oneself is the peaceful dharmakaya.

The spontaneously present benefit for others is the unified sambhogakaya.

The manifold skill in means to tame beings is the way of nirmanakaya.

The distinct and unmixed appearance aspect is the abhisambodhikaya.

Their one taste as Dharmadhatu of the emptiness aspect is the vajrakaya.

Having attained the five kayas, these are the five kinds of speech expressing their meaning:

Pure and ineffable is the ultimate speech of dharmakaya.

Illustrating through bodily form is the symbolic speech of sambhogakaya.

Possessing the voice of Brahma is the verbal speech of nirmanakaya.

Distinctively manifest is the knowledge speech of abhisambodhikaya.

The nonduality of audible emptiness is the wisdom speech of
vajrakaya.

The essence of the kayas that is mind, the five wisdoms,
Manifests from Dharmadhatu as being mirror-like,
All-accomplishing, discriminating, and equality.

As sub-aspects of the kayas are the five perfect qualities
Of realm, palace, light rays, throne, and ornaments.

Through the pacifying, increasing, magnetizing, wrathful, and
spontaneously accomplishing activities,
For as long as the sky exists, without knowing interruption,
For that long, the benefit of all beings filling space
Will occur spontaneously and free from effort.

Closing Prayers

The conventionally visualized being (*samayasattva*) and the being of
primordial awareness (*jnanasattva*) are not two different things,

So there is no need to make a request to remain.

They arise from myself and are transformations of my own free will,

My own awareness being the ground and source,

So what need is there for empowerment or full establishment?

Furthermore, the many desirable sense qualities

Are ornaments of the play of primordial awareness, my own mind,

Emanated from myself and offered to myself.

Do not seek samaya in other substances of offering.

The measureless palace of phenomena, the spiritual preceptor and
deities,

Are all a great mandala setting its seal on reality.

Just as the appearances in the mandala of water

Are devoid of self-nature, for example,

View them as arising from a state free of taking things as real.

Penetrating insight beyond word or expression, the unwavering
enlightened dimension of absolute reality (*dharmakaya*),

Chief of the five families, the enlightened dimension of perfect enjoyment of the qualities of great bliss (*sambhogakaya*),

And the great enlightened dimension of manifest appearance, the hundredfold skillful means of compassion (*nirmanakaya*),

To all the deities of the three dimensions of enlightened presence I bow down (*bell*).

Mantra of Increasing Mantras: **OM Sambara Sambara Bimana Sara Maha Zambaba Hung Phat Soha**

Purification mantras:

Sanskrit vowels: **OM a, aa   i, ii   u, uu   ri, rii   li, lii   e, ey   o, oh ang, ah**

Sanskrit consonants:

ka kha ga gha nga/

tsa ts'a dza dz'a nya/

ta t'a da d'a na/

ta t'a da d'a na/[191]

pa p'a ba b'a ma/

ya ra la wa/

sha kha sa ha kya SOHA/

Mantra of Dependent Origination:

OM Yedharma Hetu Prabawa

Hetun-Tekhan Tatagato Hyawadata

Tekhantsa Yo Niroda Evam-Wadi

Maha-Shramana-Ye Soha

100 Syllable Mantra of Vajrasattva:

OM Benza Sato Samaya

Manu Palaya

Benza Sato Tenopa

Tishta Drido Me Bhawa

Suto Khayo Me Bhawa

---

[191] The second line has a silent "r" and is represented here phonetically.

Supo Khayo Me Bhawa

Anu Rakto Me Bhawa

Sarwa Siddhi Me Pra Yatsha

Sarwa Karma Sutsa Me

Sit-Tam Shriya Kuru Hung

Ha Ha Ha Ha Ho

Bhagavan

Sarwa Tathagata

Benza Mame Muntsa

Benzi Bhawa

Maha Samaya

Sato Ah

Long Life Prayers

H.H. the Dalai Lama

For this realm encircled by snow-covered mountains

You are the source of every benefit and bliss without exception.

Tenzin Gyaltso, you who are one with Avalokiteshvara,

May you remain steadfast until Samsara's end!

Khenchen Lama

In the Dharmadhatu appearing as Amitabha,

In the Sambhogakaya form as wisdom Buddha Manjushri,

Padmasambhava's heart son Sangye Yeshe,

Incarnated as Padma Dagnag Lingpa in previous life

And Paljea pa Dorjee in this lifetime,

May your life be longer than the duration of samsara

So that all your virtuous intentions can be accomplished.

Please give me your heart blessings so that

My mind is united with yours in the Buddha nature.

So, I pray!

Wish for Bodhicitta:

OM Ah Hung Shri

Ananta Benza Sarwa Siddhi Phala Hung Ah!

Glorious, precious root lama,
Sit on the lotus seat on the crown of my head.
With your great kindness please accept me.
Please bestow the realizations of body, speech, and mind.
In all the activities of the glorious lama,
May no wrong view arise even for a moment.
By the devotion of seeing whatever he does as perfect
May the blessing of the lama enter my mind.
Throughout the succession of my lives, from the perfect lamas
May I never be separated and, enjoying the glory of the Dharma,
Perfect all the qualities of the stages and the paths
And swiftly attain the stage of Vajradhara.
The lamas who have become the glory of the Dharma, may their lives
    be stable;
May the land be entirely filled with Doctrine-holders;
May the wealth and power of the patrons of the Doctrine increase,
And may the auspiciousness of the Doctrine remain forever.

Bodhichitta, the excellent and precious mind.
Where it is unborn, may it arise.
Where it is born, may it not decline,
But ever increase, higher and higher.

Dedication:

With the mind of enlightenment, Bodhicitta, I dedicate all merit
from this practice for the enlightenment of all sentient beings. (3X)

*Abide softly and deeply in pure naked awareness without attachment or aversion
with lovingkindness and compassion for all ... always and all ways!*

*****

*This sadhana was written by Khenpo Drimed Dawa to the best of my limited
ability for the benefit of all sentient beings in July, 2009, Tucson Arizona. Please
forgive all errors or omissions. They are my own.*

Sealed   Sealed   Sealed

72441601R00246

Made in the USA
San Bernardino, CA
25 March 2018